ON RHETORIC

ARISTOTLE

ON RHETORIC

A THEORY OF CIVIC DISCOURSE

Translated with Introduction, Notes, and Appendices by

GEORGE A. KENNEDY

Second Edition

New York   Oxford

OXFORD UNIVERSITY PRESS

2007

Oxford University Press, Inc., publishes works that further Oxford University's
objective of excellence in research, scholarship, and education.

Oxford New York
Auckland   Cape Town   Dar es Salaam   Hong Kong   Karachi
Kuala Lumpur   Madrid   Melbourne   Mexico City   Nairobi
New Delhi   Shanghai   Taipei   Toronto

With offices in
Argentina   Austria   Brazil   Chile   Czech Republic   France   Greece
Guatemala   Hungary   Italy   Japan   Poland   Portugal   Singapore
South Korea   Switzerland   Thailand   Turkey   Ukraine   Vietnam

Copyright © 2007 by Oxford University Press, Inc.

Published by Oxford University Press, Inc.
198 Madison Avenue, New York, New York 10016
http://www.oup.com

Oxford is a registered trademark of Oxford University Press

Library of Congress Cataloging-in-Publication Data

Aristotle.
    [Rhetoric. English]
    On rhetoric : a theory of civic discourse / by Aristotle ; translated with
introduction, notes, and appendices by George A. Kennedy. — 2nd ed.
        p. cm.
    Includes bibliographical references and index.
    ISBN 13: 978-0-19-530508-1 (alk. paper) — ISBN 13: 978-0-19-530509-8
(pbk. : alk. paper)

    1. Rhetoric—Early works to 1800. 2. Aristotle. Rhetoric. I. Kennedy, George
Alexander, 1928– II. Title.

PN173.A7K46 2006
808.5—dc22

                                                        2005055487

To My Grandson,
Alexander Kennedy Morton,
The Original Rhetoric *for a Later Alexander*

CONTENTS

PROOEMION

The study of rhetoric in the western world began in Greece in the fifth century B.C.E. Democratic government was emerging in Athens, based on the assumption that all citizens had an equal right and duty to participate in their own government. To do so effectively, they needed to be able to speak in public. Decisions on public policy were made in regularly held assemblies composed of adult male citizens, any of whom had the right to speak. Not surprisingly, however, the leadership role in debate was played by a small number of ambitious individuals called *rhētores*, who sought to channel the course of events in a direction they thought was best for the city or for themselves. There were no professional lawyers in Greece, and if citizens needed to seek redress in the courts for some wrong or if they were summoned to court as defendants, they were expected in most instances to speak on their own behalf. There were also occasions for public address on holidays or at funerals, as well as more informal speeches at symposia or private meetings.

Some people seem to have a natural gift for communication; others can develop these skills by studying the principles of speech and composition, by observing the method of successful speakers and writers, and by practice. To meet the needs of students in Greece, teachers called "sophists" emerged who took students for pay and taught them how to be effective in public life by marshaling arguments, dividing speeches into logical parts, and carefully choosing and combining words. One of the most famous of these teachers was a man named Gorgias, who came from Sicily to Athens in 427 B.C.E. and made a great impression on his audiences by his poetic style and paradoxical arguments. Others began to publish short handbooks on the "art" of speeches, concerned primarily with showing how a person with little or no experience could organize a speech for delivery in a court of law and how to argue on the basis of the probability of what someone might have done in a given situation. These handbooks contained examples of techniques that could be adapted to different needs. Socrates and his student Plato distrusted the teaching of the sophists and handbook writers. In Plato's dialogue *Gorgias* Socrates criticizes civic rhetoric in fifth-century B.C.E. Athens as essentially a form of flattery—morally irresponsible and not based on knowledge of truth or sound logic.

The debate over the role of rhetoric in society has existed ever since, and there are still people today for whom the word "rhetoric" means empty words, misleading arguments, and appeal to base emotions. There are dangers in rhetoric—political extremism, racism, and unscrupulous sales techniques, for example—but by studying rhetoric we can become alert to its potential for misuse and learn to recognize when a speaker is seeking to manipulate us. There is great positive power in rhetoric as well, which we can use for valid ends. The American Founding Fathers organized public opinion in the cause of American independence by use of the logical, ethical, and emotional power of rhetoric. Rhetoric has helped black leaders, women, and minority groups begin to secure their rights in society. It has also been an essential feature in the preaching and teaching of the world's religions, in the transmission of cultural values, and in the judicial process.

Aristotle was perhaps the first person to recognize clearly that rhetoric as an art of communication was morally neutral, that it could be used for either good or ill. In the second chapter of *On Rhetoric* he says that persuasion depends on three things: the truth and logical validity of what is being argued, the speaker's success in conveying to the audience a perception that he or she can be trusted, and the emotions that a speaker is able to awaken in an audience to accept the views advanced and act in accordance with them. Modern rhetoricians use terms derived from Aristotle to refer to these three means of persuasion, though they have somewhat broadened his definitions: logical argument is called *logos*; the projection of the speaker's character is called *ēthos*; awakening the emotions of the audience is called *pathos*.

Aristotle composed his treatise *On Rhetoric* in the third quarter of the fourth century B.C.E. as a text for lectures he planned to give in his philosophical school. Although it influenced the view of rhetoric of Cicero, Quintilian, and other teachers in Rome and became known in the western Middle Ages in a Latin translation, it has been more studied in modern times than ever before. Most teachers of composition, communication, and speech regard it as a seminal work that organizes its subject into essential parts, provides insight into the nature of speech acts, creates categories and terminology for discussing discourse, and illustrates and applies its teachings so that they can be used in society. Although Aristotle largely limited the province of rhetoric to public address, he took a broader view of what that entails than do most modern writers on communication. This may surprise and interest readers today. He addresses issues of philosophy, government, history, ethics, and literature; and in Book 2 he includes a comprehensive account of human psychology. In Aristotle's view, speakers need to understand how the minds of their listeners work, and in the process we come to understand something of who we are and why we do what we do.

On Rhetoric can be a difficult work for modern readers, and many need help to understand it. Some difficulties may come from a lack of familiarity with the history and thought of the period in which it was composed. Other difficulties come from the compressed style in which it is written: words, thoughts, transitions, or explanations often need to be added to make the argument clear. Some problems result from apparent inconsistencies. Aristotle seems to have written different portions of the work at different times, he sometimes changed his views, and he never made a complete revision of the whole, nor did he add as many illustrations and examples as we would like. Finally, his attitude toward rhetoric was ambivalent. He wanted his students to understand the dangers of sophistic rhetoric as dramatically portrayed by Plato, and at the same time to be able to defend themselves and be effective if they engaged in public life. The differing views found in the text, especially when taken in conjunction with Plato's criticism or Isocrates' celebration of rhetoric, can provide a good starting point for discussions by modern students about the nature and functions of rhetoric in society.

This translation attempts both to convey something of Aristotle's distinctive style and way of thinking and to render the work more accessible to modern readers through introductory comments, supplemental phrases in the text, and extensive notes and appendices. Earlier translators often paraphrased or avoided technicalities to make the text more readable, but in our age, one reason for studying Aristotle is to learn his technical language. I have kept this and offered explanations of it.

As is the case with most Greek literature, our knowledge of what Aristotle wrote is based on manuscripts copied by scribes from older manuscripts, which were in turn copied from still earlier ones, going back to Aristotle's personal copy, with opportunity for mistakes at every stage in the transmission. The earliest existing evidence for the text dates from over a thousand years after Aristotle died. Since the invention of printing in the fifteenth century there have been numerous editions of Aristotle's writings, but no single version of the text of the *Rhetoric* is entirely satisfactory. I have worked primarily from the text as edited by Rudolf Kassel (1976) but have also consulted editions by Médéric Dufour and André Wartelle (1960–1973) and W. David Ross (1950). In addition, I have accepted some textual suggestions made by Fr. William Grimaldi in his commentary (1980–1988) and by others in recent publications.

Two features of my translation may be worth pointing out in advance. A major doctrine of *On Rhetoric* is the use of the enthymeme, or rhetorical syllogism. In Aristotle's own writing enthymemes often take the form of a statement followed by a clause introduced by the Greek particle *gar*, which gives a supporting reason. These occur on every page but are often obscured by other translators. I have kept them, using a semicolon and the English particle "for" as a way of drawing the attention of the reader and making the device familiar. A second feature is avoidance of some of the sexist language seen in older translations, which often speak of "men" when Aristotle uses a more general plural. I have used *man* or *men* only in those few instances in which the word *anthrōpos* or *anēr* appears in the Greek; otherwise I use *someone, people,* or *they.* On the other hand, to alter Aristotle's many uses of *he, his,* or *him* in reference to speakers or members of a Greek assembly or jury would be unhistorical and would involve an actual change to the text. Aristotle usually envisions only males as speaking in public, but he clearly did not think that rhetoric was a phenomenon limited to males, for he draws examples of rhetoric from Sappho (a woman poet of the early sixth century B.C.E.) and from female characters in epic and drama. In 1.5.6 he remarks that "happiness" is only half present in states where the condition of women is poor.[1]

The initial impetus for making a new edition of this work came from the need to correct a large number of typographical errors in the

---

1. Greek nouns have grammatical gender, and as a result of the conventions of Greek word formation most rhetorical terms in Greek are feminine, as the glossary at the end of this volume reveals. The Greek words for *city, political assembly,* and *law court* are also feminine. It is not clear, however, whether the ancient Greeks were conscious of rhetoric as operating in feminine space.

original version plus a few factual mistakes and a few passages in which words had been left out of the translation. It also offered an opportunity to make some significant changes in the format, which readers had found confusing, and in the content as well, primarily in the introductions, notes, and appendices, where my own views had changed or needed to be better expressed. I undertook a review of scholarly publication on Aristotle over the last twenty-five years (over five thousand items, of which several hundred dealt in whole or part with *On Rhetoric*), updating and enlarging the bibliography, and making changes in the translation and notes on the basis of new interpretations when I believed these were sound. Especially important publications since the appearance of the first edition of my translation include *Aristotle's Rhetoric: Philosophical Essays* (1994), edited by David J. Furley and Alexander Nehamas; *Essays on Aristotle's "Rhetoric"* (1996), edited by A. O. Rorty; and *Rereading Aristotle's "Rhetoric"* (2000), edited by Alan G. Gross and Arthur E. Walzer. I have also benefited from reviews of the original edition published in journals, from suggestions that have come to me from readers over the years, and from evaluations solicited by Oxford University Press. I want particularly to thank Janet Atwill, Thomas Cole, Christine D'Antonio, David Fleming, William Fortenbaugh, Richard Graff, David Mirhady, Victor Vitanza, and Cecil Wooten for their encouragement and thoughtful suggestions.

George A. Kennedy
Fort Collins, Colorado
August 2005

NOTES ON THE TRANSLATION

The title of the work in the manuscripts is *Tekhnē rhētorikē* (*Art Rhetorical*, or *Art of Rhetoric*). When Aristotle himself refers to the treatise in *Poetics* 19.2 he calls it *Peri rhētorikēs* (*On Rhetoric*). It is frequently simply called "Aristotle's *Rhetoric*."

The division of the text into books can be attributed to Aristotle himself and presumably reflects the convenient length of a papyrus scroll in his time. The division into numbered chapters was first made by George of Trebizond in his fifteenth-century Latin translation as a convenience for teachers and readers and is generally logical, though some discussions are divided into separate chapters where the Greek suggests they should be read as continuous. The division of the chapters into numbered sections originated in the Bipontine Edition of J. T. Buhle (Zweibrucken 1793) and is occasionally misleading. The numbers in the margins (e.g., **1354a**) indicate pages and columns in the Berlin edition (1831) of the complete works of Aristotle, edited by Immanuel Bekker. These numbers are used by scholars to refer to passages and lines in the Greek text. In a translation their location is necessarily only approximate.

Words and phrases in square brackets [. . .] within the translated text supply the Greek term used by Aristotle or words and phrases implied but not stated in the text that may elucidate the meaning.

Words and phrases in parentheses (. . .) indicate what appear to be parenthetical remarks by Aristotle.

A macron over vowels (ē and ō) in transliterations of Greek words indicates Greek eta (long e) and omega (long o).

INTRODUCTION

A. ARISTOTLE'S LIFE AND WORKS

Aristotle tells us almost nothing about the events of his life, though he reveals his mind and values fully, especially in *Nicomachean Ethics*. What we know (or think probable) about the sequence of his activities and relationships with others derives from later sources, including a short biography and a long list of his works in *Lives of the Philosophers* (5.1–35) by Diogenes Laertius, probably written in the third century C.E. but derived from much earlier sources. The most important facts that contribute to an understanding of Aristotle's writings are his ties with the kings of Macedon, Philip and Alexander, and his association with Plato as a student and colleague for twenty years.[1]

Aristotle was born in Stagiros (later called Stagira) in northern Greece in 384 B.C.E. This was a Greek city but near the Macedonian kingdom, which was only partially Hellenized. Aristotle's father was a friend of and personal physician to the king of Macedon, and his mother, Phaestis, also came from a family of doctors. Aristotle probably spent some of his youth in Macedon, and he continued to have ties with the court, culminating forty years later in his being given responsibility for directing the education of the young prince who became Alexander the Great. His Macedonian connection rendered him somewhat suspect to Athenians in later life. Aristotle's own education had probably included the usual study of language, poetry, music, and geometry, as well as athletic training in the gymnasium. A few references (e.g., *Rhetoric* 1.11.15) suggest that as a young man

---

1. For further information, see Düring 1957 and Rist 1989.

1

he had particularly enjoyed hunting with dogs. His father died when Aristotle was quite young, but the family's connections with medicine may have been a source of his unusual interest in biology and his inclination to see change in terms of organic development.

After Aristotle's father's death a man named Proxenus, probably a relative, became his guardian and in 367 B.C.E. arranged for Aristotle to go to Athens and to become a student-member of the Academy, a center for advanced studies in philosophy and science that Plato had established in the outskirts of the city.[2] This was a sign of an early serious interest in philosophy. By this time Aristotle had doubtless read Plato's early Socratic dialogues, as well as *Gorgias*, with its criticism of sophistic rhetoric, and *Republic*, Plato's search for understanding of justice by imagining the creation of an ideal city where philosophers would be kings. As it happened, Plato was not present in Athens during the first few years of Aristotle's residence there, for he had gone to Sicily in a vain attempt to help create an ideal kingdom in Syracuse. During Plato's absence the intellectual life of the Academy went on, probably under the direction of the mathematician and astronomer Eudoxus and Heracleides Ponticus, a scientist and historian. Aristotle would have participated in symposia and dialectical disputes and attended occasional lectures, as well as pursued research projects of his own. His major project came to involve developing a theory of logical argument, which was to lead to the composition of works called *Categories* and *Topics*. He would also have experienced the cultural and political life of the Athenian democracy, attending plays in the theater and perhaps listening to debates in the Assembly, which probably gave him his first experience of political oratory.

Plato returned to Athens in 365 B.C.E., and it was probably between 365 and 361 (when he again went to Syracuse for two years) that his personal influence on Aristotle was its greatest. Aristotle retained throughout his life personal affection for Plato and learned much from him, but his instinctive feeling for philosophy came to be far more pragmatic than Platonic idealism. Whatever his initial attitude, Aristotle eventually rejected some fundamental Platonic concepts, such as the reality of transcendent ideas. In particular, the Forms of the Good, the Beautiful, and the True—which Plato accorded the status of the only absolute reality—were to Aristotle not independent

---

2. For information on the Academy and life there, see *Brill's New Pauly: Encyclopaedia of the Ancient World*, vol. 1, coll. 41–42.

entities but abstractions created by the human mind.[3] His interest in political theory clearly developed out of Plato's work but again was more pragmatic, based on study of existing constitutions in their historical development and defining the checks and balances that might create stability in a mixed constitution rather than seeking to imagine an ideal state. Though conventionally pious, Aristotle preferred to live in the real world and was curious about almost all its details. Although he always shared many of Plato's ethical values, his theory of ethics is not based on religious belief of reward and punishment in the afterlife (as was Plato's) but on how to achieve happiness in a secular society by rational control of the emotions.

The writings of Aristotle that survive in complete form, including *On Rhetoric*, are treatises—systematic expositions of subjects which he probably sometimes used as notes for lectures. They were not published—that is, multiple copies were not made for sale in bookstores—but were kept in his own library for his use and revision and probably for study by others. They are therefore known as his "esoteric" works. This status probably explains their lack of literary polish. We may be allowed to hope that when he used the texts for lecture notes Aristotle expanded and illustrated what he said and perhaps even entertained questions. Although the Aristotelian corpus —the collected esoteric works—was regarded by the philosophers of later antiquity and the medieval scholastic philosophers as constituting a single consistent system of thought, inconsistencies in terminology and even in doctrine indicate that most of the texts as we read them now, including *On Rhetoric*, represent a development of Aristotle's thinking over many years with repeated revision and additions to the texts. The nature and extent of this development in each area of Aristotle's thought is a controversial subject much discussed by modern students of Aristotelian philosophy.[4] In writing systematic accounts of philosophy Aristotle departed from the model of Plato who, like his teacher, Socrates, favored dialogue over lectures as a teaching method and resisted authoritative written statements of philosophical doctrines.[5]

---

3. See especially Aristotle's discussion in *Nicomachean Ethics* 1.6 and in *Metaphysics* 1.6.

4. A seminal work was that of Jaeger (1934), which argued for initial acceptance of Platonic doctrines and a growing independence of thought over time; for criticism and more recent views, see Wians 1996.

5. The most famous passage in which Socrates (i.e., Plato) criticizes writing comes at the end of Plato's *Phaedrus*.

Aristotle also published some works, mostly in the form of dialogues, especially during the years he was a member of the Academy and under the eye of Plato. These were read in antiquity and admired for their style as well as for their arguments. They did not survive the devastations of later antiquity and are known today only from quotations, abstracts, and allusions by others. The dialogues included *On the Poets*, which probably anticipated some of the ideas found in the *Poetics*, and a dialogue on rhetoric, entitled *Gryllus*, named after the son of the historian Xenophon whose death in battle in 363 B.C.E. had evoked a series of eulogies.[6] According to the Roman rhetorician Quintilian (2.17.14), it contained an argument that rhetoric is not an "art," reminiscent of Socrates' claim in Plato's *Gorgias*; this could also be read as a criticism of Isocratean epideictic. Since the work was in dialogue form, it is apt to have argued both sides of the question and thus may have anticipated some of the ideas in *On Rhetoric*,[7] for in that later work Aristotle unhesitatingly regards rhetoric as an art (1.1.2).

This change was perhaps a result of a more thorough consideration of the nature of rhetoric. Sometime in the mid-350s B.C.E., now a senior member of the Academy, Aristotle is said to have begun to offer a course on rhetoric.[8] Our information comes from much later sources and may not be entirely reliable, but the course seems to have been open to the general public—offered in the afternoons as a kind of extension division of the Academy and accompanied by practical exercises in debate. According to the reports, a reason for offering the course was a desire to counteract the influence of Isocrates, whose school was the Academy's main competitor and rival. Isocrates was teaching his own form of sophistic rhetoric, which he called "philosophy," to numbers of students from Athens and abroad. We do not know whether Aristotle was asked by Plato to undertake this teaching or whether it was his own idea. Although not an Athenian and thus with limited personal experience of civic oratory, Aristotle's interest in logical argument led easily into consideration of public argumentation. Isocrates' defense of his teachings in the

---

6. Discussion by Chroust 1965.

7. See Lossau 1974.

8. The sources are Cicero, *On the Orator* 3.141, *Tusculan Disputations* 1.4.7, and *Orator* 46; Philodemus, *On Rhetoric* 2.50–51 ed. Sudhaus; Quintilian 3.1.14; Diogenes Laertius 5.3; Syrianus 2.5 ed. Rabe. Philodemus severely blames Aristotle for abandoning philosophy to teach rhetoric; see Chroust 1964.

Antidosis dates from 353 B.C.E. and may represent, at least in part, his own reaction to Aristotle's teaching. (See Appendix I.E.2 at the end of this book.) Some of the text of *On Rhetoric* as we read it today probably is a revision of what was said in the "afternoon" lectures. That would include much of Book 1 (except for the two opening chapters) and probably much of the discussion of style and arrangement in the second half of Book 3. The reasons for believing that these chapters date from an early period include the presence of practical advice about what to say in a speech, the presence of some philosophical views known to have been current in the Academy but inconsistent with those Aristotle held later, the absence of cross-references (except for a few that could easily have been inserted later) to other treatises of Aristotle, and numerous historical references to events and people of the 350s.[9] In what we can see of the early lectures, Aristotle seems to be developing a system of rhetoric along the lines proposed by Plato in *Phaedrus*, emphasizing the importance of knowledge of the subjects to be discussed and of logical argument, though he probably had not yet developed his theory of the enthymeme and of the role of *ēthos* and *pathos* in oratory. It was probably in preparing to teach rhetoric that Aristotle compiled, or had assistants compile, the *Synagōgē tekhnōn*, a survey of the rhetorical doctrines found in handbooks of the fifth and fourth centuries. We shall return in the next section to the relationship of Aristotle's views of rhetoric to what was found in the handbooks and to the teachings of Isocrates and Plato.

Although Aristotle was recognized in the Academy as potentially the ablest of the followers of Plato, since he was not an Athenian he could not succeed him as Scholarch (head of the school), a position which went to Plato's nephew, Speusippus. Thus in 347 B.C.E., in anticipation of or soon after the death of Plato, Aristotle left Athens and went first to Assos in Asia Minor and then to the island of Lesbos, where he did much of his biological research and where his most famous pupil, Theophrastus, joined him. Then in 343 or 342 King Philip persuaded him to come to Macedon as tutor to Alexander, about thirteen years old at this time. Aristotle probably offered him instruction in logic, literature, rhetoric, political theory, and ethics. A letter from Isocrates to Alexander that was enclosed in a letter to Philip praises the young man for studying rhetoric but expresses

---

9. See Rist 1989:136–144.

carefully worded reservations about exercises in dialectic, which would certainly have been part of Aristotle's instruction.[10] Isocrates never mentions either Plato or Aristotle by name in any of his writings.[11] Aristotle probably revised his earlier lectures on rhetoric and somewhat adapted them to Alexander's potential needs, including adding references to Isocrates' speech *Philippus*, addressed to Alexander's father and doubtless of great interest at the Macedonian court. This speech was completed in 346, so Aristotle's references must have been added after that date.

Aristotle's work with Alexander ended by 340 B.C.E. From then until 335 he was probably living in Macedon or Stagiros and continuing philosophical research with a few private students. He apparently worked on a revision of his notes on rhetoric at this time, for it contains references to historical events of the period. In 338 Philip defeated the Athenians and their allies at the Battle of Chaeronea, ending the political significance of the Greek city states in the ancient world (though Athens remained a cultural center, a kind of university town, for centuries). In 336 Philip was assassinated and Alexander succeeded to the throne. In 335 Aristotle returned to Athens and opened his own school there in the *peripatos* ("colonnade," thus the name "Peripatetic" school) of the gymnasium of the Lyceum, not far from where the Hilton Hotel now stands. In the gymnasium, or nearby, were a library, study rooms, and a dining room where he could meet with students and friends for symposia.[12] Whereas Plato's Academy was a residential community in an ideal rustic setting, Aristotle's students found their own housing in the busy city.

It seems possible that Aristotle had long been hoping to return to Athens and that he had been preparing to teach popular subjects, including rhetoric, politics, ethics, and poetics, as a way of attracting students. We do not, however, have any specific testimony that Aristotle actually used the text of *On Rhetoric* as a basis for lectures at this time, and he eventually turned his attention to the more abstruse subject of metaphysics. On the death of Alexander in 323 B.C.E., when anti-Macedonian sentiment was strong in Athens,

---

10. Isocrates, *Epistle* 5. He says that Alexander "does not even reject eristic" and regards it as a valuable private exercise but realizes it is unsuitable for a ruler to allow anyone to contradict him.

11. Plato names Isocrates only once, in an enigmatic passage at the end of *Phaedrus*. Aristotle quotes or refers to Isocrates some thirty-nine times in the *Rhetoric*, but rarely elsewhere.

12. See Lynch 1972.

Aristotle turned his school over to Theophrastus and went to live in Chalcis on the island of Euboea, which was the original home of his mother's family. He died there in 322.

Although probably not a wealthy man, Aristotle seems to have had adequate resources to finance his school and research. Plato had not charged tuition of his students; Isocrates did and Aristotle may have done so as well. Diogenes Laertius, drawing on earlier sources, preserves Aristotle's will and a brief personal description of his appearance in later life. According to this Aristotle had thin legs, was partially bald, liked to wear rings, and spoke with a lisp. He was married, had one daughter, and, after his wife's death, fathered a son, Nicomachus, by a concubine. For the subsequent history of his library, including the text of *On Rhetoric*, see Appendix II.B.

B. RHETORIC BEFORE ARISTOTLE

Rhetoric, in the most general sense, can be regarded as a form of mental or emotional energy imparted to a communication to affect a situation in the interest of the speaker. Help! HELP! **HELP!** utilizes simple rhetorical devices—repetition (a figure of speech) and pitch and volume (features of delivery)—to convey a message whose intent and energy are compelling.

So understood, rhetoric is a feature of all human communication, even of animal communication. Traditional nonliterate societies all over the world—the aboriginal Australians are a good example—use a variety of rhetorical devices in their deliberations and have terms to describe rhetorical genres and procedures. Even when thought of as the theory and practice of public address in a literate society rhetoric is not solely a western phenomenon. The earliest known rhetorical handbook is *The Instructions of Ptahhotep*, composed by an Egyptian official sometime before 2000 B.C.E.; it gives advice about how to speak and when to keep silent if brought before a judge or ruler. Some of what is said resembles precepts in the Old Testament, as in Psalm 16: "Pleasant speech increases persuasiveness. . . . Pleasant words are like a honeycomb, sweetness to the soul and health to the body." There is an extensive rhetorical literature, both collections of speeches and writing about rhetoric, from ancient China and India. These matters are discussed, with examples and bibliography, in a book entitled *Comparative Rhetoric* (Kennedy 1998).

The earliest surviving work of Greek literature is the *Iliad*, traditionally attributed to a nebulous figure named Homer who perhaps lived about seven hundred years before Christ. It originated as part of a cycle of oral epic poems and was written down by scribes after the introduction of the alphabet in the Greek-speaking world, achieving its present form by around 550 B.C.E. The *Iliad* and its companion poem, the *Odyssey*, place a high value on eloquent speech, almost equal to military prowess, and contain many poetic versions of debates and speeches that already utilize features of argument, arrangement, and style later described in rhetorical handbooks (Kennedy 1999:5–12). Aristotle sometimes quotes the *Iliad*, other early poetry, and speeches in Greek tragedy to illustrate rhetorical practice. The important role of public address in Greece in the two centuries before Aristotle is well illustrated by the numerous speeches that the historians Herodotus, Thucydides, and Xenophon included in their works. These speeches are reconstructions of what may have been said, but many examples of actual Greek speeches survive, the works of the Attic Orators of the late fifth and fourth centuries B.C.E. The most famous of these orators are Antiphon, Lysias, Isocrates, Aeschines, and Demosthenes. Aristotle could have read some of their speeches and may have heard other speeches when they were first delivered. Modern students beginning their study of the history of rhetoric should read some Greek speeches in English translation in order to better understand the context of Aristotle's rhetorical theories. Appendix I contains translations of Lysias' speech *Against the Grain Dealers*, an example of a speech given in a court of law, and of Demosthenes' *Third Philippic*, an example of a speech given in the Athenian Assembly. The most famous speech given in Aristotle's lifetime is Demosthenes' defense of his policies in resisting Philip of Macedon, known as *On the Crown* and delivered in 330. Aristotle may have heard it, but he does not mention Demosthenes' orations. His sympathies, of course, were with Philip and Macedon.

The English word "rhetoric," and its various forms in European languages, is derived from the Greek world *rhētōr*, a speaker, especially a speaker in a public meeting or court of law, sometimes equivalent to what we might call a "politician." The first datable appearance of the abstract noun *rhētorikē*, meaning the art of a public speaker, occurs in Plato's dialogue *Gorgias* (448d9), probably written around 380 B.C.E., where Socrates mentions "what is called rhetoric" and Gorgias acknowledges that this is what he teaches. This suggests the currency of the word "rhetoric" in Athens by the dramatic date of that dialogue, sometime in the last quarter of the fifth century, and in any event the word, a derivative of *rhētōr*, would have been easily understood by a speaker of Greek. Its use by Plato and Aristotle established it as a distinct area of study and eventually part of the curriculum of the liberal arts. Before and after "rhetoric" came into use there were other terms current. One was *peithō*, which means "persuasion"; more common was use of the word *logos*, meaning word or speech, in combination with other words: a *dēmiourgos logōn* was a "worker of words," and thus an orator; *tekhnē logōn*, "art of words," was used to describe the technique or art of speech and became the common title for a handbook of public speaking.

The art of rhetoric as studied in modern times had its birth in Greece, and, though it shared many features with rhetoric in non-western society, it has also had distinctive qualities that differentiate it culturally from other traditions. These qualities are closely connected with the development of democracy in Athens and some other Greek cities. The Greeks, already as seen in the *Iliad*, were a highly argumentative, contentious people; their city states were almost constantly at war with each other, and in times of peace they turned their energies into competitive athletics. Their rivalries and arguments contrast with values commonly found in Middle Eastern and Far Eastern cultures, where strong central governments discouraged or prevented public debate (and where organized athletics did not develop). Under democratic governments in Athens and some other Greek cities in the fifth and fourth centuries B.C.E., all important decisions about public policy and actions were made after debate in an assembly of the adult, male citizens, any one of whom could speak. Chaos could easily have resulted, but in order to arrive at some closure and avoid fighting, the Greeks invented the practice of deciding issues by vote of the majority, something unique to the democratic process. The Athenian law courts were also remarkably democratic. Both criminal and civil cases were heard before large juries, sometimes a thousand or more jurors, chosen by lot from the male citizens. Since there were no professional lawyers and no public prosecutors, criminal prosecutions had to be brought by an interested party, defendants were ordinarily expected to deliver one or more speeches on their own behalf, and prosecution and defense in civil cases similarly demanded an ability to address the jury in person in a set speech. In order to help litigants effectively plan and present a case, handbooks of judicial rhetoric were written and could be bought for a modest sum.

The earliest of these was apparently composed by a Sicilian named Tisias, called Corax, or the "Crow," sometime around 460 B.C.E.[13] Copies of it were brought to Athens and other, more extensive handbooks were written there. In *Phaedrus* (266d–267d) Plato gives a brief, somewhat belittling, survey of them, showing that they were organized around the conventional parts of a judicial oration: prooemion, narration, proof, and epilogue. Examples of what to say were given and could be adapted to actual situations. In connection with his earliest teaching of rhetoric around 355 Aristotle compiled a work in two books entitled *Synagōgē tekhnōn*, or "Collection of the Arts," which summarized the teaching of each of the handbooks known to him. He found them lacking in most respects and repeatedly criticizes them in *On Rhetoric* (e.g., 1.1.9; 3.13.3). They were, he complains, concerned only with judicial rhetoric and its parts and neglected deliberative oratory, a finer genre, and they gave too much attention to arousing emotions to the neglect of logical argument. In Appendix II.A, at the end of this volume, can be found a more detailed account of "The Earliest Rhetorical Handbooks," together with documentation and bibliography.

A second influence on the development of rhetorical teaching in Greece against which Plato and Aristotle reacted was that of the sophists. Among the most famous were Protagoras, Gorgias, and Hippias. A sophist was a teacher, often a foreigner who had come to Athens, who promised to provide practical verbal skills to students for a fee. Although some of the sophists made use of the question-and-answer method of instruction adopted by Socrates,[14] their more characteristic teaching technique, whatever the subject chosen, was *epideixis*, a demonstrative speech, long or short, often flamboyant, in which the sophist undertook to demonstrate some proposition artistically. Sometimes myth or allegory was employed; sometimes the argument was an indirect one in which all possibilities were enumerated, all but one disposed of, and the last accepted as valid. Sometimes the audience was asked to choose the form of the sophist's demonstration.[15] Among surviving examples of sophistic *epideixis*

---

13. It used to be thought that Corax and Tisias were two different people, but it is likely that Corax was a nickname for Tisias; see Cole 1991b and Appendix II.A.

14. Cf., e.g., Plato, *Gorgias* 449c.

15. According to Philostratus, *Lives of the Sophists* 1.9.11, Gorgias was the first to do this. Types of sophistic discourse can be seen in Socrates' encounters with sophists; see especially *Protagoras* 320c.

are speeches in Plato's *Phaedrus*,[16] Gorgias' *Encomium of Helen* (English translation in Appendix I.A) and *Palamedes*, the *Ajax* and *Odysseus* of Antisthenes, and the *Odysseus* of Alcidamas. All of these can be read as illustrating methods of speech. They make use of logical and stylistic devices that could be imitated by students, and some pretend to be addressed to a jury in a court of law. Sophistic instruction was largely oral, but such speeches could be copied down and serve as examples of oratory to be studied or imitated or quarried for commonplaces by the sophist's pupils, who could thus acquire not only the master's theory of oratorical partition, but also his techniques of argument, features of his style, and perhaps something of his delivery, all parts of later rhetorical teaching. We see this system of learning in practice in the opening pages of Plato's *Phaedrus*. The young Phaedrus has much admired a sophistic speech by Lysias,[17] secured the autograph (228a–b), and is trying to memorize it when he encounters Socrates, who shows him how to compose a speech on the same theme that will be better in structure and argument, and later delivers a speech on the opposite side of the issue. Speeches of this type are to be distinguished from serious expositions of an idea by a sophist, some of whom deserve to be regarded as philosophers: Prodicus' "Choice of Heracles," for example, which is a moral allegory, or Alcidamas' "On Those Writing Written Speeches," or the rhetorical pamphlets of Isocrates. In these works the subject matter definitely counted very much; in the former, more sophistic type, it was a way of holding the audience's attention while demonstrating a method. Some sophistic *epideixis*, of course, fell in between these extremes. Gorgias' *Helen* (of which a translation can be found in Appendix I.A) illustrates a method and expounds some serious ideas about the nature of speech and human psychology, but at the end he refers to the speech as a *paignion*, or "plaything." In the surviving works of Athenian orators of the fifth and fourth centuries B.C.E. only the three tetralogies attributed to Antiphon are certainly to be regarded as having been written to furnish models of oratory. They do not refer to specific occasions and are excellent illustrations of argument. For actual courtroom use their arguments could be adapted

---

16. The speeches in Plato's *Symposium* are also sophistic in style, but not ostensibly intended to teach rhetorical technique.

17. We do not know whether the speech in the text was actually a work by Lysias or, more likely, a deliberately bad imitation by Plato.

by introduction of documents and witnesses, by development of commonplaces, and by combination of sources. There was, thus, no reason why collections of examples of argument or style should consist of complete speeches. We read that collections of introductions and conclusions were made by Antiphon, Critias, Cephalus, and Thrasymachus,[18] and the works of Demosthenes contain a collection of prooemia for political speeches.

A crucial passage for understanding how rhetorical technique was taught by a leading sophist is what Aristotle says at the end of his short treatise on *Sophistical Refutations* (183b16–184b7). Aristotle was trying to create a theoretical and systematic art of dialectic to replace an unscientific sophistic eristic;[19] the beginning is difficult, he says (183b23), but once started, progress will be made, as has been the case in rhetorical studies (*tous rhētorikous logous*) with a succession of writers leading from Tisias,[20] to Thrasymachus, Theodorus, and others. With this he contrasts (183b36) the educational technique of the sophist Gorgias in which, he says, students were assigned ready-made speeches to memorize, "as though a shoemaker were to try to teach his art by presenting his apprentice with an assortment of shoes." In Plato's dialogue *Gorgias* (449b), Gorgias claims to be able to make people into *rhētores* like himself, but as he appears in both Plato and Aristotle he lacks the ability to conceptualize his views of rhetoric. His students were expected to learn by imitation; perhaps he offered some criticism of their efforts. Gorgias did publish prose works other than speeches, including a treatise that seeks to prove that nothing exists, that if it did exist it could not be apprehended by human beings, and if it were apprehended by someone knowledge of it could not be communicated to another.[21] But the references to his statements about rhetoric do not seem to include a judicial handbook like those described earlier.[22]

---

18. See Radermacher 1951:B X 13–15; B XVII 1; B XVIII 1.

19. This word will recur from time to time in later passages. "Eristic" is a derivative of *eris*, "strife," and refers to argument for the sake of argument with little recourse to sound logic.

20. "Tisias after the first." Whom Aristotle regarded as "the first" is uncertain. One possibility is Empedocles (Diogenes Laertius 7.57–58; Quintilian 3.1.8). "The first" probably did not refer to Corax; see Appendix II.A.

21. For a translation of this unusual work, see Sprague 1972:42–46.

22. Dionysius of Halicarnassus says (*On Composition of Words* 12; p. 84) that Gorgias tried to define *kairos*, what was timely said, but did not write anything worth mentioning about it. Perhaps he just gave examples of timely statements.

Isocrates (436–338 B.C.E.) was the most influential teacher of rhetoric in Aristotle's time. Around 390, before Plato created the Academy, Isocrates opened a school in Athens to train future leaders of Greek society in the skills of civic life, especially speech; it attracted a large number of students from Athens and abroad and continued in existence for fifty years. He had probably been a student of Gorgias. The method of his school resembled the teaching of Gorgias and other sophists in that he composed speeches for students to imitate, but he probably also lectured on rhetoric, using his own speeches as examples of method, and since he had come under the influence of Socrates, he presents his teaching as "philosophy" (see the selection from *Against the Sophists* in Appendix I.E.1). In his own way, Isocrates sought to answer one criticism of rhetoric attributed to Socrates in Plato's *Gorgias* by proposing a special subject matter for rhetoric: not speeches in legal disputes, but the great issues of Greek society and its historical tradition, especially the need for the union of the Greek states against threats from Persia. By composing speeches on such themes (as described in his *Antidosis* and elsewhere), he sought to condition students' moral behavior so that they would think and speak noble, virtuous ideas and implement them in civic policy, thus providing a response to claims that rhetoric was an art of deception and flattery. His own speeches were not delivered in public but published as pamphlets. Aristotle had clearly read them, quotes examples of rhetorical technique from them, and largely refrains from criticism of Isocrates in *On Rhetoric*. Later sources, however, record a tradition of hostility between the two men. Isocrates' school was in direct competition with the Academy of Plato, and when Aristotle first taught rhetoric in the Academy in the 350s he is said to have been motivated by opposition to Isocrates' teaching.[23] The most evident difference between Aristotelian and Isocratean teaching is the great emphasis put on truth, knowledge of a subject, and logical argument by Aristotle in contrast to Isocrates' inclination to gloss over historical facts and his obsession with techniques of amplification and smoothness of style. Aristotle doubtless thought that Isocrates was at heart a sophist, that his philosophy was shallow, and that as a teacher of rhetoric he failed to give his students an adequate understanding of logical argument—which many at the time regarded as tiresome verbal pedantry.[24] Although Aristotle quotes Isocrates' speeches

---

23. See, e.g., Cicero, *On the Orator* 3.141.
24. See Isocrates' remarks in *Against the Sophists* and the *Letter to Alexander*.

repeatedly, and although they both had close connections with the Macedonian court, it seems clear that Aristotle retained his early objections to Isocrates as a rhetorician (see, e.g., *On Rhetoric* 1.9.38). It has become a commonplace of the history of rhetoric to speak of two traditions: the Aristotelian, which stresses the logical side of the subject, and the Isocratean, emphasizing the literary aspects of rhetoric.[25]

The influence of Plato (429–347 B.C.E.) on Aristotle's view of rhetoric is strong but complex. As Plato describes in his *Seventh Epistle*, he had been embittered against contemporary rhetoric by his own frustrated attempts to participate in politics and by the trial and execution of his master, Socrates, at the hands of the Athenian democracy in 399. His criticism is most shrill in the dialogue *Gorgias*, completed about the time Aristotle was born. In the first two parts of the dialogue (the conversations of Socrates with Gorgias and Polus), the existence of any valid art of rhetoric is called into question, though some of what is said is ironic or deliberately provocative on Socrates' part. This is true of Socrates' argument, found in Appendix I.B, that since a rhetorician "knows" justice he must necessarily always be just, and his analogy between rhetoric and cookery as sham arts of flattery. Socrates demands that rhetoric have some subject matter particular to itself, but none of the possibilities (e.g., politics or justice) satisfy him. As noted in the first section of this introduction, Aristotle's early work, the dialogue *Gryllus*, contained arguments that rhetoric was not an "art," that is, not something capable of being reduced to a system. However, Aristotle's study of dialectic led him to realize that rhetoric, like dialectic, was an art, capable of systematic description, which differed from most other arts and disciplines in teaching a method of persuasion that could be applied to many different subject matters. Plato himself had led the way to the development of a philosophical rhetoric in a passage toward the end of *Gorgias* (504e):

> Will not the orator, artist and good man that he is, look to justice and temperance? And will he not apply his words to the souls of those to whom he speaks, and his actions too, and . . . will he not do it with his mind always on this purpose: how justice may come into being in the souls of the citizens and how injustice may be removed, and how temperance may be engendered and intemperance removed, and every other virtue be brought in and vice depart?

---

25. See Cicero, *On Invention* 2.8; Solmsen 1941.

In Plato's *Phaedrus*, written ten years or more after *Gorgias*, Socrates is made to develop the possibility of this ideal, philosophical rhetoric—something quite different from that flourishing in Greece or that taught by Isocrates. Near the end of the dialogue (277b5–c6) he summarizes what he has been saying as follows:

> Until someone knows the truth of each thing about which he speaks or writes and is able to define everything in its own genus, and having defined it knows how to break the genus down into species and subspecies to the point of indivisibility, discerning the nature of the soul in accordance with the same method, while discovering the logical category which fits with each nature, and until in a similar way he composes and adorns speech, furnishing variegated and complex speech to a variegated soul and simple speech to a simple soul—not until then will it be possible for speech to exist in an artistic form in so far as the nature of speech is capable of such treatment, neither for instruction nor for persuasion, as has been shown by our entire past discussion.

This ideal rhetoric, intended primarily for one-to-one communication, is clearly highly unrealistic if applied to public address, where the audience is made up of a variety of "souls" with differing patience and grasp of detailed argument. What Aristotle does in *On Rhetoric* is adapt the principles of Plato's philosophical rhetoric to more realistic situations. A speaker, he says (1.1.12), should not seek to persuade the audience of what is "debased." He posits three modes of persuasion that are an adaptation of Plato's call for fitting the speech to the souls of the audience (1.2.3). These become Aristotle's *ēthos*, or the projection of the character of the speaker as trustworthy; *pathos*, or consideration of the emotions of people in the audience; and *logos*, inductive and deductive logical argument. He seeks to provide a speaker with a basis for argument in "truth": that is, in knowledge of the propositions of politics and ethics and of how to use this knowledge to construct arguments (1.5–14, 2.18–26). He also supplies an understanding of psychology (2.1–11) and advice about adapting a speech to the character of an audience, viewed as types (2.12–17). His response to Plato on the subject of rhetoric (though without naming him) is analogous to his responses on the subject of the value of poetry, the nature of politics, ethics, and other subjects—less idealistic and more pragmatic, but based on philosophical values and methods.

C. ARISTOTLE'S CLASSIFICATION OF RHETORIC

Aristotle was the first person to give serious consideration to drawing a map of learning and to defining the relationship between the various disciplines of the arts and sciences, which were emerging as separate studies for the first time in the fourth century B.C.E. Aristotle's map of learning is the ultimate ancestor of library catalogues and the organization of the modern university in departments of arts and sciences. His own scheme can be found in Book 6 of *Metaphysics*, in Book 6 of *Nicomachean Ethics*, and in passing references elsewhere.

Aristotle divided intellectual activity into (1) theoretical sciences, where the goal is "knowing," knowledge for knowledge's sake, and which include mathematics, physics, biology, and theology; (2) practical arts, where the goal is "doing" something, including politics and ethics; and (3) productive arts of "making" something, including architecture, the fine arts, the crafts, and also medicine (which produces health). In addition, there are (4) methods or tools (*organa*), applicable to all study but with no distinct subject matter of their own. Logic and dialectic belong in that class. Aristotelian scholars of late antiquity and the Middle Ages regarded rhetoric as one of these methods or tools, largely on the basis of what is said in *On Rhetoric* 1.1. Modern scholars have tended to attribute to Aristotle the view that rhetoric is a productive art, like poetics. What he actually says in 1.2.7, however, is that rhetoric is a mixture. It is partly a method (like dialectic) with no special subject of its own, but partly a practical art derived from ethics and politics on the basis of its conventional uses. In *Nicomachean Ethics* 1.2.4–6 he calls rhetoric a part of the architectonic subject of politics. In defining rhetoric in *On Rhetoric* 1.2.1, however, he says that it is an ability of "seeing" the available means of persuasion (thus not necessarily using them oneself) and employs a verb related to the word *theory*. Thus, rhetoric in Aristotle's view also has a theoretical element and in addition clearly does often "produce" persuasion, speeches, and texts. In reading *On Rhetoric* we perceive a gradual shift of focus, moving from the use of rhetoric as a tool (like dialectic) in 1.1 to its theoretical aspects in 1.2, its political and ethical content in the rest of Books 1 and 2, and its productive aspects in Book 3. There are some excellent comments on the classification of rhetoric, showing Aristotle's influence, in Quintilian's great treatise, *The Education of the Orator* (2.18.2–5), leading to the conclusion that its primary role is that of a "practical" art.

D. ARISTOTLE'S ORIGINAL AUDIENCE AND HIS AUDIENCE TODAY

Since the publication of the first edition of this book there has been a resumption of the ongoing scholarly discussion about the audience for which *On Rhetoric* was composed and about how it should be read today.[26] In a prize-winning article entitled "Aristotle's *Rhetoric* Against Rhetoric: Unitarian Reading and Esoteric Hermeneutics," Carol Poster (1997) argued that Aristotle remained faithful to the ethical values of Plato's philosophical rhetoric and hostile to rhetoric as generally understood. In the aftermath of the execution of Socrates, however, he recognized that philosophers could be in danger. *On Rhetoric*, she concludes,

> is provided as a manual for the student trained in dialectic who needs, particularly for self-defense or defense of Platonic-Aristotelian philosophy, to sway an ignorant or corrupt audience or to understand the functioning of rhetoric within the badly ordered state. The techniques described are dangerous, potentially harmful to both the speaker and audience, and ought not be revealed to the general readership of Aristotle's dialogues, but only taught within the controlled environment of Aristotle's school, as part of the esoteric corpus of Platonic-Aristotelian teaching. (244)

A few years later, in "The Audience for Aristotle's *Rhetoric*," Edward W. Clayton (2004) examined the possible audiences Aristotle might have had in mind, including the legislator of an ideal city, the Athenian public or an elite subset of that public, the students in his philosophical school, or different audiences in different parts of the work, written at different times. He concludes that the students in his school are the most likely audience, agreeing in this with Poster, though without her emphasis on moral urgency.

The text of *On Rhetoric* that we read today is substantially the text left by Aristotle at his death and preserved in his personal library.[27] It

---

26. An earlier discussion was that of Lord 1981.

27. In a paper at the 2005 convention of the National Communication Association, Brad McAdon argued that the text we call *On Rhetoric* is a compilation of material by Aristotle, Theophrastus, and others, which was made in the first century B.C.E. by Andronicus. This is an extension of views found in McAdon 2001 and 2004 and is, at most, probably exaggerated; see further, Appendix II.B.

was one of his "esoteric" works, not published and not available to readers generally until three hundred years later. Thus there is little doubt about the audience he envisioned for this text: students in his school in Athens in the years 335–323 B.C.E. It remains the case, however, that different parts of the text were originally composed at different times for a different audience, even if somewhat revised later. The part of the text most in question is what Rist (1989:84–85) called "the early core"—Book 1, chapters 5–15—though most parts of Book 3 are perhaps also early. By "early" is meant the 350s when Aristotle was a member of the Academy and is said to have given the "afternoon lectures" to a general audience.[28] Aristotle had earlier written and published the dialogue *Gryllus* in which he is said to have argued, perhaps with the school of Isocrates in mind, that rhetoric is not an "art" in the sense of a system or method. This is the position advanced by Socrates in Plato's *Gorgias*, but we know that Aristotle subsequently abandoned it, for in 1.1.2 he defines rhetoric as an art. Thus his ideas on rhetoric did develop from their Platonic base, perhaps in connection with teaching the subject for the first time, studying real speeches, and reading the handbooks, but he also never abandoned Plato's view of what rhetoric should be in an ideal society. He made a systematic collection of teachings from rhetorical handbooks, the *Synagōgē tekhnōn*, and though he criticizes these handbooks, in *Sophistical Refutations* he also acknowledges that progress had been made over time in constructing a systematic art of rhetoric. Poster's statement that Aristotle did not think the techniques of rhetoric should be revealed to a general readership is clearly an overstatement.

Aristotle's *Poetics* shows that he did not share Plato's moral scruples about poetry, but neither does he seem to regard it as a moral force. Indeed, unlike Plato and many later critics, Aristotle apparently did not believe that it was a function of poetry to provide ethical patterns of conduct, good or bad, for listeners or readers; at most, they might experience a beneficial and brief psychological catharsis of pity and fear. Much of his other research was devoted to physics and biology, and in these scientific works his ethical philosophy is temporarily set aside in the interests of discovering all that can be known. Aristotle, unlike Plato, was a formalist in the sense that he was interested in describing phenomena of the natural and social world on the basis of observation; he clearly became interested in rhetoric as a social phenomenon and potentially as a practical application of his

---

28. For the sources, see above, Introduction A, n. 8.

theories of logic, and he was capable of giving a detached, objective account of it as of other subjects and of describing this to students.[29] This material he revised and inserted in *On Rhetoric* as we read it today, incorporating moral caveats against its improper use at the beginning of Books 1 and 3 and justifying study of it by philosophers on the basis of the corruption of contemporary society. It seems likely that Aristotle taught rhetoric to the young Alexander, and if so, what he would have taught him were practical skills in public speaking and an ability to evaluate speeches by others who came before him, with warnings about the moral dangers inherent in rhetoric.

Modern audiences for *On Rhetoric* fall roughly into four main groups, with considerable overlapping and many individual differences of opinion. One group consists of the classical philologists, specialists in Greek language, literature, and culture. Their special interest is textual and contextual, including comparisons of Aristotle's teaching with the practice of oratory, historiography, and other literature of his time and with political procedures in Athens, and it also includes efforts to date different parts of Aristotle's works on the basis of content, development of thought, and style. As a result of these studies, the philologists tend to pounce on inconsistencies in the text and thus resist viewing it as a unity.

A second group is that of the philosophers, largely scholars who study and teach ancient philosophy. They are naturally most interested in the philosophical content of *On Rhetoric* and in the relation of it to Aristotle's other philosophical works, as well as to the dialogues of Plato. Like their late-antique and medieval predecessors, they tend to approach Aristotelianism as a consistent whole, and they often defend the unity of *On Rhetoric* against the philologists. As skilled dialecticians, they are good at what they do and can easily overwhelm the average reader with their subtlety and learning, sometimes at the expense of distorting what Aristotle actually says.

The third group is that of teachers of English composition and speech communication, whose primary interest is in the rhetorical theory found in the work. They are understandably inclined to use it as the basis of developing a comprehensive system of rhetoric, following out the implications of the text or imaging what Aristotle ought to have said but didn't. They are especially interested in argumentation and in problems involving Aristotle's understanding of the enthymeme and its implications.

---

29. Cf. Hill 1981.

The fourth and smallest group is that of the literary scholars and critics. Their interest in the *Rhetoric* is largely confined to the third book, where Aristotle's theory of metaphor is of special interest, and they read the *Rhetoric* in conjunction with the *Poetics*.

E. THE STRENGTHS AND LIMITATIONS OF *ON RHETORIC*

The great strength of *On Rhetoric* derives from its clear recognition (in contrast to views expressed by Plato) that rhetoric is a technique or tool applicable to any subject and from the universality and utility of its basic, systematically organized, concepts. It provides a method for looking at rhetoric as a human phenomenon, for learning how to use it, and also for a system of criticism, in that the features of speech that Aristotle describes can be used not only to construct a speech, but also to analyze and evaluate other forms of discourse. The most important of the concepts that Aristotle uses as frameworks for his discussion are:

1. The identification of three (and only three) *pisteis*, or forms of persuasion, derived from the factors in any speech situation:
   a. Presentation of the trustworthy character of the speaker
   b. The logical argument set out in the text
   c. The emotional effect created by the speaker and text on the audience or reader
2. The distinction of three (and only three) species of rhetoric, based on whether the audience is or is not a *judge*, in the sense of being able to take specific action as a result of being persuaded to do so, and the *time* with which each species is concerned:
   a. If a judge of past actions, the species is *judicial*
   b. If a judge of future action, the species is *deliberative*
   c. If an observer of the speech, not called on to take action, the species is *epideictic*

Each of these species has its characteristic "end," the principal issue with which it is concerned:
   a. The end of judicial rhetoric is justice
   b. The end of deliberative rhetoric is the best interest of the audience
   c. The end of epideictic rhetoric is praise or blame of the subject

3. Forms of persuasion are either:
   a. *Non-artistic*: direct evidence (facts, witnesses, documents, etc.) that the speaker uses but does not—or should not—invent; or
   b. *Artistic*: logical arguments constructed by the speaker, of two types:
      i. Inductive argument, called paradigm, or example, drawing a particular conclusion from one or more parallels
      ii. Deductive argument, called enthymeme, or rhetorical syllogism, drawing a conclusion from stated or implied premises
4. In rhetoric the speaker or writer almost always deals with probabilities—what could have happened or can happen based on what happens for the most part in such situations.
5. The materials of enthymemes come from the premises of other disciplines, especially politics and ethics, but their formal structure draws on *topics*, strategies of argument useful in dealing with any subject.

On Rhetoric is strong in its emphasis on the importance of logical validity. There are also valuable concepts in the discussion of style, especially the demand for clarity, the understanding of the effect of different kinds of language and sentence structure, and the explication of the role of metaphor. The work is also of interest in that it summarizes many of the political and moral assumptions of contemporary Greek society and preserves many quotations from writers or speakers that we would not otherwise have.

As in all of his philosophy, in describing rhetoric Aristotle sought to discover what was universally true, and to a considerable extent he was successful. His system of rhetoric can, and has been, used to describe the phenomenon of speech in cultures as diverse from the Greeks as the ancient Hebrews, the Chinese, and primitive societies around the world; and it can be used to describe many features of modern communication.

The treatise nevertheless has limitations and needs to be expanded or revised to provide a complete, general rhetoric. With only occasional exceptions, its focus is on public address or civic discourse and is somewhat conditioned by the circumstances and conventions of the forms with which he was familiar. Epideictic discourse, in particular, needs to be looked at in a variety of ways not recognized by Aristotle.

He thought of it as the rhetoric of praise or blame, as in a funeral oration or a denunciation of someone, and failed to formulate its role in the instilling, preservation, or enhancement of cultural values, even though this was clearly a major function, as seen in Pericles' famous *Funeral Oration* or the epideictic speeches of Isocrates. His apparent lack of interest in the moral value of epideictic rhetoric is perhaps influenced by scorn for Isocrates, but it is also analogous to his feelings about poetry mentioned earlier.

Aristotle's theory of *ēthos* is striking, but he limits it to the effect of character as conveyed by the words of a speaker and he fails to recognize the great role of the authority of a speaker as already perceived by an audience.[30] He limits non-artistic means of persuasion to direct evidence that can be used in a trial, while the concept should perhaps be enlarged to include the appearance and authority of a speaker, features of the setting and the context of a speech that affect its reception, and other factors that a speaker can use for persuasive ends.

Another problem with the work is Aristotle's failure to illustrate and relate to rhetoric many of the political and ethical topics he discusses. Chapters 4 and 5 of Book 1, for example, give no suggestions about how to use political topics in a speech, and chapters 6–14 could have benefited from showing more clearly how this material can be employed. Similarly, the description of the emotions in Book 2, chapters 2–11, fails to draw examples from the rhetorical situation. Aristotle probably had a rather limited knowledge of Greek political oratory; in addition to epideictic orations, which he quotes, some deliberative and judicial orations were available in published form, but he seems to have made no effort to construct his theory of rhetoric by analysis of real speeches.[31] Instead, he relies on constructing arguments based on his understanding of the goals of politics and ethics. Great emphasis is put on understanding the enthymeme as the key to logical persuasion, but its theoretical importance is probably exaggerated, since its syllogistic qualities are very slippery, and Aristotle's precepts can be reduced to a recommendation that a speaker give a reason (or apparent reason) for what is asserted. Although he

---

30. This probably results from the fact that speakers in the law courts and political assemblies were often not well-known individuals. What counted was not who they were but what they said.

31. See Trevett 1996.

mentions different kinds of questions that may be at issue in a trial—questions of fact or definition of the law, for example—he fails to give adequate priority to a method for determining these questions in planning a speech, something which was later supplied by the development of stasis theory.[32] Some problems with the work result from different parts having been written at different times, and though there are signs of revisions and addition of cross-references, Aristotle never completed the process, leaving not only precepts unapplied to public address, but also inconsistencies both in doctrine and in terminology—for example, his varying uses of *pistis* and *topos*. Nor does Aristotle take a strong stand against the common Greek preference for circumstantial evidence over the direct evidence of documents and witnesses.

F. CHAPTER-BY-CHAPTER OUTLINE OF *ON RHETORIC*

To clarify the overall structure of *On Rhetoric* and to give readers an initial understanding of its coverage, a chapter-by-chapter outline of the work follows. The book divisions originated with Aristotle and represent convenient lengths for a papyrus scroll in Aristotle's time. The chapter divisions were first made by George of Trebizond in the fifteenth century and in most cases represent logical units.

Books 1–2: *Pisteis*, or The Means of Persuasion in Public Address

Book 1: Introduction; Definition and Divisions of the Subject to be Discussed; Special Topics Useful in Deliberative, Epideictic, and Judicial Rhetoric

Chapters 1–3: Introductory

Chapter 1: Introduction to Rhetoric for Students of Dialectic
2: Definition of Rhetoric; Means of Persuasion; Topics
3: The Three Species of Rhetoric: Deliberative, Judicial, Epideictic

---

32. Cf. Liu 1991.

BOOK 1
Pisteis, or The Means of Persuasion in Public Address

■ Books 1 and 2 discuss the means of persuasion available to a public speaker by presentation of the speaker's character as trustworthy, by use of persuasive arguments, and by moving the emotions of the audience. Although this part of rhetoric has come to be known as "invention" (from Latin, *inventio*) Aristotle himself offers no general term for it until the transition section at the end of Book 2, where it is referred to as *dianoia*, "thought." Throughout Books 1 and 2, discovering the available means of persuasion is treated as constituting the whole of rhetoric, properly understood, and until the last sentence of 2.26 there is no anticipation of the discussion of style and arrangement that follows in Book 3. To judge from Diogenes Laertius' list of Aristotle's works, Books 1 and 2 constituted the text for lectures in the Lyceum as Aristotle originally planned, Book 3 being a separate work on style and arrangement that came to be combined with it.

Chapters 1–3: Introduction

Chapter 1: Introduction to Rhetoric for Students of Dialectic

■ The first chapter of Book 1 was written for students in Aristotle's philosophical school who had completed a study of dialectic and who perhaps had little practical knowledge of rhetoric, though they may have been aware of the existence of handbooks on the subject and probably also of Plato's strictures on rhetoric in the dialogues *Gorgias* and *Phaedrus*. Thus they would be interested to hear what Aristotle had to say in reaction to those works. The chapter as a whole is very Platonic and contains echoes of several of Plato's dialogues (see Schütrumpf 1994a), but neither here nor elsewhere in this work does Aristotle criticize Plato by name.

Dialectic as taught by Aristotle was the art of philosophical disputation. Practice in it was regularly provided in his philosophical school, and his treatise know as *Topics* is a textbook of dialectic. (The opening chapter of the *Topics* describing dialectic can be found in Appendix I.D at the end of this volume.) The procedure in dialectical disputation was for one student to state a thesis (e.g., "Pleasure is the only good" or "Justice is the power of the stronger") and for a second student to try to refute the thesis by asking a series of questions that could be answered by "yes" or "no." If successful, the interlocutor led the respondent into a contradiction or logically indefensible position by means of definition and divisions of the question or by drawing analogies, much as Socrates is shown doing in the earlier Platonic dialogues; however, the respondent might be able to defend his position and win the argument. Dialectic proceeds by question and answer, not, as rhetoric does, by continuous exposition. A dialectical argument does not contain the parts of a public address; there is no introduction, narration, or epilogue, as in a speech—only proof and refutation. In dialectic only logical argument is acceptable, whereas in rhetoric (as Aristotle will explain in chapter 2), the impression of moral character conveyed by the speaker and the emotions awakened in the audience contribute to persuasion. While both dialectic and rhetoric build their arguments on commonly held opinions (*endoxa*) and deal with what is probable (not with logical certainty), dialectic examines general issues (such as the nature of justice), whereas rhetoric usually seeks a specific judgment (e.g., whether or not some specific action was just or whether or not some specific policy will be beneficial). Although Aristotle lists the similarities between rhetoric and dialectic, somewhat oddly he does not specify their differences.

After discussing the similarities between dialectic and rhetoric, Aristotle criticizes (sections 3–11) the Arts, or handbooks, of previous writers, which he finds unsatisfactory in several ways. Into this discussion are inserted parenthetical remarks (sections 7–9) on the specificity desirable in framing good laws, something feasible only in an ideal state. The chapter continues (sections 12 and 13) with a discussion of why rhetoric is useful—remarks that can be thought of as addressed to students of philosophy who, under the influence of Plato, may be indifferent or hostile to rhetoric. To a general Greek audience, the usefulness of rhetoric, especially in democratic assemblies and courts of law, would have been obvious, whereas they might well have been more dubious about dialectic, which could easily seem pedantic hairsplitting (see, e.g., Isocrates' criticisms in *Against the Sophists* and in the prooemion of his *Encomium of Helen*). Finally, the chapter concludes with consideration of the function of rhetoric and a definition of sophistry (section 14).

Chapter 1 is generally recognized as creating problems for the unity of the treatise.[1] Aristotle here seems firmly to reject using emotional appeals, identifies rhetoric entirely with logical argument, and gives no hint that style and arrangement may be important in rhetoric (as will emerge in Book 3). In section 6 he even seems to say that the importance and the justice of a case are not appropriate issues for a speaker to discuss; they should be left for a jury to judge. But the justice of a speaker's case, its importance, and its amplification subsequently will be given extended treatment. Some interpreters have sought to force the point of view of chapter 1 into conformity with what follows by making careful distinctions about Aristotle's terms. This involves claiming, for example, that *pisteis*, "proofs," in section 3 already includes the use of character and emotion as means of persuasion; that ethical and emotional proofs are "enthymematic"; and that verbal attack, pity, and anger in section 4 refer to expressions of emotion rather than to the reasoned use of an understanding of psychology and motivation.[2] None of this is entirely satisfactory. A better approach is that of Sprute (1994), who regards chapter 1 as describing an ideal rhetoric in an ideal state where the laws prohibit speaking outside the subject, whereas Aristotle then provides in chapter 2 a second introduction for a more realistic account of rhetoric in contemporary society. Aristotle regarded contemporary society, especially Athenian democracy, as corrupt. What he says in Book 3 (3.1.5) about the need to consider oratorical delivery applies generally to his conception of the study of rhetoric: "But since the whole business of rhetoric is with opinion, one should pay attention to delivery, not because it is right, but because it is necessary, since true justice seeks nothing more in a speech than neither to offend nor to entertain, with the result that everything except demonstration is incidental; but, nevertheless, [delivery] has great power, as has been said, because of the corruption of the audience." Other relevant passage are 1.1.12, 2.5.7, 2.21.14, 3.14.8, and 3.18.4. Among Aristotle's students he could expect some to be interested in a public career, and they needed to understand, and perhaps sometimes use, rhetoric as it was practiced in contemporary society.

Some of the apparent inconsistency between 1.1 and later parts of Book 1 results from the fact that Aristotle included in the final text, with only minor revisions, material he had originally written for the course on practical rhetoric he gave to a general audience twenty years earlier. This applies

---

1. See most recently McAdon 2004.
2. These views were argued by Grimaldi 1972, 1980, 1988.

to material in chapters 4–15 and includes, for example, chapter 9 with its specific recommendations about what to say in an epideictic speech, with no mention of ethical problems that might arise.

1. Rhetoric[3] is an *antistrophos* to dialectic;[4] for both are concerned with such things as are, to a certain extent, within the knowledge of all people and belong to no separately defined science.[5] A result is that all people, in some way, share in both; for all, up to a point, try both to test and uphold an argument [as in dialectic] and to defend themselves and attack [others, as in rhetoric]. 2. Now among the general public, some do these things at random and others through an ability acquired by habit,[6] but since both ways are possible, it is clear that it would also be possible to do the same by [following] a path; for it is possible to observe[7] the cause why some succeed by habit and

---

3. *Hē rhētorikē* (the rhetorical), a feminine singular adjective used as an abstract noun; cf. *dialektikē, poiētikē*. Neither dialectic nor rhetoric assumes knowledge of any technical subject, and both build a case on the basis of what any reasonable person would believe. Aristotle takes the term *rhetoric* from Plato. Others usually spoke of the "art of speech"; see Schiappa 1990.

4. This famous statement has been much discussed; important publications since the first edition of this translation include Brunschwig 1996 and McAdon 2001, both with earlier bibliography. *Antistrophos* is commonly translated "counterpart." Other possibilities include "correlative" and "coordinate." The word can mean "converse." In Greek choral lyric, the metrical pattern of a strophe (stanza) is repeated with different words in the antistrophe. Aristotle is more likely thinking of and rejecting the analogy of the true and false arts elaborated by Socrates in *Gorgias*, where justice is said to be an *antistrophos* to medicine (464b8) and rhetoric, the false form of justice, is compared to cookery, the false form of medicine (465c1–2). Isocrates (*Antidosis* 182) speaks of the arts of the soul (called philosophy, but essentially political rhetoric) and the arts of the body (gymnastic) as *antistrophoi*. This view is equally unacceptable to Aristotle, for whom rhetoric is a tool, like dialectic, though its subject matter is derived from some other discipline, such as ethics or politics; see 1.2.7. Aristotle thus avoids the fallacy of Plato's *Gorgias*, where Socrates is obsessed with finding some kind of knowledge specific to rhetoric. On later interpretations of *antistrophos*, see Green 1990.

5. The first sentence of the treatise, with its proposition and supporting reason, is an example of what Aristotle will call an enthymeme. The reader should become sensitive to the constant use of enthymemes throughout the text, often introduced by the particle *gar* (for).

6. The former hardly know what they are doing, but the latter, by trial and error, have gained a practical sense of what is effective.

7. *Theōrein*, lit. "see," but with the implication of "theorize." This is an instance of the visual imagery common in the *Rhetoric*.

others accidentally,[8] and all would at once agree that such observation is the activity of an art [*tekhnē*].[9]

3. As things are now,[10] those who have composed *Arts of Speech* have worked on a small part of the subject; for only *pisteis*[11] are artistic (other things are supplementary), and these writers say nothing about enthymemes, which is the "body" of persuasion,[12] while they give most of their attention to matters external to the subject; 4. for verbal attack and pity and anger and such emotions of the mind [*psykhē*] do not relate to fact but are appeals to the juryman.[13] As a result, if all trials were conducted as they are in some present-day states and especially in those well-governed [the handbook writers] would have nothing to say; 5. for everyone thinks the laws ought to require this, and some even adopt the practice and forbid speaking outside the subject, as in the Areopagus too,[14] rightly so providing; for it is wrong to warp the jury by leading them into anger or envy or

---

8. Here, as often, Aristotle reverses the order of reference: *accidentally* refers back to *at random*. Such *chiasmus* is a common feature of Greek.

9. In contrast to Socrates in *Gorgias* and to his own earlier position in the dialogue *Gryllus*, Aristotle now has no doubt that rhetoric is an art. Awareness of the cause of success allows technique to be conceptualized and taught systematically. In *Nicomachean Ethics* 6.4 Aristotle defines a *tekhnē* as "a reasoned habit of mind" in making something.

10. In 1.2.4 Aristotle again criticizes contemporary technical writers. He thus appears to be thinking primarily of the handbooks of the mid-fourth century B.C.E., such as those by Pamphilus and Callippus cited in 2.23.21. On the development of rhetorical handbooks in Greece, see Introduction section B and Appendix II.A.

11. *Pistis* (pl. *pisteis*) has a number of different meanings in different contexts: "proof, means of persuasion, belief," etc. In 1.2.2–3 Aristotle will distinguish between artistic and non-artistic *pisteis* and divide the former into three means of persuasion based on character, logical argument, and arousing emotion. Here in ch. 1 readers familiar with dialectic have no knowledge yet of persuasion by character or emotion and will assume that *pistis* means "logical proof."

12. *Body* is here contrasted with "matters external" in the next clause. In 1.2.7 rhetoric is said "to dress itself up in the clothes of politics."

13. Cf. Socrates' criticism of the handbooks in *Phaedrus* 269b4ff. The handbooks offered examples of argument from probability, but they did not identify its logical structure. The concept of the logical syllogism and its rhetorical counterpart, the enthymeme (to be discussed in ch. 2), are Aristotelian contributions. The handbooks probably treated the emotions in discussing the prooemion and epilogue (on which see Aristotle's account in 3.14 and 19). There were separate collections of emotional commonplaces such as the *Eleoi* of Thrasymachus (see 3.1.7).

14. In Aristotle's time the jurisdiction of the Athenian court of the Areopagus was chiefly limited to homicide cases. That its rules of relevance were strict is also attested in Lycurgus' speech *Against Leocrites* 12.

pity: that is the same as if someone made a straight-edge ruler crooked before using it. 6. And further, it is clear that the opponents have no function except to show that something is or is not true or has happened or has not happened; whether it is important or trivial or just or unjust, in so far as the lawmaker has not provided a definition, the juror should somehow decide himself and not learn from the opponents.

■ The following passage on framing laws resembles some of what Plato says in *Laws* 9.875–76 (see Schütrumpf 1994a) and is apparently a parenthetical remark of Aristotle to students of political philosophy; he may well have said something of this sort to young Alexander. Aristotle probably had little personal experience with cases at law and thus did not quite appreciate the impossibility of providing by law for every conceivable future circumstance; however, he will modify the position in 1.13.13 when the practical problems are considered. Section 9 will take up were section 6 leaves off.

(7. It is highly appropriate for well-enacted laws to define everything as exactly as possible and for as little as possible to be left to the judges: first because it is easier to find one or a few than [to find] many who are prudent and capable of framing laws and judging; second, legislation results from consideration over much time, while judgments are made at the moment [of a trial or debate], so it is difficult for the judges to determine justice and benefits fairly; but most important of all, because the judgment of a lawmaker is not about a particular case but about what lies in the future and in general, while the assemblyman and the juror are actually judging present and specific cases. For them, friendliness and hostility and individual self-interest are often involved, with the result that they are no longer able to see the truth adequately, but their private pleasure or grief casts a shadow on their judgment. 8. In other matters, then, as we have been saying, the judge should have authority to determine as little as possible; but it is necessary to leave to the judges the question of whether something has happened or has not happened, will or will not be, is or is not the case; for the lawmaker cannot foresee these things.)

9. If this is so, it is clear that matters external to the subject are described as an art by those who define other things: for example, why it is necessary to have the introduction [*prooemion*] or the narration [*diēgēsis*] and each of the other parts;[15] for [in treating these matters]

1354b

---

15. The *Arts*, or handbooks of rhetoric, were organized around discussion of what kind of thing should be said in each of the parts usually found in a judicial speech. These included *prooemion*, *diēgēsis*, *pistis*, and *epilogos*; see Introduction section B and Book 3, chs. 13–19.

they concern themselves only with how they may put the judge in a certain frame of mind,[16] while they explain nothing about artistic proofs; and that is the question of how one may become *enthymematic*.[17] 10. It is for this reason that although the method of deliberative and judicial speaking is the same and though deliberative subjects are finer and more important to the state than private transactions, [the handbook writers] have nothing to say about the former, and all try to describe the art of speaking in a law court, because it is less service-able to speak things outside the subject in deliberative situations;[18] for there the judge judges about matters that affect himself, so that nothing is needed except to show that circumstances are as the speaker says.[19] But in judicial speeches this is not enough; rather, it is first serviceable to gain over the hearer; for the judgment is about other people's business and the judges, considering the matter in relation to their own affairs and listening with partiality, lend themselves to [the needs of] the litigants but do not judge [objectively]; thus, as we said   1355a earlier, in many places the law prohibits speaking outside the subject [in court cases]; in deliberative assemblies the judges themselves adequately guard against this.

11. Since it is evident that artistic method is concerned with *pisteis* and since *pistis* is a sort of demonstration [*apodeixis*][20] (for we most believe when we suppose something to have been demonstrated) and since rhetorical *apodeixis* is enthymeme (and this is, generally speaking, the strongest of the *pisteis*)[21] and the enthymeme is a sort of syllogism (and it is a function of dialectic, either as a whole or one of its parts, to see about every syllogism equally), it is clear that he who is best able to see from what materials, and how, a syllogism arises would also be most enthymematic—if he grasps also what sort of things an enthymeme is concerned with and what differences it has

---

16. This was regarded as a major function of the prooemion (cf. 3.14.9–11) and epilogue (3.19.1).

17. The meaning of this term will be explained in the next paragraph.

18. Contrary to what Aristotle says, speeches like Demosthenes' *On the Crown* show that speeches in trials could be as fine and as politically significant as speeches in the democratic assembly and were by no means limited to "private transactions," or contracts, as Aristotle implies. In the manuscripts the sentence continues, "and deliberative oratory is less mischievous than judicial, but of more general interest." This is probably a comment by a later reader.

19. In deliberative rhetoric the "judges" are members of a council or assembly, making decisions about public matters that affect themselves.

20. Aristotle's technical term for logically valid, scientific demonstration.

21. This clause was bracketed by Kassel (1976) as added by a later reader.

from a logical syllogism; for it belongs to the same capacity both to see the true and what resembles the true, and at the same time humans have a natural disposition for the true and to a large extent hit on the truth; thus an ability to aim at commonly held opinions [*endoxa*][22] is a characteristic of one who also has a similar ability in regard to the truth.

■ In composing this complex and important sentence, Aristotle has assumed that students already understand from earlier study of dialectic the concepts of *pistis, apodeixis,* and *enthymēma.* Enthymeme literally means "something in the mind" and had been used by Isocrates (*Against the Sophists* 17; see Appendix I.E.1, sec. 16) to mean a "striking thought," or idea used to adorn a speech. In *Rhetoric for Alexander* (see Appendix I.F, ch. 10) enthymemes are described as considerations that run counter to the speech or action in question. In *Prior Analytics* 2.27 Aristotle defines enthymeme as "a syllogism from probabilities or signs," and he sometimes uses syllogism in the general sense of a reasoning, as in 1.2.8; he also occasionally uses "syllogism" where he means "enthymeme"; e.g., 1.10.1, 3.17.15. In contrast, a valid syllogism in the technical sense is a logical certainty, "true," and most perfectly seen only when expressed symbolically: e.g.: "If all A is B, and some A is C, then some C is B." The traditional example in post-Aristotelian logic is, "If all men are mortal, and Socrates is a man, then Socrates is mortal." In 1.2.14 Aristotle says that "few" of the premises of enthymemes are necessarily true. In 1.2.13 and 2.22.3 he says that an enthymeme need not express all its premises. The Aristotelian distinction between a syllogism and an enthymeme is largely one of context—tightly reasoned philosophical discourse in the case of the syllogism versus popular speech or writing with resulting informality in the expression of an argument in an enthymeme. In public address an argument may be a worthwhile consideration even if it is not absolutely valid. An example of a typical enthymeme might be "Socrates is virtuous; for he is wise" or "Since / If Socrates is wise, he is virtuous." Here the premises are only probable and a universal major premise (not necessarily valid), "All the wise are virtuous," is assumed. Aristotle gives examples of enthymemes in 2.21.2 and at the end of 3.17.17. Modern scholars often misunderstand Aristotle's concept of an enthymeme or warp it for their own purposes; see the excellent critique by Robert N. Gaines in Gross and Walzer (2000: 3–23).

---

22. On *endoxa*, see *Topics* 1.1 in Appendix I.D.

THE USEFULLNESS OF RHETORIC

That other writers describe as an art things outside the subject [of a speech] and that they have rather too much inclined toward judicial oratory is clear; 12. but rhetoric *is* useful, [first] because the true and the just are by nature[23] stronger than their opposites, so that if judgments are not made in the right way [the true and the just] are necessarily defeated [by their opposites]. And this is worthy of censure.[24] Further, even if we were to have the most exact knowledge, it would not be very easy for us in speaking to use it to persuade [some audiences]. Speech based on knowledge is teaching, but teaching is impossible [with some audiences]; rather, it is necessary for *pisteis* and speeches [as a whole] to be formed on the basis of common [beliefs], as we said in the *Topics*[25] about communication with a crowd. Further, one should be able to argue persuasively on either side of a question, just as in the use of syllogisms, not that we may actually do both (for one should not persuade what is debased)[26] but in order that it may not escape our notice what the real state of the case is and that we ourselves may be able to refute if another person uses speech unjustly. None of the other arts reasons in opposite directions; dialectic and rhetoric alone do this; for both are equally concerned with opposites.[27] Of course the underlying facts are not equally good in each case; but true and better ones are by nature always more productive of good syllogisms and, in a word, more persuasive. In addition, it would be strange if an inability to defend oneself by means of the body is shameful, while there is no shame in an inability to use

---

23. Aristotle believed that truth was grounded in nature (*physis*) and capable of apprehension by reason. In this he differs both from Plato (for whom truth is grounded in the divine origin of the soul) and from the sophists [for whom judgments were based on *nomos* (convention), which in turn results from the ambivalent nature of language as the basis of human society].

24. On the text and interpretation of this sentence, see Grimaldi 1980:1.25–28.

25. *Topics* 1.1.2; see Appendix I.D.

26. What is debased (*ta phaula*) refers to whatever is bad, cheap, or morally and socially useless. This principle, important as a response to Plato's criticism of rhetoric, appears only in a parenthetical remark and is not repeated in prescriptive parts of the treatise but should probably be assumed.

27. There is, however, the difference that in dialectic, opposite trains of argument are actually expressed in the dialectical situation, whereas in rhetoric the speaker has usually tried to think out the opposing arguments before speaking to be able to answer them if need arises. But occasionally an orator will both express and refute an opposing argument (e.g., "Now my opponent might here argue that . . .), or even be seen debating with himself about what is right.

speech; the latter is more characteristic of humans than is use of the body. 13. And if it is argued that great harm can be done by unjustly using such power of words, this objection applies to all good things except for virtue, and most of all to the most useful things, like strength, health, wealth, and military strategy; for by using these justly one would do the greatest good and unjustly, the greatest harm.

14. That rhetoric, therefore, does not belong to a single defined genus of subject but is like dialectic and that it is useful is clear—and that its function [*ergon*] is not to persuade but to see the available means of persuasion in each case, as is true also in all the other arts; for neither is it the function of medicine to create health but to promote this as much as possible; for it is nevertheless possible to treat well those who cannot recover health. In addition, [it is clear] that it is a function of one and the same art to see both the persuasive and the apparently persuasive, just as [it is the function] in dialectic [to recognize] both a syllogism and an apparent syllogism;[28] for sophistry is not a matter of ability but of deliberate choice [*proairesis*] [of specious arguments].[29] In the case of rhetoric, however, there is the difference that one person will be [called] *rhētōr* on the basis of his knowledge and another on the basis of his deliberate choice, while in dialectic *sophist* refers to deliberate choice [of specious arguments],[30] *dialectician* not to deliberate choice, but to ability [at argument generally]. Let us now try to reach our objectives.[31] Starting again, therefore, as it were from the beginning, after defining what rhetoric is, let us say all that remains [to be said about the whole subject].

---

28. The apparently persuasive and an apparent syllogism include fallacious arguments that initially may sound valid but will not hold up under scrutiny. Both the orator and the dialectician need to be able to recognize these.

29. In modern linguistic terminology, *sophist* is the "marked" member of the pair *dialectician/sophist* in that the first includes the second; but *rhētōr* is "unmarked" and may be interpreted either as any effective speaker or as a speaker who uses tricky arguments; see Garver 1994.

30. In classical Greek *rhētōr* means any public speaker, though often referring to a person who plays a leadership role in public debate or is active in the law courts. In the Roman period, *rhētōr* frequently meant "rhetorician, teacher of rhetoric." Latin *orator* (orig. "envoy") and thus English "orator" are translations of *rhētōr* but take on an implication of eloquence not necessarily present in the Greek word.

31. For some speculations on Aristotle's objectives, see Lord 1981 and Introduction section D. Aristotle's major objective is clearly an understanding of the nature, materials, and uses of rhetoric; but he has pointed out that the art is useful, and as the treatise unrolls it will often take on the tone of a prescriptive handbook on how to compose a persuasive speech.

Chapter 2: Definition of Rhetoric; Pisteis, *or the Means of Persuasion in Public Address; Paradigms, Enthymemes, and Their Sources; Common Topics;* Eidē *and* Idia

■ In the following chapter Aristotle identifies the genus to which rhetoric belongs as *dynamis:* "ability, capacity, faculty." In his philosophical writing *dynamis* is the regular word for "potentiality" in matter or form that is "actualized" by an efficient cause. As stated here, the actuality produced by the potentiality of rhetoric is not the written or oral text of a speech, or even persuasion, but the art of "seeing" how persuasion may be effected. In *Nicomachean Ethics* 6.4 Aristotle defines all art as a reasoned capacity (*hexis*) to make something and says that it is concerned with the coming-into-being of something that is capable of either being or not being. Art is thus for him not the product of artistic skill, but the skill itself. Later rhetoricians often amplified Aristotle's definition by adding "through speech"; however, the root of the word rhetoric, *rhē-*, refers specifically to speech. Though Aristotle uses *poetics* to refer to arts other than poetry (dance, painting, sculpture), he never uses rhetoric to refer to any art except that of speech. As is clear from chapter 3, Aristotle primarily thinks of rhetoric as manifested in the civic context of public address, but he often draws examples of rhetoric from poetry or historical writing, and in the *Poetics* (19.1456a–b) the "thought" of a speaker in tragedy is said to be a matter of rhetoric.

It may help the reader if other terms in Aristotle's definition of rhetoric are explained in advance. "In each case" (*peri hekaston*) refers to the fact that rhetoric deals with specific circumstances (e.g., particular political or judicial decisions). "To see" translates *theōrēsai,* "to be an observer of and to grasp the meaning or utility of." English *theory* comes from the related noun *theōria.* "The available means of persuasion" renders *to endekhomenon pithanon,* "what is inherently and potentially persuasive" in the facts, circumstances, character of the speaker, attitude of the audience, etc. *Endekhomenon* often means "possible."

1. Let rhetoric be [defined as] an ability, in each [particular] case, to see the available means of persuasion.[32] This is the function of no

---

32. Aristotle uses the phrase *estō dē,* "Let X be . . . ," commonly of a working hypothesis rather than a final definition and occasionally to resume a definition made earlier. The definition here was anticipated in 1.1.14 on the *ergon* of rhetoric. In *Topics* 6.12.149b26–28 Aristotle quotes a definition of an orator as one having the ability to see the persuasive in each case and omit nothing.

other art;[33] for each of the others[34] is instructive and persuasive about its own subject: for example, medicine about health and disease and geometry about the properties of magnitudes and arithmetic about numbers and similarly in the case of the other arts and sciences. But rhetoric seems to be able to observe the persuasive about "the given," so to speak. That, too, is why we say it does not include technical knowledge of any particular, defined genus [of subjects].

2. Of the *pisteis*, some are atechnic ("non-artistic"), some entechnic ("embodied in art, artistic").[35] I call *atechnic* those that are not provided by "us" [i.e., the potential speaker] but are preexisting: for example, witnesses, testimony from torture,[36] contracts, and such like; and *entechnic* whatever can be prepared by method and by "us"; thus one must use the former and invent[37] the latter. 3. Of the *pisteis* provided through speech there are three species; for some are in the character [*ēthos*] of the speaker, and some in disposing the listener in some way, and some in the speech [*logos*][38] itself, by showing or seeming to show something.

1356a

4. [There is persuasion] through character whenever the speech is spoken[39] in such a way as to make the speaker worthy of credence; for we believe fair-minded people to a greater extent and more quickly [than we do others], on all subjects in general and completely so in cases where there is not exact knowledge but room for doubt.[40] And

33. Dialectic comes closest but deals with general questions, not specific cases, and for dialectic the final term, *means of persuasion (pithanon)*, would presumably be *means of reasoning (syllogismos)*. See *Topics* 1.1 in Appendix I.D.

34. Except, of course, dialectic.

35. Later writers sometimes call these *extrinsic* and *intrinsic*, respectively. Aristotle discusses atechnic proof in 1.15. In 3.16.1 he also refers to the "facts" in an epideictic speech as atechnic.

36. In Greek law, the evidence of slaves was only admissible in court if taken under torture. There was much debate about its reliability; see 1.15.26.

37. *Heurein*, "to find"; *heuresis* becomes the regular Greek word for rhetorical invention.

38. Greek *logos* means "what is said," speech, a speech, a word, but often also the reason or argument inherent in speech.

39. Aristotle is not thinking of style and delivery but of the thought and contents. On antecedents in Greek literature for persuasion through character, see Fortenbaugh 1992:211–220.

40. Here and in 1.9.1 and 2.1.5–7 the role of character in a speech is regarded as making the speaker seem trustworthy. The extended discussion of types of character in Book 2, chs. 12–17, relates to the somewhat different matter of the adaptation of the speech to the character of an audience. Aristotle's later treatment of character in rhetoric is in fact somewhat wider than this initial definition.

this should result from the speech, not from a previous opinion that the speaker is a certain kind of person;[41] for it is not the case, as some of the handbook writers propose in their treatment of the art, that fair-mindedness [epieikeia] on the part of the speaker makes no contribution to persuasiveness;[42] rather, character is almost, so to speak, the most authoritative form of persuasion.

5. [There is persuasion] through the hearers when they are led to feel emotion [pathos] by the speech; for we do not give the same judgment when grieved and rejoicing or when being friendly and hostile. To this and only this we said contemporary technical writers try to give their attention. The details on this subject will be made clear when we speak about the emotions.[43]

6. Persuasion occurs through the arguments [logoi] when we show the truth or the apparent truth from whatever is persuasive in each case.

7. Since pisteis come about through these [three means], it is clear that to grasp an understanding of them is the function of one who can reason logically and be observant about characters and virtues and, third, about emotions (what each of the emotions is and what are its qualities and from what it comes to be and how). The result is that rhetoric is like some offshoot [paraphues] of dialectic and ethical studies (which is rightly called politics). Thus, too, rhetoric dresses itself up in the form of politics, as do those who pretend to knowledge of it, sometimes through lack of education, sometimes through boastfulness and other human causes.[44] Rhetoric is partly [morion ti] dialectic, and resembles it, as we said at the outset; for neither of them

---

41. Unlike Isocrates (Antidosis 278), Aristotle does not include in rhetorical ethos the authority that the speaker may possess due to position in government or society, previous actions, reputation, or anything except what is actually said in the speech. Presumably, he would regard all other factors, sometimes highly important, as inartistic. One reason for Aristotle's position may be that speakers in the law courts were often ordinary people unknown to the jury, and a relatively unknown person might speak in the Assembly as well.

42. Why would they say this? Possibly it was thought to weaken a speaker's position if at the beginning of a speech he showed himself as too mild rather than took an uncompromising position or demonstrated outrage.

43. In Book 2, chs. 2–11. Aristotle's inclusion of emotion as a mode of persuasion, despite his objections to the handbooks, is a recognition that among human beings judgment is not entirely a rational act. There are morally valid emotions in every situation, and it is part of the orator's duty to clarify these in the minds of the audience. On this question, see Johnstone 1980:1–24.

44. Aristotle is probably thinking of Isocrates.

is identifiable with knowledge of the contents of any specific subject, but they are distinct abilities of supplying arguments. Concerning their potentiality and how they relate to each other, almost enough has been said. 8. In the case of persuasion through proving or seeming to prove something, just as in dialectic there is on the one hand induction [*epagōgē*] and on the other the syllogism and the apparent syllogism, so the situation is similar in rhetoric; for the *paradeigma* ["example"] is an induction, the *enthymēma* a syllogism. I call a rhetorical syllogism an enthymeme, a rhetorical induction a paradigm. And all [speakers] produce logical persuasion by means of paradigms or enthymemes and by nothing other than these. As a result, since it is always necessary to show something either by syllogizing or by inducing (and this is clear to us from the *Analytics*),[45] it is necessary that each of these be the same as each of the others.[46] 9. What the difference is between a paradigm and an enthymeme is clear from the *Topics* (for an account was given there earlier of syllogism and induction):[47] to show on the basis of many similar instances that something is so is in dialectic induction, in rhetoric paradigm; but to show that if some premises are true, something else [the conclusion] beyond them results from these because they are true, either universally or for the most part, in dialectic is called syllogism and in rhetoric enthymeme. 10. And it is also apparent that either species of rhetoric[48] has merit (what has also been said in the *Methodics*[49] is true in these cases too); for some rhetorical utterances are paradigmatic, some enthymematic; and similarly, some orators are paradigmatic, some enthymematic. Speeches using paradigms are not less persuasive, but those with enthymemes excite more favorable audience reaction.

1356b *(left margin)*

---

45. *Prior Analytics* 2.23; *Posterior Analytics* 1.1.

46. Not identical, in which case there would be no need for two sets of terms, but *formally* the same in their underlying structure. In formal logic an induction consists of particular observations from which a general conclusion is drawn; in rhetoric it takes the form of a particular statement supported by one or more parallels, with the universal conclusion left unstated. Similarly, an enthymeme rarely takes the full syllogistic form of major premise, minor premise, and conclusion; more often a conclusion is offered and supported by a reason, as in the first sentence of the treatise. On the logic of this passage, see Schröder 1985.

47. There is some discussion of syllogism in *Topics* 1.1, and 1.12 offers a definition of induction with an example: "If the skilled pilot is best, and [similarly in the case of] the charioteer, then in general the skilled is the best in each thing."

48. The "species" using example or that using enthymeme.

49. A lost logical work by Aristotle of which the extant *On Interpretation* may have been a part; see Rist 1989:84.

11. The cause—and how each should be used—we shall explain later;[50] now we shall explain these things themselves more clearly.

Since the persuasive is persuasive to someone (and is either immediately plausible and believable in itself or seems to be shown by statements that are so), and since no art examines the particular— for example, the art of medicine does not specify what is healthful for Socrates or Callias but for persons of a certain sort (this is a matter of art, while particulars are limitless and not knowable)—neither does rhetoric theorize about each opinion—what may seem so to Socrates or Hippias—but about what seems true to people of a certain sort, as is also true with dialectic.[51] For the latter does not form syllogisms from things at random (there are things only madmen believe) but from that in need of argument, and rhetoric [forms enthymemes] from things customarily deliberated.[52] 12. Its function [ergon] is concerned with the sort of things we debate and for which we do not have [other] arts and among such listeners as are not able to see many things all together or to reason from a distant starting point. And we debate about things that seem capable of admitting two possibilities; for no one debates things incapable of being different either in past or future or present, at least not if they suppose that to be the case; for there is nothing more [to say]. 13. It is possible to form syllogisms and draw inductive conclusions either from previous arguments or from state- ments that are not reasoned out but require a syllogism [if they are to be accepted] because they are not commonly believed [endoxa]; but the former of these [i.e., a chain of syllogisms] is necessarily not easy to follow because of the length [of the argument] (the judge is assumed to be a simple person),[53] and the latter is not persuasive because the premises are not agreed to or commonly believed. Thus, it is necessary for an enthymeme and a paradigm to be concerned with things that are for the most part capable of being other than they are— the paradigm inductively, the enthymeme syllogistically—and drawn from few premises and often less than those of the primary syllo- gism;[54] for if one of these is known, it does not have to be stated, since

1357a

---

50. In Book 2, chs. 20–24.

51. Rhetoric as an art seeks general rules; orators, of course, commonly deal with the beliefs of specific individuals. Dialectic builds its proof on the opinions of all, the majority, or the wise; cf. *Topics* 1.1 in Appendix I.D.

52. On the text, see Grimaldi 1980, 1:53–54.

53. By "judge" (*kritēs*) Aristotle means a member of an assembly or of a jury.

54. The fully expressed syllogism that is logically inherent in the enthymeme.

the hearer supplies it: for example, [to show] that Dorieus has won a contest with a crown it is enough to have said that he has won the Olympic games, and there is no need to add that the Olympic games have a crown as the prize; for everybody knows that.[55]

14. Since few of the premises from which rhetorical syllogisms are formed are necessarily true (most of the matters with which judgment and examination are concerned can be other than they are; for people deliberate and examine what they are doing, and [human] actions are all of this kind, and none of them [are], so to speak, necessary) and since things that happen for the most part and are possible can only be reasoned on the basis of other such things, and necessary actions [only] from necessities (and this is clear to us also from the *Analytics*),[56] it is evident that [the premises] from which enthymemes are spoken are sometimes necessarily true but mostly true [only] for the most part. Moreover, enthymemes are derived from probabilities [*eikota*] and signs [*sēmeia*], so it is necessary that each of these be the same as each [of the truth values mentioned];[57] 15. for a probability [*eikos*] is what happens for the most part, not in a simple sense, as some define it,[58] but whatever, among things that can be other than they are, is so related to that in regard to which it is probable as a universal is related to a particular.[59]

1357b

---

55. Later writers, including many moderns, often regard an enthymeme as an abbreviated syllogism in which one premise, usually the major, is not expressed but is assumed, e.g., "Socrates is mortal, for he is a man," assuming "all men are mortal." Aristotle notes that this is often the case but is not a necessary feature of the enthymeme. The real determinant of an enthymeme in contrast to a syllogism is what a popular audience will understand without tiresome pedantry. Aristotle regards rhetoric, and thus the enthymeme, as addressed to an audience that cannot be assumed to follow intricate logical argument or will be impatient with premises that seem obvious.

56. *Prior Analytics* 1.8 and 12–14; *Posterior Analytics* 1.6 and 30, 2.12.

57. I.e., probabilities correspond to things true for the most part, signs to things necessarily true, but Aristotle will modify this in what follows: some signs are necessary, others only probable. Both probabilities and signs are statements about human actions, though they may be based on physical manifestations, as the following examples show.

58. The handbook writers, for whom *eikos* was any argument that might seem possible at the time; see *Rhetoric for Alexander* in Appendix I.F., sec. 7 and Goebel 1989.

59. Cf. *Prior Analytics* 2.27. Grimaldi (1980, 1:62) instances "Children love their parents"; it is a probability because a general observation—universal in form and probably but not necessarily true in a particular instance.

16. In the case of signs [*sēmeia*], some are related as the particular to the universal, some as the universal to the particular. Of these, a necessary sign is a *tekmērion*, and that which is not necessary has no distinguishing name.[60] 17. Now I call *necessary* those from which a [logically valid] syllogism can be formed; thus, I call this kind of sign a *tekmērion*; for when people think it is not possible to refute a statement, they think they are offering a *tekmērion*, as though the matter were shown and concluded [*peparamenon*]. (*Tekmar* and *peras* ["limit, conclusion"] have the same meaning in the ancient form of [our] language.) 18. An example of signs [*sēmeia*] related as the particular to the universal is if someone were to state that since Socrates was wise and just, it is a sign that the wise are just. This is indeed a sign, but refutable, even if true in this case; for it is not syllogistically valid. But if someone were to state that there is a sign that someone is sick, for he has a fever, or that a woman has given birth, for she has milk, that is a necessary sign. Among signs, this is only true of a *tekmērion*; for only it, if true, is irrefutable. It is an example of the relation of the universal to the particular if someone said that it is a sign of fever that someone breathes rapidly. This, too, is refutable, even if true [in some cases]; for it is possible to breathe rapidly and not be feverish. Thus, what probability and what sign and *tekmērion* are and how they differ has now been explained. In the *Analytics*[61] they are defined more clearly, and the cause explained why some are not syllogistic and others are.

19. It has been explained that a paradigm is an induction and with what kinds of things it is concerned. It is reasoning neither from part to whole nor from whole to part but from part to part, like to like, when two things fall under the same genus but one is better known than the other.[62] For example, [when someone claims] that Dionysius is plotting tyranny because he is seeking a bodyguard; for Peisistratus also, when plotting earlier, sought a bodyguard and after receiving it made himself tyrant, and Theagenes [did the same] in Megara, and others, whom the audience knows of, all become examples for Dionysius, of whom they do not yet know whether he makes his

---

60. See Weidemann 1989 and compare *Rhetoric for Alexander* in Appendix I.F.7.

61. *Prior Analytics* 2.27.

62. Logically, there is an "unmeditated inference" of the universal proposition, but as a practical feature of rhetorical argument "part to part" should be taken literally; see Hauser 1968, 1985.

demand for this reason. All these actions fall under the same [genus]: that one plotting tyranny seeks a guard.[63]

The sources of *pisteis* that seem demonstrative [*apodeiktikai*] have now been explained. 20. But in the case of enthymemes, a very big difference—and one overlooked by almost everybody—is one that is also found in the case of syllogisms in dialectical method; for some [enthymemes] are formed in accord with the method of rhetoric, just as some syllogisms are formed in accord with the method of dialectic, while others accord with [the content of] other arts and capabilities, either those in existence or those not yet understood.[64] Hence, [the differences] escape the notice of the listeners; and the more [speakers] fasten upon [the subject matter] in its proper sense, [the more] they depart from rhetoric or dialectic. This statement will be clearer if explained in more detail.[65]

THE "TOPICS" OF SYLLOGISMS AND ENTHYMEMES

■ *Topos* literally means "place," metaphorically that location or space in an art (more literally perhaps the place in a handbook) where a speaker can look for "available means of persuasion." Although the word accords with Aristotle's fondness for visual imagery, he did not originate its use in the sense of a rhetorical topic. Isocrates, earlier in the century, had so used it,

---

63. It could be argued that seeking a bodyguard is a "sign" of intent to establish a tyranny, and certainly paradigm and signs have some similarity; but Aristotle seems to think of a paradigm as useful in indicating motivation or the probable course of events that the audience might not otherwise anticipate, whereas a sign is usually an existing fact or condition that anyone might recognize. More import to him, however, is the logical difference that the paradigm moves from the particular premises to a particular conclusion, with the universal link not expressed (just as the universal major premise of an enthymeme need not be expressed), whereas the sign moves either from universal to particular or particular to universal.

64. It is characteristic of Aristotle to feel that there were other subjects not yet systematically studied.

65. This passage is regarded as textually corrupt by the editors. Kassel (1976) indicates that something has been lost after *listeners*; Ross (1959) rejects *the more*. The basic thought is that people do not realize that rhetoric and dialectic, though they have a method, lack content or facts and must borrow these from other disciplines, such as politics or ethics. Enthymemes are rhetorical strategies but also usually substantive arguments; and the more the argument comes from the premises of politics, ethics, or other subjects, the more the enthymeme becomes an argument of that discipline and the less it is purely rhetorical. In practice, the limits are never reached; any argument has some strategy (what Aristotle will call "topics" in 2.23) and some content (what he will call *idia* and discuss in Books 1, chs. 4–14, and 2, chs. 1–7).

and probably others did before him. In Isocrates' *Encomium of Helen* (section 4) *topos* refers to forms of argument, such as fact or possibility—what Aristotle will call *koina*. In the same speech (section 38) *topos* refers to the use of an ancient witness, Theseus' opinion of Helen—what Aristotle regards as "non-artistic" *pistis*. The word may also already have been used in mnemonic theory of the physical setting against which an object or idea could be remembered. Neither in *Topics* nor in *Rhetoric* does Aristotle give a definition of *topos*, a sign that he assumed the word would be easily understood; he does, however, give his own special twist to its meaning, usually distinguishing it from *koina* and *idia* and using it primarily of strategies of argument, as discussed in 2.23. (See Sprute 1982:172–182.)

21. I am saying that dialectical and rhetorical syllogisms are those in which we state *topoi*, and these are applicable in common [*koinēi*] to questions of justice and physics and politics and many different species [of knowledge]; for example the *topos* of the more and the less;[66] for to form syllogisms or speak enthymemes from this about justice will be just as possible as about physics or anything else, although these subjects differ in species.[67] But there are "specifics"[68] that come from the premises of each species and genus [of knowledge]; for example, in physics there are premises from which there is neither an enthymeme nor a syllogism applicable to ethics; and in ethics [there are] others not useful in physics. It is the same in all cases. The former [the common *topoi*] will not make one understand any genus; for they are not concerned with any underlying subject. As to the latter [the specifics], to the degree that someone makes better choice of the premises, he will have created knowledge different from dialectic and rhetoric without its being recognized; for if he succeeds

---

66. To be discussed in 2.23.4.

67. The *topos* does not tell one anything about these subjects but can be applied to each; for example, "If it is just to punish offenses, it is more just to punish great offenses"; "If a small force will move a body, a larger force will move it as well"; and "If public revenues will support a large army, they will support a smaller army."

68. *Idia* (n. pl. of the adjective from *eidos*), "specificities, specific or particular things." The word is chosen to denote things characteristic of the species. Aristotle here does not call these specifics "topics," but he does so refer to them in 1.15.19, and in sec. 22, as well as in 1.6.1, he speaks of them as *stoikheia* ("elements"), which he says later (2.22.13; 2.26.1) are the "same" as topics. Thus some rhetoricians have found it convenient to speak of "special, specific, particular, material" topics belonging to the separate disciplines, in contrast to "common" or "formal" topics, which are rhetorical or dialectical strategies of argument.

in hitting on first principles [*arkhai*], the knowledge will no longer be dialectic or rhetoric but the science of which [the speaker] grasps the first principles.[69] 22. Most enthymemes are derived from these species that are particular and specific, fewer from the common [topics].[70] Just as in the case of *topoi*, so also in the case of enthymemes, a distinction should be made between the species and the *topoi* from which they are to be taken. By "species" I mean the premises specific to each genus [of knowledge], and by the *topoi* those common to all. But let us take up first the genera of rhetoric so that having defined how many there are, we may separately take up their elements[71] and premises.

Chapter 3: The Three Species of Rhetoric: Deliberative, Judicial, and Epideictic

■ Of all Aristotle's rhetorical teaching, the division of rhetoric and oratory into three and only three species was most consistently associated with him. It was, however, probably only a clarification of existing classifications, seen in the conventions of different genres of Greek oratory. The identification of two genres, deliberative and judicial, is attributed by Quintilian (3.4.9) to Anaximenes of Lampsacus, and six of the seven species identified in *Rhetoric for Alexander*, chapter 1 (exhortation, dissuasion; eulogy, vituperation; accusation, defense) easily fall into three larger categories. (There is a translation of this chapter in Appendix I.F.) Aristotle's rigorous characterization does not take into consideration the use of epideictic passages in deliberative speeches (e.g., Cicero's speech *For the Manilian Law*) or casting an epideictic speech into judicial form (e.g., Isocrates' *Antidosis*), or other combinations and permutations.

Aristotle's use of *genos*, *eidos*, and *idia* in this passage may make it somewhat difficult to follow. He is probably not seeking to make a logical statement on the basis of genus and species, but in a general way, he can perhaps be said to view knowledge as a genus of which particular forms

---

69. For the concept of "first principles" see the note on 1.7.12. Part or all of a discourse may be thought of as falling in a spectrum, varying from the most general and popular to the most technical. A speech in a law court, for example, will become less "rhetorical" and more "jurisprudential" as it undertakes detailed discussion of the law; see Garver 1988.

70. This is because of the need for "content"; rhetoric constantly employs the special knowledge of other arts, such as politics and ethics.

71. *Stoikheia*, which are the same as topics; see 2.22.13, 2.26.1.

(e.g., physics, politics, ethics, rhetoric) are species (*eidē*). The premises of the *eidē* are their *idia*. In 1.2.21 he calls the kinds of rhetoric genera (*genē*), but in the first sentence of this chapter they are referred to as *eidē* (species) and in 1.3.3 he reverts back to *genē*.

Aristotle's concept of epideictic is the most problematic of the species and it has remained a problem in rhetorical theory, since it becomes the category for all forms of discourse that are not specifically deliberative or judicial. Later ancient rhetoricians sometimes regarded it as including poetry and prose literature,[72] and since the Renaissance it has sometimes included other arts, like painting, sculpture, and music. Aristotle, however, thinks of epideictic primarily as funeral oratory or praise of a mythological figure. In such speeches, praise corrects, modifies, or stregthens an audience's belief about the civic virtues or the reputation of an individual (see Oravec 1976; Hauser 1999).

There are variant names in English for each of Aristotle's species. Deliberative is called "parliamentary oratory" in some older translations; judicial is often referred to as "forensic" (a usage that should be resisted).[73] Epideictic has had a number of names: in later antiquity it was usually called "panegyric," which strictly speaking is a speech at a festival. Sometimes the term is literally translated as "demonstrative." Many subspecies of epideictic were identified in later antiquity and are discussed in detail in two handbooks attributed to a rhetorician named Menander.[74]

For an example of a Greek deliberative speech, see the translation of Demosthenes' *Third Philippic* in Appendix I.H; for an example of a Greek judicial speech, see the translation of Lysias' *Against the Grain Dealers* in Appendix I.C.

1. The species [*eidē*] of rhetoric are three in number; for such is the number [of classes] to which the hearers of speeches belong. A speech consists of three things: a speaker and a subject on which he speaks and someone addressed, and the objective [*telos*] of the *speech* relates to the last (I mean the hearer).[75] 2. Now it is necessary for the　**1358b**

---

72. Cf., e.g., Hermogenes, *On Types of Style*, chap. 12.

73. "Forensic" is inappropriate since the forum (as in Rome) was the scene of all three species of oratory; it is also open to confusion with "forensics," meaning mock debates, and "forensics," meaning medical evidence.

74. See *Menander Rhetor*, ed. with trans. and commentary by D. A. Russell and N. G. Wilson (Clarendon Press, 1981).

75. Eighteenth-century rhetoricians added *the occasion* to Aristotle's three factors in the speech situation, and modern linguists have suggested other approaches, e.g., "addresser, message, addressee, context, common code, and contact."

hearer to be either an observer [*theōros*] or a judge [*kritēs*], and [in the latter case] a judge of either past or future happenings. A member of a democratic assembly is an example of one judging about future happenings, a juror an example of one judging the past. An observer is concerned with the ability [*dynamis*] [of the speaker].[76] 3. Thus, there would necessarily be three genera of rhetorics:[77] *symbouleutikon* ["deliberative"], *dikanikon* ["judicial"], *epideiktikon* ["demonstrative"]. Deliberative advice is either protreptic ["exhortation"] or apotreptic ["dissuasion"]; for both those advising in private and those speaking in public always do one or the other of these. In the law courts there is either accusation [*katēgoria*] or defense [*apologia*]; for it is necessary for the disputants to offer one or the other of these. In epideictic, there is either praise [*epainos*] or blame [*psogos*].[78] 4. Each of these [species] has its own "time"; for the deliberative speaker, the future (for whether exhorting or dissuading he advises about future events);[79] for the speaker in court, the past (for he always prosecutes or defends concerning what has been done); in epideictic the present is the most important;[80] for all speakers praise and blame in regard to existing qualities, but they often also make use of other things, both reminding [the audience] of the past and projecting the

---

76. This sentence was rejected by Kassel (1976) as an insertion by a later reader. The audience in epideictic is not called upon to take a specific action, in the way that the assembly or jury is asked to vote; but epideictic may be viewed as an oratorical contest, either with other speakers or previous speakers (cf., e.g., Isocrates' *Panegyricus* 1), and later (2.18.1) Aristotle notes that the observer is in this sense also a judge. A very different interpretation is that of Mirhady 1995. He takes *dynamis* to refer not to ability of the speaker but to "the moral capacity of the person being praised or blamed."

77. The appearance here of "rhetorics" in the plural is very unusual in Greek and probably results from the use of *genē* in the plural. Aristotle may use *genē* here of the kinds of rhetoric earlier called *eidē* because in the next sentence he is going to divide them further into species.

78. Although passages of invective are frequent in classical deliberative and judicial oratory (e.g., in Demosthenes' *Philippics*), with the possible exception of Isocrates' *Against the Sophists, psogos* can only be illustrated from iambic poetry and drama; see Rountree 2001. In later antiquity antagonism toward Christians, pagans, or Jews produced some speeches devoted to blame [e.g., Gregory Nazianus' *Orations* 4–5 (against Julian) and 27 (against the Arians)].

79. In 1.9.40 Aristotle notes that deliberative rhetoric makes extensive use of examples from past history, since the past is the only basis for judging what is likely to occur; cf. also 2.20.8.

80. Perhaps meaning the occasion on which the speech is being given.

course of the future.[81] 5. The "end"[82] of each of these is different, and there are three ends for three [species]: for the deliberative speaker [the end] is the advantageous [*sympheron*][83] and the harmful (for someone urging something advises it as the better course and one dissuading dissuades on the ground that it is worse), and he includes other factors as incidental: whether it is just or unjust, or honorable or disgraceful; for those speaking in the law courts [the end] is the just [*dikaion*] and the unjust, and they make other considerations incidental to these; for those praising and blaming [the end] is the honorable [*kalon*] and the shameful, and these speakers bring up other considerations in reference to these qualities. 6. Here is a sign [*sēmeion*] that the end of each [species of rhetoric] is what has been said: sometimes one would not dispute other factors; for example, a judicial speaker [might not deny] that he has done something or done harm, but he would never agree that he has [intentionally] done wrong; for [if he admitted that,] there would be no need of a trial. Similarly, deliberative speakers often advance other facts, but they would never admit that they are advising things that are not advantageous [to the audience] or that they are dissuading [the audience] from what is beneficial; and often they do not insist that it is not unjust to enslave neighbors or those who have done no wrong. And similarly, those

---

81. Aristotle's attempt to assign a "time" to each species is somewhat strained. As he will acknowledge, since the future probabilities can only be known from past experience a deliberative speech is often much concerned with the past. In funeral oratory, speakers praise past actions, but often with the intent of celebrating virtues and inculcating models for future actions; cf., e.g., Pericles' "Funeral Oration" in Thucydides (2.35–46) and Lincoln's "Gettysburg Address." In sec. 6 Aristotle cites praise of Achilles as an example of epideictic, but even for him, Achilles' actions were in the distant past.

82. *Telos*, the final objective of the speaker and his art, which is actualized in the persuasion of an audience. Later rhetoricians sometimes call these "final headings" or "headings of purpose." Each *telos* often becomes a specific topic in a speech; see, for example, the discussions of expediency and justice in the debate of Cleon and Diodotus reconstructed in Thucydides 3.37–48.

83. *Sympheron* is often translated "expedient"; literally, it means whatever "brings with it" advantage. Later rhetoricians were troubled by the moral implication and sought to modify what they saw as Aristotle's focus on expediency; see Cicero, *On the Orator* 2.334–36, and esp. Quintilian 3.8.1–3. Since Aristotle has said in 1.1.12 that we must not persuade what is bad, he would presumably recommend that a speaker seek to identify the enlightened, long-term advantage to the audience, not immediate expediency. But in sec. 6 Aristotle again recognizes that in practice deliberative orators are often indifferent to the question of the injustice to others of some action.

who praise or blame do not consider whether someone has done
actions that are advantageous or harmful [to himself] but often they
include it even as a source of praise that he did what was honorable
without regard to the cost to himself; for example, they praise
Achilles because he went to the aid of his companion Patroclus knowing that he himself must die,[84] though he could have lived. To him,
such a death was more honorable; but life was advantageous.

PROPOSITIONS COMMON TO ALL SPECIES OF RHETORIC

■ No technical term appears in this chapter to denote the four subjects of
propositions described here, but in 2.18.2 they are called *koina*, "common
things, commonalities," in contrast to *idia*, "specifics, particularities." They
are discussed in greater detail in 2.19. Since the *koinon* "greater and
smaller" discussed in section 9 seems similar to the topic of "the more and
the less" mentioned in 1.2.21, these *koina* have often been called "topics"
or "common topics." Grimaldi (1980, 1:85–86) objected to this, with some
reason, though in 3.19.2 Aristotle speaks of "topics" of amplification and
seems to be referring to 2.19. Generally, however, Aristotle keeps them distinct. The topic of "the more and the less" discussed separately in 2.23.4 is
a strategy of argument, always involving some contrast, whereas "greater
and small," discussed in 1.7, 1.14, and 2.19.26–27, are arguments about
the degree of magnitude (that term occurs in 2.18.4) or importance of
something and are analogous to such questions as whether something is
possible or has actually been done. Whether something is possible, actually
true, or important are fundamental issues in many speeches; thus Aristotle
mentions them immediately after identifying the basic issues of the advantageous, the just, and the honorable.

7. It is evident from what has been said that it is first of all necessary
[for a speaker] to have propositions [*protaseis*] on these matters.[85]
(*Tekmēria* and probabilities and signs are rhetorical propositions. A
syllogism is wholly from propositions, and the enthymeme is a syllogism consisting of propositions expressed).[86] 8. And since impossibilities

---

84. Not exactly what is described in *Iliad* 18–20. Achilles makes it possible for the
Greeks to rescue Patroclus' dead body for proper burial and then kills Hector in
revenge. Possibly Aristotle knew another version of the story.

85. The advantageous, the just, the honorable, and their opposites.

86. The propositions inherent in an underlying syllogism are not necessarily all
expressed in the related enthymeme; some may be assumed before a popular audience.

cannot be done nor have been done, but possibilities [can and have been], and since it is not possible for things that have not occurred or are not going to do so to have been done or to be done in the future, it is necessary for the deliberative, judicial, and epideictic speaker to have propositions about the possible and the impossible and [about] whether something has happened or not and [about] whether it will or will not come to be. 9. Further, since all speakers, praising and blaming and urging and dissuading and prosecuting and defending, not only try to show what has been mentioned but that the good or the evil or the honorable or the shameful or the just or the unjust is great or small, either speaking of things in themselves or in comparison to each other, it is clear that it would be necessary also to have propositions about the great and the small and the greater and the lesser, both generally and specifically; for example, [about] what is the greater or lesser good or injustice or justice, and similarly about other qualities.[87] The subjects about which it is necessary to frame propositions have [now] been stated. Next we must distinguish between each in specific terms; that is, what deliberation, and what epideictic speeches, and thirdly, what lawsuits, are concerned with.

Chapters 4–15: *Idia*, or Specific Topics, in Each of the Three Species of Rhetoric

■ These chapters constitute a kind of introduction to knowledge about politics, ethics, and psychology at a popular level that Aristotle regards as requisite for responsible and effective argument in public address. They are part of his attempt to provide an intellectual basis for rhetoric in response to criticism of its vacuity and dangers attributed to Socrates by Plato.

In *Topics* 1.14 Aristotle says there are three classes of dialectical propositions: ethical, physical, and logical. Ethical can be understood to include political propositions. Since rhetoric does not ordinarily deal with questions of physics, ethical and logical propositions are those useful to a speaker. In these chapters, and continuing in Book 2, chapters 1–17, Aristotle gives lists of opinions (called *endoxa* in dialectic) on political and ethical matters that are commonly held and could be used as premises in the formation of

---

87. The subjects of propositions common to all species of rhetoric are thus the possible and impossible, past fact (or its nonexistence), future fact (or its nonexistence), and degree of magnitude or importance. These are discussed further in 2.19.

arguments; however, he does not provide much in the way of illustrating how they might be used in practice. Logical propositions will be discussed when he returns to the dialectical features of rhetoric in Book 2, chapters 18–26. Chapters 2–17 of *Rhetoric for Alexander* treat some of the same matters; they use some of the same terminology, but often defined differently, and they are far more practical in their advice for application of topics, making an interesting comparison with what we find in Aristotle's text.[88]

Chapters 4–8: Deliberative Rhetoric

Chapter 4: Political Topics for Deliberative Rhetoric

■ As noted on 1.2.21–22, Aristotle's term for the propositions discussed here is *idia*, "specifics," or in 1.6.1 *stoikheia*, "elements"—later (2.22.13 and 2.26.1) equated with "topics," but meaning those derived from some specific body of knowledge. His discussion of the specifics of each species of rhetoric may be viewed as a partial response to Plato's complaints (especially in *Gorgias*) that civic orators lack knowledge of the subjects they discuss. Although Aristotle views rhetoric as a tool subject—like dialectic and in contrast to politics, ethics, and other disciplines—he recognized that an effective civic orator needs to acquire practical knowledge, at least at a popular level, of the subjects under discussion; and he presents this knowledge as familiarity with the sources of propositions. Those discussed in this chapter all relate to the subjects of deliberation[89] in councils and assemblies in Greek cities and fall into the area of "political" thought; this subject is continued in chapter 8 with discussion of constitutions. The intervening chapters (5–7) deal with ethical thought and the propositions it provides. Aristotle discusses the various types of constitutions existing in Greece, together with their strengths and weaknesses, in his treatise *On Politics*.

1. First, then, one must grasp what kinds of good and evil the deliberative speaker advises about, since [he will be concerned] not with

---

88. See Appendix I.F for a translation selections. A complete English translation appears in volume 2 of the Loeb Classical Library edition of Aristotle's *Problems* (Harvard University Press, 1957). For discussion of *Rhetoric for Alexander*, see Appendix II.A.

89. In 1.1.10 Aristotle indicated that deliberative rhetoric was the finest form. He thus discusses it first and demotes judicial rhetoric (with which the handbooks were most concerned) to last.

all, but [only] with those that can both possibly come to pass or not. 2. As to whatever necessarily exists or will exist or is impossible to be or to have come about, on these matters there will be no deliberation. 3. Nor is there deliberation about all contingent matters; for some benefits among those that can come to pass or not are the work of nature or happen by chance, on which deliberation is not worthwhile. But the subjects of deliberation are clear, and these are whatever, by their nature, are within our power and of which the inception lies with us. [As judges] we limit our consideration to the point of discovering what is possible or impossible for us to do. 4. It is not necessary at the present moment to enumerate each of these in detail, particular by particular, and to divide them into species on the basis of what is customary in deliberation nor is there need in the present context to say fully what would be a true definition of them, since that is not a matter for the rhetorical art but for a more profound and true [discipline]—and much more than its proper area of consideration has currently been assigned to rhetoric;[90] 5. for what we said earlier[91] is true, that rhetoric is a combination of analytical knowledge and knowledge of characters and that on the one hand it is like dialectic, on the other like sophistic discourses. 6. Insofar as someone tries to make dialectic or rhetoric not just mental faculties but sciences, he unwittingly obscures their nature by the change, reconstructing them as forms of knowledge of certain underlying facts, rather than only of speech. 7. Nevertheless, let us now say what it is worthwhile to analyze, while leaving the full examination to political science.

1359b

The most important subjects on which people deliberate and on which deliberative orators give advice in public are mostly five in number, and these are finances, war and peace, national defense, imports and exports, and the framing of laws.[92]

8. Thus, one who is going to give advice on finances should know what and how extensive are the revenues of the city, so that if any have been left out they may be added and if any are rather small they may be increased; and all the expenses of the city as well, so that if any is not worthwhile it may be eliminated and if any is too great it

---

90. By sophists and Isocrates.

91. In 1.2.7.

92. This list, except for framing laws, is mentioned by Socrates in Xenophon's *Memorabilia* 3.6.4–13. In *Rhetoric for Alexander*, ch. 2, the subjects are listed as religious matters, legislation, the form of the constitution, alliances and treaties, war or peace, and finance.

may be reduced; for people become richer not only by adding to what they have but by cutting down expenses. It is not only possible to get an overall view of these matters from experience in the affairs of one's own city, but it is necessary also to be willing to do research about what has been discovered elsewhere in regard to deliberation about these things.

9. On war and peace, [it is necessary] to know the power of the city, both how great it is already and how great it is capable of becoming, and what form the existing power takes and what else might be added and, further, what wars it has waged and how (it is necessary to know these things not only about one's native city but about neighboring cities) and with whom there is probability of war, in order that there may be a policy of peace toward the stronger and that the decision of war with the weaker may be one's own. [It is necessary to know] their forces also, whether they are like or unlike [those of one's own city]; for it is possible in this respect as well to be superior or inferior. Additionally, it is necessary to have observed not only the wars of one's own city but also those of others, in terms of their results; for like results naturally follow from like causes. 10. Furthermore, in regard to national defense [it is necessary] not to overlook how it is kept up and also to know both the size of the defense force and its character and the location of fortifications (this knowledge is impossible without familiarity with the countryside), in order that it may be increased if it is rather small and may be removed if unneeded and suitable places may be guarded instead.

11. Further, in regard to food [it is necessary to know] what expenditure is adequate for the city and what kinds are on hand and what can be imported, and what items need to be exported and what imported, in order that contracts and treaties may be made with appropriate parties. It is necessary to keep the citizens constantly free from complaints from two [foreign] groups: those that are stronger and those that are useful for commerce.

12. For the security of the state it is necessary to observe all these things, but not least to be knowledgeable about legislation;[93] for the safety of the city is in its laws, so it is necessary to know how many

1360a

---

93. Greek cities did not usually have written constitutions, and what are described as laws approximated what we would call constitutional provisions. Change in them was deliberately made difficult. "Decrees" on specific subjects performed functions that we might think of as ordinary legislation.

forms of constitution there are and what is conducive to each and by what each is naturally prone to be corrupted, both forces characteristic of that constitution and those that are opposed to it. By *characteristic forces of corruption* I mean that except for the best constitution,[94] all the others are destroyed by loosening or tightening [their basic principles of governance]; for example, democracy not only becomes weaker when its [principle of equality is] relaxed so that finally it leads to oligarchy but also if the principle is too rigidly applied.[95] Like a hook nose and a snub nose, not only do they reach a mean [i.e., look like a straight nose] if their characteristic features are relaxed, but if they become very hooked or snub the result is that they do not look like noses at all! 13. In legislation, it is useful to an investigator not only to know what constitution is advantageous on the basis of past history but also to know the constitutions in effect in other states, observing what constitutions are suitable to what sort of people.[96] Thus, it is clear that in constitutional revision the reports of travelers are useful (for there one can learn the laws of foreign nations) and [that] for debates about going to war the research of those writing about history [is useful].[97] But all these subjects belong to politics, not to rhetoric. These are the most important subjects on which someone who is going to give counsel ought to have [propositions].   1360b

Let us return to the sources from which arguments of exhortation or dissuasion about these and other matters should be derived.

---

94. That based on the mean, or rule by the middle class, described in *Politics* 4.11. The forces leading to corruption of constitutions are discussed in *Politics* 5.

95. "Relaxing" the principle of equality of all citizens means that the superiority (whether by birth, wealth, or knowledge) of some is recognized, which is a step toward oligarchy, or government by the few; "tightening" the principle means a doctrinaire insistence that all citizens are equal, depriving the city of needed leadership and moving to choice of officials by lot and potential anarchy.

96. Aristotle made or sponsored a study of many different constitutions as part of his research into politics, but only the account of the *Constitution of the Athenians* has survived.

97. A number of geographical and ethnographical works had been published by travelers before Aristotle's time. Among those Aristotle may have had in mind are the now lost work of Hecataeus and the surviving *Histories* of Herodotus, which includes description of Persian, Egyptian, Scythian, and other societies as well as the history of the wars between Greece and Persia. *About going to war* is Kassel's (1976) emendation of the manuscripts, which read "political," and is supported by the Latin translation of Hermannus Alemannus.

Chapter 5: Ethical Topics for Deliberative Rhetoric

■ Chapters 5–15 are perhaps the "early core" of the *Rhetoric*, largely written in the mid-350s B.C.E., but somewhat revised twenty years later (cf. Rist 1989:84–85). Chapter 8, however, is probably a later addition; see the introductory note thereto. The evidence for early composition of the chapters are some differences (e.g., 1.11.1 on pleasure) between the ethical thought set forth here and Aristotle's developed views on the subject, even allowing for the fact that Aristotle here gives a popular account of ethical views, as well as the relative lack of cross-references to other treatises, the citation of examples that are not later in date than about 350 B.C.E., and the absence of some of the terminology (e.g., "topics") on which Aristotle later settled. But portions of these chapters have been touched up in the later revision of the work as a whole in the early 330s, for example, addition of a reference to the *Poetics* in 1.11.29. In addition to specifically political propositions as discussed in chapter 4, the deliberative orator, in his effort to demonstrate that a course of action is in the best interest of the audience, needs an understanding of the objectives and values of human life, which may provide additional premises for argument. In chapter 5 Aristotle identifies the goal of human action with "happiness" and describes the factors contributing to it. The chapter is a more popular, and probably earlier, version of philosophical discussions of happiness found in his *Endemian* and *Nicomachean Ethics* and again helps to answer some of the objections to rhetoric when not based on knowledge as voiced by Plato. In contrast to the political issues of the previous chapter, the ethical ones outlined here have less application in Greek deliberative oratory than in epideictic; some, however, are relevant for modern debates on social issues. A few premises (e.g., those relating to wealth) are applicable in judicial oratory on matters of property, contracts, or inheritance. Justification for Aristotle's discussion here lies partly in the fact that these were probably frequent matters for private deliberation (which he included under deliberative rhetoric in 1.3.3) and more importantly that awareness of them on the part of a deliberative speaker contributes to an overall understanding of what is best for the state. (On Aristotle's ethical thought, see Hardy 1980, Nussbaum 1986, and the chapters by John M. Cooper and Stephen Halliwell in Furley and Nehamas 1994:193–230.)

1. Both to an individual privately and to all people generally there is one goal [*skopos*] at which they aim in what they choose to do and in what they avoid. Summarily stated, this is happiness [*eudaimonia*] and its parts. 2. Let us, then, for the sake of giving an example [of

what might be more fully explored elsewhere,] grasp what happiness is, simply stated, and the sources of its parts; for all forms of exhortation and dissuasion are concerned with this and with the things that contribute, or are opposed, to it; for one should do things that provide happiness or one of its parts or that make it greater rather than less, and not do things that destroy it or impede it or effect its opposites.

3. Let happiness be [defined as] success [*eupraxia*] combined with virtue, or as self-sufficiency [*autarkeia*] in life, or as the pleasantest life accompanied with security, or as abundance of possessions and bodies,[98] with the ability to defend and use these things; for all people agree that happiness is pretty much one or more or these.[99]

4. If happiness is something of this sort, it is necessary for its "parts" to be good birth, numerous friendships, worthy friendships, wealth, good children, numerous children, a good old age, as well as the virtues of the body (such as health, beauty, strength, physical stature, athletic prowess), reputation, honor, good luck, virtue;[100] for a person would be most self-sufficient if he had these goods, both internal and external; for there are no others beyond these. Internal goods are those relating to the mind and the body, while good birth and friends and wealth and honor are external. And further, we [all] believe that the power to take actions and good luck should be present; for thus life would be most secure. Let us now, in a similar way,[101] grasp what each of these is.

5. *Good birth*, in the case of a nation or city, is to be autochthonous[102] or ancient and for its first inhabitants to have been

---

98. *Sōmatōn*, probably including slaves and free employees in a house or on an estate, possibly also including herds and flocks; cf. 2.5.20.

99. The multiple definitions reflect varying popular understanding of happiness. Aristotle makes some use of all but the last in his dialectical discussion of happiness in *Nicomachean Ethics* 1.7–10; but his preferred definition there is "activity [*energeia*] in accordance with virtue," and the highest virtue is found only in the contemplative life.

100. Some manuscripts add "or also its parts; practical wisdom, courage, temperance, justice"; but editors generally have regarded this as an addition to the text by a later reader. These are the four cardinal virtues of the common philosophical tradition of antiquity and the Middle Ages and constitute the "virtues of the mind," complementing the virtues of "body" and "estate" that Aristotle has listed previously.

101. I.e., in accord with popular definition, since this is what is useful in deliberative rhetoric.

102. Lit., "sprung from the soil," as claimed in myth, or at least not immigrant within historical times, a topic in epideictic more than in deliberative rhetoric. The Athenians claimed to be autochthonous; cf. Isocrates, *Panegyricus* 24 and *Panathenaicus* 124.

leaders and have had numerous descendants distinguished in estimable qualities. For an individual, good birth may be traced either on the father's or mother's side and includes legitimacy on both lines, and, as in the case of a city, [implies that] the earliest ancestors were known for virtue or wealth or another of the things that are honored and [that] there have been many outstanding men and women in the family, both among the young and the older.[103]

6. *Good children* and *numerous children* is not unclear. As applies to the community if there are many good young men—and good in excellence of body, for example in stature, beauty, strength, athletic prowess; in the case of the mind, temperance and courage are a young man's virtues. In an individual, being blessed with good and numerous children means having many of one's own and of the quality described, both female and male. In the case of female children, excellence of body means beauty and stature, [excellence] of mind [means] temperance and industry, without servility. Equally in private life and in the community, both among men and among women, there is need to seek the existence of these qualities. Among those like the Lacedaimonians where the condition of women is poor happiness is only half present.

7. The parts of *wealth* are abundance of cash, land, possession of tracts distinguished by number and size and beauty and also possession of implements and slaves and cattle distinguished by number and beauty; and all these things [should be] privately owned[104] and securely held and freely employed and useful. Things that are productive are more useful, but things for enjoyment are [more] freely employed; and by productive I mean what produces income, by enjoyable that from which there is no gain worth mentioning beyond the use of it. The definition of *securely held* is that which is possessed in such a place and in such a way that use of it lies with the owner; and whether things are *privately owned* or not depends on who has the right of alienation, and by alienation I mean gift and sale. All in all, wealth consists more in use than in possession; for the actualization of the potentialities of such things and their use is wealth.

---

103. Good birth is also a topic more characteristic of epideictic; cf. Isocrates, *Helen* 43 and *Evagoras* 13–19, 71–72.

104. "Privately owned": not in the manuscripts, but added by recent editors on the basis of what follows.

8. *Good reputation* [*eudoxia*] is a matter of achieving the respect of all people, or of having something of the sort that all or the general public or the good and prudent desire.

9. *Honor* [*timē*] is a sign of a reputation for doing good, and benefactors, above all, are justly honored, although one with the potentiality of doing good is also honored. Benefaction confers safety (and the things that cause it) or wealth or some other good of which the possession is not easily come by or not completely or not in a particular situation or moment; for many people obtain honor through things that [in other situations] seem trifles, but the place and occasion make the difference. The components of honor are sacrifices [made to the benefactor after death], memorial inscriptions in verse or prose, receipt of special awards, grants of land, front seats at festivals, burial at the public expense, statues, free food in the state dining room; among barbarians such things as proskynesis[105] and rights of precedence and gifts that are held in honor in each society; for a gift is a grant of a possession and sign of honor, and thus those ambitious for money or honor desire them. Both get what they want: those ambitious for money get a possession, those for honor an honor.   1361b

10. In the case of the body, excellence is *health*, in the form of making use of the body without illness; for many are healthy in the way said of Herodicus, whom no one would envy for his health since [to keep it] he had to refrain from all, or nearly all, human enjoyments.[106]

11. *Beauty* is different at each stage of life. In the case of a young man it is a matter of having a body fit for endurance both on the racecourse and in contests of strength, pleasant to look at for sheer delight; thus pentathletes are most beautiful because they are equipped by nature at one and the same time for brawn and for speed.[107] When someone is in his prime, he should be adapted to the toils of war and be thought attractive as well as fear-inspiring. An old man should have adequate strength for necessary exertions and not be painful to look at, lacking any of the characteristic disfigurements of old age.

---

105. The requirement in Asiatic states that those approaching an important person prostrate themselves on the ground before him, which was offensive to Greek feelings.

106. See Plato, *Republic* 3.406a–c. Herodicus was a gymnastics teacher who wore himself and others out by constant exercise.

107. The Greek pentathlon was an athletic event consisting of running, jumping, discus and javelin throwing, and wrestling; it thus required grace and coordination as well as stamina and brawn.

12. *Strength* is the ability to move another person physically as one wills; and it is necessary to move another by dragging or shoving or raising or squeezing or crushing, so strength is strength in all or some of these things.[108]

13. Excellence of *stature* consists in surpassing many others in height, length [of the limbs], and breadth [of the torso] but in such a way that motions are not too slow as a result of great size. 14. Bodily excellence in competitive athletics is a combination of size and strength and swiftness (and swiftness is actually a form of strength); for one who can throw his legs in the right way and move quickly and for a distance is a runner, and one who can squeeze and hold down is a wrestler, and one who can thrust with the fist is a boxer, and one who can do both of the latter two has the skills needed for the pancration, and one who can do them all [has the skills] for the pentathlon.

15. *A good old age* is to age slowly without pain; for no one is enjoying a happy old age if he ages quickly or if gradually but with pain. A good old age is a matter of bodily excellences and luck; for unless one is without disease and is strong, he will not lack suffering, and he will not continue without hardship to advanced old age unless he is lucky.[109] Apart from strength and health there is another faculty of longevity; for many are long-lived without the excellences of the body, but detailed discussion of this is not useful for present purposes.[110]

16. The meaning of *many friendships* and *good friendships* is not unclear if friend is defined: a *friend* is one who is active in providing another with the things that he thinks are benefits to him. One who has many friends of this sort is a person of many friends; if they are worthy men,[111] he is a person of good friends.

17. *Good luck* [*eutykhia*] means to get and keep those good things of which chance [*tykhē*] is the cause, either all or most or the most important.[112] Chance is the cause of some things that can also be

1362a

---

108. Aristotle continues to think in terms of athletics, here wrestling.

109. On the text here, see Grimaldi 1980, 1:117–118.

110. This is perhaps a late addition. The other faculty is a certain "natural vitality" or capacity for self-renewal; see Aristotle's discussion "On Length and Shortness of Life" in *Parva naturalia* 464b–467b.

111. *Andres*, "males," one of the rare specifications of sex in the *Rhetoric*.

112. There was a strong belief in Greece in *Tykhē* (Fate or Fortune), even worshiped as a goddess. To Aristotle this was superstition, but he allows that some people are luckier than others. One factor in happiness is *eutykhia*, discussed at greater length in *Eudemian Ethics* 8.2. A reputation for good luck could be a factor in securing an appointment, as in the case of the Roman dictator Sulla, called "Felix" ("Lucky"); see also Cicero, *On the Manilian Law* 47–48 about Pompey's "luck."

created by the arts and of many things unrelated to art, for example, things caused by nature (but it is possible for chance to be contrary to nature); art is the cause of health, nature the cause of beauty and stature. In general, the kinds of good things that come by chance are those that incur envy. Chance is also the cause of good things that are unaccountable, as when brothers are all ugly except one who is handsome; or when others do not see a treasure but one person finds it; or when a missile hits one bystander rather than another; or if a person who always frequents some place was [on one occasion] the only one not to come, and others, going there for the first time, were killed. All such things seem to be matters of good luck.

18. *Virtue*, since it is a topic [*topos*] most closely connected with forms of praise, must be left for definition when we give an account of praise.[113]

Chapter 6: Ethical Topics Continued: Definition of a "Good"

■ Since public address necessarily builds persuasion on popularly held assumptions, the ethical values discussed in this chapter are of a rather conventional sort (see Pearson 1962 and Dover 1974). In his ethical treatises, and especially in *Nicomachean Ethics*, Aristotle shows a greater sense of urgency toward knowing and doing what is morally right and gives higher priority to the contemplative life than to active political life. Beginning in section 19 Aristotle for the first time illustrates the use of some ethical topics in deliberation.

1. Now it is clear what future or existing things should be aimed at in exhortation and dissuasion; for the latter are the opposite of the former. But since the objective of the deliberative speaker is the advantageous [*sympheron*], and since [people] do not deliberate about this objective but about means that contribute to it and these [means] are things advantageous in terms of actions, and since the advantageous is a good, one should grasp the elements of good and advantageous in the abstract.

2. Let a good [*agathon*] be [defined as] whatever is chosen for itself and that for the sake of which we choose something else and what everything having perception or intelligence aims at or what everything would [aim at] if it could acquire intelligence.[114] Both

---

113. In 1.9.4; but the next chapter contains some remarks on the virtues. In this sentence *topos* is perhaps not to be understood in a technical sense.

114. I.e., what might be said to be "good" for a plant or animal.

what intelligence would give to each and what intelligence does give to each in individual cases is the good for each; and whatever by its presence causes one to be well-off and independent; and independence itself; and what is productive or preservative of such things; and what such things follow upon; and what is preventative and destructive of the opposite. 3. Things *follow upon* another in two senses: either simultaneously or subsequently; for example, knowledge is subsequent to learning but living is simultaneous with health. Things are *productive* in three senses: some as being healthy is productive of health; some as food is productive of health; some as exercise is, in that it usually produces health. 4. On these premises it necessarily follows that both the acquisition of good things and the elimination of evil things are goods; for in the latter case not having the evil follows simultaneously [with the action and] in the former having the good is subsequent. 5. [And it necessarily follows] that acquisition of a greater good rather than a lesser one and of a lesser evil rather than a greater one [are goods]. For when the greater thing exceeds the lesser there is acquisition of one and elimination of the other. 6. And the virtues are necessarily a good; for those having them are well-off in regard to them, and virtues are productive of good things and matters of action. Something must be said about each [virtue] separately, both what it is and what quality it has. 7. *Pleasure*, too, is necessarily a good;[115] for all living things by nature desire it. Thus, both pleasant things [*hēdea*] and fine things [*kala*] are necessarily goods [*agatha*]; for some are productive of pleasure; and in the case of fine things some are pleasant, others desirable in themselves.[116]

8. To speak of these one by one, the following are necessarily good: happiness (it is both desirable in itself and self-sufficient, and we choose other things to obtain it); 9. justice, courage, temperance, magnanimity, magnificence, and similar dispositions (for they are virtues of the soul);[117] 10. and health and beauty and such things (for they are virtues of the body and productive of many things, for example health of pleasure and life, so health seems to be the best because it is the cause of the two things most honored by most people—pleasure and life); 11. wealth (for it is the virtue of possession and productive of many things); 12. a friend and friendship (for

---

115. Aristotle gives a critical assessment of this in *Nicomachean Ethics* 10.2.

116. *Kala*, here translated "fine," can mean both things that are beautiful (and thus sources of pleasure) and things that are morally good (thus good in themselves).

117. On these virtues of the soul, see 1.9.11.

a friend is desirable in himself and productive of many things); 13. honor, reputation (for they too are pleasant and productive of many things, and the possession of things for which people are honored usually follows with them); 14. the ability to speak, to act (for all such things are productive of goods); 15. in addition, natural talent, memory, ease in learning, quick wittedness, all such things (for these abilities are productive of goods); similarly, all forms of knowledge and art; and life 16. (for even if no other good should follow, it is desirable in itself); 17. and justice (for it is a thing advantageous to society).

These, then, are what are more or less agreed upon as goods; 18. and syllogisms are drawn from [premises about] them in discussions of debatable cases. 19. [Thus, it can be argued that] a thing is good if its opposite is bad and if its opposite is advantageous to our enemies;[118] for example, if it is especially advantageous to our enemies for us to be cowardly, it is clear that courage is especially advantageous to our citizens. 20. And, in general, the opposite of what enemies want or [of] what makes them happy seems advatageous; thus, it was well said, "Yea, Priam would rejoice. . . ."[119] But this is not always the case, only generally true; there is no reason why the same thing may not sometimes be an advantage to both sides. As a result, it is said that evils bring men together when the same thing is harmful to both sides. 1363a 21. And a thing is good when it is not in excess, but whatever is greater than it should be is bad.[120] 22. And what has cost much labor and expense [is good]; for it is an apparent good already, and such a thing is regarded as an "end" and an end of many [efforts]; and the "end" is a good. This is the source of the following: "And it would be a boast left to Priam. . . ."[121] And "It is a disgrace for you to have stayed long. . . ."[122] And the proverb "[to break] the pitcher at the door."[123] 23. And what many desire and what seems an object of contention [is good]; for the good was [earlier defined as] what all

---

118. Variations on this topic are frequent in Demosthenes' *Olynthiac* and *Philippic* orations.

119. *Iliad* 1.255, said by Nestor of the advantage to the Trojans from the quarrel between Achilles and Agamemnon.

120. The basic Aristotelian doctrine of virtues and other goods as a mean between extremes.

121. *Iliad* 2.160. It would be something for Priam to boast of if the Greeks left Troy without securing Helen, which is the "end" for which they had suffered much toil.

122. *Iliad* 2.298. It would be a disgrace for the Greeks to have spent ten years fighting at Troy and return home empty-handed.

123. Presumably when carrying water from a well. But the proverb is not otherwise known in Greek, and whether it is right to understand "to break" is uncertain.

desire and *the many* resembles *all*. 24. And what is praised [is good]; for no one praises what is not good. And what the enemy and the evil praise [is good]; for like all others, they already acknowledge [its goodness]. And what those who have suffered from [praise is good]; for they would agree because it was self-evident, just as those are unworthy whom their friends blame and their enemies do not.[124] Thus, the Corinthians thought they had been slandered when Simonides wrote the verse "Ilium blames not the Corinthians."[125] 25. And what any of the wise or good men or women has shown preference for, as Athena [for] Odysseus and Theseus [for] Helen and the goddesses [for] Paris and Homer [for] Achilles. 26. And in general, things that are deliberately chosen [are good]: people prefer to do the things that have been mentioned, both evil things to their enemies and good things to their friends, and things that are possible. 27. But the latter has two senses: things that might be brought about and things that are brought about easily. Easy things are done either without trouble or in a short time; for the difficult is defined either by trouble or length of time. And [things are good if they turn out] as people want; but they want either nothing bad or [an evil] less than [the accompanying] good; the latter will be the case if the cost is either unnoticed or slight. 28. And [people value] things that are peculiarly their own and that no one else [has or does] and that are exceptional; for thus there is more honor. And [people value] things that are suited to them and such things as are befitting their family and power. And [people value] things they think they are lacking in, even if small; for nonetheless, they choose to get these things. 29. And [people value] things easily done; for since they are easy, they are possible. (The most easily done are things in which all people or most or those like themselves or those [they regard as] inferior have been successful.) And [people value] what they are naturally good at and experienced in; for they think to succeed there rather easily. And [people value] what no common person does; for these deeds are more praiseworthy. And [people value] things they happen to long for; for this seems not only pleasant but also rather good. 30. And most of all, each category of people [values as a good] that to which their character is disposed; for example, those fond of victory [value something] if it will be a victory, those fond of honor if it will be an honor, those fond of money

1363b

---

124. Translating Kassel's (1976) text in this sentence.
125. Simonides of Ceos, frag. 572. But Aristotle has somewhat misremembered the line.

if there will be money, and others similarly. Persuasive arguments [*pisteis*] on the subject of a good and the advantageous should be taken from these [elements or topics].

Chapter 7: The Koinon *of Degree of Magnitude—Greater or Smaller—as Applicable to Questions of the Advantageous and the Good in Deliberative Rhetoric*

■ In 1.3.9 Aristotle identified greater and smaller, the degree of magnitude or importance, as a form of argument common to all species of rhetoric, analogous to questions of possibility or fact. In 2.18.2 these types of argument are called *koina* and apparently are to be distinguished from topics. The topic of "the more and the less," mentioned in 1.2.21, is a logical strategy applied to a particular argument, whereas the *koinon* of degree, although sounding much the same, is an aspect of the subject being discussed. A speaker needs to show that something is important or not important much as he needs to show that it is possible or impossible. This chapter resumes the discussion as applied to deliberative rhetoric, the "end" of which is the advantageous; but as in the case of ethical knowledge discussed in the two previous chapters, the question of the degree of good is applicable to all species of rhetoric. The chapter has some common elements with *Topics* 3.1–3 and is one of the most torturous, largely because of Aristotle's persistence in trying to list and define in detail what often seem to be rather simple conceptions rather than giving a series of possible examples of application to deliberative oratory.

1. Since both sides in a debate often agree about what is advantageous but disagree about what is more advantageous [among possible courses of action], something should next be said about greater good and the more advantageous. 2. Let *exceeding* mean being as great and more in quantity [than something else] and *exceeded* mean [having a quantity that can be] contained [by something else]; and let *greater* and *more* always be in comparison with *less*, but *great* and *small* and *much* and *little* be in comparison to the magnitude of most things (the great exceeding, while that falling short is small), and similarly *much* and *little*.

3. Since, then, we call something good that is chosen for itself and not for the sake of something else and what all things aim at and what something that has mind and practical wisdom would choose and the productive and the protective (or what follows on such things)[126] and

---

126. Cf. 1.6.2.

since what exists for itself is an "end" (and since the "end" is that for the sake of which other things exist) and since to an individual the good is what has these attributes in relation to him, it necessarily follows that the more is a greater good than the one or the fewer, the one or the fewer being counted together; for it exceeds and [the fewer] being contained is surpassed.[127] 4. And if the greatest [in one class of things] exceeds the greatest [in another], the former also exceeds the latter; and when the former exceeds the latter, the greatest [individual item in one class] also exceeds the greatest [individual item in the other].[128] For example, if the largest man is larger than the largest woman, then as a group men are larger than women; and if men are as a group larger than women, [conversely] the largest man is larger than the largest woman; for the superior [in size] of classes and of the greatest within them are analogous.

5. And [what precedes is the greater] when one thing follows from another but the relationship is not reciprocal (using *follows* in the sense of resulting simultaneously or successively or potentially); for the use of what follows is already inherent in what precedes. Life follows from health simultaneously but not health from life; knowledge is subsequent to learning, and theft is the potential result of sacrilege; for one violating a holy place might also steal from it.[129]

---

127. Aristotle's effort to be precise about what might otherwise seem self-evident leads him to compose a complicated sentence that has confused editors and commentators, resulting in efforts at textual emendation; cf. Grimaldi 1980, 1:145 and Lear 2004:64.

128. A difficult passage, but clarified by the following example. Aristotle is speaking in universal terms; it is perhaps conceivable that the largest person alive in Athens at some time might be a woman, but taking the human race as a whole over all time it seems a principle of nature that the largest man has been larger than the largest woman; and the largest mouse could not exceed the size of the largest elephant.

129. Thus, health can be said to be better than mere living, and active learning more valuable than passive knowledge, and unwarranted entry into a sacred place a more heinous act than the potential theft that may follow. This is the interpretation of Cope ([1877] 1970, 1:122), and Grimaldi, (1980, 1:149), which is probably right. But the crucial clause "what precedes is the greater" is implied rather than expressed in the Greek, resulting in some possible confusion. Aristotle has said in 1.6.10 that health seems best because it is the source of life. The opposite could, of course, be argued in each case; and despite what Aristotle says, there is some reciprocity inherent in the examples: although health carries the potential for continued life, life itself carries the potential for health and is prior to it, and learning could not exist without knowledge nor knowledge without learning. Aristotle is, however, here setting out lines of possible rhetorical argument, not making absolute judgments.

6. And things exceeding something equal to a greater entity are greater than it; for they necessarily also exceed the greater.[130] And things that are productive of greater good are greater; 7. for this was the meaning of *productive of the greater.*[131] And [the good] of which the producer is greater [is greater] in the same way; for if health is greater than pleasure, it is also a greater good, and health *is* greater than pleasure. 8. And what is more preferable in itself [is a greater good] than what is not, for example, strength [is a greater good] than what is wholesome; for the latter is not sought for itself, while the former is, which was the meaning of the good. 9. And if one thing is an "end" and another is not [the "end" is a greater good]; one is sought for its own sake, the other for something else, for example, exercise for the sake of bodily fitness. 10. And what has less need than another for other things [is a greater good than what has more]; for it is more independent, and "to have less need" is to need fewer things or things easily gotten. 11. And when one thing cannot come into being without another but the latter can exist without the former[, the latter is the greater good]; for what does not have this need is more independent, so that it seems a greater good. 12. And if it is a first principle [*arkhē*] but the other is not, [it is greater]. And if it is a cause and the other is not, [it is greater] for the same reason; for existence or coming to be is impossible without a cause and first principle.[132] And if there are two first principles [of two different things], that from the greater is the greater. And if there are two causes, what comes from the greater cause is greater; and conversely, of two first principles, the first principle of the greater thing is the greater, and of two causes the cause of the greater is the greater cause. 13. It is clear, then, from what has been said that a thing seems greater in two senses; for if one thing is a first principle and another is not, the former seems to be greater, and if one is not a first principle but the other is [what is not a first principle seems greater]; for [in the second sense] the "end" is greater and not the beginning, as Leodamas said in his accusation of Callistratus that the one giving the advice did more wrong than the one who

1364a

---

130. The interpretation of Grimaldi 1980, 1:150–151.

131. In 1.7.3.

132. The concept of a first principle (*arkhē*, lit. "beginning") is basic to Aristotle's physics and metaphysics. In *Metaphysics* 5.1.1–3 he gives seven meanings of *arkhē* but says all have the common property of being the "starting point" from which something exists or comes into being or becomes known. All causes are *arkhai*, but all *arkhai* are not causes: e.g., the keel of a ship or the foundation of a house are starting points in construction but not causes.

carried it out (for the latter would not have acted if the other had not given the advice), but against Chabrias he claimed that the one who acted [did greater wrong] than the one who advised; for there would have been no effect if there had not been a doer; for this is the purpose of plots, that people may execute them.[133]

14. And what is scarcer is greater than what is abundant (for example, gold than iron), though less useful; for possession of it is a greater thing through being more difficult. But in another way the abundant [is greater] than the scarce, because it exceeds in usefulness; for *often* exceeds *seldom*; thus, it is said, "Water is best."[134] 15. And as a whole, the more difficult [is greater] than the easier; for it is rarer. But in another way the easier [is greater] than the more difficult; for that is what we want things to be. 16. And something whose opposite is greater and whose loss is greater [is greater].[135] And virtue is a greater thing than non-virtue, and vice a greater thing than non-vice; for the former are "ends," the latter not.[136] 17. And those things are greater whose effects are finer or more shameful. And where the vices and virtues are greater, the actions are greater too, since these [vices and virtues] are like causes and first principles, and the results [are greater]; and in proportion to the results so also the causes and the first principles. 18. And things whose superiority is preferable or finer [are greater]; for example, it is preferable to be keen of sight rather than of smell; for sight is also preferable to a sense of smell; and to be fond of friends is a finer thing than to be fond of money, so love of friends [is greater] than love of money.[137] And correspondingly, excesses of better things are better and of finer things finer. 19. And things of which the desires are finer or better [are greater]; for the stronger emotions are for greater things. And desires are finer or better for finer or better things for the same reason.

1364b

---

133. The incident involved the betrayal of Oropus to the Thebans and took place in 366 B.C.E., soon after Aristotle first arrived in Athens. Although a good example of contrasting judgment, the speeches cited appear to have been given in the law courts (thus drawn from judicial rhetoric), not in deliberation in the assembly.

134. Pindar, *Olympian* 1.1.

135. E.g., as Grimaldi notes (1980, 1:157), the opposite (loss) of health is a greater evil than the opposite (loss) of wealth.

136. This sentence is much discussed by the commentators, some of whom were troubled by an implied moral ambivalence. Aristotle is, however, talking about the difference in degree, not in morality, of active versus passive qualities, as is seen in the next sentence.

137. Kassel (1976) double-bracketed these examples as a later addition by Aristotle. On the superiority of sight to other senses, see the opening lines of *Metaphysics* 1.1.

20. And things [are greater] of which the forms of knowledge are finer or more serious and the subjects are finer and more serious; for as knowledge prevails, so does truth; each science commands its own subject. The sciences of more serious and finer things are analogous for the same reasons. 21. And what the wise—either all or many or most or the most authoritative—would judge or have judged the greater good are necessarily so regarded, either absolutely or in terms of the practical wisdom [*phronēsis*] by which they made their judgment.[138] This applies in common to other things; for substance and quantity and quality[139] are regarded as whatever science and practical wisdom say. But we have said this in the case of goods;[140] for that has been defined as good which [living] things would choose, in each case, if they had practical wisdom. It is clear, therefore, that what practical wisdom has more to say about is also greater. 22. And what belongs to better people [is greater], either absolutely or insofar as they are better, as courage belongs to the strong. And what a better person would choose [is greater], either absolutely or insofar as he is better, for example, to be wronged rather than to wrong;[141] for this the juster person would choose. 23. And the more rather than the less pleasant [is greater]; for all things pursue pleasure, and for its sake they long to be pleased; and it is in these terms that the good and the "end" have been defined.[142] And pleasure is sweeter that is less accompanied by pain and longer lasting. 24. And the finer [is] more [great] than the less fine [*kalon*]; for the fine is either the pleasant or what is chosen for itself. 25. And things of which people wish to be the cause to a greater extent, themselves to themselves or to their friends, these are greater goods, and of what [they wish to be the cause] the least, [these are] greater evils. 26. And things that last a longer time rather than those that last a shorter time, and more secure things [are greater] than the less secure; for the utility of the former exceeds over time and [the utility] of the latter [exceeds] in voluntary control; for use of something secure is readier when people want it.

---

138. Cf. *Topics* 1.100b 18 in Appendix I.D.

139. The first three of the ten Aristotelian categories of being; see *Categories* 4 and the note on 2.7.6.

140. See 1.6.8.

141. The principle repeatedly enunciated by Socrates, as in *Gorgias* 469c2.

142. E.g., by Eudoxus; see *Nicomachean Ethics* 10.2, where Aristotle criticizes the definition.

27. And just as would result from etymological connections among words and grammatical inflexions [in the use of other arguments],[143] so, too, other conclusions follow [here]; for example, if *courageously* is finer [than] and preferable to *temperately*, courage is preferable to temperance and being courageous to being temperate. 28. And what 1365a all people prefer [is preferable] to what all do not. And what more rather than fewer prefer [is preferable]; for *good* was what all desire, so *greater* is what more people [desire]. And what opponents [regard as a greater good] or enemies or judges or those whom judges judge [to be wise is preferable]; for in the former case it is as though all people would say so, in the latter what authorities and experts [more approve]. 29. And sometimes the greater is what all share (for not to share in it is a disgrace); but sometimes [the greater is] what no one else or a few [have] (for it is rarer). 30. And things that are more praiseworthy [are greater]; for they are finer. And similarly, things of which the rewards are greater [are greater]; for reward is a kind of evaluation; and [conversely,] that for which the punishments are greater [is greater]. 31. And things that are greater than those agreed [to be] or seeming to be great [are greater]. And the same things when divided into their parts seem greater; for there seems to be an excess of more things present. As a result, the poet[144] also says that [the following words] persuaded Meleager to rise up [and fight]:

> Whatsoever ills are to men whose city is taken:
> Folk perish, and fire levels the city to the dust,
> And others led off children.

And combination and building up [of phrases or clauses make something seem greater], as Epicharmus does,[145] both because this is the same as division (for combination points to much excess) and because it seems to be the first principle and cause of great things. 32. And since the more difficult and rarer is greater, so opportunities and

---

143. *Etymological connections among words* = systoikha (coordinates); *grammatical inflexions* = homoioi ptōseis (similar cases); see *Topics* 2.9.114a–b.

144. Homer, in *Iliad* 9.592–594. Aristotle probably quoted from memory and his version does not entirely agree with our texts.

145. *Combination* (syntithenai, synthesis) is "accumulation," as in the Homeric example; *building up* (epoikodomein) is apparently the figure of speech called "climax," exemplified in some lines of the comic poet Epicharmus quoted by Athenaeus 2.36c–d: "After the sacrifice, a feast; after the feast, drinking; after the drinks, . . . insult; after the insults, a lawsuit; after the suit, a verdict; after the verdict, chains, stocks, and a fine."

ages in life and places and times and powers make things great; for if a person [acts] beyond his power and beyond his age and beyond such things, and if [the actions are done] in such a way or place or at such a time, he will have greatness of fine and good and just things and their opposites. Thus, too, the epigram on the Olympic victor:

> In the past, having on my shoulders a rough yoke.
> I used to carry fish from Argos to Tegea.

And Iphicrates lauded himself, speaking of his origins.[146] 33. And what is self-generated [is greater] than what is acquired. Thus, the poet, too, says, "But I am self-taught."[147] 34. And the greatest part of the great [is greater]; for example, Pericles said in the Funeral Oration that the youth had been taken from the city, "as if the spring had been taken from the year."[148]

35. And things that are useful in greater need [are greater], for example, those useful in old age and illness. And of two [goods], that which is nearer the "end" [is greater]. And what is useful to a particular person [is] more [great] than what is generally useful.[149] And the possible [is greater] than the impossible; for one is useful in itself, the other not. And those things involved in the "end" of human life; for ends are more [important] than things supplementary to the end.[150] 36. And things related to truth [are greater] than things related to opinion. The definition of *related to opinion* is what a person would **1365b** not choose if he were going to escape notice. As a result, to get a benefit would seem to be more [often] chosen than to do good; for a person will choose the former even if it escapes [others'] notice, but it is not the general view that one would choose to do good secretly.[151]

---

146. Cf. 1.9.31. Iphicrates came from a humble background but became the best Athenian general of the period of Aristotle's first residence in Athens. Aristotle quotes his speeches several times, apparently from memory of having heard them, since there is no reason to believe they were published.

147. Said by the bard Phemius in *Odyssey* 22.347; but as in 1.7.31, "the poet" is apparently Homer.

148. This celebrated simile, quoted again in slightly different form in 3.10.7, does not appear in the version of the Funeral Oration attributed to Pericles in Thucydides 2.35–46. Memory of it may have been otherwise transmitted from the speech on that occasion (431 B.C.E.), or Pericles may have given more than one funeral oration.

149. See Grimaldi 1980, 1:173–174, on problems in this passage, but the translation follows the text of Ross (1959) and Kassel (1976).

150. As Grimaldi (1980, 1:175) indicates, "end" is probably to be taken teleologically, not temporally.

151. Cf. the story of Gyges' ring in Plato, *Republic* 2.359–360.

37. And things people wish to exist in reality [are preferable] to their semblance; for they are more related to truth. Thus, people say that even justice is a small thing, because it rather seems to be preferable than is.[152] But this is not the case with health. 38. And what is useful in many respects [is preferred to what is not], for example, what relates to life and living well and pleasure and doing fine things. Thus, wealth and health seem to be the greatest goods; for they have all these qualities. 39. And what is less painful and what is accompanied by pleasure [is preferred]; [here there is] more than one thing, so that both pleasure and absence of pain are present as a good. 40. And of two goods, that which added to one makes the whole greater [is greater]. And things that do not escape attention when present [are greater] rather than what does; for these point to the truth. Thus, being wealthy would appear to be a greater good than seeming to be. 41. And what is cherished, both by some alone and by others together with other things[, is greater than what is not]; thus, the punishment is not the same if one blinds a one-eyed man or one having two eyes;[153] for someone has taken away what is cherished. Now the sources of *pisteis* in exhortation and dissuasion have pretty much been stated.

Chapter 8: Topics About Constitutions Useful in Deliberative Rhetoric

■ Aristotle here resumes discussion of the premises of legislation mentioned in 1.4.12–13, where it was pointed out that the deliberative orator must understand the forces that strengthen or weaken an existing form of constitution. The chapter is probably a late addition to the early core of the *Rhetoric*; note that the last sentence of chapter 7 seems to indicate the end of the discussion of deliberative rhetoric. The cross-reference to *Politics* in 1.8.7 suggests that that work had been completed, but Aristotle here speaks of four forms of constitution, as Plato had in *Republic* 8.544c, rather than the three discussed in *Politics* 3.7, where oligarchy is treated as a perversion of aristocracy. The division into four forms is less scientific but a valid practical description of what was known in Greece and thus more appropriate for rhetoric. Although democracies, like those of Athens and its allies, provided the most opportunity for public debate, both in councils and

---

152. The view of Thrasymachus in Plato, *Republic* 2.358a, and of Callicles in the *Gorgias*.

153. An actual law in Locris according to Demosthenes, *Against Timocrates* 140–141.

assemblies, oligarchic governments like that of Sparta had councils of elder or wealthy citizens that determined policy and thus engaged in debate; and even within a monarchy like Macedon debate took place among advisers of the king. Familiarity with differing constitutions could be especially important when ambassadors from a city living under one form of government were sent to a city living under another form of government to try to persuade it that some course of action was in its own best interest, as is clear from numerous ambassador speeches in the historical writings of Thucydides and others. Rather surprisingly, Aristotle does not specifically mention ambassador speeches, nor do later rhetoricians give them much attention (see Wooten 1973). In the case of the founding of a new city or after a revolution, such as that of 411 B.C.E. in Athens, there might be internal discussion of the advantages of a particular form of government. The earliest extant example of deliberation about the advantages of different forms of constitution is found in Herodotus 3.80–87, describing an imaginary debate in Persia in 521 B.C.E., which was perhaps in Aristotle's mind as he wrote this chapter. As he pointed out in 1.4.13, and repeats in 1.8.7, detailed study of the subject belongs to the discipline of politics rather than to the art of rhetoric.

1. The greatest and most important of all things in an ability to persuade and give good advice is to grasp an understanding of all forms of constitution [*politeia*] and to distinguish the customs and legal usages and advantages of each; 2. for all people are persuaded by what is advantageous, and preserving the constitution is advantageous. Furthermore, the edict of the central authority is authoritative, and central authorities differ in accordance with constitutions; for there are as many different central authorities as there are constitutions. 3. There are four forms of constitution: democracy, oligarchy, aristocracy, monarchy; thus, the central authority and decision-making element would always be some part of these or the whole.[154]

4. *Democracy* is a constitution in which offices are distributed by lot and *oligarchy* one in which this is done on the basis of owning property,[155] and *aristocracy* one in which it is based on education

---

154. That is, it will always be one of the elements (the people, the rich, the educated, or the royal) that predominates in one of these, or a combination in the case of a mixed constitution.

155. That is, only those could hold office who had a certain minimum of ratable property. The higher the requirement, the smaller the governing elite. The Founding Fathers of the United States were fearful of radical democracy and property qualification for voting was a feature of early state constitutions.

[*paideia*].[156] By *education* I mean that laid down by law [*nomos*];[157] for those who have remained within the legal traditions [of the city] rule in an aristocracy. These people necessarily seem "best," which is also why it has this name. And *monarchy* is, in accordance with its name, that in which one person is sovereign over all; of these, some are a kingdom with orderly government, some a tyranny where power is unlimited.[158]

5. [A deliberative speaker] should not forget the "end" of each constitution; for choices are based on the "end." The "end" of democracy is freedom, of oligarchy wealth, of aristocracy things related to education and the traditions of law, of tyranny self-preservation. Clearly, then, one should distinguish customs and legal usages and benefits on the basis of the "end" of each, since choices are made in reference to this. 6. Now, since *pisteis* not only come from logical demonstrations but from speech that reveals character (for we believe the speaker through his being a certain kind of person, and this is the case if he seems to be good or well disposed to us or both), we should be acquainted with the kinds of character distinctive of each form of constitution; for the character distinctive of each is necessarily most persuasive to each.[159] What these [kinds of character] are will be grasped from what has been said above; for characters become clear by deliberate choice, and deliberate choice is directed to an end.

7. Thus, a statement has been given of what should be sought while advising about future or present circumstances and of the sources from which one should take *pisteis* about the advantageous, as well as of the means and manner of acquiring knowledge about characters distinctive of constitutions and legal traditions (insofar as

---

156. Thus effectively on a combination of birth plus some inherited wealth and an understanding of the traditional culture of the city. Aristocracy is literally "rule by the best," oligarchy "rule by the few"; and many writers regarded aristocracy as a good form of oligarchy, which degenerates by admitting the newly rich to office.

157. Primarily, "unwritten law, custom," the traditional educational pattern observed by the upper classes and including for the Greeks *gymnastikē* (athletic training) and *mousikē* (learning to read and write, with some instruction in geometry, music, poetry, and the history and legal customs of the city).

158. Aristotle discusses the forms of constitution at length in *Politics*, Books 3–4.

159. Thus, an envoy should exhibit democratic, oligarchic, aristocratic, or monarchical sympathies as appropriate to the audience, or at least show an understanding of the political views of the community. This widens the concept of ethos beyond what was described in 1.2.4 and anticipates what will be said about adapting a speech to an audience in 2.13.16 and at the end of 2.18.1.

was appropriate for the present, for the details about these matters are described in the *Politics*).

[Chapter 9: Epideictic Rhetoric]

Chapter 9: Topics for Epideictic Rhetoric; Definition of the Virtues and the Honorable as Sources of Praise; Amplification as Characteristic of Epideictic Rhetoric

■ This chapter discusses the virtues and the concept of *to kalon*, the "honorable," "fine," or "noble," and to a lesser extent its opposite, *to aiskhron*, the "shameful," which are the bases of praise or blame in epideictic rhetoric. In 3.19.1 what is said here is described as the "topics" from which portrayal of moral character can be derived. As Aristotle indicates in the first section, knowledge of such matters is very useful in a speaker's efforts to secure the trust of the audience so that it will believe what is said. This trust can also be important in judicial rhetoric, where a speaker may be personally unknown to the jury or be under a cloud of distrust. Many of the ways to establish a positive ethos can be illustrated from private orations written on behalf of clients by Lysias, Demosthenes, Hyperides, and other logographers. Further, in sections 35–37 Aristotle points out how epideictic premises can be converted into deliberative ones by applying them to advice about future action rather than praise of what has been done in the past. The views Aristotle sets out here provide an interesting sample of the conventional values of Greek society in his time; though often consistent with his discussions of moral values in his ethical treatises, they are here couched in a popular form (as more appropriate for rhetoric) and as a whole place somewhat greater emphasis on social and financial success than on the intellectual and moral values he himself elsewhere stresses as the most worth attaining.

1. After this, let us speak of virtue and vice and honorable and shameful;[160] for these are the points of reference for one praising or

---

160. *Aretē, kakia, kalon, aiskhron*, respectively. Although here predominantly used in a moral sense, all carry an implication of what is or is not "fine, seemly." *Aretē* is basically any excellence (in early Greek it often refers to excellence in fighting); e.g., in 3.2.1 the *aretē* of prose style is said to be clarity. *Kalon* means "good" in the sense of having something beautiful about it; in previous chapters it has often been translated "fine," but here it seems to mean what is admired as a fine thing, with a moral connotation, hence "honorable." Older translators preferred "noble." The other common word for "good" in Greek is *agathon*, more general in meaning, though often moral and with no necessary aesthetic connotation.

blaming. Moreover, as we speak of these, we shall incidentally also make clear those things from which we [as speakers] shall be able to make both ourselves and any other person worthy of credence in regard to virtue. 2. But since it often happens, both seriously and in jest, that not only a man or a god is praised but inanimate objects and any random one of the other animals,[161] propositions on these subjects must be grasped in the same way. Thus, only for the sake of giving an example [of what might be more thoroughly explored] let us speak about these propositions also.

3. Now *kalon* describes whatever, through being chosen itself, is praiseworthy or whatever, through being good [*agathon*], is pleasant because it is good. If this, then, is the *kalon*, then virtue is necessarily *kalon*; for it is praiseworthy because of being good [*agathon*]. 4. Now virtue [*aretē*] is an ability [*dynamis*],[162] as it seems, that is productive and preservative of goods, and an ability for doing good in many and great ways, actually in all ways in all things.

1366b

5. The parts [or subdivisions] of virtue are justice, manly courage, self-control, magnificence, magnanimity, liberality, gentleness, prudence, and wisdom.[163] 6. Since virtue is defined as an ability for doing good, the greatest virtues are necessarily those most useful to others. For that reason people most honor the just and the courageous; for the latter is useful to others in war, and the former in peace as well. Next is liberality; for the liberal make contributions freely and do not quarrel about the money, which others care most about. 7. *Justice* [*dikaiosynē*] is a virtue by which all, individually, have what is due to them and as the law requires; and injustice [is a vice] by which they have what belongs to others and not as the law requires. 8. *Manly courage* [*andreia*] [is a virtue] by which people perform fine actions in times of danger and as the law orders and obedient to the law, and cowardice is the opposite. 9. *Self-control* [*sophrosynē*] is the virtue through which people behave as the law orders in regard to the

---

161. Isocrates (*Helen* 12) mentions encomia of salt and bumblebees; from later antiquity we have Dio Chrysostom's *Encomium of Hair* and Synesius' *Encomium of Baldness*; and from the Renaissance Erasmus' *Encomium of Folly*. See Pease 1926.

162. In *Nicomachean Ethics* 2.5–6 Aristotle insists that virtue is a state of habit (*hexis*), not a *dynamis*, but that probably represents a view he later developed, and in any event such a fine distinction is not relevant to rhetoric; see Grimaldi 1980, 1:194 and Allard-Nelson 2001.

163. These and other moral virtues are further defined in *Nicomachean Ethics*, Books 3–4.

pleasures of the body, and lack of control [is] the opposite.[164] 10. *Liberality* [*eleutheriotēs*] is the disposition to do good with money, illiberality [is] the opposite. 11. *Magnanimity* [*megalopsykhia*] is a virtue, productive of great benefits [for others], 12. and *magnificence* [*magaloprepeia*] is a virtue in expenditures, productive of something great, while little-mindedness [*mikropsykhia*] and stinginess [*mikroprepeia*] are the opposites.[165] 13. *Prudence* [*phronēsis*] is a virtue of intelligence whereby people are able to plan well for happiness in regard to the good and bad things that have been mentioned earlier.

14. Now enough has been said about virtue and vice in general and about their parts for the present occasion, and it is not difficult to see the other things [that were proposed for discussion];[166] for it is clear that things productive of virtue are necessarily honorable (for they tend to virtue), as well as things that are brought about by virtue; and both the signs [*sēmeia*] and works of virtue are of such a sort. 15. But since the signs [of virtue] and such things as are the workings or experiencings of a good man are honorable, necessarily whatever are the works of courage or signs of courage or have been done courageously are honorable; also just things and works justly done [are honorable] (but not things justly suffered; for in this alone of the virtues what is justly experienced is not always honorable, but in the case of being punished, to suffer justly is more shameful than to suffer unjustly), and similarly in the case of other virtues. 16. [The following things are all honorable:] things for which the rewards are a *kala*, especially those that bring honor rather than money; and whatever someone has

---

164. In most cases, this would be unwritten law, the norms of the community. Laws of Greek cities did not usually regulate conduct in matters of sexual acts, drinking, etc., unless violence or an affront to the community was involved, though some cities had "sumptuary" laws restricting personal ostentation.

165. In *Nicomachean Ethics* 4.1–2 Aristotle explains the differences between liberality and magnificence more clearly and why the latter is a virtue. The *liberal* person is not necessarily wealthy but is generous and not disposed to bicker about small sums; the *magnificent* person (one might think of Lorenzo the Magnificent in Renaissance Italy) is wealthy and expends large sums in a grand manner on public projects and in good taste. Like all virtues, magnificence must be a mean; it lies between vulgar excess and niggardliness. *Eleutheriotēs* might well be translated "generosity," but "liberality" preserves the connection with *eleutheros*, "free." In Plato's writings "liberality" is the virtue of a free man, and *megaloprepeia* is "high-mindedness," but Aristotle here gives them economic connotations. In 1.9.25–27, however, *eleutheros* means a man free of the need to toil for a living.

166. In 1.9.1–2, the topics and propositions relating to the "honorable," useful in praise or blame.

done not for his own sake; 17. and things absolutely good and whatever someone has done for his country, overlooking his own interest;
and things good by nature and that are not benefits to him, for such
1367a   things are done for their own sake; 18. and whatever can belong to
a person when dead more than when alive (for what belongs to a
person in his lifetime has more the quality of being to his own advantage); 19. and whatever works are done for the sake of others (for they
have less of the self); and good deeds done for others but not for the
self and acts of kindness (for they are not directed to oneself); 20. and
things that are the opposites of those of which people are ashamed
(for they feel shame when speaking and doing and intending shameful things), as also Sappho has written in a poem:

> (Alcaeus speaking) I wish to say something, but shame hinders me.
> [Sappho] If you had a longing for noble or honorable things
> And your tongue had not stirred up some evil to speak,
> Shame would not have filled your eyes,
> But you would have been speaking about what is just.[167]

21. [Those things are honorable] also for which people contend
without fear; for they put up with suffering in regard to goods that
contribute to their reputation. 22. And the virtues and actions of those
who are superior by nature are more honorable, for example, those of
a man more than those of a woman. 23. And those that give pleasure
to others more than to oneself; thus, the just and justice are honorable;
24. and to take vengeance on enemies and not to be reconciled; for to
retaliate is just,[168] and the just is honorable, and not to be defeated is
characteristic of a brave man. 25. And victory and glory are among
honorable things; for they are to be chosen even if they are fruitless,
and they make clear a preeminence of virtue. And things that will be
remembered [are honorable]; and the more so, the more [honorable].
And what follows a person when no longer alive (and glory does
follow) and things extraordinary and things in the power of only one
person are more honorable; for [they are] more memorable. And possessions that bring no fruit [are more honorable]; for [they are] more
characteristic of a free man.[169] 26. And things peculiar to each nation
are honorable [among them]. And whatever are signs of the things
praised among them [are honorable]; for example, in Lacedaimon it

---

167. Sappho, frag. 138.
168. By the definition of 1.9.7: for each to have what is due to him is just.
169. Or perhaps, are more "freely held"; see Lear 2004:134–135.

is honorable to have long hair, for a sign of a free man. (It is not very easy with long hair to do the work of a hired laborer.) 27. And not to work at a vulgar trade [is honorable]; for it is characteristic of a free man not to live in dependence on another.

HOW TO EMPLOY TOPICS OF PRAISE AND BLAME

■ At this point Aristotle becomes prescriptive, for the first time seeming to lay down rules that the orator should follow if he is to succeed in persuading an audience. Probably he is drawing on his "afternoon" lectures addressed to a general audience interested in learning how to speak well. In so doing he may seem to ignore moral considerations, but rhetoric is useful in arguing on both sides of a question (1.1.13), and what he describes are "available means of persuasion" as included in the definition of rhetoric in 1.2.1. It is clear from Book 1 up to this point that a speaker should have a virtuous moral intent and an understanding of the good. That a speaker can be allowed a certain amount of cleverness in obtaining legitimate ends, given the unsophisticated nature of popular audiences, is an assumption of traditional rhetoric; Quintilian, for example, insists (12.1.36–45) that an orator must be "a good man" but allows him to bend the truth when he regards it as necessary. This is perhaps easier to justify in epideictic, such as a funeral oration, than in deliberative or judicial oratory, since the epideictic observer will expect the orator to give the most favorable picture possible of his subject. Even Plato indulges this in the funeral oration in his *Menexenus*.

28. One should assume that qualities that are close to actual ones are much the same as regards both praise and blame; for example, that a cautious person is cold and designing and that a simple person is amiable or that one who does not show anger is calm; 29. and [when praising] one should always take each of the attendant terms in the best sense; for example, [one should call] an irascible and excitable person "straightforward" and an arrogant person "high-minded" and "imposing" and [speak of] those given to excess as actually in states of virtue, for example, the rash one as "courageous," the spendthrift 1367b as "liberal"; for this will seem true to most people and at the same time is a fallacious argument drawn from "cause"; for if a person meets danger unnecessarily, he would be more likely to do so where the danger is honorable, and if he is generous to those he meets, all the more to his friends; for to do good to everyone is overdoing virtue. 30. Consider also the audience before whom the praise [is spoken]; for, as Socrates used to say, it is not difficult to praise Athenians in

Athens.[170] And one should speak of whatever is honored among each people as actually existing [in the subject praised], for example, among the Scythians or Laconians or philosophers.[171] And all in all, attribute what is honored to what is honorable, since they seem related. 31. [Do the same with] whatever is appropriate, for example, if deeds are worthy of the subject's ancestors or his earlier actions; for to acquire additional honor is a source of happiness and honorable. Also [do the same] if something goes beyond the norm in the direction of the nobler and more honorable: for example, if someone shows restraint in times of good fortune but is magnanimous in adversity or in becoming greater becomes nobler and more conciliatory. Such were the remarks of Iphicrates about his [humble] origins and success and of the Olympic victor, "the past having on my shoulders a rough [yoke] . . . ,"[172] and of Simonides, "She whose father and husband and brothers were tyrants."[173]

32. Since praise is based on actions and to act in accordance with deliberate purpose is characteristic of a worthy person, one should try to show him acting in accordance with deliberate purpose. It is useful for him to seem to have so acted often. Thus, one should take coincidences and chance happenings as due to deliberate purpose; for if many similar examples are cited, they will seem to be a sign of virtue and purpose.

33. *Praise* [*epainos*] is speech that makes clear the great virtue [of the subject praised].[174] There is thus need to show that actions have been of that sort. *Encomium*, in contrast, is concerned with

---

170. Something like this is attributed to him by Plato, *Menexenus* 235d.

171. Aristotle cites extreme cases: barbarians, doctrinaire oligarchs, and intellectuals.

172. See 1.7.32.

173. In praise of Archedice, daughter of Hippias, tyrant of Athens in the sixth century B.C.E. The point is that despite these influences, she was a modest woman; cf. Thucydides 6.59.

174. Further explained in *Eudemian Ethics* 2.1.12, where it is said that *epainos* is a matter of praising the subject's general character, *enkōmion* of praising particular deeds. In most Greek usage, *epainos* is a general term for praise and found in many contexts, whereas *enkōmion* is usually a rhetorical genre, such as Gorgias' or Isocrates' *Enkōmia* of Helen. *Epainos* and *psogos* (blame) are the two species of epideictic (demonstrative oratory). The term "panegyric" originally meant a speech at a festival (*panēgyris*), but in later Greek rhetorical treatises it came to refer to all laudatory oratory. *Eulogia* is another Greek word for praise; though not commonly employed by ancient rhetoricians of a speech genre, *eulogy* has subsequently acquired that meaning and is now often used of funeral orations, which in Greek are *epitaphioi logoi*.

deeds.[175] [Mention of] attendant things contributes to persuasion, for example, good birth and education; for it is probable that good children are born from good parents and that a person who is well brought up has a certain character. Thus, too, we "encomi-ize" those who have accomplished something. The deeds are signs of the person's habitual character, since we would praise even one who had not accomplished anything if we believed him to be of the sort who could. 34. (*Blessing* [*makarismos*] and *felicitation* [*eudaimonismos*] are identical with each other, but not the same as *praise* and *encomium*; but just as happiness embraces virtue, so felicitation includes these.)

35. Praise and deliberations are part of a common species [*eidos*] in that what one might propose in deliberation becomes encomia when the form of expression is changed. 36. When, therefore, we know what should be done and what sort of person someone should be, [to adapt this to deliberative oratory] we should change the form of expression and convert these points into propositions: for example, that one ought not to think highly of things gained by chance but of things gained through one's efforts. When so spoken, it becomes a proposition but as praise [of someone] it takes the following form: "He did not think highly of what came by chance but of what he gained by his own efforts." Thus, when you want to set out proposals in deliberation, see what you would praise. 37. The form of expression will necessarily be the opposite when negative advice is given instead of positive.

1368a

38. [In epideictic] one should also use many kinds of amplification;[176] for example, if the subject [of praise] is the only one or the first or one of a few who most has done something; for all these things are honorable. And [praise can be taken] from the historical contexts or the opportunities of the moment, especially if the actions surpass expectation; and if the subject has often had success in the same way (for that is a great thing and would seem to result not from chance but from the person himself); and if incitements and honors have been invented and established because of him; and if he was the first to

---

175. Kassel (1976) double-brackets secs. 33–37 as a late addition by Aristotle and further brackets sec. 34 as an addition by a later reader. In the manuscripts the entire passage 33–34 is repeated at the end of 3.16.3, where it seems to have been used by the scribes to fill a lacuna in the thought; see Grimaldi 1980, 1:213.

176. *Ta auxētika* = *auxēsis*, Lat. *amplificatio*. Amplification is especially characteristic of epideictic and a major factor in demonstrating the speaker's cleverness. It is also characteristic of other species when they are given literary revision and development for publication.

receive an encomium, as in the case of Hippolochus; and [if for him,] as for Harmodius and Aristogeiton, statues were set up in the maketplace.[177] And similarly in opposite cases. And if you do not have material enough with the man himself, compare him with others, which Isocrates used to do because of his lack of experience in speaking in court.[178] One should make the comparison with famous people; for the subject is amplified and made honorable if he is better than [other] worthy ones.

39. Amplification [*auxēsis*], with good reason, falls among forms of praise; for it aims to show superiority, and superiority is one of the forms of the honorable. Thus, even if there is no comparison with the famous, one should compare [the person praised] with the many, since superiority [even over them] seems to denote excellence. 40. In general, among the classes of things common to all speeches,[179] amplification is most at home in those that are epideictic; for these take up actions that are agreed upon, so that what remains is to clothe the actions with greatness and beauty. But paradigms are best in deliberative speeches; for we judge future things by predicting them

---

177. Hippolochus is unknown. Harmodius and Aristogeiton assassinated Hipparchus, brother of the tyrant Hippias, at Athens in 514 B.C.E. and were subsequently regarded as heroes of the democracy. Kassel (1976), consistent with his view of references to encomia in this passage, double-bracketed the first half of the sentence as a late addition by Aristotle.

178. *Lack of experience* is the reading of the oldest manuscript, of the medieval commentary by Stephanus, and of the medieval Latin translation by William of Moerbecke; other manuscripts read *because of his experience*; see the *apparatus criticus* in Kassel (1976). Earlier in his career Isocrates did write speeches for clients to deliver in court (six survive), but he never delivered a speech in person. The point here seems to be that Isocrates' lack of practical and personal experience in court, where such comparisons could have been seen as outside the case, led him to indulge amplification in his published oratory, including the extended comparison of Theseus and Heracles in his *Encomium of Helen* and of Athens and Sparta in his *Panegyricus*. The use of the imperfect tense, *used to do*, might imply that this passage was added after Isocrates' death in 338, or that Isocrates' later speeches made less use of such comparisons, which seems arguable. Given Isocrates' leading role in epideictic and Aristotle's numerous references to him elsewhere, it is somewhat surprising that this is the only occurrence of his name in this chapter. The somewhat belittling reference, however, is consistent with a source in Aristotle's "afternoon" lectures, intended to reduce Isocrates' influence.

179. As Aristotle will point out in 2.26.1, amplification is not a *topos*; rather, it is a *koinon* and form of *pistis* (see 2.18.5), a technique of persuasion, analogous to—though logically weaker than—*paradeigma* and *enthymēma*, as discussed immediately.

from past ones; and enthymemes are best in judicial speeches, for what has happened in some unclear way is best given a cause and demonstration [by enthymematic argument].

41. These, then, are the things from which speeches of praise and blame are almost all derived, as well as what to look for when praising and blaming; for if we have knowledge of these [sources of praise], their opposites are clear; for blame is derived from the opposites.[180]

Chapters 10–15: Judicial Rhetoric

Chapter 10: Topics About Wrongdoing for Use in Judicial Rhetoric

■ In considering what constitutes wrongdoing, Aristotle reveals some interesting cultural values that differ from the teaching of modern society, though not necessarily from modern practice and unspoken beliefs. One is the assumption that it is natural for people to have personal "enemies" who will seek opportunities to do them harm and whom they will seek to harm if the opportunity arises. Another is the right of people to take vengeance on others who have harmed them or their family and friends. The Greeks, a highly contentious people, tended to view life in competitive terms, which found expression in athletics, politics, commerce, speech, and personal relationships. The infliction of harm on a rival was not a source of guilt to an average Greek. Indeed, we hear in Greek texts, including those of Aristotle, many references to feelings of shame at being defeated, wronged, or belittled, and virtually none to feelings of guilt at actions done to another person.

1. Holding to our plan, we should [next] speak of accusation [*katēgoria*] and defense [*apologia*]: from how many and what sort of sources should their syllogisms[181] be derived? 2. One should grasp three things: first, for what, and how many, purposes people do wrong; second, how these persons are [mentally] disposed; third, what kind of persons they wrong and what these persons are like. 3. Let us discuss these questions in order after defining wrongdoing.[182]   **1368b**

---

180. On Aristotle's relative neglect of rhetorical invective, see note on 1.3.3 and Rountree 2001.

181. I.e., enthymemes, arguments.

182. Motives are discussed in chs. 10–11, the mental disposition of wrongdoers and those wronged in ch. 12.

Let wrongdoing [*to adikein*] be [defined as] doing harm willingly in contravention of the law. Law is either specific [*idion*] or common [*koinon*]. I call *specific* the written law under which people live in a polis and *common* whatever, though unwritten, seems to be agreed to among all.[183] People "willingly" do whatever they do knowingly and unforced. Now everything they do willingly they do not do by deliberate choice, but whatever they do by deliberate choice they do knowingly; for no one is ignorant of what he has chosen. 4. Vice [*kakia*] and weakness [*akrasia*] are the reasons why people make the choice of harming and doing bad things contrary to law; for if certain people have one or more depravity, it is in relation to this that they are in fact depraved and are wrongdoers; for example, one is ungenerous with money, another is indulgent in the pleasures of the body, another is soft in regard to comforts, another cowardly in dangers (they abandon comrades in danger through fear), another ambitious for honor, another short-tempered through anger, another fond of winning because of desire for victory, another embittered through vindictiveness, another foolish through misunderstanding of justice and injustice, another shameless through contempt for public opinion, and similarly each of the others in regard to each of their underlying vices.

5. But these things are clear, partly from what has been said about the virtues,[184] partly from what will be said about the emotions.[185] It remains to say for what reason people do wrong and in what state of mind and against whom. 6. First, therefore, let us define what people long for and what they are avoiding when they try to do wrong; for it is clear that the prosecutor should consider, as they apply to the opponents, the number and nature of the things that all desire when they do wrong to their neighbors, and the defendant should consider what and how many of these do not apply.

7. All people do all things either not on their own initiative or on their own initiative. Of those things done not on their own initiative they do some by chance, some by necessity; and of those by necessity,

---

183. See further 1.13.1 and 1.15.3–8. The common law is the traditional understanding of right and wrong shared among all Greeks: e.g., standards of civilized behavior including respect for gods, suppliants, and women, and the right of self-defense. Aristotle does not use the term *natural law*, but in 1.13.2 he does describe common law as based on a natural principle. His usage should not be confused with *common law* in the Anglo-American tradition, which is the law of precedent and equity as established by judicial decisions.

184. In 1.9.

185. In 2.2–11.

some by compulsion, some by nature. So that all the things people do that are not by their own initiative are done some by chance, some by nature, or some by compulsion. But whatever they do on their own initiative and of which they are the causes, these things are done by habit or by desire, sometimes rational desire, sometimes irrational.[186] 8. In one case there is will, desire for some good (no one wills something except when he thinks it a good); but anger and longing are irrational desires. Thus, necessarily, people do everything they do for seven causes: through chance, through nature, through compulsion, through habit, through reason, through anger, through longing. 9. (To distinguish actions further on the basis of age or habitual character or other things is beyond the present task; for if it incidentally results that the young are prone to anger or longing, they do not act in this way because of their youth but because of anger and longing. Nor [do those disposed to longing feel this desire] because of wealth or poverty, but it incidentally results that the poor long for money because of lack of it and [that] the rich long for unnecessary pleasures because of excess [of money]. But these, too, will act not because of wealth or poverty but because of longing. And similarly, both the just and the unjust (and others said to act by their habitual character) will do things either through reason or through emotion; but the former will do good things by character or emotion, the latter the opposite. 10. Yet there surely are consequences of having specific characters or emotions; for good reputation and sentiments in regard to his pleasures follow immediately and equally for the temperate person from his temperance, and to the intemperate person the opposites [follow] in regard to the same things. 11. As a result, though careful distinctions should be left aside [here], there should [later] be consideration of what follows what; for if someone is light or dark or large or small, nothing[187] is ordained as a consequent of such qualities; but if [someone is] young or old or just or unjust, it immediately makes a difference. And generally, [there should be consideration of] what attributes make the moral characters of human beings differ; for example, seeming to oneself to be rich or poor will make some difference, and [thinking oneself] to be lucky or unlucky. We shall discuss these later,[188] but now let us speak first about the remaining matters.)

---

186. What is meant by *irrational* will be explained in 1.11.5.

187. That is, nothing relevant to wrongdoing.

188. In 2.12–17. This long parenthetical passage, with its anticipation of Book 2, is probably a later addition by Aristotle.

12. Things that happen by chance are those whose cause is undefined and which do not occur for a purpose and not always, or not usually, in some ordained way. All this is clear from the definition of *chance*. 13. [Things that happen] by nature are those whose cause is in themselves and ordained; for the result is always or for the most part similar. As for things that happen contrary to nature,[189] there is no need to seek exactness as to whether they occur by a natural principle or some other cause [that is not understood]; chance would also seem to be the cause of such things. 14. By compulsion [occur things] that come into being through the actions of the doers themselves [but] contrary to their desire and reasonings. 15. By habit [occurs] what they do because of having often done it. 16. Through reasoning [occur] things that seem to be advantageous on the basis of goods that have been mentioned or as an "end" or as means to an "end", whenever they are done for the sake of the advantage; for the intemperate also do advantageous things, but because of pleasure, not for the advantage. 17. Through anger and desire [come] things that are vengeful. But revenge and punishment differ; for punishment is for the sake of the sufferer,[190] revenge for the sake of the doer, that he may get a sense of fulfillment. What anger is will become clear in the discussion of the emotions,[191] 18. and through longing is done whatever seems pleasurable. The familiar and the habitual are among the pleasurable; for people even do with pleasure many things that are not pleasurable when they have grown accustomed to them. In short, all things that people do of their own volition are either goods or apparent goods or pleasures or apparent pleasures. But since they do willingly whatever they do on their own initiative and not willingly whatever is not at their own initiative, everything that they do willingly would be goods or apparent goods or pleasures or apparent pleasures. (I place removal of evils or apparent evils or exchange of greater for less [evil] among the goods; for they are somehow preferable, and [so is] removal of pains or what appears so; and exchange of lesser for greater similarly among pleasures.) 19. Things that are advantageous and pleasurable, their number and nature, should therefore be understood. Since the subject of the advantageous in deliberative oratory has been discussed earlier,[192] let us now speak about the

---

189. E.g., the birth of a deformed offspring of healthy parents.
190. To correct the fault, a view also of Plato; see *Gorgias* 507–508.
191. See 2.2; probably a later addition.
192. In 1.6.

pleasurable. Definitions should be thought sufficient if they are neither unclear nor inexact on each subject.

Chapter 11: Topics About Pleasure for Use in Judicial Rhetoric

■ In this chapter Aristotle adopts the definition of pleasure as *kinēsin tina tēs psykhēs*, "a certain movement of the soul." The subject had been much discussed in Plato's Academy during Aristotle's residence there between 367 and 347 B.C.E., and this definition can be attributed to Speusippus, who was probably in charge during Plato's absences and who eventually became Plato's successor (see Fortenbaugh 1970, para. 4; Guthrie 1978, 5:468–469). Later, in *Nicomachean Ethics* 10.4.2, Aristotle denies that pleasure is to be viewed as *kinēsis*. Rist (1989:84) regards the statement here as evidence that this section of the *Rhetoric* is one of the earliest parts of the work, written many years before the development of Aristotle's final views of pleasure and the soul. The word traditionally translated "soul" (*psykhē*) literally means "breath." Aristotle, as always, uses it for the vital principle of life found in all living things. In the case of human beings it can often be best translated "mind." To him the word had a scientific, not a religious, connotation. As in some earlier chapters, Aristotle here provides basic knowledge and understanding of human psychology that he regards as needed by a speaker, in this case a speaker in a court of law, but without attempting to show how the topics might be applied in a speech.

1. Let us assume that pleasure [*hēdonē*] is a certain movement [*kinēsis*] of the mind [*psykhē*] and a collective organization of sensual perception reaching into [an individual's] fundamental nature and that pain is the opposite.[193] 2. If pleasure is something of this sort, it is clear that what is productive of the condition mentioned is also pleasurable [*hēdu*] and that what is destructive [of it] or is productive of the opposite organization is painful. 3. Movement into a natural state is thus necessarily pleasurable for the most part, and especially whenever a natural process has recovered its own natural state. And habits [are pleasurable]; for the habitual has already become, as it were, natural; for habit is something like nature. (What happens often is close to what happens always, and nature is a matter of "always," habit of "often.") 4. What is not compulsory also [is pleasurable]; for

1370a

---

193. Pain, too, might be called a movement of the soul, but instead of collecting and organizing perceptions, thus inducing a feeling of well-being, it disrupts and distracts or focuses all sensation on what is alien to the natural state of the organism.

compulsion is contrary to nature. Thus, constraints are painful, and it has been rightly said, "Every necessary thing is naturally trouble-some."[194] Duties and studies and exertions are painful; for these too are necessarily compulsions unless they become habitual; then habit makes them pleasurable. And their opposites are pleasurable; thus, ease and freedom from toil and carefreeness and games and re-creations and sleep belong among pleasures; for none of these is a matter of necessity. 5. And everything is pleasurable for which there is longing; for longing is a desire for pleasure. (Some longings are *irrational*, some in accordance with reason. I call *irrational* those in which people do not long for something on the basis of some opinion in the mind. Those that are said to be natural are of that sort, like those supplied from the body; for example, thirst and hunger for nourish-ment and longing for a particular kind of food and longing concerned with taste and sex and in general things that can be touched and things concerned with smell and hearing and sight. [I call things] *in accor-dance with reason* what people long for on the basis of persuasion; for they desire to see and possess many things after hearing about them and being persuaded [that they are pleasurable].)[195]

6. Since to be pleased consists in perceiving a certain emotion, and since imagination [*phantasia*][196] is a kind of weak perception, and since some kind of imagination of what a person remembers or hopes is likely to remain in his memory and hopes—if this is the case, it is clear that pleasures come simultaneously to those who are remem-bering and hoping, since there is perception there, too. 7. Thus, nec-essarily all pleasurable things are either present in perception or past in remembering or future in hoping; for people perceive the present, remember the past, and hope for the future.

8. Memories are thus pleasurable, not only about things that were pleasant when they were going on but even about some unpleasant things if their consequences are honorable and good. Thus, too, it has been said,

But sweet it is to remember toils when saved[197]

and

194. Quoted also in *Eudemian Ethics* 2.7.4, where it is attributed to the fifth-century B.C.E. elegiac poet Evenus of Paros.
195. The parenthetical passage was double-bracketed by Kassel (1976) as a later addition by Aristotle.
196. For Aristotle's theory of the imagination, see *On the Soul* 3.3.11.
197. From Euripides' lost *Andromeda*, frag. 131.

For when he remembers later, a man rejoices at his pains,
He who suffers much and does much.[198]

The cause of this is that not having an evil is also pleasurable. 9. And things hoped for [are pleasurable] that, when present, seem to confer great delights or benefits and to benefit without giving pain. Generally, things that give delight when present [are pleasurable], both when we hope for them and (for the most part) when we remember them. Thus, even anger is pleasurable as Homer also [said in the verse he] composed about anger,

Which is much sweeter than honey dripping from the comb;[199]

for no one feels anger at someone who apparently cannot get revenge, and people are not angry—or are less angry—at those much above them in power.

10. A kind of pleasure also follows most desires; for people enjoy a certain pleasure as they remember how they got something or as they hope they will get it; for example, those afflicted with thirst in a fever take pleasure both in remembering how they drank and in hoping to drink, 11. and those in love enjoy talking and writing and continually doing something concerned with the beloved; for in all such things they think, as it were, to have sense perception of the beloved. The starting point of love is the same to all; [it occurs] when [people] not only delight in the beloved's presence but delight in remembering one absent; and they are in love also when there is grief at absence.[200] 12. And similarly, a certain pleasure is felt in mourning and lamentation; for the grief applies to what is not there, but pleasure to remembering and, in a way, seeing him and what he used to do and what he was like. Thus, too, it has been reasonably said,

Thus he spoke, and raised in them all the sweet longing of tears.[201]

13. And to be revenged is pleasurable; for if not attaining something is grievous, getting it is pleasurable, and angry people who do not get revenge are exceedingly pained, but while hoping for it, they rejoice. 14. And winning is pleasurable not only to those fond of it but to all; for there is an imagining of superiority for which all have desire either

---

198. An approximate quotation (doubtless from memory) of *Odyssey* 15.400–401.
199. *Iliad* 18.109.
200. The Greek text of this sentence is corrupt and variously reconstructed; see Grimaldi 1980, 1:255.
201. *Iliad* 23.108, of Patroclus, and *Odyssey* 4.183, of Odysseus.

mildly or strongly. 15. Since winning is pleasurable, necessarily, games of physical combat and mental wit are pleasurable (winning often takes place in these) and games of knucklebone and dice and backgammon. And similarly in the case of serious sports; for pleasure results if one is practiced [in them], and some are pleasurable from the start, such as tracking with dogs and all hunting; for where there is a contest, there is victory. That is also the source of pleasure in lawsuits and contentious debates to those who are practiced and adept.

16. And honor and reputation are among the pleasantest things, through each person's imagining that he has the qualities of an important person; and all the more [so] when others say so who, he thinks, tell the truth. Such ones are neighbors (rather than those living at a distance) and his intimates and fellow citizens (rather than those from afar) and contemporaries (rather than posterity) and the practical (rather than the foolish) and many (rather than few); for those named are more likely to tell the truth than their opposites, [who are disregarded,] since no one pays attention to honor or reputation accorded by those he much looks down on, such as babies or small animals,[202] at least not for the sake of reputation; and if he does, it is for some other reason.

17. A friend is also one of the pleasures; for to be fond of something is pleasurable (no one is fond of wine unless he takes pleasure in wine), and to be liked is pleasurable. There, too, the good is present to someone in his imagination, which all who perceive desire. To be liked is to be cherished for one's own sake. 18. And to be admired is pleasurable because it is the same as being honored. And to be flattered and have a flatterer is pleasurable; for a flatterer is an apparent admirer and apparent friend. 19. To do the same things often is pleasurable; for it was noted above that the habitual is pleasurable. 20. And [conversely] change is pleasurable; for change is a return to nature, because doing the same thing all the time creates an excess of the natural condition.[203] This is the origin of the saying "Change in all things is sweet."[204] For this reason things seen only at intervals are also pleasurable, both human beings and objects; for there is a change

---

202. *Thērion* is usually a wild animal; thus Grimaldi 1980, 1:258 thought the reference was to barbarians. But it is a diminutive of *thēr*, "beast," and can be a tame animal; in 2.6.23, where it is also coupled with "babies" (*paidia*), the reference seems to be to small creatures that cannot speak or judge an action as shameful.

203. E.g., to learn is pleasant, and thus studying is pleasant, but without an occasional respite from the routine the pleasure is diminished.

204. Euripides, *Orestes* 234.

from what is present, and at the same time what comes at intervals is rare. 21. And to learn and to admire are usually pleasurable; for in admiration there is desire,[205] so the admirable is desirable, and in learning there is the achievement of what is in accordance with nature. 22. And to benefit [others] and to be well treated are among   1371b pleasurable things; for to be well treated is to attain what people desire, and to confer benefits is to have [the resources to do so] and to surpass [others], both of which people want. Since conferring benefits is pleasurable, it is also pleasant for people to set their neighbors right and to supply their wants.[206] 23. Since to learn and to admire is pleasurable, other things also are necessarily pleasurable, such as, for example, a work of imitation, as in painting and sculpture and poetry, and anything that is well imitated, even if the object of imitation is not in itself pleasant;[207] for the pleasure [of art] does not consist in the object portrayed; rather there is a [pleasurable] reasoning [in the mind of the spectator] that "this" is "that," so one learns what is involved [in artistic representation].[208] 24. And peripeteias[209] and narrow escapes from dangers [are pleasurable]; for all of these cause admiration. 25. And since what accords with nature is pleasurable and related things are related in accordance with nature, all things that are related and similar are, for the most part, a source of pleasure; for example, human being to human being, horse to horse, and youth to youth. This is the source of the proverbs "Coeval delights coeval,"[210] "Always like together," "Beast knows beast," "Jackdaw by jackdaw,"[211] and other such things. 26. But since all likeness and relationship is pleasurable to an individual, necessarily all are more or less lovers of themselves; for all such things apply most to oneself. And since all are lovers of themselves, necessarily their own things are also pleasurable to all, for example, their deeds and words. Thus, people are for the most part fond of flatterers, lovers, honors, and children;

---

205. "Desire *to learn*" in the Greek text, but perhaps a misunderstanding by a scribe; see Grimaldi 1980, 1:261–262.

206. Section 22 has been questioned by some editors as interrupting the train of thought. Kassel (1976) double-bracketed it as a later addition by Aristotle.

207. Such as fearful animals or dead bodies; cf. *Poetics* 4.4.1448b10–12.

208. Cf. *Poetics* 4.4.1448b15–17. As seen throughout the *Poetics*, Aristotle's aesthetics are cognitive. The spectator comes to understand cause and effect and the relation of universals to particulars.

209. Sudden changes, as from good fortune to disaster or the reverse. Aristotle seems to be thinking primarily of the pleasure of a spectator.

210. I.e., people take pleasure in those of their own age.

211. "Birds of a feather flock together."

for children are their own doing. And to supply things that are lacking is pleasurable; for it becomes their own doing. 27. Further, since people are, for the most part, given to rivalry, it necessarily follows that it is pleasurable to criticize one's neighbors; and to be the leader. (And since to be the leader is pleasantest, to seem to be wise is also pleasurable; for to be wise in a practical way is a quality of leadership, and wisdom is a knowledge of many and admirable things.)[212] 28. And to spend time at what one thinks he is best at [is pleasurable], as the poet also says:

> Each one presses on to this,
> Allotting the most part of the day
> To what happens to be his best endeavor.[213]

29. And similarly, since games are among pleasurable things, all relaxation is, too; and since laughter is among pleasurable things, necessarily laughable things (human beings and words and deeds) are also pleasurable. The laughable has been defined elsewhere in the books *On Poetics*.[214] Let this much, then, be said about pleasurable things; and painful things are clear from their opposites.

1372a

Chapter 12: Topics in Judicial Rhetoric About Wrongdoers and Those Wronged

■ In the following discussion Aristotle provides, without specifically noting it, many premises for argument from probability resembling techniques taught in the rhetorical handbooks of his time.

1. The reasons why people do wrong are those [just described]. Let us now discuss their dispositions of mind and whom they wrong. Now, then, [people do wrong] whenever they think that something [wrong] can be done and that it is possible for themselves to do it—if, having done it, they [think they] will not be detected or if detected they will not be punished or will be punished but [that] the penalty will be less

---

212. In the manuscripts, this sentence is found at the beginning of sec. 27, and one good manuscript (F) omits "and to be leader." Kassel (1976) regarded the parenthesis as a late addition by Aristotle. Possibly it was inserted in the wrong place.

213. From Euripides' lost *Antiope*, frag. 183.

214. Presumably in the lost second book, though there is a short definition in *Poetics* 5.1449a32–34: "some kind of mistake and ugliness that is not painful or destructive." The cross-reference is a late addition by Aristotle.

than the profit to themselves or to those for whom they care. What sort of things seem possible or impossible will be discussed later (these are common to all speeches);[215] 2. but those most think they can do wrong without penalty who are skilled at speaking and disposed to action and experienced in many disputes and if they have many friends and if they are rich. 3. They most think they can get away with it if they themselves are among those enumerated; but if [they are] not, [they think so] if they have friends like that or helpers or accomplices; for through these means they are able to act and escape detection and not be punished. 4. [They] also [think so] if they are friends of those being wronged or of the judges; for friends are not on guard against being wronged and seek reconciliation before undertaking legal procedures, while the judges favor their friends and either completely acquit them or assign a small punishment.[216]

5. [Wrongdoers] are likely to be unsuspected if [their appearance and condition in life is] inconsistent with the charges; for example, a weak man [is not likely to be suspected] on a charge of assault, and a poor man and an ugly man on a charge of adultery; and [people are able to get away with] things that are done in the open and in the public eye (no precaution being taken because no one would ever have thought of it) and things so great and of such a sort that no one person [would be thought able to do it]; 6. for these things also are not guarded against: everybody is on guard against usual diseases and wrongs but nobody takes precautions about an affliction that no one has yet suffered. 7. And [people do wrong] who have either no enemy or many enemies; the former think that they will escape because no precautions are being taken against them, the latter do escape because it does not seem likely they would attack those on their guard and [so] they have the defense that they would not have tried. 8. And those [do wrong] who have a means of concealment, either by artifices or hiding places, or abundant opportunities for disposal [of stolen property]. For those who do not escape detection there is [the possibility] of quashing the indictment or postponing the trial or corrupting the judges. And if a penalty is imposed, there is avoidance of full payment or postponement of it for a while, or through lack of means a person will have nothing to pay. 9. Then there are those for whom the profits

---

215. See 2.19.1–15.

216. This, and the possibility of bribing the judges mentioned later, was made difficult in the Athenian courts by the very large number of juror-judges, a minimum of 201 and often many more.

are clear or great or immediate and the punishments are small or unclear or remote. And [there are those] for whom the feared punishment is not equal to the benefit, as is thought to be the case with

1372b   tyranny.[217] 10. And [there are those] for whom the unjust acts bring substantial reward but the punishments are only disgrace; and conversely, [there are] those whose wrongful acts lead to some praise; for example, if the results include vengeance for a father or mother, as in the case of Zeno,[218] while the punishments lead [only] to fines or exile or something of that sort. People do wrong for both reasons and in both states of mind, except that those who do so are opposites in character. 11. And [people do wrong] when they have often been undetected or not punished. Those [do wrong,] too, who have often been unsuccessful; for there are some among these, too, as among the warlike, who are [always] ready to fight again. 12. And those for whom the pleasure is immediate but the pain comes later, or the profit [is] immediate but the punishment [comes] later; for the weak are like that, and their weakness of character applies to everything they desire. 13. And conversely, those [do wrong] for whom the pain or the penalty is immediate but the pleasure and advantage come later and are long-lasting; for the strong and those who are more prudent pursue such things. 14. And those [do wrong] who can seem to have acted by accident or by necessity or by natural instinct or by habit and all in all seem to have made a mistake rather than committed a crime. And those [do wrong] to whom there is a chance of fair consideration.[219] 15. And those in need [do wrong]. But need is of two sorts: for either it is a matter of necessities, as in the case of the poor, or a result of excess, as in the case of the rich. 16. And those [do wrong] who are very well thought of, and those with very bad reputations—the former as not being suspected, the latter as being no worse thought of.

CHARACTERISTICS OF THOSE WHO ARE WRONGED

People take in hand a wrongful action when disposed as just described, and they wrong people of the following sort and in the following ways. 17. [They wrong] those having something they lack, either as necessities of life or for surfeit or for enjoyment, both those afar and

---

217. This sentence was double-bracketed by Kassel (1976) as a later addition by Aristotle.

218. Incident unknown.

219. Before a court.

those near; 18. for in the latter case they get what they want quickly, and in the former retribution is slow, as in the case of those robbing the Carthaginians.[220] 19. And [they wrong] those who do not take precautions and are not on guard, but trusting; for it is rather easy to take all these unawares. And [they wrong] those who are easy-going; for it is characteristic of a careful person to initiate prosecution. And [they wrong] those who are shy; for they are not likely to make a fight about proceeds. 20. And [they wrong] those who have been wronged by many and have not prosecuted, since these are, as the saying goes, "Mysian spoil."[221] 21. And [they wrong] those who have never and those who have often [been wronged]; for both are off their guard, the former since it has never happened, the latter on the ground that it will not happen again. 22. And [they wrong] those who have been slandered or are easy to slander; for they do not choose to go to court for fear of the judges, nor could they persuade them. Those who are hated and despised are in this class. 23. And [they wrong] those against whom they have the pretext that those persons' ancestors or themselves or their friends either harmed, or were going to harm, them or their ancestors or those for whom they care; for as the proverb has it, "Wickedness only needs an excuse." 24. And [they wrong] both enemies and friends; for the latter is easier, the former sweet. And [they wrong] those who are friendless. And [they wrong] those not good at speaking or taking action; for either they do not undertake prosecution or they come to an agreement or accomplish nothing. 25. And [they wrong] those to whom there is nothing to gain by wasting time in attending on the court or awaiting settlement, for example, foreigners and the self-employed; for they are willing to abandon the suit cheaply and are easily put down. 26. And [they wrong] those who have done many wrongs to others or the [same] kind of wrongs [as are] being done to them; for it almost seems to be no wrong when some one is wronged in the way he himself is in the habit of wronging others. 27. And [they wrong] those who have done bad things [to the person who now reciprocates] or wanted to or want to now or are going to; for this is both pleasurable and honorable and seems almost no wrong. 28. And [they wrong] those whom people wrong as favors to their friends or to those they admire or love or regard as their

1373a

---

220. Aristotle is probably thinking of attacks by Greek pirates on Carthaginian shipping; Carthage seemed far away, and the pirates would not be soon caught if at all.

221. "Easy prey." For speculation on why the Mysians in Asia Minor may have been so regarded, see Cope's commentary ([1877] 1970) on this passage.

masters or, generally, depend on in their lives. And [they wrong] those in regard to whom there is a chance of fair consideration.[222] 29. And [they wrong] those against whom they have made complaints and have had previous differences, as Calippus did with Dion;[223] for such things seem almost no wrong. 30. And [they wrong] those who are going to be wronged by others if the doers do not act [first] themselves, since it is no longer possible to deliberate, as Aenesidemus is said to have sent the *kottabos* prize to Gelon after the latter had enslaved a city, because Gelon did first what Aenesidemus was planning.[224] 31. And [they wrong] those for whom they can do many just things after they have wronged them, thus easily remedying the wrong, as Jason of Thessaly said he had to do some few unjust things in order to do many just ones.

SOME REMARKS ON THE NATURE OF WRONGS

32. [People do those things] that all or many are in the habit of doing wrongfully; for they think they will get pardon. 33. [They steal] things easy to conceal and the kind that are quickly consumed, like eatables, or easily altered in shape or color or by mixing [them with other things] or which there is an opportunity to hide in many places. 34. Such things include those that are easily carried and can be concealed in small places 35. and those that are indistinguishable and similar to many others that the criminal already has. And [they commit crimes] that those wronged are ashamed to mention; for example, outrages against the women of their household or against themselves or their sons. And [they commit] actions in regard to which a complaint would seem to be litigious and such as are small matters for which there is forgiveness.[225]

The characteristics of those whom people wrong and what sort of wrongs they do and against what sort of people and for what reason are more or less these.

---

222. From the person wronged; cf. 1.12.14.

223. Calippus had a role in the death of Plato's friend Dion of Syracuse in 354 B.C.E. when Aristotle was at the Academy.

224. *Kottabos* was a game played by tossing disks into a basin, popular at drinking parties in Sicily. The usual prizes were sweets. Aenesidemus apparently cynically complimented Gelon on success at playing the "game" of tyranny. The date was around 485 B.C.E.; see Grimaldi 1980, 1:283.

225. Cf. the legal principle *De minimis non curat lex*, "The law does not care about trifles."

Chapter 13: Topics About Justice and Injustice for Judicial Rhetoric

1. Let us now classify all unjust and just actions, beginning first with   **1373b**
the following points. Just and unjust actions have been defined in
reference to two kinds of law and in reference to persons spoken of in
two senses. 2. I call law on the one hand specific, on the other common,
specific being what has been defined by each people for themselves,
some of this unwritten, some written,[226] and *common* that which is
based on nature; for there is in nature a common principle of the just
and unjust that all people in some way divine, even if they have no
association or commerce with each other, for example what Antigone
in Sophocles' play seems to speak of when she says that though forbidden, it is just to bury Polyneices, since this is just by nature:

> For not now and yesterday, but always, ever
> Lives this rule, and no one knows whence it appeared.[227]

And as Empedocles says about not killing living things,

> 'Tis not just for some and unjust for others,
> But the law is for all and it extends without a break
> Through the wide-ruling ether and the boundless light.[228]

And as Alcidamas says in the *Messeniacus*, . . .[229]
3. And law is divided in two ways in regard to persons; for what
one ought to do or not do is defined in regard to the community or in
regard to individual members of the community.[230] Thus, unjust and
just actions are matters of being unjust and doing justly in two senses,
either in respect to one defined individual or in regard to the community. Committing adultery and beating someone up are wrongs to
some defined individual; refusing to serve in the army wrongs the
community.

---

226. Aristotle here allows for unwritten specific law in a particular state, a
refinement of the definition made in 1.10.3.
227. Sophocles, *Antigone* 456–457.
228. Empedocles, frag. 31.B.135.
229. Alcidamas was a sophist of the generation before Aristotle. The work
mentioned was probably an epideictic oration. Although the manuscripts of Aristotle
do not supply a quotation, a medieval commentator offers "God has left all free,
nature has made no one a slave."
230. Greek law distinguished between a public offense (*graphē*) and violation of
private rights (*dikē*); the distinction differs from modern understanding of criminal
and civil law in that many actions that today would be regarded as criminal, including
murder, were regarded as violation of private rights.

4. Since all kinds of unjust actions have been classified, some being against the community, others against one or another person or persons, let us take up the matter again and say what it means to be wronged. 5. To be wronged is to suffer injustice at the hands of one who acts voluntarily; for to do injustice has earlier been defined as voluntary.[231] 6. Since a person who suffers injustice is necessarily harmed and harmed against his will, the forms of harm are clear from what has been said earlier. (Things good and bad in themselves have been discussed earlier, as have things that are done voluntarily, which is whatever is done knowingly.)[232] 7. Thus, all accusations are either in regard to [wrongs done to] the community or to the individual, the accused having acted either in ignorance and involuntarily or voluntarily and knowingly and in the latter case either with deliberate choice or through emotion. 8. Anger [*thymos*] will be discussed in the account of the emotions;[233] and what sort of things are deliberately chosen and in what disposition of character has been said earlier.

1374a

9. Since people often admit having done an action and yet do not admit to the specific terms of an indictment or the crime with which it deals—for example, they confess to have "taken" something but not to have "stolen" it or to have struck the first blow but not to have committed "violent assault" or to have had sexual relations but not to have committed "adultery" or to have stolen something but not to have committed "sacrilege" ([claiming] what they took from a temple did not belong to the god) or to have trespassed but not on state property or to have had conversations with the enemy but not to have committed "treason"—for this reason, [in speaking we] should give definitions of these things: What is theft? What [is] violent assault?[234] What [is] adultery?[235] In so doing, if we wish to show that some legal term applies or does not, we will be able to make clear what is a just verdict. 10. In all such cases the question at issue [*amphisbētēsis*]

---

231. See 1.10.3.

232. Aristotle here refers to various parts of the discussion in chapters 6, 7, 9, and 10.

233. In 2.2 (where, however, the word for anger is *orgē*). This is probably a late addition by Aristotle.

234. The word translated "violent assault" is *hybris*, which in Greek law describes any violent assault on another person, including rape.

235. Aristotle's observations here were further developed by Hermagoras (second century B.C.E.) and later rhetoricians into what is called stasis of definition; e.g., a defendant on a murder charge can perhaps deny that he killed anyone (stasis of fact) but, if unable to do that, can plead that his actions were justifiable homicide, not fitting the legal definition of murder. See further 3.15.

relates to whether a person is unjust and wicked or not unjust; for wickedness and being unjust involve deliberate choice; and all such terms as "violent assault" and "theft" signify deliberate choice; for if someone has struck another it does not in all cases mean he has "violently assaulted" him, [only] if he has done so for a certain reason, such as to dishonor him or to please himself. Nor has he committed "theft" in all cases if he took something but [only] if for harm and his own advantage. The situation in other cases is similar to this.

11. Since there are two species of just and unjust actions (some involving written, others unwritten laws), our discussion has dealt with those about which the [written] laws speak; and there remain the two species of unwritten law. 12. These are, on the one hand, what involved an abundance of virtue and vice, for which there are reproaches and praises and dishonors and honors and rewards—for example, having gratitude to a benefactor and rewarding a benefactor in turn and being helpful to friends and other such things[236]—and on the other hand things omitted by the specific and written law. 13. Fairness,[237] for example, seems to be just; but fairness is justice that goes beyond the written law.[238] This happens sometimes from the intent of the legislators but sometimes without their intent when something escapes their notice; and [it happens] intentionally when they cannot define [illegal actions accurately] but on the one hand must speak in general terms and on the other hand must not but are able to take account only of most possibilities; and in many cases it is not easy to define the limitless possibilities; for example, how long and what sort of weapon has to be used to constitute "wounding";[239] for a lifetime would not suffice to enumerate the possibilities. 14. If, then, the action is undefinable, when a law must be framed it is necessary to speak in general terms, so that if someone wearing a ring raises his hand or strikes, by the written law he is violating the law and does wrong, when in truth he has [perhaps] not done harm, and this [latter judgment] is fair.

---

236. The unwritten law, requires gratitude and generosity. Conversely, it regards as unacceptable and cause for reproach such things as ingratitude and rudeness.

237. *Epieikes*, often translated "equity"; but *epieikes* is a broader concept and applies to both public and private law.

238. Rigid application of the written law may sometimes go against its intent and be inequitable, as the following discussion notes.

239. The legislators cannot list all possible weapons. The court must decide in terms of the intent of the law and fairness to those involved.

1374b   15. If, then, fairness is what has been described, it is clear what kind of actions are fair and what are not fair and what kind of human beings are not fair: 16. those actions that [another person] should pardon are fair, and it is fair not to regard personal failings [*hamartēmata*] and mistakes [*atukhēmata*] as of equal seriousness with unjust actions. Mistakes are unexpected actions and do not result from wickedness; personal failings are not unexpected and do not result from wickedness; [and] unjust actions are not unexpected and do result from wickedness. 17. And to be forgiving of human weakness is fair. And [it is also fair] to look not to the law but to the legislator and not to the word but to the intent of the legislator and not to the action but to the deliberate purpose 18. and not to the part but to the whole, not [looking at] what a person is now but what he has been always or for the most part. And [it is fair] to remember the good things one has experienced [because of him] rather than the bad, and good things experienced [because of him] rather than done for him. And [it is fair] to bear up when wronged. And [it is fair] to wish for an issue to be decided by word rather than by deed. 19. And [it is fair] to want to go into arbitration rather than to court; for the arbitrator sees what is fair, but the jury looks to the law, and for this reason arbitrators have been invented, that fairness may prevail.[240] On the subject of things that are fair let definitions be made in this way.

Chapter 14: The Koinon *of Degree of Magnitude as Applicable to Questions of Wrongdoing in Judicial Rhetoric*

■ This chapter parallels 1.7, where the same *koinon* was applied to deliberative questions. The first sentence is linked grammatically to the last sentence of the previous chapter, indicating no real break in Aristotle's thinking. The division of the text into chapters was first made in the fifteenth century by George of Trebizond and here seems inappropriate.

1. And a wrong is greater insofar as it is caused by greater injustice. Thus, the least wrong [can sometimes be] the greatest, as, for example, the accusation of Callistratus against Melanopus, that he defrauded the temple builders of three consecrated half-obols.[241] But in the case

---

240. On the use of arbitrators, see Aristotle's *Constitution of the Athenians* 53.2–4. Official arbiters (*diaitētai*) were appointed from among men fifty-nine years of age.

241. A paltry sum, as is explained later. The incident is otherwise unknown, but Callistratus and Melanopus were political rivals in the period around 370 B.C.E. On Callistratus, see also 1.7.13 and 3.17.14.

of justice it is the opposite.[242] This results from the fact that [injustice] inheres in the potentiality; for he who steals three consecrated half-obols would be capable of doing any wrong. Sometimes the greater is judged this way, sometimes from the harm done. 2. And [a wrong is greater] where there is no equal punishment but all are too little. And [it is greater] where there is no healing the wrong; for it is difficult, even impossible [to undo]. And [it is greater] where the victim cannot have recourse to a trial; for in such cases there is no healing [the wrong]; for a trial and punishment are a form of healing. 3. And [it is greater] if the victim who is wronged has [as a result] inflicted some great punishment on himself; for the doer should justly be punished with the greater [suffering], as Sophocles,[243] speaking on behalf of Euctemon after he had killed himself because of the outrage he suffered, said he would not fix the penalty as less than the victim had assessed it for himself. 4. [A wrong is greater] that only one person has done or has been the first to do or is one among few to have done. And to commit the same fault often is a great thing [against someone]. Also what results in search and discovery of [new] forms of prevention and punishment [is a great wrong], as in Argos a person was punished because a law was passed [as a result of his actions], as were those for whom a prison was built.[244] 5. And the more brutal a crime, the greater [the wrong]. And the more premeditated [the crime the greater the wrong]. Rhetorical techniques adaptable to this are [to say] that a person has broken many norms of justice and gone beyond [a single crime], for example, [breaking] oaths, handshakes, promises, marriage vows; for this is a heaping up of wrongs. 6. And [wrongs are greater when committed] in a place where wrongdoers are being punished, which is what perjurers do; for where would they not do wrong if they do it even in the law court? And things in which there is the greatest disgrace [are greater wrongs]. And [a wrong is greater] if against the very one by whom a person was benefited; for he does more wrong both because he wrongs and because he does not do good [in turn]. 7. And what contravenes the unwritten codes of justice [is a greater wrong]; for it is characteristic of a better person to be just without being required to do so; thus, what is written is a matter of

1375a

---

242. The most insignificant just actions are not the greatest.

243. Possibly the dramatist, but more likely a fifth-century B.C.E. politician of the same name, in which case perhaps the Sophocles also mentioned in 3.18.6.

244. The incident is unknown. Prisons were usually used in Greece only for short detention, as in the case of Socrates awaiting execution.

necessity, what is unwritten not. In another way [it is a greater wrong] if it contravenes what is written; for one who does wrong despite his fears and despite the existence of punishments would also do wrong that did not incur punishments. Enough, then, has been said, about greater and lesser wrong.

Chapter 15: Atechnic (Non-artistic, Extrinsic) Pisteis in Judicial Rhetoric: Laws, Witnesses, Contracts, Tortures, Oaths

■ In 1.2.2 Aristotle divided the means of persuasion into artistic techniques —use of paradigms and enthymemes—and non-artistic *pisteis* that an orator uses but does not invent. The latter are described in the following chapter and consist largely of documentary evidence that can support or weaken a case at law. In democratic law courts, such as those at Athens, the evidence of witnesses was taken down at a preliminary hearing and read out by a clerk at the trial rather than being given in person. If the witness was present, he might be asked to acknowledge the testimony. Orators sometimes also called on the clerk to read the text of laws or contracts that were relevant or in dispute; or they quoted poets, oracles, or proverbs as "witnesses." Oaths taken or refused on previous occasions could be introduced as evidence. Resemblances between this chapter and the discussion of "supplementary" *pisteis* in the *Rhetoric for Alexander* (chs. 15–17) suggest that Aristotle is drawing on some earlier handbook on the subject (see Fuhrmann 1960:138–142; Thür 1977; Mirhady 1991).

To some readers this chapter has seemed rather too tolerant of sophistry, but as in the case of the prescriptive passages in chapter 9, Aristotle is setting out the "available" means of persuasion in accordance with his definition of 1.2.1. As he states in 1.1.12, rhetoric provides arguments on both sides of a case. Under constitutional governments in Greece a defendant was entitled to state a case in the most favorable way. It may be that a defendant is legally guilty but morally justified, hence Aristotle's emphasis in 1.13.13–19 on the importance of fairness and equity.

The discussion here clearly is focused on judicial procedures in Athens. An Athenian jury, made up of 201, 501, or more citizens selected by lot, was thought of as representative of the people as a whole and could judge what if any laws should apply as well as the facts of the case. Thus, some elements of deliberation about laws could occur during trials. Though there are separate Greek words for judge (*kritēs*) and juror (*dikastēs*), in democratic states there was no presiding judge at a trial to instruct the jury and determine what was or was not admissible evidence. Thus, in most legal procedures judge and juror were identical. Aristotle often uses the words interchangeably.

There was no appeal from judicial decisions, though cases were sometimes reopened if new evidence became available or the procedure could be faulted. (On the procedures in Athenian courts, see Bonner and Smith 1930–1938; for comparison of Aristotle's remarks with the practice of Greek orators, see Carey 1994.)

In working on this technically difficult chapter the translator was much indebted to Professor David Mirhady.

1. Following on what has been said, [the next subject is] to run through what are called "atechnic" *pisteis*; for they are specifics [*idia*] of judicial rhetoric. 2. They are five in number: laws, witnesses, contracts, tortures, oaths.[245]

TOPICS AGAINST AND IN FAVOR OF WRITTEN LAWS

3. Let us first speak about laws [*nomoi*], [showing] how they can be used in exhorting and dissuading[246] and accusing and defending; 4. for it is evident that if the written law is contrary to the facts, one must use common law and arguments based on fairness as being more just. 5. [One can say] that to use [the jurors'] "best understanding" is not to follow the written laws exclusively;[247] 6. and that fairness always remains and never changes nor does the common law (for it is in accordance with nature) but written laws often change. This is the source of what is said in Sophocles' *Antigone*; for she defends herself as having performed the burial [of her brother] in violation of the law of Creon, but not in violation of what is unwritten:

> For not now and yesterday, but always, ever   1375b
>
> . . . .
>
> This I was not likely [to infringe] because of any man.[248]

7. And [one can say] that the just is something true and advantageous but what seems to be just may not be; thus, the written law

---

245. Aristotle here adds laws and oaths to those mentioned in 1.2.2.

246. *Exhorting and dissuading* is deleted by some editors as appropriate only to deliberative rhetoric, but as Mirhady (1991) argues, its presence here probably reflects the introduction of political deliberation about the validity and interpretation of law into a trial, as indicated in the next section.

247. Juries were sworn to decide a case "in accordance with the law" or, if the law was unclear, in accordance with their "best understanding."

248. An approximate quotation of *Antigone* 456 and 458; cf. 1.13.2, where line 457 is found instead of 458.

may not be; for it does not [always] perform the function of law. And [one can say] that the judge is like an assayer of silver in that he distinguishes counterfeit and true justice. 8. And [one can say] that it is characteristic of a better man to use and conform to the unwritten rather than the written [laws].[249] 9. And if [a law] somewhere is contradictory to an approved law or even to itself (for example, sometimes one law orders what has been set out in a contract to be binding while another forbids making contracts in violation of the law) 10. and if it is ambiguous, so that one can turn it around and see to which meaning it fits, whether with justice or the advantageous, one should make use of this interpretation. 11. And if, on the one hand, the situation for which the law was established no longer prevails but the law still exists, one should try to make this clear and fight with this [argument] against the law.

12. But if, on the other hand, the written law applies to the facts, one should say that *in their best understanding* does not mean that the jury is to judge contrary to the law but is there to provide that the jury not violate its oath if it does not understand what the law says. And [one should say] that no one chooses what is good in general but what is good for himself.[250] And [one should say] that it makes no difference whether a law is not passed or is not used.[251] And [one should say] that in the other arts there is no advantage to being "smarter than the doctor"; for a mistake by a physician does not do so much harm as becoming accustomed to disobey one who is in charge. And [one should say] that to seek to be wiser than the laws is the very thing that is forbidden in those laws that are praised. And let distinctions be made this way on the subject of the laws.

QUOTATION OF POETS, ORACLES, PROVERBS, AND
WELL-KNOWN PERSONS AS "WITNESSES"

13. As for witnesses [*martyres*], they are of two sorts, some ancient, some recent; and of the latter [there are] some sharing the risk [of being brought to trial for perjury], some outside it. By *ancient* I mean the poets and other well-known persons whose judgments are clear;

---

249. On unwritten law see 1.10.3 and 1.13.1.

250. This seems to be an answer to an opponent who wants to have the law, passed in the interest of the community, waived to suit a particular situation. The jury can be reminded that to uphold the law is in its interest.

251. I.e., since the law has been passed, it should be enforced.

for example, the Athenians used Homer as a witness in their claim to Salamis, and the Tenedians recently use Periander of Corinth against the Sigeans.[252] And Cleophon used the elegies of Solon [as a witness] against Critias, saying that the insolence of his family was ancient; otherwise, Solon would never have composed the line:

Tell the fair-haired Critias to listen to his father for me.[253]

Witnesses about past events are of this sort, 14. while expounders of oracles [are witnesses] about future events; for example, Themistocles [interpreted] the "wooden wall" to mean that a naval battle must be fought.[254] Also proverbs, [where the phrase] "as has been said" is a form of testimony; for example, if someone were to advise against making a friend of an old man, the proverb "Never do good to an old man" bears testimony to it.[255] And [if someone advises] killing sons whose fathers have already been killed, [he may say] "Foolish he who after killing the father leaves behind the son."[256]

1376a

15. Recent witnesses are well-known persons who have given a judgment about something; for their judgments are also useful in controversies about similar things; for example, Euboulus, attacking Chares in the law courts, made use of what Plato said to Archebius, that "confessions of vice have become common in the city."[257] [Recent

---

252. Around 600 B.C.E. Solon had cited *Iliad* 2.557–558 in support of Athenian claims to the island of Salamis against the claims of Megara. The "recent" incident involving the people of Tenedos (an island off the coast of the Troad) and Sigeum (on the coast nearby) is unknown, but Aristotle lived nearby at Assos from 347 to 345 and could have known about some local incident. Periander of Corinth had acted as an arbitrator in a dispute between Athens and Mytilene over Sigeum around 600.

253. Solon, frag. 221. Cleophon was a demagogue in late fifth-century B.C.E. Athens, often ridiculed in comedy.

254. In 480 B.C.E. Themistocles persuaded the Athenians not to rely on the walls of Athens to defend the city against the Persians but to interpret an oracle from Delphi, promising that the "wooden wall" would not fail to provide security, to mean the Athenian fleet; see Herodotus 7.141.

255. This is an actual Greek proverb of a rather cynical cast; on the character of the old (distrustful, small-minded, thinking only of themselves), see 2.13.

256. Attributed by Clement of Alexandria (*Strommata* 7.2.19) to Stasinus, author of the early epic *Cypria*. Although the Athenians in the fifth century B.C.E. repeatedly put to death all male citizens of cities that had revolted, as at Melos in 416 B.C.E., they usually spared children, and the injunction mostly applies to the heroic world as seen in Greek tragedy.

257. Euboulus was a well-known politician and slightly younger contemporary of Plato. The quotation sounds like something Plato might have said but is otherwise unknown.

witnesses] are also those who share the risk [of being brought to trial] if they seem to commit perjury. 16. Such persons are only witnesses of whether or not something has happened (whether or not something is or is not the case) but not [competent] witnesses of the quality of the act—of whether, for example, it was just or unjust or conferred an advantage or not. 17. On such matters, outsiders are [objective] witnesses, and ancient ones the most credible; for they are incorruptible.

TOPICS AGAINST AND IN FAVOR OF WITNESSES

One having no witnesses as corroborators of testimony [should say] that judgment must be made on the basis of probabilities and that this is what is meant by *in their best understanding* and that probability cannot deceive for bribes and that probabilities are not convicted of false testimony; the one who has [witnesses can say] against the one who does not that probabilities are not subject to trial and that there would be no need of witnesses if it were enough to speculate on the basis of [probable] arguments. 18. Some testimonies are about the speaker, others about the opponent, and some [are] about the facts, others about character, so it is evident that there is never a lack of useful testimony; for if there is no testimony relating to the fact or supporting the speaker or contradicting the opponent, still [there will be abundance of evidence] about his character that points to fair-mindedness or about the opponent that points to badness. 19. Other points about a witness—whether friends or enemy or in between, whether reputable or disreputable or in between, and any other differences of this kind—should be chosen from the same topics[258] from which we derive enthymemes.

TOPICS FOR AND AGAINST CONTRACTS

20. As regards contracts [*synthēkai*], argument is useful to the extent of amplifying or minimizing or making them credible or not, [that is, making them credible and valid] if they support [the speaker's]

---

258. If 1.5.18 is excluded, this is the first appearance of the word *topoi* as a technical term since 1.2.22, where it was used of *common* topics in contrast with the *eidē*, or species of arguments in particular disciplines like politics. Since the *topoi* mentioned here seem to be the specific political and ethical arguments as discussed in chapters 4–15, we are given some textual justification for calling these *specific* topics. But the sentence may be a late addition by Aristotle.

position but the opposite if they help the opponent. 21. As far as rendering them credible or not credible goes, there is no difference from the treatment of witnesses; for contracts are credible insofar as the signatories and custodians are.

If it is agreed that a contract exists, this should be amplified as long as it supports the speaker's side; for [he can say] a contract is a law that applies to individuals and particulars; and contracts do not make law authoritative, but laws give authority to contracts made in accordance with law, and in general the law itself is a certain kind of contract,[259] so that whoever disobeys or abolishes a contract abolishes the laws. 22. Further, [he can say] most ordinary and voluntary transactions are done in accordance with contracts, so that if they lack authority, the commerce of human beings with each other is abolished. And other suitable things [to say] are self-evident.

23. If the contract is opposed to the speaker and on the side of his opponent, first it is suitable [to say] those things that one might use to fight an opposing law; for [one can say] it is strange if we think we do not have to obey laws whenever they are not rightly framed and those who made them erred but necessary to obey contracts. 24. Secondly, [one can say] that the jury is an umpire of justice; it is not this [contract] that should be considered but how more justly [to treat the parties involved]. And that it is not possible to pervert justice by deceit or compulsion (for justice is based on nature) 25. but [that] contracts are among those things affected by deceit and compulsion. In addition, look to see whether the contract is contrary to any written or common laws and in the case of written laws whether those of the city or foreign ones, then [whether it is contrary] to other earlier or later contracts; for later contracts take precedence, or else the earlier ones are authoritative and the later ones fraudulent (whichever argument is useful). Further, look at the matter of what is advantageous, whether perhaps there is something [about the contracts] opposed to the interest of the judges and anything else of this sort; for these things are easy to see in a similar way.[260]

---

259. Aristotle's *Politics* begins (1.1) with the assumption that all government is a *koinonia*, or association, partially anticipating the theories of the "social contract" as developed in modern times by Rousseau and others.

260. With the Athenian system of very large juries, to appeal to the interest of the judges is to appeal to the public interest. Thus, they might invalidate a contract that cornered the market on some product.

TOPICS FOR AND AGAINST THE EVIDENCE OF SLAVES

■ The evidence of slaves was admissible in Greek courts only if extracted under torture supervised by officials, the assumption being that slaves could not be counted on to tell the truth otherwise. Occasionally slave owners tried to free their slaves to avoid having them tortured, and in practice slave evidence does not seem to have been commonly used.[261] Aristotle regarded slavery as "natural," in the sense that some human beings had irredeemably servile characters (cf. *Politics* 1.5), but as this chapter shows he did not believe that evidence extracted under torture was reliable. Most Greek states had large slave populations, used in agriculture, in mining, and in private houses as servants, and there were also publicly owned slaves. What little police force Athens had consisted of slaves. Slaves were acquired from military actions and many were themselves Greeks; few if any were racially distinct from their masters. Aristotle owned slaves; in his will (Diogenes Laertius 5.12–16) he provided that some be freed.

26. Tortures [*basanoi*] are a kind of testimony and seem to have credibility because some necessity [to speak] is involved. It is thus not difficult about them, either, to see the available [means of persuasion] from which it is possible to provide amplification if they are in favor [of the speaker], [saying] that this form of testimony is the only true one. But if they are against him and favor his opponent, one could refute them by speaking [first] about the whole concept of torture; for [slaves] do not lie any less when under compulsion, neither [those who] harden themselves not to tell the truth nor [those who] lie easily to stop the pain more quickly. There is [also] need to cite examples that the judges know, which have [actually] happened. (It is necessary to say that tortures are not reliable; for many slow-witted and thick-skinned persons and those strong in soul nobly hold out under force, while cowards and those who are cautious will denounce someone before seeing the instruments of torture, so that there is nothing credible in tortures.)[262]

1377a

---

261. See Gagarin 1996.
262. Most editors, including Kassel (1976), regard this passage as an addition to the text by some later scribe. There are also textual problems within it; the translation follows the versions in Kassel's apparatus criticus.

TOPICS RELATING TO OATHS TAKEN OR REFUSED BY
THE PRINCIPALS IN A TRIAL

■ In Greece an attempt to settle a matter before or during a trial could take the form of an "exculpatory oath." The assumption is that the gods will punish anyone who knowingly swears falsely. One or both of the disputants could challenge the other to take an oath (e.g., that the terms of a contract had been fulfilled). If the matter was not settled in this way before a trial, these challenges then could be used as evidence for or against the litigants, or a challenge to swear could be given during the trial. The passage is difficult to translate because the Greek idiom *to give an oath* means to dictate, or administer, the terms on which another person will swear, while *to take an oath*, as in English, means to swear to the terms given by another.

27. On the matter of oaths [*horkoi*], there are four distinctions to make; for either [a person both] gives and [himself] takes [an oath], or does neither, or does [only] one or the other of these, and in the last case he may give the other [an oath to swear] but not take [an oath] himself or may take [an oath] but not give one to his opponent. Further, beyond this, [there is the question] whether an oath was sworn [earlier] by one or the other.

28. If a person does not give [his opponent an opportunity to swear], he can say [at the trial] that people swear false oaths easily, and that one who has sworn does not [necessarily] allow his opponent to swear in return but thinks [a jury] will condemn one who has not sworn, and that one who has sworn does not [necessarily] allow his opponent to swear, and that the risk [of giving his opponent an oath] is greater before a jury; for [he can say] he trusts jurors but not his opponent.

29. If he does not take [an oath himself, he can say] that an oath is a substitute for something more tangible;[263] and that if he were a bad man he would have taken the oath; for it is better to be bad for some profit than for nothing, since [the one who] has sworn will win the case but [the one who has] not sworn will not; and thus [a refusal] is because of virtue, not because of a [fear of] perjury. And Xenophanes' maxim applies,[264] that the same challenge to take an oath is not equal for an irreligious man in comparison with a religious one; for it is much as if a strong man called out a weak one to hit or be hit.

---

263. *Khrēmata*, lit. "things," usually translated "money," but perhaps "hard evidence."
264. Xenophanes of Colophon, philosopher and poet who lived around 500 B.C.E. The following clause in Greek resembles iambic verse.

30. If he takes an oath, [he can say] that he trusts himself, not the opponent. And by reversing the maxim of Xenophanes, one should say that in this way it is equal if the irreligious man gives an oath and the religious one swears it. And that it would be terrible for him not to want [to decide the case by his oath][265] about matters on which he would think it right for the judges to decide only after being sworn.

31. If he gives an oath, he can say that it is pious to want to entrust the matter to the gods and that there is no need for his opponent to demand any other judges; for he [the speaker] is giving the decision to him [the opponent]. And that it would be out of place not to want to swear on a matter about which he would think it right that others swear.

32. Since it is clear how one should speak in each of these cases, it is also clear how to speak when they are combined; for example, if the speaker wishes to take [an oath] but not to give one to his opponent and if he wishes to give an oath to his opponent but does not wish to take one himself, and if he wishes both to take and to give [oaths] or if neither; for these necessarily are a combination of the positions mentioned, so that the arguments are composed of those described.

And if an oath has been taken by the speaker, and is in conflict [with what he now says, he should say] that there is no perjury; for wrongdoing is voluntary and to commit perjury is wrongdoing, but what is done under force and under deceit is involuntary.[266] 33. Here, then, one should also conclude that committing perjury is with the mind and not with the tongue.[267] If, on the other hand, [the oath] is opposed to [what] the opponent [now says] and he is the one who has sworn, [the speaker can say] that he who does not abide by what he has sworn overturns everything; for this is why [juries] administer the laws under oath. And [he can say to the jury], "[My opponents] think it right for you to abide by the oaths by which you swore you would judge, but they themselves do not abide [by their oaths]." And there are many other things one might say in amplification.

---

265. The verb to be supplied is apparently *dikazein* (Mirhady's suggestion to me). Taking an oath effectively settles the case; cf. what is said in the next section and Demosthenes 29.52–53.

266. Claiming, apparently, that he has somehow been tricked or forced into taking the oath.

267. Cf. the notorious line from Euripides, *Hippolytus* 612: "It was my tongue that swore, my heart is unsworn." Aristotle cites it in 3.15.8.

BOOK 2

Pisteis, or The Means of Persuasion in Public Address (continued)

■ In 1.2.3–6 Aristotle identified three artistic modes of persuasion, derived from presenting the character (*ēthos*) of the speaker in a favorable light, awakening emotion (*pathos*) in the audience so as to induce them to make the judgment desired, and showing the probability of what is said by logical argument (*logos*). In 2.1.1–4 he repeats this in the order *logos*, *ēthos*, *pathos*. This order is then reversed (chiasmus) in the following discussion: chapters 2–11 explore the emotions; chapters 12–17 the adaptation of the speech to the character of the audience; and chapters 18–26 return to logical techniques, including paradigms, enthymemes, and topics, concluding the discussion of rhetorical invention or thought. Arguments by L. Spengel and O. Vahlen to reverse the order of chapters, putting 18–26 before 2–17, were discussed in detail and refuted by Cope ([1877] 1970, 2:171–175) and by Grimaldi (1988, 2.12:225–228).

Chapter 1: Introduction

■ Sections 1–4 of this chapter resume the discussion in 1.2.3–5 of the character of the speaker (on which see also 1.9.1) and the emotions of the audience as artistic modes of persuasion. Sections 5–7 discuss the need for the speaker to render himself trustworthy to the audience; section 8 turns to the matter of *pathos* and outlines the method Aristotle will follow in discussing the emotions in chapters 2–11.

1. These [specifics, or special topics, set forth in Book 1] are the proper sources of exhortation and dissuasion, praise and blame, and prosecution and defense, and the kinds of opinions and propositions useful for their persuasive expression; for enthymemes are concerned with these matters and drawn from these sources, so the result is speaking in a specific way in each genus of speeches. 2. But since rhetoric is concerned with making a judgment (people judge what is said in deliberation, and judicial proceedings are also a judgment), it is necessary not only to look to the argument, that it may be demonstrative and persuasive but also [for the speaker] to construct a view of himself as a certain kind of person and to prepare the judge; 3. for it makes much difference in regard to persuasion (especially in deliberations but also in trials) that the speaker seem to be a certain kind of person and that his hearers suppose him to be disposed toward them in a certain way and in addition if they, too, happen to be disposed in a certain way [favorably or unfavorably to him]. 4. For the speaker to seem to have certain qualities is more useful in deliberation; for the audience to be disposed in a certain way [is more useful] in lawsuits;[1] for things do not seem the same to those who are friendly and those who are hostile, nor [the same] to the angry and the calm but either altogether different or different in importance: to one who is friendly, the person about whom he passes judgment seems not to do wrong or only in a small way; to one who is hostile, the opposite; and to a person feeling strong desire and being hopeful, if something in the future is a source of pleasure, it appears that it will come to pass and will be good, but to an unemotional person and one in a disagreeable state of mind, the opposite.

1378a

5. There are three reasons why speakers themselves are persuasive; for there are three things we trust other than logical demonstration. These are practical wisdom [*phronēsis*] and virtue [*aretē*] and good will [*eunoia*];[2] for speakers make mistakes in what they say through [failure to exhibit] either all or one of these; 6. for either through lack of practical sense they do not form opinions rightly; or though forming opinions rightly they do not say what they think because of a bad character; or they are prudent and fair-minded but lack good will, so that it is possible for people not to give the best advice although they

---

1. The sentence up to this point is double-bracketed by Kassel (1976) as a later addition by Aristotle.

2. Practical wisdom and virtue are aspects of character, good will of *pathos*, as section 7 makes clear.

know [what] it [is]. These are the only possibilities. Therefore, a person seeming to have all these qualities is necessarily persuasive to the hearers. 7. The means by which one might appear prudent and good are to be grasped from analysis of the virtues;[3] for a person would present himself as being of a certain sort from the same sources that he would use to present another person; and good will and friendliness need to be described in a discussion of the emotions.[4]

8. The emotions [*pathē*] are those things through which, by undergoing change, people come to differ in their judgments and which are accompanied by pain and pleasure, for example, anger, pity, fear, and other such things and their opposites.[5] 9. There is need to divide the discussion of each into three headings. I mean, for example, in speaking of anger, what is their *state of mind* when people are angry and against *whom* are they usually angry and for what sort of *reasons*; for if we understood one or two of these but not all, it would be impossible to create anger [in someone]. And similarly, in speaking of the other emotions. Just as we have drawn up a list of propositions [*protaseis*] on the subjects discussed earlier, let us do so about these and let us analyze them in the way mentioned.

Chapters 2–11: Propositions About the Emotions Useful to a Speaker in All Species of Rhetoric

■ These famous chapters on the emotions, although reflecting some ideas of Plato found in *Phaedrus* and *Philebus* (see Fortenbaugh 2000), are the earliest systematic discussion of human psychology. It is possible that they originated in some other context, for they have been only partially adapted to the specific needs of a speaker. Even if they were originally written for some version of the *Rhetoric* Aristotle seems to have given thought to the context only at a later time when he made a few revisions to try to give the work greater unity. With a few exceptions (e.g., 2.3.13 and 2.6.20 and 24) the examples given are not drawn from rhetorical situations, and some (e.g., 2.2.10–11) do not at all fit a deliberative, judicial, or epideictic audience. The primary rhetorical function of the account is apparently to provide a speaker

---

3. Topics useful for this can be found in 1.9.

4. Topics useful for this are found in ch. 4.

5. Aristotle here adopts Plato's "medical" view of emotion as a mixture of pleasure and pain, a view he rejects in his ethical writings; see Frede 1994:258–285.

with an ability to arouse these emotions in an audience and thus to facilitate the judgment sought (see 1.2.5, 2.1.4, 2.2.27, 2.3.17, 2.4.32, 2.5.15, 2.9.6, and 2.10.11). But some of the emotions (e.g., shamelessness, unkindliness, or envy) are not ones a speaker is likely to want to arouse toward himself, and a secondary purpose emerges in 2.4.32 and 2.7.5–6: how to arouse emotion against an opponent and how to refute an opponent's claims to the sympathy of an audience. All these passages seem to be afterthoughts, tacked on to the discussion to adapt them to their present context, and chapters 6, 7, 8, and 11 lack any adaptation at all. Nevertheless, chapters 2–11, taken as a whole, provide an introduction to psychology (at least to conventional Greek psychology of Aristotle's time) that could give a speaker better insight into human motivation and improve speaking in general.

The discussions come in pairs, arranged chiastically in what might loosely be described as positive/negative, negative/positive (e.g., anger/calmness, friendliness/hostility, fear/confidence, shame rightfully felt/shamelessness). George of Trebizond in the fifteenth century and subsequent editors some-what disguised the pairing by separating the first set (discussed at greater length than others) into two chapters (2–3), but the Greek text is con-tinuous. Chapters 8–9 and 10–11 also seem logical units even though the relationship between pity, indignation, and envy as discussed there is somewhat complex (see 2.9.3–5). In the case of each emotion Aristotle considers the reason for it, the state of mind of the person who feels it, and those toward whom it is directed (although not always in the same sequence and detail). This division of the subject has some resemblance to his theory of "four causes" as seen in *Physics* 2.3 (see Fortenbaugh 1975, esp. 9–18).

In 2.3.17 and 3.19.3 Aristotle refers to these chapters as setting out the "topics" of the emotions. At the end of chapter 1 he has said that he will furnish *protaseis*, or propositions, about the emotions in what follows. This raises the question as to whether what is set out in chapters 2–11 are to be regarded as premises for enthymemes. It was the view of Grimaldi (1972:147–51, also echoed in his *Commentary* 1988 vol. 2), and of Conley (1982) that they are, to which Wisse (1989) cogently objected. If this was Aristotle's view, he has done remarkably little to make it clear, and in 3.17.8 he actually advises *against* using enthymemes when seeking to arouse emotion. It is true that some emotional appeals can take the form of an enthymeme; one example would be 2.5.11: "And among those wronged and enemies or rivals it is not the quick-tempered and outspoken who are to be feared but the calm and those who dissemble and the unscrupulous;

for with these it is unclear if they are close to acting, with the result that it is never evident that they are far from doing so." One can imagine a speaker saying this to impart fear in an audience. But much of what Aristotle says would not take enthymematic form in a speech. A good example is the list of qualities that create friendly feeling, given in 2.4.11–22. The audience will feel friendly to a speaker who is pleasant and good-tempered: he can accomplish this by not criticizing other people's faults, by joking, by praising other people, by being neat in appearance, by refraining from slander, by being serious about serious things, by showing himself to be like his hearers in interests and desires, and so on.

Aristotle's discussion of the emotions here is the only extensive account of this aspect of psychology in his extant works and as such has been a part of the *Rhetoric* especially ineresting to medieval and modern students of his philosophy. There is extensive scholarship on the subject, especially on the differences between Aristotle's views here and in his ethical writings; see discussions in Rorty 1996 and Fortenbaugh 2000. Emotions in Aristotle's sense are moods, temporary states of mind—not attributes of character or natural desires—and arise in large part from perception of what is publicly due to or from oneself at a given time. As such, they affect judgments. On the influence of these chapters on Cicero and later rhetorical writers, see Wisse 1989.

At the 1990 Symposium Aristotelicum, Pierre Aubenque drew attention to the following passage in Martin Heidegger's *Being and Time* (1962:178):

> The different modes of state-of-mind and the ways in which they are interconnected in their foundations cannot be Interpreted within the problematic of the present investigation. The phenomena have long been well-known ontically under the terms "affect" and "feelings" and have always been under consideration in philosophy. It is not an accident that the earliest systematic Interpretation of affects that has come down to us is not treated in the framework of "psychology." Aristotle investigates the *pathē* [affects] in the second book of his *Rhetoric*. Contrary to the traditional orientation, this work of Aristotle must be taken as the first systematic hermeneutic of the everydayness of Being with one another. Publicness, as the kind of Being which belongs to the "they" not only has in general its own way of having a mood, but needs moods and "makes" them for itself. It is into such a mood and out of such a mood that the orator speaks. He must understand the possibilities of moods in order to rouse them and guide them aright.

Chapter 2: Orgē, *or Anger*

THE DEFINITION AND CAUSES OF ANGER

1. Let anger be [defined as] desire, accompanied by [mental and physical] distress, for apparent retaliation because of an apparent slight that was directed, without justification, against oneself or those near to one.[6] 2. If this is what anger is, necessarily the angry person always becomes angry at some particular individual (for example, at Cleon but not at an [unidentified] human being)[7] and because he has done or **1378b** is going to do something to him or to those near to him; and a kind of pleasure follows all experience of anger from the hope of getting retaliation. It is pleasant for him to think he will get what he wants, but no one wants things that seem impossible for himself to attain. Thus, it has been well said of rage [*thymos*],

> A thing much sweeter than honey in the throat,
> It grows in the breast of men.[8]

A kind of pleasure follows from this and also because people dwell in their minds on retaliating; then the image [*phantasia*] that occurs creates pleasure, as in the case of dreams.

3. Belittling [*oligōria*] is an actualization of opinion about what seems worthless[9] (we think both good and bad things worth serious attention, also things that contributed to them, but whatever amounts to little or nothing we suppose worthless), and there are three species of belittling: contempt [*kataphronēsis*], spite [*epēreasmos*], and insult [*hybris*]; 4. for one who shows contempt belittles (people have contempt for those things that they think are of no account, and they

---

6. On the text, see Wisse 1989:69. The word translated "slight" (*oligōria*) literally means a "belittling," and that rendering is more apt in some of what follows. Aristotle does not regard *orgē* as an emotion felt when a person understands that he or she has been justly treated, e.g., by a superior who issues a justifiable rebuke; nor it is an emotion felt against oneself.

7. This rules out the situation in which in modern times we say a person in angry when he does not know at whom to direct his anger, e.g., the feeling on discovering that some unknown person has run into your parked car. Here there is usually no personal slight. Aristotle also fails to notice the situation in which one group, say the Athenians, is angry at another, say the Spartans, but in fact his observations can apply to the latter situation.

8. *Iliad* 18.109.

9. That is, by word or deed one person "puts down" another as of no account, and what was only a possible opinion is given actual expression.

belittle things of no account); so, too, the spiteful person; for the spiteful person is an impediment to [another's] wishes, not to get anything himself but so that the other does not. Since, then, there is no gain for himself, he belittles; for clearly he does not suppose [the other] will harm him (or he would be afraid and would not belittle) nor that [the other] might benefit [him] in any way worth mentioning; for then he would be taking thought so as to become a friend. 5. The person who gives insult also belittles; for insult is doing and speaking[10] in which there is shame to the sufferer, not that some advantage may accrue to the doer or because something has happened but for the pleasure of it; for those reacting to something do not give insult but are retaliating.

6. The cause of pleasure to those who give insult is that they think they themselves become more superior by ill-treating others. That is why the young and the rich are given to insults; for by insulting they think they are superior. Dishonor is a feature of insult, and one who dishonors belittles; for what is worthless has no repute, neither for good not evil. Thus, Achilles, when angered, says,

> [Agamemnon] dishonored me; for taking my prize, he keeps it himself.[11]

And, as a reason for his anger,

> [He treats me] like a dishonored vagrant.[12]

7. And people think they are entitled to be treated with respect by those inferior in birth, in power, in virtue, and generally in whatever they themselves have much of; for example, in regard to money a rich man [thinks himself] superior to a poor man, and in regard to speech an eloquent one [thinks himself superior] to one unable to express himself, and a ruler [thinks himself superior] to one who is ruled, and one thinking himself worthy to rule [thinks himself superior] to one worthy to be ruled. Thus, it has been said,

---

10. The reading of Parisinus 1741; but other good manuscripts have *harming and distressing*, and there is no clear basis of choice between the two versions.

11. *Iliad* 1.356.

12. Grimaldi (1988, 2:24) denies that Agamemnon was Achilles' inferior and thus that anger in Aristotle's system is limited to reaction again inferiors. Agamemnon was the commander, but he is Achilles' inferior in fighting, in fame, and in birth. The point is that the angry person regards one who insults him as an inferior and that one who insults is trying to assert superiority.

Great is the rage of Zeus-nurtured kings.[13]

And

But still, even afterward, he has resentment.[14]

For they are vexed by their sense of [ignored] superiority. Furthermore, a person [feels belittled by adverse remarks or actions of those] by whom he thinks he should be well treated. These are those whom he has treated well [in the past] or is [treating well] now (either directly by himself or through some of those near to him) or those whom he wants or has wanted to treat well.

THE STATE OF MIND OF THOSE WHO BECOME ANGRY

9. It is now apparent from this what is the state of mind[15] of those who become angry and at whom and for what sort of reasons [they do so]; [the answer to the first question is they become angry whenever they are distressed;] for the person who is distressed desires something. If, then, someone directly opposes him in anything, for example, preventing his drinking when he is thirsty—and even if not directly, nevertheless seems to accomplish the same thing—and if someone works against him and does not cooperate with him and annoys him when so disposed, he becomes angry at all these. 10. As a result, those who are ill, in need of money, [in the middle of a battle,][16] in love, thirsty—in general, those longing for something and not getting it— are irascible and easily stirred to anger, especially against those belittling their present condition; for example, one who is ill [is easily stirred to anger] by things related to his sickness, one who is in need by things related to his poverty, one at war by things related to the war, one in love by things related to his love, and similarly also in the other cases; for each has prepared a path for his own anger because of some underlying emotion.[17] 11. Further, [a person is easily stirred

---

13. *Iliad* 2.196.

14. *Iliad* 1.82.

15. Lit. "how they have," a temporary state; in contrast, a person's character is a *hexis*, a continuing and habitual condition.

16. Not in the manuscripts, but supplied by editors in anticipation of the following examples.

17. This sentence has a number of textual and grammatical problems; see Grimaldi 1988, 2:34–38, whose reading is largely followed here. Aristotle clearly realized that outbursts of anger often result from some relatively minor slight that represents the "last straw" to someone under stress.

to anger] if he happened to be expecting the opposite [treatment]; for the quite unexpected hurts more, just as the quite unexpected also delights if what is desired comes to pass. From this, then, it is evident what seasons and times and dispositions and ages are easily moved to anger and where and when, and that when people are more in these [conditions], they are also more easily moved.

THOSE AT WHOM PEOPLE BECOME ANGRY

12. People so disposed then are easily moved to anger, and they become angry at those who laugh at them and scoff and mock; for these wantonly insult. Necessarily, these actions are of the sort that are not in response to something [done earlier by the sufferer] and not beneficial to those who do them; for only then does it seem they are done through *hybris*. 13. And [people become angry] at those who speak badly of, and scorn, things they themselves take most seriously, for example, at those taking pride in philosophy if someone speaks against philosophy or taking pride in their appearance if someone attacks their appearance, and similarly in other cases. 14. They do this much more if they suspect they do not really have [what they take pride in], either not at all or not strongly, or do not seem to have it; for whenever they confidently think they excel in the matters in which they are scoffed at, they do not care. 15. And [they become angry] at friends more than those who are not friends; for they think it is more appropriate for them to be well treated by them than not. 16. And [they become angry] at those who have been accustomed to honor or respect them if, instead, they do not associate with them in this way; for they think they are being treated with contempt by these as well; for [otherwise] they would treat them in the same way. And at those not returning favors and those not doing so on an equal basis. 17. And at those opposing them if these are inferiors; for all such evidently show contempt, the latter as though looking down [on someone] as inferior to themselves, the former as having received a benefit from inferiors. 18. And [they become angry] more at those of no account if they belittle [them] in some way; for anger resulting from being belittled is assumed to be against those who have no right to do it, and inferiors have no right to belittle. 19. And [they become angry] against friends if these do not speak well of, or benefit, them and even more if they do the opposite and if they are insensitive to those in need, as in the case of Plexippus in Antiphon's [tragedy] *Meleager*; for lack of sensitivity is a sign of belittling: what we care about does

1379b

not escape our notice. 20. And [they become angry] against those rejoicing at misfortunes and generally taking pleasure in others' misfortune; for it is a sign of being either an enemy or a belittler. And [they become angry] against those who do not care if they are suffering. Thus, people become angry at those announcing bad news. 21. And [they become angry] at those listening to bad things about them or seeing their bad side; for these are similar to belittlers or enemies; for friends share griefs, and all grieve when they see faults of those close to them.

22. Further, [they become angry] at those belittling them before five classes of people: those with whom they are rivals, those they admire, those by whom they wish to be admired, or [those] before whom they are embarrassed or [those] who are embarrassed before them. If someone belittles them among these they become all the more angry. 23. And [they become angry] at those belittling others whom it would be shameful for them not to defend, for example, parents, children, wives, dependants. And [they become angry] at those not returning a favor; for the belittlement is contrary to what is fitting. 24. And [they become angry] at those mocking them when they are being serious; for mockery [*eirōneia*] is contemptuous. 25. And [they become angry] at those who do good to others if they do not do it also to them; for this, too, is contemptuous, not to think them also worthy of what they do for all [others]. 26. And forgetfulness is also productive of anger, for example, forgetfulness of names, being such a little thing; for the forgetfulness seems to be a sign of belittlement; for forgetfulness occurs through lack of concern, and lack of concern is belittlement.

27. At one and the same time, then, the persons at whom anger is directed and the dispositions of those angry and the kinds of causes have been stated; and it is clear that it might be needful in a speech to put [the audience] in the state of mind of those who are inclined to anger and to show one's opponents as responsible for those things that are the causes of anger and that they are the sort of people against whom anger is directed.

1380a

■ A speaker might arouse the anger of an audience against an opponent by showing that the latter had "belittled" the audience or the state or the laws with contempt, spite, or insult and might transmit to an audience feelings of anger at an opponent. Demosthenes' speech *Against Meidias* (who had publicly insulted him) expressed his own anger, and his *Philippics* sought to arouse the anger of the Athenians against Philip of Macedon. The chapter gives no examples of the use of anger in a rhetorical situation, and section 27 seems to have been added to adapt the original discussion to the context, but illustration is clearly needed.

Chapter 3: Praotēs, or Calmness

■ Aristotle regards *praotēs* as the emotion opposite to anger. It is often translated "mildness," which seems rather a trait of character or absence of emotion, while Aristotle views it as a positive attitude toward others, involving an emotional change toward a tolerant understanding of a situation: in colloquial English "calming down" is perhaps the closest translation, but there is no single English word that quite captures the meaning. The appearance in a particular situation of mildness, gentleness, patience, tractability, good temper are all aspects of it. As in the case of anger, though viewed as an emotional state, it has its roots in character. (On this chapter, see Nikolaides 1982.)

THE DEFINITION OF CALMNESS AND
THOSE TOWARD WHOM PEOPLE FEEL CALM

1. Since becoming calm is the opposite of becoming angry, and anger the opposite of calmness [*praotēs*], the state of mind of those who are calm should be grasped [by a speaker] and toward whom they are calm and for what reasons. 2. Let calmness [*praünsis*] be [defined as] a settling down and quieting of anger. 3. If, then, people become angry at those who belittle and belittling is a voluntary thing, evidently they are calm toward those doing none of these things or doing them involuntarily or seemingly so. 4. And [they are calm] toward those intending the opposite of what they have done. And [they are calm toward] all who regard them as they themselves would; for no one is thought to belittle himself.[18] 5. And [they are calm] toward those who admit and repent [having belittled someone]; for regarding [the other's] distress as just retribution, they cease their anger at those who have provoked it. A sign [of this is seen] in the punishment of slaves; for we punish all the more those who argue and deny, but we cease our wrath toward those who confess themselves justly punished.

---

18. There are, at least in modern times, insecure persons who constantly belittle themselves, and at a more sophisticated level there exists the type of the "ironic" person, who seems to belittle himself to get attention or as a ploy in argument. Socrates is the most famous example of the latter. See also *Nicomachean Ethics* 4.7.14.

The reason is that to deny clear evidence is disrespectful, and disrespect is belittling and contempt; at least we do not respect those for whom we have contempt. 6. [People are also calm] toward those who humble themselves toward them and do not contradict them; for they seem to admit being inferiors, and inferiors are afraid, and no one who is afraid belittles. That anger ceases toward those who humble themselves is evident even in the case of dogs, who do not bite those sitting down.[19] 7. And [they are calm] toward those who are serious with them when they are serious; for they think they are being serious and not showing contempt. And [they are calm] toward those who have done greater kindness in the past [than any passing affront]. 8. And [they are calm] toward those begging a favor and entreating them [not to be angry]; for they are humbler. 9. And [they are calm] toward those who are not insulting or scoffing or belittling against anyone, or not against good people or against such as they are. 10. As a whole, things producing calmness should be looked at on the basis of their opposites.[20] [They are calm] also toward those whom they fear and respect; for as long as they are so disposed, they do not become angry; for it is impossible to be afraid and become angry.[21] 11. And toward those who have acted in anger people are not angry or are less angry; for they do not seem to have acted by belittling, since no one belittles when angry; for belittling is painless [to the one doing it], but anger is accompanied by pain. And [people are calm] toward those showing respect to them.

1380b

THE STATE OF MIND OF THOSE WHO ARE CALM

12. It is clear that people are calm when their state of mind is the opposite of being angry, for example, in play, in laughter, at a feast, in prosperity, in success, in fulfillment, generally in the absence of pain and in reasonable expectation of the future. Further, [they are calm if] their anger has cooled with time and is not in its first stage; for time makes anger cease. 13. Greater anger toward a different

---

19. In *Odyssey* 14.29–38 Odysseus tries this strategy when attacked by dogs. As in that case, it probably should not be counted on to work unless the dog's master is nearby.

20. Double-bracketed by Kassel (1976) as a late addition by Aristotle.

21. Though someone might "be" angry at another who is feared, it is often best not to worsen the situation by displaying anger. The emotions Aristotle discusses and that the speaker needs to understand are mostly those that come out in public.

person or vengeance already taken on another person earlier also causes anger to cease. Thus, when someone asked Philocrates at the time the people [of Athens] were angry with him, "Why do you not defend yourself?" he wisely said, "Not yet." "But when then?" "When I see someone else has been slandered."[22] For people become calm whenever they have spent their anger on someone else, which happened in the case of Ergophilos; for though [the Athenians] were more angry at him than at Callisthenes, they let him go because they had condemned Callisthenes to death on the previous day.[23] 14. And [people become calm] if they take pity[24] [on offenders] and if these have suffered greater evils than they would have done to them when angry; for they think they have obtained a kind of retaliation. 15. And [people become calm] if they think they themselves have done wrong and suffered justly; for anger does not arise against justice nor against what people think they have appropriately suffered; that was [implicit in] the definition of anger. Thus, one should first chastise in word; for even slaves are less indignant when [so] punished.

16. Also, [people are calm] when they think that [their victims] will not perceive who is the cause of their suffering and that it is retribution for what they have suffered; for anger is a personal thing, as is clear from the definition. Thus, the verse "Say it was Odysseus, sacker of cities,"[25] was rightly composed, since [Odysseus] would not have been avenged if [Polyphemus the Cyclops] had not realized both from whom and why revenge came. Thus, people do not vent their anger on others who are not aware of it nor continue it against the dead, since the latter have suffered the ultimate and will not suffer nor will they have perception, which is what angry people want. Thus, in wanting Achilles to cease his anger against Hector once he was dead, the poet spoke well: "For it is unseemly to rage at senseless clay."[26]

---

22. Largely through the efforts of Demosthenes, Philocrates was prosecuted for bribery in the peace negotiations he carried on between Athens and Macedon. He escaped into exile and was condemned to death in absentia in 343 B.C.E. This date is consistent with the revision of the *Rhetoric* into its present form in the immediately following years. Kassel (1976) double-brackets the example as a late addition by Aristotle.

23. The date is about 362 B.C.E., when Aristotle was living in Athens. Anger at Ergophilos resulted from his actions as a commander in the Hellespont. He may have been fined but was not condemned to death.

24. The reading of Parisinus 1741; other manuscripts have *if they convict*.

25. *Odyssey* 9.504.

26. *Iliad* 24.504. The words are spoken by Apollo at a council of the gods.

17. Clearly, then, those wishing to instill calmness [in an audience] should speak from these topics;[27] they produce such a feeling in them by having made them regard those with whom they are angry as either persons to be feared or worthy of respect or benefactors or involuntary actors or as very grieved by what they have done.

Chapter 4: Philia, *or Friendly Feeling, and* Ekhthra, *or Enmity*

■ From the positive emotion of calmness Aristotle moves to another positive emotion, a feeling of friendliness toward someone, and then to its negative, enmity and hate, thus establishing the chiastic order followed in successive chapters. Friendliness and enmity are longer-lasting emotions than anger and calmness and thus perhaps more intimately connected with character, but Aristotle is primarily interested in them as feelings that come out in certain situations. Only in the last section of the chapter does he indicate that this material might be applied in a rhetorical situation. Most of the premises are expressed in the third person, but in sections 11 and 27 the first person plural suddenly appears. Perhaps these remarks were added at a later time.

THE DEFINITION OF FRIENDLINESS AND THOSE TOWARD
WHOM PEOPLE HAVE A FRIENDLY FEELING

1. Let us say whom people like and whom they hate and why, after having defined friendliness and being friendly.[28] 2. Let *being friendly* [*to philein*] be [defined as] wanting for someone what one thinks are good things for him, not what one thinks benefits oneself, and wanting what is potentially productive of these good things. A friend is one who loves and is loved in return,[29] and people think they are friends when they think this relationship exists mutually. 3. On these premises, a friend is necessarily one who shares pleasure in good things and distress in grievous ones, not for some other reason but because of the friend; for all rejoice when the things they want

1381a

---

27. *Topoi*, the first instance of the term in Book 2. These topics are apparently the *idia* (specifics) of ethical knowledge, which includes study of the emotions.

28. *Philia*, with its related verb *philein*, has a spectrum of meanings ranging from general friendly feelings toward someone to a special friendship and love, but as elsewhere in this book, Aristotle is discussing a particular feeling that arises under particular circumstances and may thus be useful in making a jury or other audience sympathetic to a speaker's point of view.

29. This clause is double-bracketed by Kassel (1976) as a late addition by Aristotle.

happen and grieve at the opposite, so distresses and pleasures are a sign of their wish. 4. And [friends] are those to whom the same things are good and bad and who have the same friends and the same enemies;[30] for they necessarily wish the same things, so the one who also wishes for another what he wishes for himself is evidently a friend to the former. 4. And [friends] are those to whom the same things are good and bad and who have the same friends and the same enemies;[31] for they necessarily wish the same things, so the one who also wishes for another what he wishes for himself is evidently a friend to the former. 5. And people are friendly to those who have benefited them —either to them directly or to those they care for—if they have done them great benefit or done it eagerly or at opportune times and for their sake; also to those who they think wish to benefit them. 6. [They are friendly] also to the friends of their friends and those friendly with those they themselves like and those liked by those they themselves like. 7. And [they are friendly to] those who have the same enemies they have and who hate those they themselves hate and who are hated by those they hate; for the same things seem good to all these as to themselves, so that they wish the same things as they do, which was the characteristic of a friend. 8. Further, [they are friendly to those] who are disposed to do good to others in regard to money and safety; therefore, they honor generous and brave people. 9. [They are friendly] also to those who are just. And they suppose those who do not live at the expense of others to be of this sort; such also are those who live by their own efforts and, of these, especially those who live from the land or else are craftsmen.[32] 10. And [they are friendly to] those who are self-controlled, because not unjust and to those who mind their own business for the same reason.

11. [We are friendly] also to those with whom we want to be friends if they seem to want it; such are those who are morally good and respected, either among all or among the best people or among those admired by themselves or those who admire them. 12. Further, [they are friendly to] those who are pleasant to deal with and to pass the day with; such are those who are good-tempered and not critical

---

30. This clause is also double-bracketed by Kassel (1976). Note the characteristic Greek assumption that a man will have enemies.

31. This clause is double bracketed by Kassel (1976) as a late addition by Aristotle.

32. The key words in this sentence are *they suppose*. Aristotle is setting out the assumptions of a typical Athenian jury, largely made up of small landowners, craftsmen, and the like.

of people's faults and not contentious or quarrelsome; for all such are pugnacious, and those always fighting clearly want the opposite. 13. And [they are friendly to people like] those who are ready to make or receive a joke; for in both cases they are intent on the same thing as their neighbor, able to be kidded and kidding in good sport. 14. And [they are friendly to] those who praise the presence of good qualities [in others] and especially who praise the qualities that these people **1381b** fear they do not really have. 15. And [they are friendly to] those who are neat in appearance and in dress and in all their way of life. 16. And [they are friendly to] those who are not critical of mistakes or of bene- factions; for in both cases they are not reproachful. 17. And [people are friendly to] those not mindful of wrongs done to them nor inclined to cherish their grievances but who are easily appeased; for people think the attitude they suppose shown to others will also be shown to themselves. 18. And [they are friendly to] those who do not say or want to know bad things about neighbors or friends but [look for] good things; for the good person acts this way. 19. And [they are friendly to] those who do not oppose others when [the latter are] angry or being serious; for such persons are pugnacious. And [they are friendly to] those taking them seriously in some way, for example, admiring them and regarding them as serious people and finding pleasure in them; 20. and especially those feeling this way about what they wish to be admired in themselves or in regard to what they want to be serious about or what they find pleasure in 21. And [they are friendly to] those who are like themselves and have similar interests, provided they do not become annoying or get their livelihood from the same source; for then it becomes the case of "potter against potter."[33] 22. And [they are friendly to] those who long for the same things when it is possible to share them at the same time; but if that is not possible, the same result follows as in the previous case.

23. [People have friendly feelings] also toward those with whom their relationship is such that they are not ashamed [in their presence] of things that might be thought, unless [the others] show contempt. 24. And [they are friendly] toward those whose prestige they would like to attain and [those] by whom they wish to be emulated and not envied; they like them or want to be their friends. 25. And [they are friendly to] those with whom they join in doing good, unless greater evils are going to result for themselves. 26. [They are] also [friendly to] those who show equal affection for their friends both

---

33. Hesiod, *Works and Days* 25, on rivalry among craftsmen.

absent and present. Therefore, all people like those who are such in regard to the dead. And all in all, [people like those] who are very fond of their friends and not inclined to leave them in the lurch; for among the good they most like those who are good at being friends. 27. And [they like] those who are not deceitful with them; such are those who even tell them their faults. (It was said earlier that we do not feel shame before friends in regard to things that might be thought; if then one who feels shame is not a friend, one who does not is like a friend.) And [we like] those [who are] not intimidating and with whom we feel secure; for no one likes a person he fears.

THE CAUSES OF FRIENDSHIP

28. The species of friendship are companionship, intimacy, kinship, and other such things. 29. [Doing] a favor is productive of friendship and doing it unasked and not advertising what has been done; for in this case it seems to have been done for the sake of the friends and not for some other reason.

ENMITY AND HATE

■ Aristotle regarded hostile emotions as awakened by the perception that someone belongs to a detested class of individuals, such as thieves or sycophants. The negative feeling toward the class is a permanent one, but the identification of an individual with the class may be established or disproved in a speech.

30. The nature of enmity [*ekhthra*] and hating [*to misein*] is evident from the opposites [of what has been said about friendliness]. Anger, spite, and slander are productive of enmity. 31. Now anger comes **1382a** from things that affect a person directly, but enmity also from what is not directed against himself; for if we suppose someone to be a certain kind of person, we hate him. And anger is always concerned with particulars, directed, for example, at Callias or Socrates, while hate is directed also at types (everyone hates the thief and the sycophant).[34] The former [anger] is curable in time, the latter [hatred of types] not curable; the former is the desire [that the other may feel] pain, the

---

34. A sycophant in Greek was an "informer," specifically one who denounces another to the government for trading in contraband (*sykon* = fig, the trade in figs being controlled). Since such a person often hopes to gain from the action, the word came to mean "self-server" or "servile flatterer for his own advantage."

latter [that he may suffer] evil; for one who is angry wants his anger perceived, but to the one who hates it does not matter [whether the object of his hatred knows it]. Painful actions [inflicted by one person on another] are all perceived by the senses, but the greatest evils—injustice and thoughtlessness—are least perceived; for the presence of evil causes no pain. Anger is also accompanied by pain [to the one who feels anger], but hate is not accompanied by pain; for the angry person is himself pained, the one who hates is not. One who is angry might feel pity when much has befallen [the person he is angry at], but one who hates under no circumstances; for the former wants the one he is angry at to suffer in his turn, the latter wants [the detested class of persons] not to exist.

32. From this, then, it is evident that it is possible [for a speaker] both to demonstrate that people are enemies and friends and to make them so when they are not and to refute those claiming to be[35] and to bring those who through anger or enmity are on the other side of the case over to whatever feeling he chooses. But what sort of things people fear and whom and in what state of mind will be evident from what follows.

Chapter 5: Phobos, *or Fear, and* Tharsos, *or Confidence*

THE DEFINITION OF FEAR AND ITS CAUSE

1. Let fear [*phobos*] be [defined as] a sort of pain and agitation derived from the imagination of a future destructive or painful evil; for all evils are not feared; for example, [a person does not fear] that he will become unjust or slow-witted but [only] what has the potential for great pains or destruction, and these [only] if they do not appear far off but near, so that they are about to happen; for what is far off is not feared: all know that they will die, but because that is not near at hand they take no thought of it.[36]

2. If this is what fear is, such things are necessarily causes of fear as seem to have great potential for destruction or for causing harms

---

35. This introduces a new function, the demonstration or refutation of claims of enmity or friendship by the opponent. Some examples of doing this in public address would have been welcome, but must be supplied by the student.

36. In modern times, especially with awareness of Alzheimer's disease, some old people do fear they may become slow-witted, or worse. Fear of death often is a sudden panic in dangerous situations and must have occurred in Greek times as it does today.

that lead to great pains. Therefore, even the signs of such things are causes of fear; for that which causes fear seems near at hand. (This is danger: an approach of something that causes fear.) 3. Such [signs] are enmity and anger from those with the power to do something; for it is clear that they wish to, and thus they are near doing it. 4. And injustice [is such a sign] when it has power; for the unjust person is unjust by deliberate choice. 5. And outraged virtue [is such a sign] when it has power; for it is clear that when a person is outraged, he **1382b** always chooses to act, and now he can. 6. And [another sign] is fear on the part of those with the power to do something; for necessarily such a person is also in readiness [to act].

THOSE WHO ARE FEARED

7. Since most people are rather bad, slaves of profitmaking and cowardly in danger, being at the mercy of another is in most cases a cause of fear, so that the accomplices of one who has done something dreadful are feared [by him], in that they may inform on him or leave him in the lurch, and those able to do wrong [are a cause of fear] to those able to be wronged; 8. for human beings usually do wrong when they can. And [others who are feared] are those who have been wronged or think they have been wronged; for they are always watching for an opportunity [for revenge]. Also those who have done wrong, if they have power, are feared, being apprehensive of suffering in their turn; for this sort of thing is inherent in what is feared. 9. And those who are rivals for the same things [are feared], insofar as it is not possible for both to share at the same time; for people are always fighting against such rivals. 10. And [people fear] those [that seem a cause of fear] to others who are stronger than they are; for they could harm them more if they could even harm those who are stronger. And for the same reason those [are feared] who attack those weaker than they are; for they are either cause for fear or [will be] when they have grown stronger. And among those wronged and enemies or rivals it is not the quick-tempered and outspoken [who are feared] but the calm and those who dissemble and the unscrupulous; for with these it is unclear if they are close [to acting], with the result that it is never evident that they are far from doing so.

12. All fearful things are more fearful insofar as something cannot be set right by those who have made a mistake and is either wholly irremediable or not in their power but in the power of their opponents. And [they are more fearful] when there are no sources of help or no

easy one. In a word, things are fearful that are pitiable when they happen or are going to happen to others. Fearful things, then, and what people fear are pretty much (so to speak) the greatest things. Let us now speak about the state of mind of those who are afraid.

THE STATE OF MIND OF THOSE WHO FEAR

13. If fear is accompanied by an expectation of experiencing some destructive misfortune, it is evident that no one is afraid if he is one of those who thinks he will suffer nothing. [People fear] neither things they do not think they will suffer nor others by whom they do not think [they will be harmed] and not at a time when they do not think so. Necessarily, then, people who think they might suffer something are in fear, and those [who think they are going to suffer] at the hands of those [from whom they expect to suffer]; and they fear these things and at this time. 14. Those experiencing, and thinking they **1383a** experience, great good fortune do not think they might suffer; therefore, they are insolent and belittlers and rash (wealth, strength, an abundance of friends, power, makes them so); nor [are those afraid] who think they have already suffered all dreadful things possible and have become coldly indifferent to the future, like those actually being done to death. [For fear to continue,] there must be some hope of being saved from the cause of agony. And there is a sign of this: fear makes people inclined to deliberation, while no one deliberates about hopeless things. 15. The result is that whenever it is better [for a speaker's case] that they [i.e., the members of the audience] experience fear, he should make them realize that they are liable to suffering; for [he can say that] others even greater [than they] have suffered, and he should show that there are others like them suffering [now] (or who have suffered) and at the hands of those from whom they did not expect it and suffering things [they did not expect] and at a time when they were not thinking of [the possibility].[37]

CONFIDENCE AND THOSE WHO INSPIRE IT

16. Since it is evident what fear and fearful things are and [what is] the state of mind of those who are afraid, it is evident from this also what it is to be confident and what sort of things people are confident

---

37. Thus, awakening fear is especially useful in deliberative oratory, e.g., in showing the danger from a foreign state.

about and what their state of mind is when they are confident; for confidence [*tharsos*] is opposed [to fear, and what inspires confidence][38]
to what is fearful.[39] Thus, hope of safety is accompanied by an imagination that it is near, while fearful things either do not exist or are far
away. 17. Dreadful things being far off plus sources of safety being
near at hand equal feelings of confidence.[40] And if there are remedies
and many sources of aid or great ones or both and if people have
not been wronged or done wrong and if antagonists do not exist at
all or do not have power or, having power, are friends or have been
benefactors or have received benefits, [then people are confident].
Or if those with the same interests are numerous or stronger or both
[people are confident].

THE STATE OF MIND OF THOSE WHO FEEL CONFIDENT

18. People are themselves confident when they have the following
states of mind: if they think they have often succeeded and not suffered or if they have often come into dangers and have escaped; for
human beings become free from emotions [of fear] in two ways:
either by not having been put to the test or by having the resources
needed, just as in dangers at sea both those who are inexperienced
with a storm and those with the resources of experience are confident.
19. And [people become confident] when something is not a source
of fear to those like them, nor to those [who are] inferior and whose
superiors they think themselves to be; and they so regard those they
have defeated, either these themselves or their superiors or their equals.
20. And [people feel confident] if they think they have more and
better resources, by which they are rendered especially formidable.   1383b
These are a supply of money and bodies[41] and friends and territory
and preparations for war, either all these or the greatest. And [people
feel confident] if they have done no wrong to anybody or not to many
or not to those from whom they fear anything. 21. And on the whole,
[people feel confident] if their relationship to the gods is good, both

---

38. Not in the manuscripts, but added by most editors.

39. *Tharsos* is often translated "courage," but courage (often *andreia* in Greek) is
a virtue, a habitual state of character, just as cowardice is a vice. Fear and confidence,
as Aristotle discusses them here, are feelings under certain circumstances, analogous
to becoming angry or calm. A speaker might instill fear or confidence in an audience
but would not thereby make they audience cowardly or courageous.

40. The Greek text is uncertain but the meaning seems clear.

41. Cf. note on 1.5.3.

as known from signs and oracles and in other ways.[42] (Anger is a confident thing, and to be wronged rather than to do wrong is productive of anger, but the divine is supposed to come to the aid of those who are wronged.) 22. And [people feel confident] when, laying hands to some task, they think they are not likely to suffer [now] or will succeed. So the matters relating to fear and confidence have been discussed.

Chapter 6: Aiskhynē, *or Shame, and* Anaiskhyntia, *or Shamelessness*

■ Shamelessness is explicitly mentioned only at the beginning and end of the chapter, but the many actions listed as shameful can be taken as signs of shamelessness. Though the society of ancient Greece is too complex to be labeled a "shame culture" in the sense used by Ruth Benedict and other anthropologists, it is true that Greek literature, beginning with the *Iliad*, shows a relatively highly developed personal fear of being shamed in the eyes of society—what in the Orient is called "losing face"—and conversely, a relatively undeveloped sense of inner personal guilt, which is found somewhat more among ancient Hebrews and Romans. In 2.2.14 Aristotle notes what might be thought of as an "inferiority complex," but as seen in chapter 6 (esp. section 14) shame only occurs if someone else, or society in general, perceives disgrace to an individual.

THE DEFINITION AND CAUSES OF SHAME

1. What sort of things people are ashamed of and feel no shame about and toward whom and in what state of mind is clear from the following. 2. Let shame [*aiskhynē*] be [defined as] a sort of pain and agitation concerning the class of evils, whether present or past or future, that seem to bring a person into disrespect, and [let] shamelessness [*anaiskhyntia*] [be defined as] a belittling about these same things. 3. If what has been defined is shame, necessarily being shamed applies to such evils as seem [in the eyes of others] to be disgraceful to a person or one about whom he cares. Such are those actions that result from vice, for example, throwing away a shield or fleeing in battle; for these come from cowardice. And [such is] refusing to pay back a deposit; for this comes from injustice. 4. And [such is] having sexual relations with those with whom one should not or

---

42. This sentence is double-bracketed by Kassel (1976) as a late addition by Aristotle.

where one should not or when one should not; for this comes from licentiousness. 5. And [such is] making a profit from petty or shameful things or from helpless people, for example, the poor or the dead, whence the proverb "He would even rob a corpse"; for this comes from shameful profiteering and stinginess. 6. And [such is] not giving aid with money when one can or giving less aid. And [such is] being aided from those with fewer resources. 7. And [such is] to seek a loan under the guise of asking a favor, to ask a favor under the guise of demanding a return of something owed, to ask for the return of something under the guise of asking a favor, to praise with the apparent aim of asking a favor and, when unsuccessful, nonetheless [continuing to ask];[43] for all these are signs of stinginess. 8. And [such is] praising those present; [for it is a sign] of flattery.[44] And [such are] over-praising good things and glossing over bad ones and showing excessive distress for one in distress when he is present and all such things; for they are signs of flattery. 9. And [such is] not standing up under labors that older people bear or those who are delicate or higher in rank or, on the whole, less able; for all these are signs of softness. 10. And [such are] accepting favors from another, and often, and reproaching someone for a good deed; for all these are signs of smallness of mind and meanness. 11. And [such are] talking about oneself and making pronouncements and claiming the achievements of another for one's own; for [these are signs] of boastfulness. Similarly, too, the deeds and signs and the like that result from other vices of character; for these are disgraceful and things to be ashamed of.

1384a

12. And in addition [it is shameful] not to share in the fine things of which all have a share, or all those like oneself or most of them. By *those like oneself* I mean those of the same nation, fellow citizens, those of the same age, relatives—generally, one's equals; for in the first place it is shameful not to share to the same extent in education and similarly in other ways, but all these [lacks] are more shameful if they seem to be one's own fault; for thus they now [seem to come] more from vice if one is the cause of [one's own] past, present, or future [deficiencies].

13. People feel shame when they suffer or have suffered or are going to suffer such things as contribute to dishonor and censures,

43. A difficult sentence. The translation follows Grimaldi 1988, 2:110 but remains uncertain.

44. This sentence is double-bracketed by Kassel (1976) as a late addition by Aristotle.

and these are things that include providing the services of the body or engaging in shameful actions, of which being physically violated is one (and though actions voluntary and involuntary are a part of licentiousness, the involuntary are done by force); for submission and lack of resistance comes from effeminacy or cowardice.[45] These then, and things like them, are the things of which people are ashamed.

THOSE BEFORE WHOM PEOPLE FEEL SHAME

14. Since shame is imagination [*phantasia*] about a loss of reputation and for its own sake, not for its results, and since no one cares about reputation [in the abstract] but on account of those who hold an opinion of him, necessarily a person feels shame toward those whose opinion he takes account of. 15. He takes account of those who admire him and whom he admires and by whom he wishes to be admired and those to whose rank he aspires and those whose opinions he does not despise. 16. Now people want to be admired by those and admire those who have something good in the way of honors or from whom they happen to be greatly in need of something those people have in their control, as lovers [want love or sexual favors]; 17. but they aspire to the rank of those [they regard as] like themselves, and they take account of prudent people as telling the truth, and their elders and educated people are of such a sort. 18. And they feel more shame at things done before these people's eyes and in the open; hence, too, the proverb "Shame is in the eyes."[46] For this reason people feel more shame before those who are going to be with them and those watching them, because in both cases they are "in" their eyes. 19. And [they feel more shame] before those not liable to the same charge; for it is clear that the opposite values seem right to them. And [they feel more shame] before those not inclined to be forgiving to people who have clearly made a mistake;[47] for it is said that one

1384b

---

45. Frequenting prostitutes and engaging as an "active" partner in male homosexual activity was in Greece not a source of shame, but to take money for sexual favors was (and in the case of a male could lead to loss of civil rights), and it was shameful for a man to allow another man to insert his sexual organ into any part of his body. Thus, pederasty, out of respect for the boy, often took the form of intercrural rather than anal or oral intercourse; see Dover 1978:98–99. There was apparently no shame in homosexual activity among women, but heterosexual activity outside of marriage was shameful for the woman, and a woman who was raped was regarded as shamed.

46. Probably not, as Grimaldi thought (1988, 2:117), in their own eyes ("a guilty look"), but in the eyes of the person disappointed, such as a parent or teacher.

47. This clause is double-bracketed by Kassel (1976) as a late addition by Aristotle.

is not angry at neighbors when they do things one does oneself, so clearly one *is* angry when they do what one does not do. 20. And [they feel more shame] before those inclined to tell about it to many others; for not to tell the tale is no different from not thinking it [a fault].[48] Those inclined to tell tales are those who have been wronged, because they keep on the watch, and slanderers; for if [they tell something false] about those who have committed no error, they will all the more [tell] about those who have. And [people feel shame before those] whose employment is watching the errors of their neighbors, for example, professional jokesters and comic poets; for these are in a way slanderers and talebearers. And among those from whom they have never failed to get what they want; for [among them] they are in the position of those that are admired. Thus, too, they feel shame [in refusing] those who have asked for something for the first time, since they have not yet been held in disrespect among these. Such are those who have recently wanted to become their friends (these have seen their best side, and thus the reply of Euripides to the Syracusans applies)[49] and among old acquaintances those not cognizant of anything wrong.

21. And people are ashamed not only of the shameful things that have been mentioned but of all the signs [of shameful deeds], as those who freely indulge their sexual feelings [are ashamed] not only of it but of the signs of it. And [people feel shame] not only in doing but even in saying disgraceful things. 22. Similarly, people are not only ashamed before those who have been mentioned but also before those who will reveal their faults to them, for example, servants and friends of these others. 23. But on the whole they are not ashamed before those whose reputation of telling the truth they much look down on (no one feels shame before babies and small animals); nor [are they ashamed] of the same things before acquaintances and strangers, but before acquaintances [they are ashamed] of things truly regarded [as wrong and] before those from abroad [they are ashamed] of things conventionally so regarded.[50]

---

48. This would have been clearer if Aristotle had avoided the triple negative: "For when a gossiper tells a tale, it is a sign that he thinks it casts the doer in a shameful light."

49. According to a medieval commentator, Euripides, as Athenian ambassador to Syracuse in Sicily, said, "You ought, Syracusans, even if for no other reason except that we are just now feeling the need of you, to be ashamed to reject us, your admirers."

50. The parenthesis really applies to those who cannot speak at all, infants and animals; cf. 1.11.16. The second half of the sentence deals with a different matter.

THE STATE OF MIND OF THOSE WHO FEEL SHAME

24. People would feel shamed if they were in the following situations: first, if certain others were in the relationship to them that we said was characteristic of those before whom they feel shame (and these were those who are admired or admirers or those by whom they want to be admired or from whom they have some need that they will not attain if they lose their reputation) and, [second, if] these [were] either seeing [what is going on] (as Cydias said to the people in the debate about the allotment of land in Samos; for he thought the Athenians should imagine [all] the Greeks standing around them in a circle, actually seeing and not only later hearing about what they might vote)[51]—or if such persons are nearby or are going to learn of it. Thus, too, people fallen into misfortune do not want to be seen by those who have ever been their rivals; for rivals are admirers. 25. And [people feel shame] whenever they have in their backgrounds deeds or facts that they will [be seen to] disgrace, whether these are their own or those of their ancestors or certain others with whom there exists to them some tie of kinship. And on the whole [they feel shame] on account of those on whom they themselves bring shame. These are the people mentioned and those who have been entrusted to them, either those of whom they have been teachers or advisers or if there are others like themselves to whose rank they aspire; 26. for people do and do not do many things out of a sense of shame because of the existence of such people. 27. And if they are going to be seen and be associated in public with those who know their guilt, they are more embarrassed. Thus, too, Antiphon the poet, when on the point of being crucified and beaten to death on the orders of Dionysius, made this remark, seeing that those who were going to die by his side covered their faces as they went through the gate: "Why do you cover your faces?" he said. "You don't think, do you, that any of these [standing near by] will see you tomorrow?"[52] Now these things apply to shame. Clearly, we shall find good material on shamelessness from their opposites.

51385a

---

51. The speech was probably given in 365 B.C.E., just before Aristotle first arrived in Athens. Athens had captured the island of Samos and debated sending out settlers there, apparently in violation of terms of the League of 377/376.

52. Dionysius I, tyrant of Syracuse during the first third of the fourth century B.C.E., composed tragedies that were ridiculed by others, among whom Antiphon, himself a dramatist, may have been one.

■ Aristotle fails to add here (also at the end of chapters 7,8, and 11) any application to public address. The example in section 24 shows, however, that inducing shame might occasionally be useful in deliberative oratory. It is difficult to imagine any situation in which an orator would want to create a deliberate feeling of shamelessness, though he might want to show that the conduct of others was shameless.

Chapter 7: Kharis, *or Kindliness, and* Akharistia, *or Unkindliness*

■ *Kharis* has a number of meanings in Greek—"kindliness, benevolence, good will, a favor, gratitude, grace," etc.—and is also frequently used in the accusative case as a preposition meaning "for the sake of." Aristotle's definition in section 2 makes it clear that he is speaking here about an altruistic feeling of kindness or benevolence that at a particular time gratuitously moves a person to do something for another. This short chapter differs from others on the emotions in that it focuses on what *kharis* is, neglecting the state of mind of those who exhibit it, and in that its concluding paragraph deals with how to make an opponent seem to lack kindliness. The noun *akharistia*, "unkindliness," does not actually occur in the chapter, but Aristotle does use the related negative adjective and verb.

DEFINITION OF KINDLINESS

1. To whom people show kindliness and for what reasons and in what state of mind will be clear [to us] after having defined *kharis*. 2. Let *kharis*, in the sense that one is said to "have *kharis*," be [defined as] a service to one in need, not in return for anything nor that the one rendering the service may get anything but as something for the recipient.[53] [*Kharis*] would be great if [the recipient] is either greatly in need or in need of what is great and difficult [to get] or in times of crisis of this sort or if [the giver] is the only one or the first or the one who most confers it. 3. Needs are desires [*orexeis*] and, among desires, especially those accompanied with pain because of something not present. Longings [*epithymiaia*] are such things as love and those [things] felt in sufferings of the body and in times of danger; for one who is in danger and one who is in pain "longs." Thus, those who stand by someone in poverty and those in exile [exhibit *kharis*], even if their services are small, because of the greatness of the need and their having shown kindliness at the opportune time, for example, the

---

53. Thus excluding *kharis* in the sense of gratitude.

person who gave the mat in the Lyceum.[54] 4. Necessarily, then, it is most a matter of offering service in these cases or, if not, in cases of equal or greater need. Thus, since it is evident to whom and for what reasons kindliness is offered and in what state of mind,[55] it is clear that [speakers] should derive it from these sources, showing that some people either were or had been in such pain and need and that others had performed some such service in time of want or were doing so.

HOW TO CREATE AN IMPRESSION OF UNKINDLINESS

5. It is also evident how it is possible to refute claims of kindliness and make people seem unkindly; for [it might be shown that] either they were performing or had performed a service for their own advantage (and this [by definition] was not *kharis*) or that it fell out by chance or that they had been acting under constraint or that they gave back rather than freely gave [a favor], either knowingly or not knowingly; for in both cases there is a return for something and thus it would not be *kharis*. 6. And the matter should be considered in terms of the "categories"; for *kharis* is either [determined by] substance or quantity or quality or time or place.[56] And it is a sign [of unkindliness] if a small service is not rendered and if the same or greater services are rendered to enemies; for it is clear that in neither case they do these things for "our" sake. Or [it is a sign of unkindliness] if knowingly [someone renders a service] of little value; for no one

1385b

---

54. The incident is unknown. The reference need not imply a time when Aristotle was teaching in the Lyceum. It was in use as a gymnasium before and during Aristotle's first residence in Athens, and one might imagine a scene in which someone was injured and a bystander gave him a straw mat to lie on. Since the Lyceum was one of the places frequented by Socrates, the story may have been well known in philosophical circles.

55. The last point has not been directly treated. One might have expected something about why or what puts them in that state of mind, as in other chapters. Perhaps Aristotle intended to add this but never got around to it; just possibly, something may have been lost in the text.

56. Aristotle here uses *categories* in the technical sense discussed in the logical treatise of that name; cf. also 1.7.21, where, however, the term *category* is not used. In addition to the five categories mentioned here, there are five others that Aristotle apparently regarded as not applicable: relation, condition, position, activity, and receptivity. *Substance* would refer to what was given (e.g., money or a drink of water), *quantity* to amount (much or little), *quality* to something like used clothes compared with a new coat, *time* to how opportune the gift or service was, *place* perhaps to whether it was conferred publicly or privately.

admits having need of what is of little value. This finishes the discussion of being kindly or being unkindly.

Chapter 8: Eleos, *or Pity*

■ Pity is also an important concept in Aristotle's *Poetics*; see especially the definition of tragedy in *Poetics* 6.2 and the discussion in 14.6–9. Given the frequent importance of arousing pity for a defendant in a trial, it is remarkable that Aristotle has added nothing to adapt this chapter to its place in the *Rhetoric*. (On rhetorical appeals to pity, see Walton 1997:35–61.)

THE DEFINITION OF PITY

1. Let us say what sort of things are pitiable and whom people pity and in what state of mind. 2. Let pity be [defined as] a certain pain at an apparently destructive or painful event happening to one who does not deserve it and which a person might expect himself or one of his own to suffer, and this when it seems close at hand; for it is clear that a person who is going to feel pity necessarily thinks that some evil is actually present of the sort that he or one of his own might suffer and that this evil is of the sort mentioned in the definition or like it or about equal to it. 3. Therefore, those who are utterly ruined do not feel pity (they think there is nothing left for them to suffer; for they *have suffered*) nor [do] those thinking themselves enormously happy; they demonstrate insolent pride [*hybris*] instead. (If they think all good things are actually present, clearly they also think it is not possible to experience any evil; for this [impossibility of suffering] is one if the good things.)

THE STATE OF MIND OF THOSE WHO FEEL PITY

4. The kind of people who think they might suffer are those who have suffered in the past and escaped and older people because of their practical wisdom and experience and the weak and those who are cowardly and those who have been educated; for they are discerning. 5. Also those that have parents or children or wives; for these are their "own" and subject to the sufferings that have been mentioned. 6. And those who are not in a courageous emotional state, for example not in a state of anger or confidence (these feelings do not take account of the future) nor in one of violent insolence (these people, too, take no account of suffering anything) nor, conversely, in a state of extreme

fear (those who are scared out of their wits do not feel pity because so taken up with their own suffering) but [only] those who are in between these states. 7. And [people feel pity] if they think certain individuals are among the good people of the world; for one who thinks no good person exists will think all worthy of suffering. And on the whole, [a person feels pity] when his state of mind is such that he remembers things like this happening to himself or his own or expects them to happen to himself or his own.

1386a

THE CAUSES OF PITY

The state of mind, then, of those who feel pity has been described, and what things they pity is clear from the definition: 8. all things are pitiable that are destructive, consisting of grief and pains, and things that are ruinous, and whatever evils, having magnitude, are caused by chance. 9. Deaths and torments and diseases of the body and old age and sicknesses and lack of food are painful and destructive; 10. and the evils of which chance is the cause are lack of friends, scarcity of friends (thus, too, it is pitiable to be separated from friends and companions), ugliness, weakness, mutilation. [It is] also [pitiable] for some evil to come from a source that ought to have supplied something good. And [it is pitiable] for this to happen often. 11. And [it is pitiable] for some good to have happened [only] after a person has suffered, as when the presents from the king [of Persia] were sent to Diopeithes after he had died.[57] And [it is pitiable] either for nothing good [ever] to have happened [to someone] or, if it happened, for there to have been no enjoyment of it.

THOSE FOR WHOM PITY IS FELT

Now those for whom people feel pity are the following and those like them. 12. They pity their acquaintances, unless they are very closely connected to their household, and in that case they feel for them as they feel about their own future suffering; this is why Amasis, according to reports,[58] did not weep when his son was led off to death but

---

57. Diopeithes led Athenian settlers to the Chersonese, thus bringing Athens in conflict with Macedon, about 342 B.C.E. and was subsequently honored by the king of Persia. This is one of the later historical references in the *Rhetoric*.

58. The story is told in Herodotus 3.14, but of Psammenitus (= Psammetichus III), king of Egypt about 525 B.C.E. Amasis was his father. Aristotle may have misremembered or is following a different source.

did [weep] for a friend reduced to begging; for the latter was pitiable, the former dreadful; for the dreadful is something different from the pitiable and capable of expelling pity and often useful to the opponent;[59] 13. for people no longer pity when something dreadful is near themselves. And they pity those like themselves in age, in character, in habits, in rank, in birth; for in all these cases something seems more to apply to the self; for in general, one should grasp here, too, that people pity things happening to others insofar as they fear for themselves. 14. And since sufferings are pitiable when they appear near at hand and since people do not feel pity, or not in the same way, about things ten thousand years in the past or future, neither anticipating nor remembering them, necessarily those are more pitiable who contribute to the effect by gestures and cries and display of feelings and generally in their acting [*hypokrisis*]; for they make the evil seem near by making it appear before the eyes either as something about to happen or as something that has happened, 15. and things are more pitiable when just having happened or going to happen in a short space of time. For this reason signs and actions [contribute   **1386b** to pity]; for example, the clothes of those who have suffered and any other such things,[60] and words and any other such things of those in suffering; for example, of those on their deathbed; for all such things, through their appearing near, make pity greater.[61] And most pitiable is for good people to be in such extremities, since one who is unworthy [is suffering] and the suffering is evident before our eyes.

Chapter 9: To Nemesan, *or Being Indignant*

■ Aristotle uses the verbal noun *to nemesan*, "being indignant," rather than the related noun *nemesis*, throughout this chapter except once, in section 3, perhaps because, as noted in section 2, *nemesis* had often taken on the meaning of "divine retribution."

---

59. Adopting the interpretation of Radt (1979:297–298).

60. In Greek epic and drama, suffering characters sometimes appear in rages (Euripides' portrayal of Telephus was the most notorious example), roll in the dirt, etc. Defendants in Greek courts probably sometimes dressed for the part to awaken sympathy.

61. The translation follows Kassel's (1976) transposition of this clause from the next sentence.

DEFINITION OF BEING INDIGNANT AND ITS RELATION TO OTHER EMOTIONS

1. On the other hand, what is most opposed to pity is what people call being indignant; for it is in some way opposed to feeling pain at undeserved *mis*fortune, and being pained at undeserved *good* fortune arises from the same moral character [as does pity], and both emotions are characteristic of a good character; 2. for it is right to sympathize with and pity those who suffer undeservedly and to feel indignation at those who [undeservedly] fare well; for what takes place contrary to deserts is unjust, and thus we attribute being indignant to the gods.

3. But it might seem that envy [*phthonos*] is also opposed to feeling pity in the same way, as being closely related and much the same thing as being indignant; and yet it is different. Envy is both agitated pain and directed at success, but of an equal and a like rather than of someone who is unworthy. What is similarly present in all cases [of indignation or envy] is not the feeling that some unpleasant change will befall a person himself but [a feeling of pain] because of [what good befalls] his neighbor; for it will be neither envy, on the one hand, nor indignation [*nemesis*] on the other, but fear if the pain and agitation are present because [he thinks] something bad will come to him as a result of the other person's success. 4. It is evident that opposite feelings will also follow these [reactions]; for one who is distressed at undeserved misfortunes will take pleasure or be unmoved by misfortunes of the opposite sort [i.e., deserved]; for example, no good person would be distressed when parricides and bloodthirsty murderers meet punishment; for it is right to rejoice in such cases, as in the case of those who deservedly fare well; for both are just things and cause a fair-minded person to rejoice; for necessarily there would be hope that what has befallen [one] like himself will befall himself. 5. All these feelings come from the same moral character, and opposite feelings from the opposite; for one who is malicious is also envious; for when someone is distressed at the acquisition or possession of something, he necessarily rejoices at its deprivation or destruction. As a result, all these things are hindrances to pity and differ for the reasons mentioned, so that they are similarly useful [to a speaker] in counteracting feelings of pity.

1387a

THOSE TOWARD WHOM INDIGNATION IS FELT AND ITS CAUSES

6. First, then, let us speak about being indignant: at whom people are indignant and for what reasons and in what state of mind, then after

this about the other emotions. 7. The former is evident from what has been said; for if being indignant is being distressed at the evidence of unworthy success, it is clear, first of all, that it is not possible to be indignant at all good things [that others acquire or possess]; 8. for if someone is just or brave or if he takes on some virtue of character, no one will feel indignation at him (nor are there feelings of pity at the opposites of these) but at [undeserved] wealth and power and such things as, in general, good people are worthy of, for example, noble birth and beauty and things like that [when the possessor is not a morally respected person]. 9. Since what is long established seems close to nature, necessarily people are indignant at those having the same advantage if they have recently gotten it and do well because of it; for the newly rich cause more annoyance than those wealthy a long time and by inheritance. 10. And similarly, when they are in public office and in power and with numerous friends and fine children and anything of that sort. And if some other good comes to them because of these things, similarly; for in this case the newly rich cause more distress when they hold office owing to their wealth than do the old rich, and similarly in other cases. The reason is that the latter seem to have what belongs to them, the former not; for when something [such as inherited wealth] has always been evident in this way it seems truly to belong to those who have it, with the result that others seem to have what is not their own. 11. And since each good thing is not deserved by any chance person, but there is a kind of analogy and propriety [about who has it] (for example, beauty of weapons suits a courageous rather than a just person, and distinguished marriages fit the wellborn, not the newly rich), then it is a source of indignation if someone who is good does not attain what is fitting. [It is] also [a source of indignation] for a lesser person to dispute with a greater one, especially those engaged in the same activity, whence, too, this has been said, "But he avoided battle with Ajax, son of Telamon",[62]   **1387b** for Zeus was angry at him when he fought with a better man. But if [the activity] is not the same, even if a lesser person [disputes] with a greater in any way at all, [there is indignation], for example, if a musician [does so] with a just person; for justice is better than music.

---

62. *Iliad* 11.542.

THE STATE OF MIND OF THOSE WHO ARE INDIGNANT

At whom, then, people feel indignant and why is clear from this; for they are these and things like them. 12. People are prone to indignation [first] if they happen to be worthy of the greatest advantages and have acquired them; for [they think] it is not just for those unlike them to think themselves worthy of the advantages they have. 13. Second, [they are prone to indignation] if they happen to be virtuous and serious; for [then] they make sound judgments and hate unjust things. 14. And [they are prone to indignation] if they are ambitious and desirous of certain things and, especially, are ambitious in regard to things that others are really unworthy of. 15. And generally, those who think themselves deserving of things they do not believe others deserve are prone to indignation toward the latter and about these things. Thus, the servile, the worthless, and the unambitious are not given to indignation; for there is nothing of which they regard themselves as worthy. 16. It is evident from this at what sort of people in misfortune and evildoing and lack of success one should rejoice or [at least] not feel distressed; for the opposites are clear from what has been said. And so if the speech puts the judges into this [hostile or indifferent] frame of mind [toward the opponent] and shows that those who think they deserve to be pitied (and to be pitied on certain grounds) are unworthy to attain it and worthy not to attain it, it is impossible for pity to be felt.

Chapter 10: Phthonos, *or Envy*

■ Both indignation and envy are emotions opposed to pity. For the distinction between them, see 2.9.3–5.

1. It is clear for what reasons and against whom and in what state of mind people are envious, since envy [*phthonos*] is [defined as] a certain kind of distress at apparent success on the part of one's peers in attaining the good things that have been mentioned, not that a person may get anything for himself but because of those who have it. The kind of people who feel envy are those who have, or seem to themselves to have, [more fortunate acquaintances among] those like themselves. 2. I mean those like themselves in terms of birth, relationship, age, disposition, reputation, possessions, as well as those who just fall short of having all of these on an equal basis. Therefore, those who do great things and are fortunate are envious; for they think everybody is trying to take what is theirs. 3. And those [are envious]

who are exceptionally honored for something, and especially for wisdom or happiness. And the ambitious are more envious than the unambitious. And those [are envious] who are wise in their own conceit; for they are ambitious for wisdom. And on the whole, those fond of fame in some way are envious in that regard. And the small-souled [are envious]; for all things seem great to them.

THE CAUSES OF ENVY AND THE PEOPLE WHO ARE ENVIED

4. The good things that people envy have been mentioned; for almost all things that cause people to love fame and honor, whether deeds **1388a** or possessions, and make them desire attention and whatever things are the gifts of fortune are, almost all of them, objects of envy, and especially those that they themselves desire or think they ought to have or things they possess only slightly more than others or slightly less. 5. It is evident, too, whom people envy; for these have been just now stated; for they envy those near to them in time and place and age and reputation, whence it has been said, "Kinship, too, knows how to envy."[63] And [they envy] those they rival; for they rival those mentioned, [feeling] the same way toward them and on the same grounds,[64] but no one rivals people ten thousand years in the future or dead nor those who live at the Pillars of Heracles[65] nor those they or others regard as inferior or much superior. 6. But since people seek honor in comparison with antagonists and rivals in love and in general those wanting the same things, necessarily they are most envious of these. This is the source of the saying "Potter [against] potter."[66] 7. And people are envious of those who have acquired something or been successful. These, too, are near and like; for clearly, they do not attain this good because of themselves, so distress at this causes envy. 8. And [they envy] those who have or have acquired whatever naturally belongs to themselves or what they once had. This is why the older [envy] the younger. 9. And those who have spent much money envy those who have spent little for the same object. 10. And those who got something with difficulty or did not get it at all envy those who got it quickly.

---

63. Attributed by a medieval commentator to Aeschylus. Kassel (1976) double-bracketed this as a late addition by Aristotle.

64. The translation transposes this otherwise troublesome phrase from the end of the section.

65. Gibraltar, the nominal limit of the known world.

66. Cf. 2.4.21.

THE STATE OF MIND OF THOSE WHO ENVY

11. It is also clear what such people rejoice at and for what causes and in what state of mind; for the state of mind that accompanies distress is also the state of mind in which people take pleasure in the opposite situations. So if [speakers] have created this [envious] state of mind [in the audience] and if persons of the sort described have thought themselves deserving to be pitied or to attain some good, clearly they will not attain pity from those in authority.

Chapter 11: Zēlos, or Emulation

■ This chapter belongs with the preceding in that emulation is regarded as the positive counterpart of envy. Both are feelings that may result from a sense of rivalry with those a person regards as in some sense an equal. In Hellenistic and later rhetoric, *zēlos* becomes an important aspect of literary imitation, referring to the "zeal" on the part of a writer to equal the quality of the great writers of the past. This chapter concludes the chiastically arranged survey of positive and negative emotions.

1. But the state of mind of those who feel emulation [*zēlos*], and at what sort of things and what people [feel it] is clear from what follows; for if emulation is [defined as] a kind of distress at the apparent presence among others like him by nature of things honored and possible for a person to acquire, [with the distress arising] not from the fact that another has them but that the emulator does not (thus emulation is a good thing and characteristic of good people, while envy is bad and characteristic of the bad; for the former, through emulation, is making an effort to attain good things for himself, while the latter, through envy, tries to prevent his neighbor from having them)—[if this definition is posited,] then necessarily those are emu-
1388b lous who think themselves deserving of goods they do not have (for no one thinks himself worthy of things that seem impossible).[67] For this reason the young and the great-souled are emulous. Also those [are emulous] who possess such goods as are worthy of men [*andrōn*] who are honored, and these are wealth and numerous friends and offices and all such things; for since it is right to be good, people zeal-ously seek goods of this sort because they are appropriate attributes

---

67. Kassel (1976) double-bracketed this sentences as a late addition by Aristotle.

of the good. 2. And those are given to emulation whom others think worthy [of such goods] 3. and whose ancestors or relatives or household or nation or city are honored on these grounds; for they think these things properly belong to them and that they are worthy of them. 4. But if honored goods are the objects of emulation, necessarily the virtues are such things and whatever is a source of advantage and benefit to others; for people honor benefactors and the good. And goods [are causes of emulation] when their enjoyment can be shared with neighbors, for example, wealth and beauty more than health.

THOSE WHO ARE EMULATED

5. What persons are emulated is also evident; for they are those who have acquired these things and things like them. These things are those mentioned, for example, bravery, wisdom, public office; for public officials, including generals, politicians [*rhētores*], [and] all having this kind of power, can benefit many people. 6. And those [are emulated] whom many want to be like, or many of their acquaintances or many of their friends. Or [those are emulated] whom many admire or whom the emulators admire. 7. And those [are emulated] whose praises and encomia are spoken by poets and prose writers. But people feel contempt for the opposite [types]; for contempt [*kataphronēsis*] is the opposite of emulation and *to emulate* the opposite of *to feel contempt for*. Necessarily, those in a situation to emulate or be emulated are contemptuous of others (and for these reasons) who have the bad attributes that are opposites of the emulated good ones. As a result, they are often contemptuous of those who are fortunate, whenever good fortune comes to the latter without [bringing with it] those things that are really valued. This concludes an account of how the emotions are created and counteracted, from which are derived *pisteis* related to them.[68]

---

68. Or "and [the topics] from which are derived. . . ." *And* is found only in some late manuscripts and medieval Latin translations. It was restored to the text by Kassel (1976) and has been defended by Conley (1982). The interpretative issue is the extent to which topics about the emotions are to be regarded as primarily premises for enthymemes. If *and* is not inserted (as in the translation here), the sentence claims only that the creation or counteracting of emotions, as described in these chapters, produces persuasion based on emotional feelings.

Chapters 12–17: Topics About Ethos, Useful in Adapting the Character of the Speech to the Character of the Audience

■ In Plato's *Phaedrus* (see esp. 271d–272b and 277b–c) Socrates argues that there cannot be a true art of speech without a knowledge of the soul (*psykhē*), enabling a speaker to fit the appropriate argument to the soul of the hearer. Although this emphasis on audience psychology was an important contribution to rhetoric, Socrates does not mention the problem inherent in addressing a group with diverse characters. Aristotle takes up the subject in these chapters and develops it by considering character in terms of groups, classified by age and as affected by birth, wealth, power, and fortune. The picture of youth, prime of life, and old age that he gives reflects the common stereotypical views of antiquity and can be seen in the comedies of Menander and his Roman imitators, Plautus and Terence.

The predominant meaning of *ēthos* in Aristotle is "moral character" as reflected in deliberate choice of actions and as developed into a habit of mind. At times, however, the word seems to refer to qualities, such as an innate sense of justice or a quickness of temper, with which individuals may be naturally endowed and which dispose them to certain kinds of action. In 1.2.4 one of the three modes of persuasion was identified as provided by *ēthos*. In that sense the word refers to the trustworthy character of a speaker as artistically created in a speech. Students of the *Rhetoric* have taken different views as to whether the brief passage in 2.1.5–7 or the longer passage—Book 2, chapters 12–17—should be regarded as Aristotle's principal discussion of character presentation as a mode of persuasion. It seems clear, however, that 2.1.5–7 resumes the original statement of 1.2.3–5, noted also in 1.9.1, and that Book 2, chapters 12–17 is aimed at something rather different: the adaptation of a speech to the character of the audience, which was anticipated in 1.8.6. The need to discuss the effect of age, wealth, and fortune on character was pointed out in 1.10.10–11, and these chapters provide that account. In 2.22.16 Aristotle seems to refer to Book 2, chapters 12–17, as listing "topics" relating to *ēthos*; these may include, but are not limited to, topics for enthymemes. At the end of 2.18.1 the preceding discussion is described as a matter of making speech "ethical," and in 3.17.8 we are told that enthymemes should be avoided when the speech is being "ethical." As Grimaldi wrote (1988, 2:186), "the actual purpose of chapters 12–17 with its study of the major character types is to show the speaker how his *ēthos* must attend and adjust to the *ēthos* of varied types of auditor if he is to address them successfully." This is similar to what Socrates urges in the *Phaedrus* but more pragmatic and open to possible abuse. An extant short work by Aristotle's student Theophrastus, entitled *Characters*, contains amusing portraits of thirty character stereotypes.

Chapters 2.12–17, like 2.2–11, seem to have been inserted in the *Rhetoric* without adequate revision to integrate them into the objectives of the treatise. Note that the chapters contain no examples from oratory and, beginning with the second sentence, link character and emotion. Wisse (1989:9–43) reasonably concluded that these chapters are an "appendix" to the account of both *ēthos* and *pathos*.

Chapter 12: Introduction; the Character of the Young

■ In this chapter Aristotle gives the stereotypical Greek view of young men as pleasure-loving, impulsive, and optimistic. In 2.13.16 he indicates that awareness of this is useful in addressing the young, but the chapter does not indicate any situations in which that might be done. What is actually found in Greek oratory is the use of some of the topics Aristotle mentions to explain the actions and motivations of a young man when he is accused before a jury of some crime. An example is the sixteenth speech of Lysias, *For Manitheus* (esp. sections 11 and 15–16). Juries have often been disposed to excuse youthful high jinks, as in the case Cicero successfully pleaded *For Caelius* (see esp. sections 37–47).

1. Next let us go through the kinds of character, considering what they are like in terms of emotions and habits and age of life and fortune. 2. By emotions I mean anger, desire, and the like, about which we spoke earlier, and by habits virtues and vices, which have also been discussed earlier, including what sort of things each type of person chooses and does.[69] The ages of life are youth, prime, and old age. By fortune I mean good birth and wealth and powers and their opposites and in general good fortune and misfortune.   1389a
3. In terms of their character, the young are prone to desires and inclined to do whatever they desire. Of the desires of the body they are most inclined to pursue that relating to sex and they are powerless against this. 4. They are changeable and fickle in desires, and though they intensely lust, they are quickly satisfied; for their wants, like the thirst and hunger of the sick, are sharp rather than massive. 5. And they are impulsive and quick-tempered and inclined to follow up their anger [by action]. And they are unable to resist their impulses; for through love of honor they cannot put up with being belittled but become indignant if they think they are done a wrong. 6. And though they love honor, they love victory more; for youth longs for superiority

---

69. Adopting the punctuation suggested by Wisse 1989:322.

and victory is a kind of superiority. They have both of these characteristics more than a love of money, and [of the age groups] they are
least lovers of money because they have not yet experienced want, as
the saying of Pittacus about Amphiaraus has it.[70] 7. And they are not
cynical but guileless, because of not yet having seen much wickedness. And [they are] trusting, because of not yet having been much
deceived. 8. And [they are] filled with hopes; for like those drinking
wine, the young are heated by their nature, and at the same time [they
are filled with hopes] because of not yet having experienced much
failure. And they live for the most part in hope; for hope is for the
future, and memory is of what has gone by, but for the young the
future is long and the past short; for in the dawn of life nothing can be
remembered and everything [can be] hoped for. And they are easily
deceived for the reason given; for they easily hope for the best. 9. And
they are more courageous [than the other age groups]; for they are
impulsive and filled with good hopes, of which the former quality
makes them lack fear, and the latter makes them brave; for no one
feels fear when angry, and to expect something good is a source. 10.
And they are sensitive to shame; for they have been educated only
by convention and do not yet understand other fine things. 11. And
they are magnanimous; for they have not yet been worn down by life
but are inexperienced with constraints, and to think oneself worthy
of great things in magnanimity and this is characteristic of a person of
good hopes. 12. And they choose to do fine things rather than things
advantageous [to themselves]; for they live more by natural character
than by calculation, and calculation concerns the advantageous, virtue
the honorable. 13. And more than other ages of life they are fond of
friends and eager for companions because they enjoy living with
others. And they do not yet judge anything on the basis of advantage;
thus, they do not judge friends that way. 14. And all the mistakes they
make are in the direction of excess and vehemence, contrary to the
maxim of Chilon;[71] for they do "everything too much"; they love too
much and hate too much and all other things similarly. And they think
they know everything and strongly insist on it; for this is the cause of
their doing everything too much. 15. And the wrongs they commit
come from insolence, not maliciousness. And they are inclined to
pity, because of supposing [that] everybody is good or better than the

1389b

---

70. The saying is otherwise unknown. Pittacus was chief of state of Mytilene about
600 B.C.E.; Amphiaraus was one of the legendary Seven Against Thebes.

71. The Spartan sage to whom was attributed the maxim "Nothing too much."

average; for they measure their neighbors by their own innocence, with the result that they suppose them to be suffering unworthily. And they are fond of laughter and, as a result, witty; for wit is cultured insolence. Such, then, is the character of the young.

Chapter 13: The Character of the Old

■ Instead of moving through the stages of life chronologically, Aristotle jumps to a description of the old as opposites of the young. In chapter 14 he will then return to describe the prime of life as a mean. The central character in Menander's *Dyskolos (The Curmudgeon)* (317 B.C.E.) has some of the traits described here by Aristotle.

1. People who are older and more or less past their prime have characters that are for the most part the opposite of these [just described]; for through having lived for many years and having been more often deceived and having made more mistakes themselves, and since most things turn out badly, they assert nothing with certainty and all things with less assurance than is needed. 2. And they "think," but do not "know" anything. And being doubtful, they always add *perhaps* and *maybe* and say everything that way, but nothing definitively. 3. And they are cynical; for a cynical disposition supposes everything is for the worse. Further, they are suspicious because of their distrust and distrustful because of experience. 4. And for these reasons they neither love nor hate strongly but, following the advice of Bias,[72] they love as if they would one day hate and hate as if they would one day love. 5. And they are small-minded because of having been worn down by life; for they desire nothing great or unusual but things necessary for life. 6. And they are stingy; for one of the necessities is money, and at the same time they know from experience that it is difficult to acquire and easy to lose. 7. And they are cowardly and fearful ahead of time about everything; for their disposition is the opposite of the young. (They are chilled, but the young are hot, so old age has prepared the way for cowardice; for fear is a kind of chilling.) 8. And they are fond of life and more so on their last day because of the presence of desire for what is gone, and people most desire what they lack. 9. And they are more fond of themselves than is right; for this is also a form of small-mindedness. And they live for what is

---

72. One of the "Seven Sages" of early Greek times.

advantageous [to themselves] (not for what is fine), more than is right, through being fond of themselves. (The advantageous is good for the individual, the fine absolutely.) 10. And they are more shameless than sensitive to shame; for since they do not care equally about what is fine and what is advantageous, they think little of their reputation. 11. And they expect the worst, through experience—[in their view] the greater part of things that happen are bad; at least most turn out for the worse—and through their cowardice, too. 12. And they live in memory more than in hope; for what is left of life is short, what is past is long, and hope is for the future, memory for what is gone. This is the cause of their garrulity; for they keep talking about things that have passed; for they take pleasure in reminiscence. 13. Their outbursts of anger are sharp but weak; and some of their desires have failed, others are weak, with the result that they are not spirited and do not act on the basis of desire, but for profit. Thus, those in this age group seem self-controlled; for their desires are gone, and they are slaves to profit. 14. And they live more by calculation than by natural character; and calculation is a matter of what is beneficial, character of virtue. And the wrongs they commit are from malice, not insolence. 15. The old are also inclined to pity but not for the same reason as the young; with the latter it is a matter of human feelings [*philanthrōpia*], with the former weakness; for they think that all kinds of sufferings are close to hand for themselves, and this was the definition of one who feels pity.[73] As a result, they are querulous and not witty nor fond of laughter; for querulousness is the opposite of love of laughter. 16. Such are the characters of the young and the older; as a result, since all people receive favorably speeches spoken in their own character and by persons like themselves, it is not unclear how both speakers and speeches may seem to be of this sort through use of words.[74]

Chapter 14: The Character of Those in the Prime of Life

1. It is evident that those in the prime of life will be between the young and the old in character, subtracting the excess of either, and neither exceedingly confident (rashness is such) nor too fearful but

---

73. See 2.8.2.

74. This concluding statement would apply best to logography, the composition of speeches by a professional speech writer for a client to memorize and deliver in court. Most of the speeches of Lysias fall into this genre. He was especially celebrated for his ability to suit a speech to the character of a speaker.

1390a

having the right amount of both, 2. neither trusting nor distrusting everybody but rather making realistic judgments and not directing their lives only to what is fine or what is advantageous but to both and neither to frugality nor to extravagance but to what is fitting. **1390b** 3. Similarly in regard to impulse and desire. And they combine prudence with courage and courage with prudence, while among the young and the old these things are separated; for the young are brave and lack self-restraint, the older prudent and cowardly. To speak in general terms, whatever advantages youth and old age have separately, [those in their prime] combine, and whatever the former have to excess or in deficiency, the latter have in due measure and in a fitting way. 4. The body is in its prime from the age of thirty to thirty-five, the mind about age forty-nine. Let this much be said about the kinds of character of youth and old age and the prime of life.

■ Aristotle first taught rhetoric in Athens about the age of thirty and returned there to open his school at the age of fifty-two. If the text of the *Rhetoric* as we have it represents a revision made a few years earlier in anticipation of a return to Athens, he may have written these words when he was about forty-nine years old. The ages specified here only approximately accord with the common Greek theory that life can be viewed in ten stages of seven years each, which Aristotle mentions in *Politics* 7.16.17.

Chapter 15: The Effect on Character of Goods That Come from Chance: Eugeneia, or Good Birth

■ *Tykhē* can mean "chance," "accident," "fortune," or "luck." To Aristotle it represented unmotivated contingency, not Fate or the predetermined will of some divinity, but he realized that some people seem consistently luckier than others. Some of the advantages Aristotle describes, for example, good birth, can be said to be a matter of chance, but power combines luck with ability and effort on the part of the person who has it.

1. Let us speak next about goods that come from *tykhē* insofar as some kinds of character also result for human beings from them. 2. The character that comes from good birth is a matter of its possessor being rather ambitious; for all people, when some advantage is theirs, usually add others to it, and good birth is rank in society that derives from ancestors.[75] Also, such persons are contemptuous, even of those

---

75. Thus, it gives the possessor an initial advantage.

[of their contemporaries] equal [in achievement] to their own ancestors, because these things are more honorable and easy to boast about when they come into existence further back in time than when recent. 3. *Good birth* [*eugeneia*] refers to the excellence of the family, whereas *noble* [*gennaion*] refers to there having been no degeneration from [the earliest] nature [of the line]; for the most part such is not the case among the wellborn, since many of them are worthless; for there is a kind of harvest in the generations of men as in what grows on the land, and sometimes, if the stock is good, outstanding men continue to be born into the family, and then again it falls off. Originally good stock [often] degenerates into rather demented forms of character, as in the case of the children of Alcibiades and Dionysius the Elder, while a previously steadfast stock [often] turns into silliness and stupidity, as in the children of Cimon and Pericles and Socrates.[76]

Chapter 16: Character as Affected by Ploutos, or Wealth

■ Aristotle's view of the wealthy is quite negative, and he does not attribute to them magnanimity or magnificence, virtues he had defined in 1.9.11. The acquisition of great wealth and the practice of philanthropy by private individuals was largely a development of the Hellenistic and Roman periods.

1. The kinds of character that follow from wealth are plain for all to see; for [the wealthy] are insolent and arrogant, being affected somehow by the possession of wealth; for their state of mind is that of those who have all good things; for wealth is a kind of standard of value of other things, so that all things seem purchasable by it. 2. And the wealthy are ostentatious and pretentious: ostentatious because of luxury and the display of their prosperity, pretentious and vulgar because all are used to spending their time with whatever they love and admire and because they think everybody else has the same values they do. At the same time, this feeling is reasonable; for there are many who need what they have. This is the reason for what Simonides said about the wise and the rich to the wife of Hieron when she asked whether it was better to be rich or wise: [he replied,] "To be

1391a

---

76. There are references to Socrates' sons, still young at the time of his death in 399 B.C.E., in Plato's *Apology* and *Phaedo*, but nothing is known about their subsequent fates.

rich"; for he said one sees the wise waiting at the doors of the rich.[77]
3. [Another result of wealth is that the rich] think they deserve to rule;
for they think they have that which makes one worthy to rule. And in
sum, the character that comes from wealth is that of a lucky fool. 4.
The characters of the newly rich and those with old wealth differ in
that the newly rich have all the vices to a greater degree and in a worse
form; for to be newly rich is, as it were, to lack education in the use
of wealth. And the wrongs that they commit are not malicious but
sometimes acts of insolence, sometimes the result of lack of self-
control, for example, personal injury and adultery.

Chapter 17: Character as Affected by Dynamis, or Power

1. Similarly with power, most of the ways it influences forms of character are evident; for power has some characteristics that are the same
as wealth, some that are better; 2. for those holding power are more
ambitious and more manly in character than the rich, because of their
power. 3. And they are more earnest, because of being in a position of
responsibility, forced to keep an eye on everything that relates to their
power. 4. And they are rather more reserved in a dignified way than
inclined to be severe; for their rank makes them quite conspicuous, so
they seek moderation. Their dignity is a mild and graceful severity,
and if they commit wrong, they do it on a large, not a small, scale.

CONCLUSION TO THE DISCUSSION OF CHAPTERS 15–17

5. Good fortune in its different forms makes for the kinds of
character described above (for the kinds of good fortune that seem
greatest tend in these directions), and in addition good fortune offers   **1391b**
an opportunity for advantages in regard to the blessings of children
and the goods of the body. 6. Although people are more arrogant and
unreasonable because of good fortune, there is one very good characteristic that follows from good fortune, namely, that these people are
lovers of the gods and have a special relationship to divinity, having
faith in the gods because of the benefits that have come to them from
fortune. Enough has now been said about types of character as related

---

77. Hieron was tyrant of Syracuse in the 470s B.C.E. and was visited there by the
poet Simonides of Ceos. To a follow-up question the philosopher Aristippus replied,
"Philosophers know what they need, the rich do not" (Diogenes Laertius 2.69).

to stage in life and fortune; for the opposite kinds of character are evident from the opposites of what has been said, for example, the character of the poor and the unfortunate and the powerless.

Chapters 18–26: Dialectical Features of Rhetoric Common to All Three Species

Chapter 18: Introduction

■ This chapter provides a transition from the discussion of character to a further consideration of premises, forms of proof, and common topics, resuming the thought of 2.1.2. There are, however, a number of obscurities that have troubled the commentators. The text of section 1 is cumbersome at best and ungrammatical at worst. Cope ([1877] 1970, 2:171–175) and Grimaldi (1988, 2:224–226) review the problems and proposed solutions in detail. Cope described the text as "incoherent" and hesitantly proposed that some words have been omitted after "discussed earlier" near the end of the section. Kassel (1974) double-bracketed section 1 up to "counsel is being given" as a later addition by Aristotle. Possibly the philosopher made some hasty notes in the margin of his copy of the text and an editor tried to integrate them as well as possible. Or perhaps section 1 was an early draft of an introduction to this part of the book which sections 2–5 were intended to replace. Section 1, as punctuated by Kassel (1976), is not really grammatically complete, there being no clear apodosis, or main clause, following on the "since" and "if" clauses. Grimaldi (1988, 2:230) regarded the last clause of section 1 as the logical apodosis, and the translation here follows that assumption.

1. Since the use of persuasive speech is directed to a judgment (there is no further need of speech on subjects that we know and have already judged), and since there is judgment even if someone, by using speech to address an individual, exhorts or dissuades, as do those giving advice or persuading [someone to do something] (a single individual is no less a judge; for a judge is, so to speak, simply one who must be persuaded), and if someone speaks against an opponent and if against a proposition, the same is true (it is necessary to use speech also to refute opposing arguments at which the speech is directed as at an opponent), and similarly in epideictic (the speech is composed for the observer as a judge); but nevertheless, only that person is purely a judge in the general sense of the word who is judging

the questions at issue in civic debates (for he inquires into the facts of the dispute [in a law court] and the subject on which counsel is being given [in a deliberative assembly] and [since] the role of characters in deliberations under [different] constitutions has been discussed earlier—as a result, the definition of how and through what means one ought to make speeches ethical should be complete.

2. Since there was a different end for each genus of speech,[78] and opinions and premises have been collected for all of them, from which [speakers] derive *pisteis* when speaking in deliberation and in demonstrations and contention, and from which, moreover, it is possible to make speeches appropriate to character,[79] and since definitions have been given on these matters, it remains to describe the *koina*;[80] 3. for it is necessary for all, in their speeches, in addition [to what has been described] to make use of [premises] concerning the possible and impossible and for some to try to show that something will be the case and others that something has taken place. 4. Further, a common feature of all speeches is the matter of magnitude [*megethos*]; for all use diminution and amplification when deliberating and when praising or blaming and when prosecuting or defending themselves. 5. Once these have been defined, let us try to speak about   1392a enthymemes in general terms, so far as we can, and about paradigms, in order that having added what remains, we may complete the program originally outlined. Of the *koina*, amplification is most proper to epideictic (as has been said),[81] past fact [is most proper] to judicial (judgment there is about past facts), and possibility and future fact [are most proper] to deliberative speeches.

Chapter 19: The Koina: *The Possible and the Impossible; Past and Future Fact; Degree of Magnitude or Importance*

■ This chapter resumes discussion of three subjects of argument, first mentioned in 1.3.7–9, that are useful in all species of rhetoric. Degree of magnitude was also discussed in 1.7.14.

---

78. According to the definitions of 1.3.5.

79. Commentators have been troubled at the absence of reference to *pathos* in this summary. Probably it is to be thought of as included in *ēthikous*, "appropriate to character" (cf. 2.12.1).

80. I.e., subjects common to all species (or genera) of rhetoric. These are the forms of argument first mentioned, but given no technical name, in 1.3.7–9.

81. In 1.9.40.

THE POSSIBLE AND THE IMPOSSIBLE

1. First let us speak about possible and impossible. If it is possible for the opposite of something to exist or to have happened, the opposite would also seem to be possible; for example, if it is possible for a human being to be healthy, it is possible also to be ill; for the potentiality of opposites is the same, insofar as they are opposites.[82] 2. And if one of two things is possible, the other is also. 3. And if the more difficult is possible, so is the easier. 4. And if something can come to be good and beautiful, it can also come to be in general; for it is more difficult for a house to be beautiful than for a house to exist. 5. And where the beginning is possible, so also is the end;[83] for no impossible thing comes to be nor begins to come to be; for example, the diagonal [of a square] could not begin to be, nor be, commensurate [with the side]. And where there is an end, the beginning is also possible; for all things come from a beginning. 6. And if what is later in existence or birth is possible, so also what is prior [is possible]; for example, if it is possible for a man to exist, so also for a boy (a boy is prior to a man); [if it is possible for a boy to exist] so also a man (a boy is also a first principle).[84] 7. And that for which there is a natural desire or longing [is possible]; for no one desires or longs for things that are impossible, at least not for the most part. 8. And where sciences or arts exist, it is possible for the subject of those studies both to exist and to have existed.[85] 9. And [things are possible] whose first principle lies in things we can compel or persuade; these are those things than which we are stronger or over which we have authority or [persons] of whom we are friends.[86] 10. And the whole is possible of which the parts are possible, and for the most part the parts

---

82. In this example, as in the following ones, note that Aristotle is talking about what is logically possible, not what is necessarily true in a particular case. The propositions here laid down are dialectical in that they are based on common assumptions that most people would accept and do not require further demonstration.

83. An axiom important in metaphysics: if the world was created, it is possible for it to come to an end; if the soul is immortal, it is possible for it to have existed before birth, etc.

84. Or "beginning" (*arkhē*); see note on 1.7.12.

85. From the popular point of view, it is thus logically possible that the subjects of astrology or magic exist, since a systematic body of thought about them seems to exist.

86. It is possible to make a statue of wood or stone because "we" have the strength to work the material; it is possible to hire or dismiss servants because "we" are the masters; it is possible to invite people to dinner because "we" have friends.

are possible if the whole is;[87] for if the sole and toe and top can be made, shoes can be made too; and if shoes [can be made], then [so can] the sole and the toe.[88] 11. And if the genus as a whole is among possible things so also the species, and if the species, also the genus; **1392b** for example, if a ship can be built, a trireme can be, and if a trireme, also a ship. 12. And if either one of two naturally corresponding things [is possible, so] also the other; for example, if double [is possible, so] also half, and if half, also double. 13. And if something is possible without art or preparation, all the more is it possible with art and care. This is the source of Agathon's saying,

> And indeed we must do something by art, and some
> Happen to us by necessity and chance.[89]

14. And if something is possible for inferior or lesser people, then [it is] also more possible for their opposites, as Isocrates said that it is strange if he himself could not understand a subject that Euthynous had learned. 15. As for the impossible, it is clear from the opposites of what has been said.

PAST AND FUTURE FACT

■ Argument from probability is a major characteristic of Greek rhetoric, in part because of the distrust of direct evidence in cases at law. Aristotle here sets out a number of useful forms that argument from probability can take, though it would have been clearer if he had furnished more examples from legal and deliberative rhetoric rather than from natural science. Possibly the account originated in some other context and was added to a revision of the *Rhetoric* with little change. Past fact is a common subject of judicial rhetoric, and the arguments here discussed roughly correspond to what is called "circumstantial evidence" in modern law; future fact—what is actually going to take place—is the subject of deliberative rhetoric. Behind what is said here lies the assumption that human actions and events follow predictable natural patterns, except in unusual circumstances.

---

87. An example of the qualification *for the most part* is the begetting of a child. Parents cannot beget the parts (e.g., limbs) separately.

88. We do not know exactly what parts of a shoe Aristotle refers to by *proskhisma*, *kephalis*, and *khiton*; the translation is only an approximation.

89. Agathon was a tragic poet of the fifth century B.C.E. (also a character in Plato's *Symposium*). These iambic lines seem to come from one of his lost plays.

16. Whether some action has or has not taken place should be considered on the basis of the following:[90] First, if what is naturally less likely to have happened [did happen], what is more so should also have happened.[91] 17. And if what usually occurs after something else has happened [did happen], the previous event has also happened; for example, if someone has forgotten something, he also once learned it. 18. And if a person had the capacity and the will [to do something], he has done it; for all act when ability to do so coincides with desire; for nothing hinders them. Further, if someone had the will to do something and no external agency hindered him, [then he acted], 19. and if he had the ability and was angry, and if he had the ability and longed for something[, then he acted]; for usually people do what they long to do if they can, the bad through lack of self-control, the good because they desire good things. 20. And if something was going to happen and someone was going to do something, [then it occurred]; for it is probable [*eikos*] that one who was going to do something also did it. 21. And if things that are naturally antecedents or causes [happened, the consequences happened]; for example, if it has lightened, it has also thundered, and if he tried, he did it. And if something has occurred that is naturally subsequent or a result, then the antecedent and cause have occurred; for example, if it has thundered, it also lightened, and if he did it, he tried. Of all these, some are related by necessity, some only for the most part. 22. As for what has not happened, that is clear from the opposites of the things mentioned.

What is going to be in the future is clear from the same arguments;
for that will be something for which there is both capacity and motivation, 23. and those things for which there is desire and the impulse of anger and calculation together with capacity to act; those things, too, that are on the verge of being done or going to be done will take place; for things that are going to be done, rather than things that are not, usually take place. 24. And if what usually precedes has preceded [what usually follows will probably happen]; for example, if it is cloudy, there is a probability it will rain. 25. And if something has been done for the sake of something else, it is probable that the latter has resulted; for example, if a foundation [has been laid], a house [has probably been built].

---

90. In judicial rhetoric, the first and sometimes the only consideration is whether or not the defendant has in fact personally committed the alleged act, such as killing, stealing, or breaking the terms of a contract.

91. E.g., if a defendant has been shown on another occasion to have stolen someone else's property, it is likely that he has attempted to recover his own property from another when the need arose.

MAGNITUDE; *AUXĒSIS*, OR AMPLIFICATION

26. The subject of largeness and smallness of things and more and less and, on the whole, large and small is evident to us from what has been said; for an account was given in the discussion of deliberative rhetoric of the magnitude of goods and of the greater and lesser in general terms.[92] As a result, since in each kind of speech the projected "end" is a good—for example, the advantageous [in deliberative rhetoric] and the honorable [in epideictic] and the just [in judicial][93] —it is evident that one should seize the opportunities for amplification [*auxēsis*] in all. 27. To go into the matter of magnitude in general and the concept of superiority in further detail is wasting words; for the particulars of subjects are controlling factors in the application of universals. Thus, let this be enough on the subject of possibility and impossibility and whether something has or has not happened and will or will not come to be and about largeness and smallness of things.

Chapters 20–22:
Koinai Pisteis, or Common Modes of Persuasion

■ These chapters resume discussion of the basic tools of logical persuasion, first defined in 1.2.3. In contrast to earlier chapters in this book, they make use of examples from public address, and they would lend themselves to a lecture format more easily than do the earlier chapters.

Chapter 20: Paradigm, or Example

1. It remains to speak about *pisteis* that are common to all [species of rhetoric], since the account of specifics has been completed.[94] These common *pisteis* are of two kinds: paradigm and enthymeme (maxim [*gnōmē*] is a part of an enthymeme). 2. First, then let us speak of

---

92. See 1.7.

93. See 1.3.5.

94. This sounds as though it originally followed 1.5–15; but see the introduction to Book 2. The common *pisteis* are those called demonstrative in 1.2.19 and should not be confused with the artistic (*entekhnoi*) *pisteis*, which are the more general modes of logical, ethical, and emotional persuasion. The term *specifics* (*idia*) is taken up from 1.2.21, where it referred to the subject matter specific to some discipline like politics and ethics, and in subsequent chapters was considered in terms of the specific subject matter of deliberative, epideictic, and judicial rhetoric. We now return to the fundamental logical devices of all rhetoric in greater detail.

paradigm; for paradigm is similar to an induction, and induction is a beginning.

There are two species of paradigms; for to speak of things that have happened before is one species of paradigm and to make up [an illustration] is another.[95] Of the latter, comparison [*parabolē*] is one kind, fables [*logoi*] another, for example, the Aesopic and Lybian.[96] 3. An instance of speaking of [historical] facts is if someone were to say that it is necessary to make preparations against the king [of Persia] and not allow Egypt to be subdued; for in the past Darius did not invade [Greece] until he had taken Egypt, but after taking it, he invaded; and again, Xerxes did not attack until he took [Egypt]. But having taken it, he invaded; thus if he [the present king] takes [Egypt], he will invade [Greece]; as a result it must not be allowed.[97] 4. Socratic sayings are an instance of comparison: for example, if someone were to say that officials should not be chosen by lot (for that would be as if someone chose athletes randomly—not those able to compete, but those on whom the lot fell); or [as if] choosing by lot any one of the sailors to act as pilot rather than the one who knew how.[98]

5. An example of a fable is that of Stesichorus about Phalaris and of Aesop about the demagogue. When the people of Himera had chosen Phalaris as dictator and were about to give him a bodyguard, after saying other things at some length, Stesichorus told them a fable about how a horse had a meadow to himself. When a stag came and

1393b

---

95. Thus the species are "historical" and "fictional." For a different division, see *Rhetoric for Alexander* in Appendix I.F., sec. 8.

96. According to Theon (*Progymnasmata* 4), the only difference between these was whether the fable is attributed to Aesop or a Lybian or some other source.

97. I.e., the Greeks should go to the aid of Egypt's independence. The structure of this argument is proposition, two historical examples with implied conclusion (whoever takes Egypt invades Greece), and application to the proposition. The "present king" is Artaxerxes III Ochus, who in 343 B.C.E. sent an embassy to Greece asking for an alliance in his efforts to regain Egypt; the passage was therefore written after that date. The king recovered Egypt but did not invade Greece and was subsequently overthrown by Alexander.

98. For Socrates' use of this comparison, see Xenophon, *Memorabilia* 1.2.9. Here we have proposition and then two comparisons, of which the latter contains another comparison that makes the point: public officials should be chosen on the basis of their knowledge. Note that Aristotle does not remark on any connection between *parabolē* as a demonstrative tool (treated here) and *eikōn* (simile) (treated as a stylistic device in 3.4 and regarded as basically poetic).

quite damaged the pasture, the horse, wanting to avenge himself on the stag, asked a man if he could help him get vengeance on the stag. The man said he could if the horse were to submit to a bit and he himself were to mount on him, holding javelins. When the horse agreed and the man mounted, instead of getting vengeance the horse found himself a slave to the man. "Thus you too," said Stesichorus, "look out, lest while wishing vengeance on your enemies you suffer the same thing as the horse. You already have the bit [in your mouth], having appointed a general with absolute power; if you give him a bodyguard and allow him to mount, you will immediately be slaves to Phalaris."[99] 6. Aesop, when speaking on behalf of a demagogue who was on trial for his life in Samos, told how a fox, while crossing a river, was carried into a hole in the bank. Not being able to get out, she was in misery for some time and many dog-ticks attacked her. A hedgehog came wandering along and, when he saw her, took pity and asked if he could remove the ticks. She would not let him and, when asked why, [said,] "These are already full of me and draw little blood, but if you remove these, other hungry ones will come and drink what blood I have left." "In your case too, O Samians," said [Aesop], "this man will no longer harm you; for he is rich. But if you kill him, other poor ones will come who will steal and spend your public funds."[100]

7. Fables are suitable in deliberative oratory and have this advantage,   **1394a** that while it is difficult to find similar historical incidents that have actually happened, it is rather easy with fables. They should be made in the same way as comparisons, provided one can see the likenesses, which is rather easy from philosophical studies.[101] 8. Although it is easier to provide illustrations through fables, examples from history are more useful in deliberation; for future events will generally be like those of the past.

---

99. The date is the second quarter of the sixth century B.C.E. in western Sicily. Stesichorus is the lyric poet, mentioned by Aristotle again in 2.21.8 and 3.116. Phalaris became the most notorious of Greek tyrants, alleged to have roasted his victims in a brazen bull.

100. Aesop is supposed to have been a slave in Samos in the sixth century B.C.E. (and thus not likely to have engaged in public debate). But very little is known about him, and the collections of fables attributed to him by oral tradition were made in later times.

101. Probably the meaning is that the dialectical exercises in the philosophical schools, with their frequent use of the Socratic technique of analogy, train a student to see likenesses.

9. If one does not happen to have a supply of enthymemes, one should use paradigms as demonstration; for persuasion [then] depends on them. But if there are enthymemes, paradigms should be used as witnesses, [i.e., as] a supplement to the enthymemes. When the paradigms are placed first,[102] there is the appearance of induction, but induction is not suitable to rhetorical discourses except in a few cases; when they are put at the end they become witnesses, and a witness is everywhere persuasive. Thus, too, when they are first, it is necessary to supply many of them; when they are mentioned at the end, one is sufficient; for even a single trustworthy witness is useful. This concludes the discussion of how many species of paradigms there are and how and when they should be used.

■ As the examples Aristotle has given show, induction is useful in deliberative oratory, where the future must be projected on the basis of past experiences. But it can be, and often is, used to create a picture of the character of a litigant in court by drawing a picture of his virtues or vices from past conduct. Aristotle's point, however, is that it is usually more effective to state the conclusion first and then support it with examples, e.g., "The king plans to invade Greece; for he is securing his position in Egypt [enthymeme]. This is what both Darius and Xerxes did in the past [example]."

Chapter 21: Gnōmē, *or Maxim*

■ What Aristotle calls gnōmē, or "maxim," is in Latin *sententia*; cf. English "sententious." Literally, gnōmē means "a thought," usually an opinion given as a judgment or advice. Pithy, epigrammatic statements have a long history as a feature of rhetoric from classical Greece to the present. Aristotle's successors, however, (e.g., Quintilian 8.5) treat the gnomic saying as a stylistic device used primarily for ornament, while he regards it as a tool of logical argument. There was an ancient gnomic tradition in Greece, seen in the utterances of sages and the elegiac poetry of Theognis, and quotable lines are a regular feature of Greek tragedy, especially the plays of Euripides. Aristotle cites a number of these.

1. As for the use of gnomic sayings, once it has been explained what a maxim is it should be very evident on what subjects and when and by whom it is appropriate to use the expression of maxims

---

102. That is, before the enthymeme, which then functions as a summary conclusion.

in speeches. 2. A maxim is an assertion—not, however, one about particulars, such as what kind of person Iphicrates is, but of a general sort, and not about everything (for example, not that the straight is the opposite of the crooked) but about things that involve actions and are to be chosen or avoided in regard to action. As a result, since enthymemes are rather like syllogisms about such things, the conclusions of enthymemes and [either of] the premises (with the [full] syllogism omitted) are maxims; for example,

> It is never right for a man who is shrewd
> To have his children taught to be too wise.[103]

This, then, is a maxim. But if the cause is added and the reason, the whole is an enthymeme; for example,

> For apart from the other idleness they have,
> They incur hostile jealousy from fellow-citizens.[104]

And this:

> There is no man who is happy in all ways.[105]

1394b

And this is a maxim:

> There is no one of men who is free.

But taken with what follows it is an enthymeme:

> For he is a slave of money or of chance.[106]

3. If a maxim is in fact what has been described, there are necessarily four species of maxim; for either it is with or without a supplement.[107] 4. Now those that need demonstration are those that say something paradoxical or disputable, but those that involve no paradox [can stand] without a supplement. 5. Of the latter, necessarily, some need no supplement because of being already known, for example,

---

103. Euripides, *Medea* 294–295.

104. Ibid., 296–297.

105. Thought to be from Euripides' lost *Sthenoboe*, see Grimaldi 1988, 2:263.

106. Euripides, *Hecuba* 864–865.

107. The supplement is the supporting reason. The four species are (1) commonly known and requiring no supplement, (2) not commonly known but self-evident when examined, (3) part of an enthymeme, (4) not part of an enthymeme but with an enthymematic character in itself when examined.

Best for a man is to be healthy, as it seems to me.[108]

(For so it seems to many.) But others, as soon as spoken, are clear to those who look at them carefully; for example,

No one is a lover who does not always love.[109]

6. Of those with a supplement, some are part of an enthymeme, as "it is never right for a man who is shrewd . . . ,"[110] others are enthymematic but not part of an enthymeme, and these are most well liked.[111] They are those in which the reason for the saying is inherently clear, for example, in the maxim "Being a mortal, do not cherish immortal anger"; for to say one should not cherish it is a maxim, but adding *being a mortal* gives the reason. Similarly, "A mortal should think mortal, not immortal, thoughts."

7. It is, then, evident from what has been said how many species of maxim there are and for what sort of context each is appropriate; for in disputed or paradoxical matters a supplement should not be lacking,[112] but use the maxim as a conclusion after first stating the supplement; for example, if someone were to say "As for me, then, since [a child] should not be an object of jealousy nor idle, I say that it is not necessary for one to be educated"; or putting the latter part first, then add the former. When the statement is not paradoxical but yet not clear, add the reason for it as tersely as possible. 8. In such cases Laconic apothegms[113] and enigmatic sayings are suitable; for example, if someone should say what Stesichorus said among the Locrians, that they should not be insolent, lest their cicadas chirp from the

1395a

---

108. Source uncertain; see Grimaldi 1988, 2:263–264.

109. Euripides, *Trojan Women* 1051.

110. The example from sec. 2. The two lines there quoted are the conclusion of an enthymeme, of which the second set of two lines is the minor premise. The implied major premise is something like, "A sensible man should want his children to be busy and well liked."

111. They are the equivalent of enthymemes (since some reason is given or implied) but do not take the form of enthymemes, which is characteristically a conclusion with a supporting clause giving a premise. The source of the two following quotations is not known with certainty; cf. Grimaldi 1988, 2:265.

112. This applies to civic discourse, which is all that concerns Aristotle. In religious discourse unsupported maxims may be effective, as in the case of many sayings of Jesus or the Buddha.

113. Laconia was the territory of Sparta. Since Spartan culture discouraged verbosity, the term *laconic* has come to mean "terse." There is a collection of Laconic apothegms in Plutarch's *Moralia* 208b–242d.

ground.[114] 9. Speaking in maxims is appropriate to those older in years and on subjects with which one is experienced, since to speak maxims is unseemly for one too young, as is storytelling; and on matters in which one is inexperienced it is silly and shows lack of education. There is an adequate sign of this: country folk are most inclined to strike maxims and readily show themselves off.

10. To speak in universal terms of what is not universal is especially suitable in bitter complaint and great indignation,[115] and in these cases either at the outset or after the demonstration. 11. And one should even use trite and common maxims if they are applicable; for because they are common, they seem true, as though everyone agreed; for example, [it is useful] for one who is exhorting [troops] to face danger without first sacrificing to the gods [to say,] "One omen [literally, one bird] is best, to fight for one's country."[116] And if they are outnumbered, [to say,] "The War God is impartial."[117] And [exhorting troops] to destroy the sons of their enemies, even though having done no wrong, [it is useful to say,] "Foolish he who after killing the father leaves the sons."[118] 12. Further, some proverbs are also maxims, for example, "an Attic neighbor."[119] 13. One should also speak maxims that are contrary to popular wisdom (by *popular wisdom* I mean such as "Know thyself" and "Nothing too much") whenever [the speaker's] character is going to be made to seem better or the maxim is stated with *pathos*. An example of a maxim with *pathos* is if someone in anger were to say that it is a lie that one should know himself: "At least, this man, if he had known himself, would never have thought himself worthy of command."[120] And his character [would appear] better [if he were to say] that contrary to what

---

114. That is, if they persist, their city many be leveled to the ground. Demetrius (*On Style* 99, 100, and 243) attributes the remark to Dionysius of Syracuse rather than to the poet Stesichorus.

115. For example, to cry, "All great men are envied" when there is really only oneself.

116. *Iliad* 12.243, when Hector disregards, as a chance occurrence, a bird flight that Polydamas regards as an unfavorable omen. Exhortation to troops about to enter battle is a form of deliberative rhetoric found both in epic poetry and in the historians.

117. *Iliad* 18.309.

118. See note on 1.15–14.

119. Cf. Thucydides 1.70. A neighbor should be a friend, but the volatile Athenians were often a trial to their neighbors.

120. "This man" may be Iphicrates, to whom Aristotle has referred earlier in several passages. Probably the statement means something like, "No one gets ahead in the world by knowing his own limits."

people say, it is not right to love as though some day one would hate, but better to hate as though later going to love. 14. One should make moral purpose clear by the choice of words [*lexis*], but if not, then add the cause; for example, saying something like, "Love should not take the form people say [i.e., able to turn to hate], but it should be as though one were always going to love; for otherwise it is a form of treachery"; or thus: "The saying does not please me; for the true lover should love as though he was always going to love"; and "That business about 'Nothing too much' isn't true either; one cannot hate the wicked too much." 15. Maxims make one great contribution to speeches because of the uncultivated mind of the audience; for people are pleased if someone in a general observation hits upon opinions that they themselves have about a particular instance. What I mean will be clear from the following and, at the same time, how one should hunt for maxims. A maxim, as has been said, is an assertion of a generality, and people enjoy things said in general terms that they happen to assume ahead of time in a partial way; for example, if someone had met up with bad neighbors or children, he would accept a speaker's saying that nothing is worse than having neighbors or that nothing is more foolish than begetting children. Thus, one should guess what sort of assumptions people have and then speak in general terms consistent with these views. 16. This is one useful aspect of employing maxims, and another is greater; for it makes the speech "ethical." Speeches have character[121] insofar as deliberate choice is clear, and all maxims accomplish this because one speaking a maxim makes a general statement about preferences, so that if the maxims are morally good, they make the speaker seem to have a good character. Concerning maxims, then, what they are and how many species there are of them and how they should be used and what advantages they have, let this much be said.

1395b

Chapter 22: Enthymemes, or Rhetorical Syllogisms

1. Let us speak about enthymemes as a whole, [first] in what way one should seek for them, and after that about their topics [*topoi*]; for each of these is different in kind. 2. That the enthymeme is a kind of syllogism has been said earlier and how it is a syllogism and in what it differs from those in dialectic; 3. for [in rhetoric] the conclusion

---

121. An unusual expression for Aristotle; otherwise only persons have *ēthos*, though speeches may be "ethical"; see Woerther 2005.

should not be drawn from far back, nor is it necessary to include everything.[122] The former is unclear because of the length [of the argument], the latter tiresome because of stating what is obvious. This is the reason why the uneducated are more persuasive than the educated [when speaking] before crowds, just as the poets say the uneducated are more "inspired by the Muses" in a crowd;[123] for [the educated] reason with axioms [*koina*] and universals, [the uneducated] on the basis of what [particulars] they know and instances near their experience. Thus, one should not speak on the basis of all opinions but of those held by a defined group,[124] for example, either the judges or those whom they respect, and the fact that what is said   1396a seems true should be clear to all or most people. And do not draw the conclusion only from what is necessarily valid, but also from what is true for the most part.

SPECIFIC TOPICS OF ENTHYMEMES

4. First, then, one should grasp that on whatever subject there is need to speak or reason it is necessary to have the facts belonging to that subject,[125] whether from political or any other argument, either all or some of them; for if you had none, you would have nothing from which to draw a conclusion. 5. I mean, for example, how could we advise the Athenians whether to go to war or not without knowing what their forces are and how great, whether naval or infantry or both; and what revenues they have or friends or enemies; further, what wars they have fought and how; and other such things. 6. Or [how could we] praise [the Athenians] if we did not know about the sea battle at Salamis or the fight at Marathon, or [how could we praise the Spartans without knowing] the things done by the Children of Heracles or something of that sort? All [speakers] base their praise on fine things that are, or seem to be, relevant facts. 7. Similarly, too, [speakers] blame [the Athenians] on the basis of the opposites,

---

122. In rhetoric, the conclusion should not be drawn from a series of premises with supporting reasons, which a popular audience will find difficult to follow, and some of the premises can be assumed as obvious. A good example of what not to do in a speech is the convoluted sentence in 2.18.1.

123. Cf. Euripides, *Hippolytus* 988–989.

124. Reading *horismenois* as conjectured by Kassel (1976).

125. *Ta hyparkhonta*; the word recurs throughout the chapter and needs to be translated as the context seems to demand. It refers to what underlies or is inherent in a subject, its natural or logical attributes, relevant facts or information, etc.

looking for something [bad that] applies to them or seems to, for example, that they subjugated the Greeks and enslaved the Aeginetans and Potidaeans, who had fought with them against the barbarian and done valorous deed, and other such things and [looking for] whether some other error in judgment is attributed to them. In the same way, those making an accusation and those making a defense do so by considering the relevant facts. 8. It makes no difference whether the subject is Athenians or Lacedaimonians or man or god; the same thing is done. In advising Achilles, [for example,] and praising or blaming him and attacking or defending him, we should take up the relevant facts—or what seem to be the facts—about him in order to say on the basis of these if there is evidence of something honorable or shameful when we are praising or blaming; and of something just or unjust when we are accusing or defending; and of something advantageous or harmful when we are advising. 9. The same is true about any subject whatever; for example, whether justice is a good or not on the basis of the attributes of justice and the good.

10. As a result, since everyone seems to demonstrate arguments in this way, whether they reason in accordance with strict logic or more loosely (they do not take propositions from all sources but from those that are relevant to each subject), and since it is impossible through speech to demonstrate anything in any other way, it is evident that it is first necessary, as [described] in the *Topics*,[126] to have selected statements about what is possible and most suited to the subject, 11. and, when unexpected problems occur, to try to follow the same method, looking not to the undefined but to what inherently belongs to the subject of the discourse and marking off as many [facts] as possible and what are most closely relevant to the subject; for the more relevant facts [are] at hand, the easier it is to offer a demonstration; and the more closely related they are, the more at home [in a particular speech] and less common. 12. By *common* I mean praising Achilles because he was a man and one of the demigods and because he went on the expedition against Ilium; for these facts apply to many others, so such remarks do not praise Achilles any more than Diomedes. *Specifics* [*idia*] are what apply to no one other than Achilles; for example, his killing of Hector, the best of the Trojans, and of Cycnus, who prevented all [the Greeks] from disembarking and was invulnerable, and [praising Achilles] because he was the

1396b

---

126. *Topics* 1.4–15.

youngest of those who went on the expedition and the one who had not sworn [to defend Menelaus' right to Helen], and anything else of this sort.

Now one way of selecting [enthymemes, and] this the first [in importance], is the "topical," 13. so let us discuss these elements [*stoikheia*] of enthymemes; and by *element* and *topic* of an enthymeme, I mean the same thing.[127] 14. But first, let us say some things that are necessary to say first; for there are two species of enthymemes: some are *demonstrative* [*deiktika*] of the fact that something is or is not the case, and others are *refutative* [*elentika*], and the difference is like that in dialectic between refutation and syllogism. 15. The demonstrative enthymeme draws a conclusion from what is agreed, the refutative draws conclusions that are not agreed to [by the opponent]. 16. Now the topics [*topoi*][128] concerned with each of the species [of rhetoric] that are useful and necessary are more or less understood by us; for the propositions concerned with each have been collected and as a result the [specific] topics that are sources of enthymemes about good or evil, or honorable or shameful, or just or unjust [are known], and topics concerned with characters and emotions and moral habits, having been collected in a similar way, are already at hand. 17. But in what follows let us take up the subject as a whole in a different way, considering [those topics that apply to] all [species of rhetoric], and let us discuss it while taking note of refutative and demonstrative [enthymemes] and those of apparent enthymemes, which are not enthymemes since they are not really syllogisms. When we have made these things clear in a supplementary discussion,[129] we shall offer definitions of the sources from which refutations and objections should be brought to bear on enthymemes.

1397a

---

127. This sentence is apparently a transition, not to what immediately follows but to ch. 23. The last clause is repeated in 2.26.1. *Topics* thus refers to the common topics of ch. 23. What Aristotle has been discussing up to this point are *idia*, or premises relating to specific subjects. Sections 14–17 are perhaps a later addition, in which case Aristotle's decision to refer to *idia* as topics was a late stage in the composition of the *Rhetoric*.

128. I.e., the *idia*, discussed in Book 1, chs. 4–14 and the premises for ethical and pathetical *pisteis* discussed in chs. 2–7 of Book 2. In neither of these passages are they called "topics."

129. *Parasēmainomenoi*. Chapters 23–24 are thus a supplement, apparently added to the work at a late stage in its development; cf. Düring 1966:143.

Chapter 23: Topoi, *or Common Topics*

■ In this chapter Aristotle lists twenty-eight *topoi* of enthymemes. These are lines or strategies of argument, useful in treating many different subject matters in all three species of rhetoric. They thus contrast with the *idia*, "specifics," or "particular topics" on politics and ethics defined in 1.2.21 and discussed throughout Book 1. On Aristotle's use of the term *topos*, see comments prefixed to 1.2.21 and note thereon. Some topics listed here are also discussed in Aristotle's *Topics*. For examples of their use in the Greek orators, see Palmer 1914; for their later history, including Cicero's discussion in his *Topica*, see Reinhardt 2003:18–35; for comparison to the topical system of Perelman and Olbrechts-Tyteca, see Barbara Warnick, "Two Systems of Invention," in Gross and Walzer 2000:107–129; for modern applications see David Fleming, "Becoming Rhetorical: An Education in the Topics," in Petraglia and Bahri 2003:93–116.

Topic 1: From opposites. 1. One *topos* of demonstrative [enthymemes] is that from opposites [*ek tōn enantiōn*]; for one should look to see if the opposite [predicate] is true of the opposite [subject], [thus] refuting the argument if it is not, confirming it if it is: for example, that to be temperate is a good thing; for to lack self control is harmful. Or, as in the *Messeniacus*,[130] "If the war is the cause of present evils, things should be set right by making peace." [Or]

> For since it is unjust to fall into anger
> At those who have unwillingly done wrong,
> If someone benefits another perforce
> It is not appropriate for thanks to be owed.[131]

[Or]

> But since, old man, false statements are persuasive
> Among mortals, you should believe the opposite too:
> That many truths turn out to be incredible to mortals.[132]

Topic 2: From grammatical form. 2. Another is from [different] grammatical forms of the same word [*ek tōn homoiōn ptōseōn*]; for the same [predicate] should be true or not true; for example, [to say] that the just is not entirely good; for then what is done *justly* would be a good, but as it is, to be put to death justly is not desirable.

---

130. The speech of Alcidamas mentioned in 1.13.2.
131. The passage is in iambic trimeter and thus probably comes from some lost drama.
132. Euripides, *Thyestes*, frag. 396; see Grimaldi 1988, 2:294.

Topic 3: From correlatives. 3. Another is from correlatives [*ek tōn pros allēla*]; for if to have done honorably or justly is predicated of one of a pair, to have experienced [it honestly or justly] belongs to the others, and if [one person has the right] to give an order, [the other has the right] also to act; for example, what Diomedon the tax farmer said about the taxes: "If it is not shameful for you to sell them, neither is it for me to buy."[133] And if something is honorably or justly predicated of one who experiences it, it is also of one who does it. But there is in this the possibility of false reckoning; for if someone has experienced something justly, he has justly experienced, but perhaps not from *you*. Thus, one ought separately to look at whether the sufferer deserves to suffer and whether the agent of the suffering is the right person to have acted, then to use whichever argument fits; for sometimes there is disagreement in such cases, and nothing prevents [a response] like this in the *Alcmeon* of Theodectes: [Alphesiboa asks,] "Did no one of mortals loathe your mother?" In reply, [Alcmeon] says, "But one should examine the statement by taking it apart." And when Aphesiboa asks how, he takes it up and says,   **1397b**

They judged she should die, but not that I should kill her.[134]

Another example is in the trial of Demosthenes and those who killed Nicanor;[135] for since the jury thought he had been justly killed, it seemed that they justly killed him. Also the case of the man murdered at Thebes, about whom [the defendant] demands a judgment as to whether he justly deserved to die, on the ground that it was not unjust to kill someone who died justly.[136]

---

133. Greek and Roman cities, like the French government under the monarchy, sold the right to collect taxes to private individuals or groups who hoped to make a profit. Numerous abuses occurred; thus, some thought the procedure shameful.

134. Theodectes is described by later writers as having been a student of Plato and Isocrates and a friend of Aristotle, who quotes him repeatedly in this chapter. He was one of the best-known tragedians of the time, as well as a prominent orator. Alcmeon, like Orestes, murdered his mother, was driven mad, and eventually was purified. Alphesiboa was his wife.

135. Most commentators agree that the Demosthenes mentioned here is not the famous orator; his life is very well known, and there is no mention in the sources of his being involved in any such trial. Dionysius of Halicarnassus (*To Ammaeus* 1.12) unconvincingly sought to identify this trial with Demosthenes' defense of Ctesiphon in 330 B.C.E., which would make it by several years the latest historical reference in the *Rhetoric*.

136. Some editors move the last two sentences of this section back to follow the story of Diomedon; Kassel (1976) double-bracketed them as a later addition by Aristotle.

Topic 4: From the more and the less. 4. Another is from the more and less [*ek tou mallon kai hētton*];[137] for example, "If not even the gods know everything, human beings can hardly do so"; for this is equivalent [to saying,] "If something is not the fact where it would be more [expected], it is clear that it is not a fact where it would be less." Also, [the argument] that "a person who had beaten his father has also beaten his neighbors" follows from [the proposition that] if the lesser thing is true, the greater is also; for people strike their father less than their neighbors. Or [one can argue] as follows: either "if something is not the fact in a case where it would be more [expected, etc.]" or "if in a case where it would be less [expected, etc.]," according to whichever there is need to show, whether that something is or is not the fact.[138]

Topic 4a: From analogy or precedent. 5. Further, [there is a related form of argument] if [something is] neither more nor less.[139] This is the source of the statement,

> Your father is pitiable for having lost his children;
> Is Oeneus not also then, for having lost a famous offspring?[140]

And [the argument] that if Theseus did no wrong [in abducting Helen], neither did Alexander [i.e., Paris, who abducted her later]; and if not the sons of Tyndareus [who abducted women], then not Alexander; and if Hector [did no wrong in killing] Patroclus, Alexander also [did no wrong in killing] Achilles. And if other professionals are not contemptible, neither are philosophers. And if generals are not contemptible because they are often put to death, neither are sophists.[141] And [the argument] that "if a private individual should care about your reputation, you should care about that of Greece."[142]

---

137. See 1.2.21.

138. This sentence has a number of textual problems, but the argument seems clear. Depending on what you want to prove, you can argue either that if B is more likely to be true of A than of C but is *not* true of A, then it is less likely to be true of C; or that if B is less likely to be true of C than of A but *is* true of C, then it is more likely to be true of A; see Grimaldi 1988, 2:298–299.

139. This would seem to deserve to be a distinct topic, though editors and translators do not so treat it.

140. The name Oeneus indicates this is from a play about his son Meleager, perhaps by Antiphon.

141. The reference is probably to the execution of the Athenian generals after the naval battle of Arginusae in 406 B.C.E. and to the execution of Antiphon the Sophist after the revolution of 411. But "often" is odd, and possibly the text is corrupt. Cope [1877] 1970, 2:249) conjectured "are defeated" for "put to death."

142. "You" is plural and presumably refers to the Athenian citizens. Source unknown.

Topic 5: From looking at the time (a fortiori). 6. Another is from looking at the time [*ek tou ton khronon skopein*];[143] for example, what Iphicrates said in the [suit] against Harmodius: "If, before accomplishing anything, I asked to be honored with a statue if I succeeded, you would have granted it. Will you not grant it [now] that I have succeeded? Do not then make a promise in anticipation but refuse it in realization."[144] Another example: on the subject of [allowing] Philip to pass through Thebes into Attica [the Macedonian ambassador said] that if [the request had been made] before [Philip] decided to help [the Thebans by moving] into Phocis, [the Thebans] would have promised [to let him pass through their territory into Attica]; it is strange, then,   if they will not let him pass [now] because he let that opportunity go and trusted them.[145]

Topic 6: From turning the argument on the opponent. 7. Another is from [turning] what has been said against oneself upon the one who said it [*ex tōn eirēmenōn kath hautou pros ton eiponta*], but the way of doing it differs [with the context]. For example, in the *Teucer* [of Sophocles]. . . .[146] And [there is] the argument Iphicrates used against Aristophon when he asked [the latter] if he would betray the fleet for money. After [Aristophon] denied it, [Iphicrates] said, "If you, being Aristophon, would not play the traitor, would I, Iphicrates?"[147] But the opponent should be the one who seems more likely to have done wrong. Otherwise, it would seem ludicrous if someone were to say

---

143. This comes to be known as a *plastos*, or "fictive" argument; cf. Quintilian 5.10.95–99, Pseudo-Hermogenes, *On Invention* 3.11. As given here it is closely related to the more and the less, for it contrasts what was or would have been true in the past with what is more true in the present. It is thus a variety of argument *a fortiori* (from the stronger).

144. In 390 B.C.E. a statue was voted in honor of the general Iphicrates for his services to Athens. When after twenty years it had not been erected he brought successful action to implement the grant. Dionysius of Halicarnassus (*Lysias* 836d) thought the speech was written for Iphicrates by Lysias.

145. The first incident took place in 346 B.C.E., the second in 339. This is one of the last datable references in the *Rhetoric*, added to the text in advance of Aristotle's return to Athens in 335. The Thebans refused permission, and the result was the definitive defeat of the Greeks, including Athens and Thebes, at Chaeronea in 338.

146. The example was either never filled in by Aristotle or has been lost.

147. The occasion was probably allegations of treachery against Iphicrates during the Social War of 357–355 B.C.E. The basis of the argument is the contrasting reputation of the two speakers. We thus have an example of an enthymeme whose topics are matters of ethos. Note that an enthymeme, like a syllogism, can take the form *if . . . then*. If B is predicated of A, and C is greater than A, then B can be predicated of C. But the statement is only possibly true, not valid in formal logic.

this in reply[, for example,] to a prosecution by Aristides,[148] but [it should be used] for discrediting the accuser; for the accuser always wants to be morally superior to the defendant. This, then, should be disproved. In general, it is out of place when someone reproaches others for [failing to do] what he does not do—or would not do—himself.

Topic 7: From definition. 8. Another is from definition [*ex horismou*]; for example, What is the divine? Is it not either a god or the work of a god? Still, whoever thinks it is the work of god must also think that gods exist.[149] And [another example is,] as Iphicrates [argued], that the best person is the most noble; for there was no noble quality in Harmodius and Aristogiton until they did something noble, while he himself was more like them [than his opponent was]: "At least, my deeds are more like those of Harmodius and Aristogiton than yours are."[150] And [another example is,] as [said] in the *Alexander*,[151] that all would agree that those who are not well-behaved are not content with the enjoyment of one [woman's] body. And [another is] the reason Socrates gave for refusing to visit Archelaus; for he said *hybris* was just as much an inability on the part of those benefited to return a favor as [it was retaliation by] those harmed.[152] For all these [speakers], by making definitions and grasping the essence of a thing, draw syllogistic conclusions about the subject they are discussing.

Topic 8: From varied meanings. 9. Another is from the varied meanings [of a word] [*ek tou posakhōs*], as discussed in the *Topics* on the meaning of *oxus*.[153]

---

148. Aristides "the Just," an early fifth-century B.C.E. statesman.

149. An apparent reference to Socrates' argument in Plato, *Apology* 27b–c.

150. From the speech mentioned in 2.23.6. Iphicrates' opponent named Harmodius was apparently a descendant, direct or collateral, of the celebrated Athenian hero of the same name, who, together with his lover Aristogiton, killed Hipparchus, brother of the tyrant Hippias, in 514 B.C.E. Though this was really a private quarrel, they were honored with statues in the marketplace as tyrannicides. As the earlier passage indicates, Iphicrates was claiming his right to a statue.

151. An epideictic speech, perhaps by Polycrates; cf. 2.24.7, 2.24.9, and 3.14.3.

152. This statement is otherwise unknown. Archelaus was king of Macedon. Though he could lavish favors, Socrates thought ill of him; see Plato, *Gorgias* 470c–471d.

153. *Oxus* (sharp)—in music the opposite of *flat*, of a knife the opposite of *dull*. See *Topics* 1.15. *Oxus* was a conjecture of Thurot, accepted by Kassel (1976) and probable correct. The manuscripts read *orthōs* (rightly), but this does not occur in the *Topics*. Grimaldi (1988, 2:309) kept *orthōs* and translated it "as has been mentioned in the topical discipline concerning the right use of a word."

Topic 9: From division. 10. Another is from division [*ek diaireseōs*]; for example, if [one says,] "All people do wrong for one of three reasons: either for this, or this, or this; now two of these are impossible, but even [the accusers] themselves do not assert the third."[154]

Topic 10: From induction. 11. Another is from induction [*ex epagōgēs*]; for example, in the case of the woman of Peparethus [it was argued] that women everywhere discern the truth about [the father of] children; for when the orator Mantias at Athens was disputing [the parentage of] his son, the boy's mother declared the truth.[155] Similarly, when Ismenias and Stilbon were in a dispute at Thebes, the woman of Dodona identified the son of Ismenias; and for this reason Thettaliscus was recognized as Ismenias' son. And again, [another example is] from the *Law* speech of Theodectes[156] [to the effect that] if people do not entrust their horses to those who take poor care of others' horses nor ships to those who have overturned others' ships—if then this is similarly true in all cases—one should not employ for one's own safety those who have poorly guarded the safety of another. And [another example is] as Alcidamas [argued], that all honor the wise; at least, Parians honored Archilochus despite the nasty things he said [about them]; and Chians Homer, though he was not a citizen; and Mytilenaeans Sappho, although a woman; and Lacedaimonians, though least fond of literature, made Chilon a member of their council of elders, and the Italiotes honored Pythagoras and the Lampsacenes buried Anaxagoras, though a foreigner, and even now still honor him. And Athenians were prosperous while using the laws of Solon, and Lacedaimonians when [using] those of Lycurgus; and at Thebes, at the time the leaders became philosophers, the city prospered.[157]

Topic 11: From authority. 12. Another [topic] is from a [previous] judgment [*ek kriseōs*] about the same or a similar or opposite matter, especially if all always [make this judgment]—but if not, at least most people, or the wise (either all of them or most) or the good;[158] or if the

1398b

---

154. The use of logical divisions in rhetoric is recommended in Plato's *Phaedrus* 265e–266a and is the method followed in Gorgias' *Helen*; see Appendix I.A.

155. Mantias was forced to recognize two illegitimate sons. The incident provides the background for Demosthenes' speeches *Against Boeotus*.

156. On Theodectes, see 2.23.13.

157. Kassel (1976) double-bracketed this sentence as a later addition by Aristotle. The "philosophers" at Thebes are presumably Epaminondas and Pelopidas in the years 371–361 B.C.E.

158. The phraseology is reminiscent of the basis of dialectic in generally accepted opinions as described in *Topics* 1.1.

judges themselves [have so decided] or those whom the judges approve or those whose judgment cannot be opposed, for example, those with legal authority to make it or whose judgment cannot be honorably opposed, for example, the gods, a father, or teachers, as Autocles said against Mixidemides: "If it is right for the Dread Goddesses to stand trial in the Areopagus, should not Mixidemides?"[159] Or as Sappho said, that it is bad to die; for the gods have so judged; for otherwise they would die. Or as Aristippus [replied] to Plato, when the latter said something rather dogmatic, as he thought: "But our companion," he said, "would have said nothing of the sort," meaning Socrates. And at Delphi Agesipolis, after earlier consulting oracles at Olympia, asked the god if his opinion was the same as his father's, implying it would be shameful for him to say contradictory things.[160] And as Isocrates wrote about Helen, that she was virtuous, since Theseus so judged; and about Alexander, whom the goddesses preferred to others; and about Evagoras, that he was virtuous, so Isocrates claims: for at any rate Conon, leaving all others aside, came to him [for help].[161]

Topic 12: From subordinate parts. 13. Another [topic] is from the parts [*ek tōn merōn*], as discussed in the *Topics*;[162] [for example,] What kind of motion is the soul? For it is this or that.[163] There is an example from the *Socrates* of Theodectes:[164] "Against what holy place has he profaned? Which gods that the city recognizes has he not believed in?"

Topic 13: From the consequence. 14. Another is to exhort or dissuade and accuse or defend and praise or blame on the basis of the consequence [*ek tou akolouthountos*], since in most instances it

---

159. The Dread Goddesses are the Furies, who appear as prosecutors of Orestes before Athena's court in Aeschylus' *Eumenides*. Autocles was active in military affairs in the 370s and 360s B.C.E. and, according to Demosthenes' *Against Phormio* (53), was prosecuted for some of his actions.

160. The god at Delphi was Apollo, son of Zeus, who was the god of Olympia.

161. Isocrates, *Helen* 18–22, 41–48; *Evagoras* 51–52.

162. *Topics* 2.4, beginning at 111a33. By *parts* is meant the species within a defined genus.

163. The kinds of motion as defined in *Categories* 14 are generation, destruction, increase, diminution, alteration, and change of place. Aristotle regarded the soul as the vital principle in living things and thus inherently some kind of motion.

164. Probably one of the *apologies* written by fourth-century B.C.E. authors, of which those by Plato and Xenophon survive. If, as it seems, Aristotle is quoting literally, use of the third person indicates that Theodectes' version took the imagined form of a speech by some advocate.

happens that something good and bad follows from the same [cause]. For example, being envied is an evil result of being educated, but the wisdom [acquired] is a good thing; therefore, [it may be argued,] one should not be educated; for one ought not be envied. On the other hand, one should be educated; for one ought to be wise. This topic constitutes the *Art* of Callippus, with the addition of the possible and other things that have been mentioned.[165]

Topic 14: From contrasting opposites. 15. Another: when there is need to exhort or dissuade on two matters that are contrasted [*peri duoin antikeimenoin*], [one needs] to use the method mentioned in both; but there is the difference that in the previous case any two things are contrasted, while here they are opposites. For example, a priestess did not allow her son to engage in public debate: "For," she said, "if you say what is just, the people will hate you, but if what is unjust, the gods will. On the other hand, you should engage in public debate; for if you speak what is just, the gods will love you, if what is unjust, the people will." This is the same as what is said about buying the marsh with the salt.[166] This dilemma [*blaisōsis*, "twist"] occurs whenever good and evil follow either of two things, each opposite to each.

Topic 15: From hypocritical deception. 16. Another: when [one's opponents] do not praise the same things openly as they do secretly [*ou phanerōs kai aphanōs*], but to a great extent openly praise the just and beautiful while privately they wish rather for what is to their advantage, try to draw the other conclusion from what they say; for this is the most effective topic in dealing with paradoxes.

Topic 16: From consequences by analogy. 17. Another is from consequences by analogy [*ek tou analogon symbainein*]. For example, when they tried to force his son who was underage to perform public services because he was tall, Iphicrates said that if they deem large boys men, they should vote that small men are boys. And Theodectes in the *Law* [speech said],[167] "Since you are making citizens of mercenary soldiers, for example, Strabax and Charidemus, because of their merits, will you not make exiles of those among the mercenaries who have wrought irreparable damage?"

1399b

---

165. Callippus was a student of Isocrates and author of a handbook. "The other things" are presumably the impossible, past and future fact, and magnitude, as described in 2.19.

166. Apparently a proverb, equal to "taking the bad with the good." Salt was chiefly obtained from evaporating seawater in marshes.

167. See 2.23.11.

Topic 17: From results to causes. 18. Another is from [arguing] that if some result is the same [*to symbainon t' auton*], the things from which it resulted are also. For example, Xenophanes[168] said that those who say that the gods are born are as impious as those who say that they die; for in both cases, the result is that at some time the gods do not exist. And in general [this topic is a matter of] taking the result of each thing as always the same. [For example,] "You are going to make a judgment not about Isocrates, but about education: whether it is right to study philosophy."[169] And that to give "earth and water" is to be a slave, and that to share in the "common peace" is to do what is commanded. One should take up whichever argument is useful.[170]

Tonic 18: From contrasted choices. 19. Another is from not always choosing the same thing before or after [an event], but the reverse [*ek tou anapalin haireisthai*]; for example, this enthymeme: "[It would be terrible] if when in exile we fought to come home, but having come home we shall go into exile in order not to fight."[171] Sometimes people have chosen to be at home at the cost of fighting, sometimes not to fight at the cost of not remaining at home.

Topic 19: From identifying purpose with cause. 20. Another is to say that the purpose [*to hou heneka*] for which something might exist or might happen is the cause for which it does exist or has happened; for example, if someone gave somebody something so that he could cause him pain after he took it away. This is also the source of the following [quotation from some unidentified tragedy]:

> God gives great good fortune to many, not out of good will,
> But so that the disasters people experience may be more obvious.

---

168. Xenophanes of Colophon, sixth-century B.C.E. philosopher and poet who criticized conventional views of the gods.

169. Though the manuscripts read "Socrates," the quotation is an approximation of what Isocrates says in *Antidosis* 173–175.

170. That is, one can argue that these results do follow or that the specific action does not have the significance being given to it. Earth and water were demanded of the Greeks by the Persian king during the invasion of 480–479 B.C.E. as a symbol of acceptance of his domination; to offer it was thus thought to lead to slavery. The "common peace" is probably that forced on the Greek cities by Macedon after the Battle of Chaeronea in 338. Ratification was not complete until 336, and this is often regarded as the latest datable reference in the *Rhetoric*. It is used by Rist (1989:85–86) as part of his argument that Aristotle completed the *Rhetoric after* his return to Athens in 335.

171. Apparently an adaptation of Lysias 34.11 on the situation in Athens in 403 B.C.E.; but see Trevett 1996:372. Aristotle has carelessly omitted the clause that justifies calling this an enthymeme.

And this from the *Meleager* of Antiphon:

> Not that they may kill the beast, but that
> They may be witnesses to Greece of the courage of Meleager.[172]

And from the *Ajax* of Theodectes, that Diomedes chose Odysseus not out of honor to him but in order that his companion might be inferior; for he could have done it for this reason.[173]

Topic 20: From reasons for and against. 21. Another that is common both to litigants and deliberative speakers is to look at what turns the mind in favor and what turns the mind against something [*ta protreptonta kai apotreponta*] and for what reasons people both act and avoid action. For these are the factors that if present, impel action [but if not present, deter action]; for example, [consider] if [an action was] possible and easy and advantageous to a person or friends or harmful to enemies and, if punishable, [consider whether] the punishment is less than the reward of the action. People are urged on for these reasons and dissuaded by their opposites, and they use these same arguments in accusation and defense: they defend themselves by drawing on reasons that deter, and they prosecute by drawing on those that encourage. This topic is the whole *Art* of Pamphilus and Callippus.[174]

Topic 21: From the implausible. 22. Another is derived from things that are thought to have taken place but yet are implausible [*ek tōn apistōn*], [using the argument] that they would not seem true unless they were facts or close to being facts. And [one can argue] that they are all the more true [for that reason]; for people accept facts or probabilities as true; if, then, something were implausible and not probable, it would be true; for it is not because of probability and plausibility that it seems true [but because it is a fact].[175] For example, when Andocles of Pittheus was speaking against a law and said, "Laws need a law to correct them," there was general outcry against him. [He continued,] "And fishes need salt" (although it is neither probable nor credible that creatures born in the sea would need salt)

1400a

---

172. See note on 2.23.5. The "beast" was a wild boar.

173. The situation is the night embassy described in *Iliad* 10.

174. Since in 2.23.14 Aristotle mentions other topics discussed by Callippus, "whole" should not be taken literally. Pamphilus is a little-known earlier rhetorician, whose handbook is described by Cicero (*On the Orator* 3.82), probably derived from Aristotle's *Synagoge*, as "puerile."

175. Cf. the argument attributed to Tertullian (though not found in his writings) that he believed in Christianity "because it is absurd."

"and pressed olives need oil" (though it is strange that things from which oil comes would need oil).[176]

Topic 22: From contradictions. 23. Another is refutative, a matter of looking at contradictions [*ta anomologoumena*] [in three ways]: once as applies only to the opponent (if something is contradicted by all dates, actions, and words);[177] for example, "And he says he loves you, but he took the oath with the Thirty";[178] once as applicable to the speaker: "And he says I am litigious, but he cannot show that I have brought any case to be judged in court"; and once as applicable to the speaker and the opponent: "And he has never lent any money, but I have even ransomed many of you."

Topic 23: From the cause of a false impression. 24. Another, in reference to human beings or actions that have been prejudged or seem to have been, is to state the cause of the false impression [*to legein tēn aitian tou paradoxou*]; for there is some reason why it seems true; for example, when a certain woman claimed that her son was the child of a different mother, because she embraced him she was thought to be involved with him as her lover, but when the reason was explained [i.e., that he really was her son] she was freed from slander. Another example is in the *Ajax* of Theodectes: Odysseus tells Ajax why he [Odysseus] does not seem braver than Ajax, although he really is.

Topic 24: From cause and effect. 25. Another is from the cause [*apo tou aitiou*] [and effect]: if the cause exists, so does the effect; if it does not, there is no effect. The cause and that of which it is the cause go together, and without cause there is nothing. For example, when Leodamas was defending himself against Thrasybulus' charge that his name had been cut out [from some inscription] in the time of the Thirty [Tyrants], he said it was not possible; for the Thirty would have trusted him more if his hatred of the democracy had remained inscribed.

Topic 25: From a better plan. 26. Another is to see if there was or is a better plan of a different sort [*ek beltion allōs*] from what is advised or is being done or has been done; for it is evident that if this is so, it has not been acted on; for no one willingly and knowingly chooses the bad.[179] But this may be false reasoning; for it often later

1400b

---

176. Andocles was an Athenian demagogue of the late fifth-century B.C.E.

177. Kassel (1976) double-bracketed what is here in parentheses as a late addition by Aristotle; other editors move it back before the previous clause.

178. "You" (plural) is the Athenian people; the Thirty are the Thirty Tyrants of 404 B.C.E.

179. The negative of this is the major argument in Demosthenes' speech *On the Crown* in defense of his policy against Macedon: there was no better plan.

becomes clear how things could have been better done but earlier it was unclear.

Topic 26: From comparison of contraries. 27. Another, when something is about to be done that is contrary to what has been done, is to look at them together [*hamaskopein*]. For example, when the people of Elea asked Xenophanes if they should sacrifice and sing dirges to Leucothea or not, he advised them not to sing dirges if they regarded her as a god, and if as a human being not to sacrifice.[180]

Topic 27: From what would have been a mistake. 28. Another topic is to accuse or defend on the basis of what would have been a mistake [*ek tōn hamartēthentōn*]. For example, in the *Medea* of Carcinus[181] some accuse her on the ground that she has killed her children. At any rate, they are not to be seen; for Medea made the mistake of sending the children away. But she defends herself on the ground that [it is improbable she has killed them, because] she would have killed Jason [then as well], not [only] the children; for she would have made a mistake in not doing so if she had done the other thing. This topic and species of enthymeme is the whole art before Theodorus.[182]

Topic 28: From the meaning of a name. 29. Another is from a name [*apo tou onomatos*], for example, as in Sophocles,

When [your mother] named you Sidero she clearly meant it.[183]

And [another example is] as people are accustomed to speak in praises of the gods,[184] and as Conon called Thrasybulus *thrasboulon* ["bold in counsel"] and as Herodicus[185] said to Thrasymachus, "You are always *thrasymakhos* ["bold in fight"] and to Polus, "You are always a *polus* ["a colt"], and of Dracon the lawgiver that his laws were not those of a human being but of a *drakon* ["snake"]; for they were harsh. And [another example is] as Hecuba in Euripides says of Aphrodite,

---

180. Leucothea (White Goddess) in Greek mythology was daughter of Cadmus, the legendary king of Thebes, and originally named Ino. She was regarded as transformed into a sea goddess. Xenophanes is the sixth-century B.C.E. philosopher and poet. For the example to be apposite the Eleans must earlier have either sacrificed to her or sung dirges.

181. Early fourth-century B.C.E. tragic poet.

182. Rhetorician of the late fifth century B.C.E.; see Appendix II.A.

183. *Sidērō* (feminine noun) means iron. Tyro, in the lost play by that name, is apparently addressing his cruel stepmother.

184. Perhaps an example has been lost here. The medieval commentator Stephanus suggests "Zeus is given his name as the cause of life (*zōēs*)."

185. Late fifth-century B.C.E. physician and apparently inveterate punster.

And rightly the name of the goddess begins like *aphrosynē*.[186]

And as Chaeremon [said]

Pentheus, named from his future unhappy fate.[187]

30. Refutative enthymemes are better liked [by audiences] than demonstrative ones because the refutative enthymeme is a bringing together of opposites in brief form, and when these are set side by side they are clearer to the hearer. In the case of all syllogistic argument, both refutative and demonstrative, those are most applauded that [hearers] foresee from the beginning, but not because they are superficial (at the same time, too, people are pleased with themselves when anticipating [the conclusion]), and [they like] those they are slower to apprehend to the extent that they understand when these have been stated.

Chapter 24: Real and Apparent, or Fallacious, Enthymemes

■ The main function of this chapter is not to teach how to compose fallacious enthymemes, though Aristotle's wording at times seems to imply that, but to help a speaker recognize them when employed by others. Grimaldi appositely quoted (1988, 2:337) Aristotle's remarks in *Sophistic Refutations* (165a24–27): "It is the task of one who has knowledge about a thing to speak the truth about what he knows, and to be able to expose the individual who makes false statements." Some of the fallacies discussed here are also treated in *Sophistic Refutations*, which is an appendix to Aristotle's *Topics*. Fallacious enthymemes doubtless often result from invalid premises, but Aristotle did not need to mention that here, where he is concerned with the structural topics that invalidate an argument.

1. But since it is possible for [a logical argument] to be a syllogism or for it not to be a syllogism but to appear to be one, necessarily [a rhetorical argument] also may be an enthymeme or not be an enthymeme but appear to be one, inasmuch as an enthymeme is a sort of syllogism.

1401a   *Fallacious topic 1: From verbal style.* 2. One kind of *topoi* of apparent enthymemes is verbal [*para tēn lexin*] and of this one part resembles what occurs in dialectic when the final statement takes the

---

186. *Trojan Women* 990, "folly," but the words come from different roots.
187. *Penthos,* or "sorrow." He was destined to go mad and kill his mother.

form of a conclusion without constituting a [valid] syllogism ("since such and such [is true], necessarily also this and that follows"), and in the case of enthymemes a statement appears to be an enthymeme whenever it is spoken compactly and antithetically; for verbal style of this sort is the place where an enthymeme is at home, and such seems to result from the shape of the expression. For purposes of speaking in verbally [i.e., not logically valid] syllogistic form it is useful to enumerate the headings of several syllogisms; [for example,] that [Evagoras] saved some, avenged others, and freed the Greeks.[188] Each of these statements has been demonstrated from other arguments, but when they are put together something else appears to result from them.

Another [verbal fallacy] is by use of homonyms,[189] as saying that a mouse [*mys*] is a worthy creature from which comes the most honored of all festivals; for the [celebration of the Eleusinian] *Mysteries* is the most honored of all. Or if someone delivered an encomium of the dog that included the Dog Star or [the god] Pan, because Pindar said [of Pan],

> O blessed one, whom the Olympians call dog
> Of the Great Goddess, taking every form.[190]

Or [if someone said that] because it is most dishonorable for there to be no "dog," thus clearly the dog is honored.[191] Or to say that Hermes is the "most sociable" [*koinōnikos*] of the gods; for he alone is called

---

188. Aristotle here draws on Isocrates' *Evagoras* (65–69), an epideictic speech honoring the king of Salamis in Cyprus, but he compresses Isocrates' argument into what he calls *kephalaia*, "headings" (actually conclusions), which then appear to support the proposition that Evagoras was brave, wise, and virtuous. By amplification of details, the audience's attention is drawn away from the logical weakness of the generalization, while at the same time a logical structure seems to be maintained that is emphasized by being stated in compact form.

189. Words that sound the same but have different meanings, thus verbal equivocations. *Mystery* is not derived from *mys* (mouse), though they sound the same, but from the verb *myein*, "to close the lips, keep secret."

190. Pindar, *Parthenia*, frag. 86. Pan was regarded as a doglike attendant on Cybele, mother goddess of all nature.

191. The metaphorical meaning of *dog* here is unclear, and the Greek could be translated "It is most dishonorable for no one to be a dog." Stephanus, the medieval Greek commentator, thought there was a reference to Diogenes the Cynic (Cynic = Dog). To call a person a dog in Greek was usually an insult, since dogs were thought shameless, but *dog* is occasionally used to mean watchman or attendant, as in the passage from Pindar, and something like that may have been in Aristotle's mind. "It is most dishonorable to have no attendant"? Compare Alexander Pope's epigram for a dog collar: "I am His Highness' dog at Kew. Pray tell me, Sir, Whose dog are you?"

"Hermes the Sharer" [*koinos*].[192] And that *logos* is the best thing, because good men are worthy not of money but of *logos* ["esteem"]; for "worthy of *logos*" has more than one meaning.

Fallacious topic 2: From combination or division; fallacy by omission. 3. Another is for the speaker to combine what is divided [*to diērēmenon syntithenta*] or divide what is combined; for since what is not the same often seems to be the same, whichever is more useful should be done. This was Euthydemus' form of argument, for example, his claim to know there was a trireme at the Peiraeus because he knew each of the terms,[193] and that by knowing the letters, he "knew" the word; for the word is the same thing [as the letters]. And since twice as much of a thing induces illness, one can say that a single portion is not healthful either; for it would be odd if two goods equaled one evil. This is in refutation, but in demonstration thus: [a double portion is healthful;] for one good thing cannot equal two bad ones. The whole topic is contrary to logic. Again, what Polycrates said in regard to Thrasybulus, that he deposed thirty tyrants; for he combines them.[194] Or what is in the *Orestes* of Theodectes; for it is from division: "It is just," for this woman to die, "who has killed a husband" and for the son to avenge the father; so then these things have been [justly]

1401b   done. But perhaps when they are combined it is no longer just. This would also be [a fallacy] by omission [*elleipsis*]; for it ignores the [just] agent.

Fallacious topic 3: From exaggeration. 4. Another topic is constructing or demolishing an argument by exaggeration [*to deinōsei kataskeuazein*]. This occurs when one amplifies the action without showing that it was performed; for when [the accused] amplifies the charge, he causes it to appear that he has not committed the action, or when the accuser goes into a rage [he makes it appear] that [the

---

192. Hermes, among other things, was god of good luck. If someone found something valuable, he exclaimed "Hermes *koinos*," meaning that he claimed a share of it.

193. He knew there was a place called the Peiraeus and such a thing as a trireme, or warship; therefore, combining things that are really separate, he knew there was a trireme at the Peiraeus, the port of Athens. Euthydemus was a sophist, best known from Plato's dialogue named for him. A fuller version of this fallacy is discussed in *Sophistic Refutations* 177b12–13.

194. Thrasybulus was a leader in ending the rule of the Thirty Tyrants in 404 B.C.E. This was really one tyranny by thirty individuals. If an award is to be paid to one who ends a tyranny, should he get thirty times the fixed amount? (Cf. Quintilian 3.6.26.) Polycrates was a sophist, active in the early fourth century B.C.E.

defendant] has. There is then no enthymeme; for the hearer falsely reckons that he did it or did not, although this has not been shown.

Fallacious topic 4: From a non-necessary sign. Another is from a [non-necessary] sign [*ek tou sēmeiou*]; for this, too, is non-syllogistic; for example, if someone were to say, "Lovers benefit cities; for the love of Harmodius and Aristogeiton destroyed the tyrant Hipparchus."[195] Or if someone were to say that Dionysius is a thief; for he is wicked. This is certainly nonsyllogistic: not every wicked man is a thief, but every thief is wicked.

Fallacious topic 5: From an accidental result. 6. Another is through an accidental result [*dia to symbebēkos*]; for example, Polycrates says of mice that they aided [the Egyptians] by gnawing the bowstrings [of the invading Assyrians].[196] Or if someone were to say that to be invited to dinner is the greatest form of honor; for Achilles' wrath against the Achaeans at Tenedos resulted from not being invited. But he was angry because of being dishonored, and not being invited to dinner was an accidental result of this.

Fallacious topic 6: From affirming the consequent. 7. Another is in terms of what follows [from a fallacious assumption] [*para to hepomenon*], for example, in the *Alexander*[197] [the claim] that [Paris] was "high-minded"; for looking down on the society of the multitude he passed his time by himself on Mount Ida. [The argument is] that because the high-minded have this quality, he, too, should be thought high-minded.[198] And when someone is a dandy and roams the streets at night, he is sexually promiscuous; for that is the way such people act. Similarly, too, because beggars sing and dance in temple precincts and because exiles can live wherever they want, since these things are true of those seeming to be happy, such people might seem to be happy. But there is a difference in the circumstances. Thus, it, too, falls under the [the fallacy of] omission.

Fallacious topic 7: From assuming "post hoc, ergo propter hoc." 8. Another is taking a non-cause as a cause [*para to anaition*]; for example, when something has happened at the same time or after [something else]; for people take what happens later as though it

---

195. See 2.23.8.
196. See Herodotus 2.141.
197. The epideictic speech mentioned in 2.23.8.
198. I.e., Paris scorned the crowd; for he lived in the mountains. The high-minded scorn the crowd. Therefore, as a consequence, Paris is high-minded. But scorning the crowd is not convertible with being high-minded.

happened because of what proceeded, and especially people involved in politics, for example, the way Demades [regarded] the policy of Demosthenes as the cause of all evils; for the war took place after it.[199]

Fallacious topic 8: From omission of when and how. 9. Another is by omission of consideration of when and how [*para tēn elleipsin tou pote kai pōs*]; for example, [the argument] that Alexander took Helen justly; for free choice [of a husband] had been given her by her father. [This is fallacious;] for presumably [the choice was] not for all time, only for the first time;[200] for the father's authority only lasts to that point. Or if someone were to say that it is *hybris* to beat those who are free; [this is fallacious;] for it is not true, only when someone strikes the first blow.

Fallacious topic 9: From confusing the particular with the general. 10. Further, just as in eristics [i.e., sophistic debate] an apparent syllogism occurs in confusing what is general and what is not general [*para to haplōs kai mē haplōs*] but some particular (for example, in dialectic [asserting that] non-being exists; for what-is-not *is* what-is-not; and that the unknown is known, for it is *known* about the unknown that it is unknown), so also in rhetoric there is an apparent enthymeme in regard to what is not generally probable but probable in a particular case. The probability is not absolute, as Agathon,[201] too, says,

> Probably one could say that this thing itself is probable:
> Many improbable things happen to mortals.

For some things happen contrary to probability, so what is contrary to probability is also probable. If this is so, the improbable will be probable. But not generally so; as in eristics, not adding the circumstances and reference and manner makes for deception, so here [in rhetoric], because the probability is not general but qualified. 11. The *Art* of Corax is made up of this topic:[202] for example, if a weak man were charged with assault, he should be acquitted as not being a likely

---

199. This is the only certain reference to the orator Demosthenes in the *Rhetoric* and one of the latest historical references. "The war" is that between Athens and its allies and Macedon, culminating in the defeat of the Greeks at Chaeronea in 338 B.C.E. Demades' statement could have been made any time thereafter.

200. Her father was Tyndareus. Her first husband was Menelaus.

201. On Agathon, see note on 2.19.13.

202. Plato, *Phaedrus* 273a–b, attributes the following argument to Tisias; Corax ("Crow") is probably a nickname for Tisias of Syracuse; see Cole 1991b and Appendix II.A.

suspect for the charge; for it is not probable [that a weak man would attack another]. And if he *is* a likely suspect, for example, if he is strong, [he should be acquitted]; for it is not likely [that he would start a fight] for the very reason that it was going to seem probable. And similarly in other cases; for necessarily a person is either a likely suspect or not a likely suspect for a charge. Both alternatives seem probable, but only one really is probable, the other so not generally, only in the circumstances mentioned.[203] And this is "to make the weaker seem the better cause."[204] Thus, people were rightly angry at the declaration of Protagoras; for it is a lie and not true but a fallacious probability and a part of no art except rhetoric and eristic.[205] This concludes discussion of real and apparent enthymemes.

Chapter 25: Lysis, *or Refuting an Opponent's Enthymemes*

■ *Lysis* literally means "unloosing" or "undoing" the logical ties of a syllo-gism or enthymeme. *Enstasis,* literally "stepping in," is used here to mean an objection to a premise in the opponent's argument. In 3.17.13 the word for "refutation" in a speech is *elengkhos.*

1. The next point in the continuing discussion is to speak about refutation [*lysis*]. It is possible to refute either by stating an opposite syllogism or by bringing an objection [*enstasis*]. 2. Now, clearly, an opposite syllogism can be made from the same topics [as the opponent

---

203. The second possibility, that the strong man would have realized he would seem to have been the aggressor, requires a specific knowledge of the circumstances and the character of the individuals involved.

204. This is what sophists were accused of doing; cf. Aristophanes, *Clouds* 889–1104; Plato, *Apology* 18b. But willingness to give a hearing to the weaker cause, in the sense of an unpopular view or something challenging the conventional views of society, e.g., the rights of minorities or women, has proved basic to freedom of speech.

205. According to Diogenes Laertius (9.52), the opening sentence of Protagoras' now lost treatise *On the Gods* caused him to be expelled from Athens and his books burned. It read, "Concerning the gods, I cannot know either that they exist or that they do not exist; for there is much to prevent one's knowing: the obscurity of the subject and the shortness of life." This declaration, although repugnant to the Athenians, was a statement of agnosticism based on reasoning and does not seem to deserve Aristotle's strong criticism. Perhaps more likely objectionable to Aristotle was the equally famous declamation of relativism that opened Protagoras' treatise *On Truth*: "Man is the measure of all things, of things that are insofar as they are, and of things that are not insofar as they are not" (Diogenes Laertius 7.60).

used but drawing the opposite conclusion]; for the syllogisms are derived from commonly held opinions [*endoxa*] and many opinions are opposed to each other.

3. Objections are brought, as has also been described in the *Topics*,[206] in four ways; for either they are derived from the original argument or from something similar or from the opposite or from what has been judged true. 4. By the original argument I mean, for example, if the enthymemes concerned love, claiming it was good, the objection [then] would be double; for it could be generally claimed that all lack is bad [and love is a feeling of lacking something]; or, taking one kind, [one could claim] that there would be no talk of Caunian love if there were not also bad forms.[207] 5. Objection is brought by the opposite if, for example, the enthymeme was that "a good man benefits all his friends"; [the objection is,] "But the wicked man does not harm [all his friends]." 6. [An objection is based] on something similar [to the original argument]; if the enthymeme was that those who suffer always hate [their oppressor], [the objection is,] "But those who are benefited do not always love [their benefactors]." 7. "Judgments" [*kriseis*] are those of well-known men; for example, if someone spoke the enthymeme that one should excuse those who are drunk, for their mistakes are made out of ignorance. The objection is that then Pittacus[208] didn't know what he was doing; for he legislated greater punishments if someone committed a misdeed when drunk.

8. Since enthymemes are drawn from four sources and these four are probability [*eikos*], paradigm, *tekmērion* [or necessary sign], and *sēmeion* [or fallible sign][209] (enthymemes from probability are drawn from things that either are, or seem for the most part to be, true; others come from example by induction of what is like, whether one thing or more, whenever a general statement is made and then supported by a particular instance; others are derived from a necessary and always existing sign; others from signs of what is generally or in part true or not) and since the probable is not always but for the most part true, it is clear that all these kinds of enthymemes can be refuted

---

206. The treatise as a whole, not any particular passage.

207. Caunian love is incest, named from Caunus' passion for his sister in mythology.

208. Author of laws at Mytilene in the early sixth century B.C.E.

209. See 1.2.14–18, where, however, paradigm (or example) is made coordinate with enthymeme rather than being one of its sources. But examples are used in enthymemes, and especially in refutation, where one example can refute a universal positive (e.g., U.S. presidents have not always lived in the White House; for George Washington never lived in the White House).

by bringing objections, but the refutation may be an apparent one, not always valid; 9. for the objector does not refute the probability but [shows] that [the conclusion in a particular case] is not necessary. 10. As a further result, the defendant always has an advantage over the prosecutor because of this fallacy; for since the prosecutor demonstrates by probabilities, and since it is not the same thing to show in refutation that an argument is not probable as to show it is not necessary, what is for the most part true is always open to objection; for otherwise it would not be *for the most part* and probable, but *always* and necessary. Yet when a refutation is made in this way, the judge thinks either that the thing is not probable or that it is not for him to decide, reasoning falsely as we said—[falsely] because he should not only judge from necessary arguments but from probable ones, too; for this is to judge "in accordance with the best understanding."[210] Therefore, it is not sufficient if one attacks an argument as "not necessary"; and one must refute it as "not probable." This will result if the objection is a more probable statement; 11. and that such is the case can be shown in two ways, either in terms of the time or the facts but most effectively if by both; for if something is often true, it is more probable.[211]   **1403a**

12. Signs [*sēmeia*] and enthymemes that draw a conclusion through a sign are refutable, even if true, as was said in the first [lectures];[212] for that every refutable sign is non-syllogistic is clear to us from the *Analytics*.[213] 13. The refutation of examples is the same as that of probabilities; for if we cite an example that does not accord with the [generalized] conclusion, the argument is refuted because it is not "necessary," even if something else is more often true or true in more cases. But if the larger number of instances is usually as the opponent says, one should contend that the present case is not similar or not in the same way or has some difference. 14. But *tekmēria* and enthymemes with infallible signs cannot be refuted as non-syllogistic (this is also clear from the *Analytics*), and what is left is to show that the alleged fact is not true. If it is evident that it is true and that there is an infallible sign of it, the argument is irrefutable from the start; for the whole demonstration is already evident.

---

210. For this phrase, part of the oath taken by jurors in Athens, see note on 1.15.5.

211. Consideration of time can involve showing that at a particular time a particular action was not, is not, or will not be probable and (to judge from the last clause) also that it is either probable as something that frequently was or is (and thus will be) done or improbable as rare.

212. In 1.2.16–18.

213. *Prior Analytics* 2.27.

Chapter 26: Amplification, Refutation, and Objection

■ Any of the topics can be amplified in a variety of ways and amplification thus has no identifiable logical structure of its own. There are additional comments on amplification as an aspect of style in 3.6.7 and 3.12.4.

1. To amplify [*to auxein*] or to deprecate [*to meioun*] is not an element [*stoikheion*] of an enthymeme. (I call the same things "element" and "topic"; for an element or a topic [is a heading] under which many enthymemes fall.)[214] To amplify and to deprecate contribute to showing that something is great or small, just as also [to showing that something is] good or evil or just or unjust and anything else, 2. but all these things are the subjects of syllogisms and enthymemes,[215] so if each of them is not a topic of an enthymeme, neither is amplification and deprecation.

3. Nor are refutative enthymemes a distinct species; for clearly, one refutes by proving something or bringing an objection, but these are a demonstration in response to the adversary's position; for example, if one side shows that something has happened, the other [tries to show] that it has not, and if the first shows that it has not, the second that it has. The result is that this would not be the difference; for they both use the same [forms of argument] and bring in enthymemes to show that something is or is not true. 4. "Objection" [*enstasis*] is not an enthymeme either; but, as in the *Topics*,[216] it is a matter of stating an opinion from which it will be clear that the opponent's argument does not constitute a syllogism or that he has introduced something false.

Transition to Book 3

Since there are in fact three things that should be systematically worked out in discussion of speech, 5. let us regard what has been said as enough about paradigms and maxims and enthymemes and in general about the thought [*dianoia*][217] and the sources of argument and how we shall refute them. It remains to go through an account of style [*lexis*] and arrangement [*taxis*].

1403b

---

214. Cf. 2.22.13.
215. That is, they are *idia* or *koina*. But *idia* have been called topics in 2.22.1 and 2.22.16 and *koina* seem to be so called in 3.19.2.
216. Perhaps *Topics* 1.10 is meant.
217. Or in later terminology, *heuresis*, "invention."

BOOK 3
Delivery, Style, and Arrangement

■ After a few remarks on delivery, chapters 1–12 contain a discussion of *lexis*, chapters 13–19 of *taxis*. *Lexis* (Latin *elocutio*) refers to the "way of saying something" in contrast to *logos*, "what is said," and is usually translated "style." In some passages Aristotle uses *lexis* in a broad sense of how thought is expressed in words, sentences, and a speech as a whole, but often he uses the term in the more restricted sense of "word choice, diction" (hence, English *lexical*). Translation needs to vary with context, and often it has seemed best to retain the Greek term and let the meaning emerge from the context. *Taxis* (Latin *dispositio*) means "arrangement" and refers to the "ordering" of the conventional parts of an oration, especially as seen in judicial speeches.

To judge from the list of Aristotle's works given by Diogenes Laertius (5.24), Book 3 was originally a separate work, and much of it was probably written during Aristotle's early teaching of rhetoric in Plato's Academy in the 350s B.C.E. Chapters 1–9 contain no references to events later than that time. Chapters 10 and 11 cite Isocrates' *Philippus* of 346 and have been written or revised after that date, perhaps when Aristotle was teaching Alexander. The *Philippus*, Isocrates' address to his father, Philip of Macedon, urging him to take leadership of the Greeks against Persia, would have been of special interest to the young man. Aristotle had a less mature grasp of the material on style than of the logical and ethical features of rhetoric discussed in Books 1 and 2. Chapters 5, 6, 8, and 9 are particularly unsatisfactory.

For a chapter-by-chapter analysis of Book 3, go to http://archelogos.com/xml/aristotleindex.htm.

Chapter 1: Introduction

Chapter 1: Summary of Books 1–2; Some Remarks on Hypokrisis,
or Delivery; the Origins of Artistic Prose

■ The first two sections of chapter 1 are a transition connecting what follows
with Book 2, which itself ended with a short transition section. This repetition is awkward and probably resulted from joining two separate works
together: the work in two books on *dianoia,* "thought," or "invention," and
a work on *lexis* and *taxis.* Perhaps Aristotle made this connection himself at
a late stage in his revision of the whole, in which case the transition at the
end of Book 2 indicated that further discussion of rhetoric continued on
another papyrus scroll, which then began with a notice that it was to be
linked with the work on invention. Perhaps, however, section 1 and 2 were
added by Tyrannio or Andronicus when the works of Aristotle were edited
and published in the first century B.C.E.; see Appendix II.B. A third beginning
is then supplied in section 3, followed by some remarks on delivery, and the
actual discussion of *lexis* does not begin until section 8.

1. Since there are three matters that need to be treated in discussion
of speech—first, what will be the sources of the *pisteis,* second concerning the *lexis,* and third how the parts of the speech ought to be
arranged—an account has been given of the *pisteis* and their number,
including the fact that they are drawn from three sources and what
sort of things these are and why there are only these [three]. (All
people are persuaded either because as judges they themselves are
affected in some way or because they suppose the speakers have certain qualities or because something has been logically demonstrated.)
An account has also been given of enthymemes and where they are to
be found. (There are on the one hand species [*eidē*] of enthymemes
and on the other hand there are topics.[1]) 2. The next subject to discuss
is *lexis;* for it is not enough to have a supply of things to say but it is
also necessary to say it in the right way, and this contributes much
toward the speech seeming to have a certain quality.

HYPOKRISIS, OR DELIVERY

3. The first thing to be examined was naturally that which came first
by nature, the facts from which a speech has persuasive effect; second

---

1. The *species* are the *idia* of Book 1, chs. 4–14; the topics are the *koina* of 2.23.

is how to compose this in language [*lexis*]; and third is something that has the greatest force but has not yet been taken in hand, the matter of the delivery [*hypokrisis*].[2] Even in regard to tragedy and rhapsody,[3] delivery was late in coming to be considered; for originally the poets themselves acted their tragedies.[4] Clearly there is something like this in rhetoric, as in poetics. Some others have given attention to the latter, among them Glaucon of Teos.[5] 4. It is a matter of how the voice should be used in expressing each emotion, sometimes loud and sometimes soft or intermediate, and how the pitch accents [*tonoi*] should be entoned, whether as acute, grave, or circumflex,[6] and what rhythms should be expressed in each case; for [those who study delivery] consider three things, and these are volume, change of pitch [*harmonia*], and rhythm. Those [performers who give careful attention to these] are generally the ones who win poetic contests; and just as actors are more important than poets now in the poetic contests, so it is in political contests because of the sad state of governments.[7]

5. An *Art* concerned with [the delivery of oratory] has not yet been composed, since even consideration of *lexis* was late in developing, and delivery seems a vulgar matter when rightly understood.[8] But since the whole business of rhetoric is with opinion, one should pay attention to delivery, not because it is right but because it is necessary, since true justice seeks nothing more in a speech than neither to offend nor to entertain; for to contend by means of the facts themselves is

1404a

---

2. The prevailing meaning of *hypokrisis* in Greek is "acting" and the regular word for an actor is *hypokritēs*. Aristotle had remarked in 2.8.14–15 on gestures used by people in affliction, which were probably sometimes acted in court, but his discussion here relates only to the voice. On the use of gestures in Greek delivery, see Boegehold 1999.

3. The recitation of epic or dithyrambic poetry.

4. Thus there was no need to consider the oral interpretation of a play separately from the presentation of it by the author. With occasional exceptions, plays were only performed once, but written copies were available to the reading public.

5. Probably the rhapsodist mentioned in Plato's *Ion* 530 and quoted in *Poetics* 25.1461b1.

6. Accents on Greek words indicate pitch, not stress: an acute accent indicates a rising tone, a grave accent a falling tone, and a circumflex accent a rising and falling tone. In addition, Greek words have a rhythmical shape determined by the arrangement of long and short syllables.

7. This point, repeated in the next section, seems to reflect the Platonic view (e.g., *Gorgias* 463a–b) that political oratory under democracy had become a form of flattery and that it offered entertainment to the mob.

8. Aristotle's negative attitude toward delivery probably also derives from Plato (e.g., *Republic* 3.397a–d); see Fortenbaugh 1986.

just, with the result that everything except demonstration is incidental; but, nevertheless, [delivery] has great power, as has been said, because of the corruption of the audience. 6. The subject of *lexis*, however, has some small necessary place in all teaching; for to speak in one way rather than another does make some difference in regard to clarity, though not a great difference; but all these things are forms of outward show and intended to affect the audience. As a result, nobody teaches geometry this way. 7. Whenever delivery comes to be considered[9] it will function in the same way as acting, and some have tried to say a little about it, for example, Thrasymachus in his *Emotional Appeals*.[10] Acting is a matter of natural talent and largely not reducible to artistic rule, but insofar as it involves how things are said [*lexis*], it has an artistic element. As a result, prizes go to those who are skilled at it, just as they do to orators on the basis of their delivery; for written speeches [when orally recited] have greater effect through expression [*lexis*] than through thought.[11]

8. The poets were naturally the first to set in motion [study of verbal expression]; for words are imitations,[12] and the voice, the most mimetic of all our parts, was there to start with. Thus, the verbal arts were established: rhapsody and acting and the others. 9. Since the poets, while speaking sweet nothings, seemed to acquire their reputation through their *lexis*, a poetic style came into existence [in prose as well], for example, that of Gorgias. Even now, the majority of the uneducated think such speakers speak most beautifully. This is not the case, but the [proper] *lexis* of prose differs from that of poetry. It is clear from what has happened [in other literary genres that the direction of development is away from the use of poetic diction]; for the makers of tragedies do not continue to use the same style, but just as they changed from tetrameters to the iambic meter because it was most like ordinary speech, so also they have abandoned the use of words that are not conversational, with which they had at first

---

9. As it was by Aristotle's student Theophrastus; see Fortenbaugh 1985: 269–288.

10. The *Eleoi* by Thrasymachus of Chalcedon, referred to by Plato in *Phaedrus* 267c9.

11. There were oratorical contests, with prizes, at festivals in Greece. *Written speeches* here probably refers to works by sophists, written and then dramatically recited. The subject of oral and written style will be discussed further in chapter 12.

12. This is consistent with some of Plato's *Cratylus* but not with Aristotle's own discussion of words in *On Interpretation* 1, where they are called "symbols" and "signs."

ornamented their diction as the writers of hexameter poetry still do.[13] As a result, it is absurd to imitate those who themselves no longer use that style of speech. 10. Thus, it is clear that we need not go into detail about all matters concerned with *lexis*, only about what applies to the subject we are discussing. Concerning the other style there is a discussion in the *Poetics*.[14]

Chapters 2–12: *Lexis*, or Style

■ Chapters 2–4 are primarily concerned with lexis in the sense of diction, or choice of words, chapters 5–12 with the composition of words into sentences, which came to be known as *synthesis*, "putting together." Aristotle's discussion applies both to oral speech and to written prose.

Chapter 2: The Aretē, *or Virtue, of Good Prose Style;* Word Choice and Metaphors

■ This chapter begins with a definition of the virtue or excellence of prose style and civic oratory as clarity, but with the accompanying requirement that a writer or speaker seek a mean between ordinary speech and poetic language as appropriate to the subject. In chapter 5 Aristotle will add a requirement of grammatical correctness and in subsequent chapters will discuss various forms of ornamentation. These concepts were reformulated by his student Theophrastus in a treatise, now lost, *On Lexis*, as "correctness, clarity, propriety, and ornamentation" and appear in some form in most subsequent Greek and Roman treatments of rhetoric; see, e.g., *Rhetoric for Herennius* 4.17; Cicero, *On the Orator* 3.37 and *Orator* 79; Quintilian 8.1–2.

1. Let the matters just discussed be regarded as understood, and let **1404b** the virtue of style [*lexeōs aretē*] be defined as "to be clear" [*saphē*] (speech is a kind of sign, so if it does not make clear it will not perform its function)—and neither flat nor above the dignity of the subject, but appropriate [*prepon*]. The poetic style is hardly flat, but it is not appropriate for speech.

---

13. The turn to ordinary diction can be seen by comparing dialogue passages of Euripides, whose diction is often conversational, with those of Aeschylus a generation earlier, where the diction is sometimes bombastic.

14. *Poetics* 20–22. Style in poetics is an aspect of imitation, in rhetoric of persuasion.

■ Aristotle here applies to word choice the concept of virtue as a mean between two extremes that is fundamental to his ethical philosophy. His emphasis on clarity as the most important requirement of good oratorical style is consistent with his stress on logical proof in the earlier books and his dislike of the style of sophists. The development of artistic prose in Greek, though influenced by Gorgianic mannerism derived from poetry, was largely a matter of the purification of diction and regularization of syntax into an efficient, elegant tool of expression. The development of artistic prose in French, and to a lesser extent in English, followed an analogous course between the sixteenth and eighteenth centuries. The great models of Attic prose are Plato, Lysias, Isocrates, and Demosthenes. On the development of a theory of style in Greece, see Graff 2005.

2. The use of nouns and verbs in their prevailing [*kyrios*][15] meaning makes for clarity; other kinds of words, as discussed in the *Poetics* [chapters 21–22], make the style ornamented rather than flat. To deviate [from prevailing usage] makes language seem more elevated; for people feel the same in regard to word usage as they do in regard to strangers compared with citizens. 3. As a result, one should make the language unfamiliar;[16] for people are admirers of what is far off, and what is marvelous is sweet. Many [kinds of words] accomplish this in verse and are appropriate there; for what is said [in poetry] about subjects and characters is more out of the ordinary, but in prose[17] much less so; for the subject matter is less remarkable, since even in poetry it would be rather inappropriate if a slave used fine language or if a man were too young for his words or if the subject were too trivial, but in these cases, too, propriety is a matter of contraction or expansion [of what is being said]. 4. As a result, authors should compose without being noticed and should seem to speak not artificially but naturally.[18] (The latter is persuasive, the former

---

15. *Kyrios* refers to the prevailing meaning in good current usage and may also be translated "proper" in the sense found in dictionary definitions; it is not necessarily the semantic, etymological, or essential meaning of the word. Modern literary critics, however, have called the concept into serious question, emphasizing the context as the determinant of meaning; cf. Richards 1936:37–41.

16. The view of literary language as "defamiliarization" has been greatly extended in modern times by the Russian Formalist School, leading to Roman Jakobson's famous definition of poetry as "organized violence committed on ordinary speech"; see Erlich 1981:219.

17. Lit. "in bare words"; Aristotle has no technical term for prose.

18. Perhaps the earliest statement in criticism that the greatest art is to disguise art.

the opposite; for people become resentful, as at someone plotting against them, just as they are at those adulterating wines.) An example is the success of Theodorus' voice when contrasted with that of other actors; for his seems the voice of the actual character, but the others' those of somebody else.[19] 5. The "theft" is well done if one composes by choosing words from ordinary language. Euripides does this and first showed the way.

Since speech is made up of nouns and verbs,[20] and the species of nouns are those examined in the *Poetics*, from among these one should use glosses[21] and double words and coinages rarely and in a limited number of situations. (We shall later [3.7] explain where; the reason has already been given: the usage departs from the appropriate in the direction of excess.) 6. A word in its prevailing and native meaning and metaphor are alone useful in the *lexis* of prose. A sign of this is that these are the only kinds of words everybody uses; for all people carry on their conversations with metaphors[22] and words in their native and prevailing meanings.

■ *Metaphora* is itself a metaphor and literally means "carrying something from one place to another, transference." The word first occurs in Isocrates' *Evagoras* 9, where the author claims to banish metaphors from his prose. In *Poetics* 21.7 Aristotle defines metaphor as "a movement [*epiphora*] of an alien [*allotrios*] name either from genus to species or from species to genus or from species to species or by analogy"; see Appendix I.G. There is a vast bibliography on Aristotle's concept of the metaphor and its subsequent influence; see Kirby 1997. On the difference between its function in poetics and rhetoric, see Ricoeur 1977:7–43. He says (p. 20) that the Aristotelian idea of *allotrios* tends to assimilate three distinct ideas: *deviation* from ordinary usage, *borrowing* from an original usage, and *substitution* for an absent word by an available ordinary word. Aristotle will discuss metaphor in greater detail in chapters 4 and 10.

---

19. The statement sounds as though Theodorus was still acting when Aristotle first wrote this passage; that would date it to the mid-350s B.C.E.; see Burkert 1975.

20. *Onomata*, "name words" (including adjectives) and *rhēmata*, "sayings, verbs, predicates," are the two major parts of speech recognized by Aristotle. In 3.5.2 he adds *syndesmoi*, "connectives." Full categorization of parts of speeches was largely a development of the study of grammar in the third to the first century B.C.E.

21. Strange or rare words; see 3.3.2.

22. Ordinary language contains many metaphorical expressions that have often lost their force, e.g. "It's raining cats and dogs," "The sun is smiling," etc.

Thus, it is clear that if one composes well there will be an unfamiliar quality and it escapes notice and will be clear. This, we said, was the virtue of rhetorical language. 7. The kind of words useful to a sophist are homonyms (by means of these he does his dirty work), to a poet synonyms. By words that are both in their prevailing meaning and synonymous I mean, for example, *go* and *walk*; for when used in their prevailing sense these are synonymous with each other.

Now what each kind of word is and how many species of metaphor there are and that metaphor has very great effect both in poetry and speeches has been said, as noted above, in the *Poetics*. 8. In speech it is necessary to take special pains to the extent that a speech has fewer resources than verse. Metaphor especially has clarity and sweetness and strangeness, and its use cannot be learned from someone else.[23] 9. One should speak both epithets and metaphors that are appropriate, and this will be from an analogy. If not, the expression seems inappropriate because opposites are most evident when side-by-side each other. But one should consider what suits an old man, just as a scarlet cloak is right for a young one; for the same clothes are not right [for both]. 10. And if you wish to adorn, borrow the metaphor from something better in the same genus, if to denigrate, from worse things. I mean, for example, since they are opposites in the same genus, saying of a person who begs that he "prays" or that a person praying "begs," because both are forms of asking, is composing in the way described; as also when Iphicrates called Callias a "begging priest" rather than a "torchbearer" and the latter replied that Iphicrates was not initiated into the Mysteries or he would not have called him a begging priest but a torchbearer;[24] for both are religious epithets, but one is honorable, one dishonorable. Then there are the "parasites of Dionysus," but the persons in question call themselves "artistes." These are both metaphors, the former one that sullies, the profession, the latter the contrary. Pirates now call themselves "businessmen." Thus, one can say that a criminal "has made a mistake" or that someone making a mistake "has committed a crime" or that a thief both took and "plundered." A phrase like that of Euripides' *Telephus*,

---

23. Cf. *Poetics* 22.17, where it is also said that an ability to use metaphor is a "sign of natural ability."

24. The incident probably took place about 390 B.C.E., when both served in a war between Athens and Sparta; see Xenophon, *Hellenica* 6.3.3. Callias was a hereditary torchbearer in the Mysteries and apparently thought Iphicrates was ignorant. Though a prominent Athenian general, he came from humble origins and had family connections with the barbarous Thracians.

"lording the oar and landed in Mysia," is inappropriate [in prose], since *lording* is too elevated; there is no "theft" [if the metaphor is too flagrant].

11. There is a fault in the syllables if the indications of sound are unpleasant; for example, Dionysius the Brazen[25] in his *Elegies* calls poetry "Calliope's screech" because both are sounds; but the metaphor is bad because it implies meaningless sounds. 12. Further, metaphor should be used in naming something that does not have a proper name of its own[26] and [it should] not be far-fetched but taken from things that are related and of similar species, so that it is clear the term is related; for example, in the popular riddle [*ainigma*], "I saw a man   1405b gluing bronze on another with fire,"[27] the process has no name, but both are a kind of application; the application of the cupping instrument is thus called "gluing." From good riddling it is generally possible to derive appropriate metaphors; for metaphors are made like riddles; thus, clearly, [a metaphor from a good riddle] is an apt transference of words.

13. And the source of the metaphor should be something beautiful; verbal beauty, as Licymnius says,[28] is in the sound or in the sense, and ugliness the same; and thirdly there is what refutes the sophistic argument: for it is not as Bryson[29] said that nothing is in itself ugly, since it signifies the same thing if one word is used rather than another; for this is false; one word is more proper than another and more like the object signified and more adapted to making the thing appear "before the eyes."[30] Moreover, one word does not signify in the same way as another, so in this sense also we should posit one as more beautiful or uglier than another; for both signify the beautiful or the ugly, but not solely as beauty or ugliness.[31] Or if they do, [it is] only in degree.

---

25. So called because he first proposed (early fifth century B.C.E.) the use of bronze rather than silver money at Athens.

26. This is known as *katakhrēsis* or *abusio*, but to regard it as metaphor is sometimes thought inconsistent with a rigorous substitution theory; cf. Genette 1982:50–52.

27. The answer to the riddle is "cupping" or "bleeding," done by a physician with a hot bronze cup (in modern times a glass) that draws out blood as it cools.

28. The rhetorician mentioned in Plato's *Phaedrus* (267c2) as having written an account of beautiful words.

29. Sophist and mathematician, contemporary with Aristotle. The view here expressed was taken up later by the Stoics; see Cicero, *Letters to His Friends* 9.22.1.

30. This concept will be discussed in chapters 10–11.

31. Cf. the difference between *vase, jar, pot,* and *jug.* Aristotle here seems to imply belief in some natural link between some words and their meaning as discussed in Plato's *Cratylus,* though elsewhere he regards words as symbols rather than icons.

These are sources from which metaphors should be taken: from the beautiful either in sound or in meaning or in visualization or in some other form of sense perception. It makes a difference whether the dawn is called "rosy-fingered"[32] or "purple-fingered" or worse still, "red-fingered." 14. In the use of epithets the transference is also sometimes from the bad or ugly, for example, *mother-slayer*, sometimes from the better, for example, *avenger of his father*.[33] When the winner in a mule race offered Simonides a paltry sum [for an ode in honor of his victory], he declined the commission as though annoyed at composing about "half-asses"; but when the winner paid enough, he wrote, "Hail, daughters of storm-footed mares!"[34] Nevertheless, they *were* daughters of asses. 15. The same effect can be achieved by diminution. A diminutive [*hypokorismos*] makes both bad and good less so, as Aristophanes does sarcastically in the *Babylonians*[35] when he substitutes *goldlet* for *gold*, *cloaklet* for *cloak*, *insultlet* for *insult*, and *diseaselet* [for *disease*]. But one should be careful and observe moderation in both [epithets and diminutives].

Chapter 3: Ta Psykhra, *or Frigidities*

■ Having discussed virtues of style, Aristotle now turns briefly to their opposites, the faults that come from violating the principles of clarity and appropriateness in choice of words and that make the language "frigid." Longinus follows the same approach in chapters 3–4 of *On Sublimity*. Frigidity, Aristotle says, may result from the use of ponderous compounds— often coined by the speaker—from unfamiliar words, from inappropriate epithets, and from far-fetched metaphors.

1. Frigidities [*ta psykhra*] in *lexis* come about in four ways: [first] in double words,[36] as in Lycophron's phrase "the many-faced heaven of the great-summited earth" and "the narrow-passaged shore" and as Gorgias spoke of "beggar-mused flatterers, forsworn and right-solemnly sworn" and as in Alcidamas' expression, "his soul full of

---

32. As frequently in the Homeric poems.
33. Either epithet could be applied to Orestes, as in Euripides, *Orestes* 1587–1588.
34. Simonides of Ceos (c. 556–468 B.C.E.), frag. 10.
35. Produced 426 B.C.E., now lost; frag. 90.
36. Or compounds, which Aristotle thinks of as poetic. Greek, like German, forms compounds easily, and though the result is intelligible, it can also be pompous. Elaborate compounds were especially characteristic of the tragic style of Aeschylus and are ridiculed in Aristophanes' *Frogs* 830–894.

anger and his face becoming fire-colored" and "end-fulfilling deemed he their zeal would be" and "end-fulfilling he made the persuasion of his words," and the foam of the sea was "copper-blue."[37] All these seem poetic because of the doubling.

2. This is one cause of frigidity, and another is the use of glosses,[38] as when Lycophron called Xerxes "a monster man"[39] and Sciron "a *sinis* man"[40] and Alcidamas spoke of "[bringing no such] *toys* to poetry" and "the *wretchedlessness* of his nature" and one who had been "*whetted* with the unmixed anger of his thought."

3. Third is use of epithets that are long or untimely or frequent.[41] In poetry it is appropriate to speak of "white milk,"[42] but in a speech such things are not only rather unsuitable, but if used immoderately they convict [the writer of artificiality] and make it clear that this is "poetry." Though there is some need to use them (for they change what is ordinary and make the *lexis* unfamiliar), nevertheless one should aim at the mean, for it does less harm than speaking carelessly; carelessness lacks merit, moderation lacks fault. As a result, Alcidamas' phrases seem frigid; for he uses epithets not as seasonings but as the main course, so frequent, extended, and conspicuous are they; for instance, not "sweat" but "wet sweat"; not "to the Isthmian games" but "to the convocation of the Isthmian games"; not "laws" but "the royal laws of cities"; not "in a race" but "in a racing impulse of the soul"; not "museion"[43] but adding "Nature's museion"; and "sullen-visaged the thought of his soul"; and the artificer not of "favor" but of "pandemic favor," and "steward of the pleasure of the listeners," and hidden not by "boughs" but "boughs of the wood," and not "he covered his body" but "he covered his body's shame," and "anti-mimicking was the desire of his soul" (this is at one and the same

---

37. Lycophron and Alcidamas, like Gorgias, were sophists of the late fifth and early fourth centuries B.C.E. who used poetic language in prose.

38. Lit. "tongues." The term *gloss* comes to be used chiefly of archaic, foreign, or rare words, but Aristotle means anything that sounds strange and might puzzle an audience; cf 3.10.2. In *Poetics* 21.6 (see Appendix I.G) a gloss is defined as a word "other people use," thus borrowed from another dialect or language. In modern usage, a *gloss* is an explanatory word or phrase.

39. *Pelōron*, "monster," is the reading of Parisinus 1741 and could be called a gloss because it was archaic.

40. *Sinis* means "ravager"; both Sciron and Sinis were famous robbers.

41. By *epithet* ("what is added on") is meant a descriptive adjective or phrase.

42. Common in the United States today, but Aristotle did not know about chocolate milk.

43. "Place, or haunt, of the Muses." English "museum."

time both a compound and an epithet, so the result is poetry), and "so extravagant an excess of wickedness." Thus, by speaking poetically in an inappropriate way [Alcidamas and other sophists] impart absurdity and frigidity, and also lack of clarity because of the verbiage; for when a speaker throws more words at someone who already understands, he destroys the clarity by the darkness. People coin double words when something has no name of its own and the word is easily formed, as is "pastime" [*to khronotribein*]. But if there is much of this, [the diction] becomes completely poetical. Thus, *lexis* using double words is most useful to dithyrambic poets, for they are sensitive to sound,[44] but glosses to epic poets, for they are stately and self-assured.[45]

4. The fourth kind of frigidity occurs in metaphors; for there are inappropriate metaphors, some because they are laughable (comic poets, too, use metaphor), some because too lofty and tragic. And they are unclear if far-fetched, for example, Gorgias' phrase about "pale and bloodless doings," or "You have sown shamefully and have reaped badly." These are too poetic. And as Alcidamas calls philosophy "a fortress against the laws"[46] and the *Odyssey* "a fair mirror of human life" and "bringing no such toys to poetry." All these are unpersuasive for the reasons given.[47] Yet Gorgias' exclamation to the swallow when she flew down and let go her droppings on him is in the best tragic manner: he said, "Shame on you, Philomela"; for if a bird did it there was no shame, but [it would have been] shameful for a maiden. He thus rebuked the bird well by calling it what it once had been rather than what it now was.[48]

---

44. A dithyramb was originally a hymn to Bacchus, thus somewhat wild and metrically varied; in the late fifth century B.C.E. it became a narrative vehicle for virtuoso performers, of whom Timotheus is the best known.

45. The manuscripts continue, "metaphor to iambic poets, for they now use these, as has been said." But this was probably a marginal comment by some later reader, then copied into the text. The cross-reference is to the end of 3.1.

46. Perhaps meaning that philosophy offers courage or consolation in the face of legal injustice, as in the case of Socrates when condemned to death (or later in Boethius' *Consolation of Philosophy*).

47. Some of the expressions Aristotle finds affected in Greek may be acceptable in English. The context of their use determines their suitability, and two thousand and more years of literature have dulled the ear for many metaphors.

48. In Greek mythology Philomela (in some versions her sister Procne) was transformed into a swallow by the gods. On this passage see Rosenmeyer 1955.

Chapter 4: Eikōn, or Simile

■ An *eikōn* is a "likeness" (cf. English *icon*). Though Aristotle views the simile as a characteristic poetic device, seen especially in the extended similes of epic poetry, simile is not discussed in the *Poetics*. In this chapter of the *Rhetoric* it is treated as an expanded form of metaphor: a metaphor, that is, with an explicit comparison, whether provided by a verb, adjective, or adverb. Later rhetoricians often reverse this concept, taking a metaphor to be an abbreviated or condensed simile and regarding a simile as a figure of speech, involving several words, while a metaphor is a trope, the "turning" of the meaning of a single word. The distinction between tropes and figures is not explicit in Aristotle's work and is a development of his successors in the Hellenistic period. Aristotle has discussed *parabolē*, or comparison, as a topic of invention in 2.20.2–7, but neither there nor here does he relate it to simile, which he regards purely as a device of style; see McCall 1969; Ricoeur 1977; Tamba-Mercz and Veyne 1979; Kirby 1997 (the latter a semiotic approach).

1. A simile is also a metaphor; for there is little difference: when the poet says, "He rushed as a lion," it is a simile, but "The lion rushed" [with "lion" referring to a man] would be a metaphor; for since both are brave, he used a metaphor [i.e., a simile] and spoke of Achilles as a lion.[49] 2. The simile is useful also in speech, but only on a few occasions; for it is poetic. [Similes] should be brought in like metaphors; for they *are* metaphors, differing in the form of expression. 3. Examples of similes are what Androtion said to Idreus, that he was "like puppies that have been chained"; for they jump to bite, and Idreus, freed from prison, was vicious.[50] And the way Theodamus likened Archidamus to "a Euxenus that does not know geometry"; this is from analogy, for Euxenus will then be an Archidamus who knows geometry.[51] And the one in the *Republic* of Plato, that those who strip the dead [on the battlefield] are like curs that snap at stones but do not bite the throwers; and the one applied to the citizen body,

---

49. The simile of Achilles and the lion occurs in *Iliad* 20.164. "The lion rushed," meaning Achilles, does not occur in the Homeric poems; thus, Aristotle says *would be*. Early Greek literature makes rather little use of metaphor, except for personification of abstract forces, but much of simile; see Stanford 1936.

50. Androtion was a fourth-century B.C.E. Athenian politician, best known from Demosthenes' speech against him in 346. Idreus succeeded Mausolus as king of Caria in 351.

51. I.e., they are equally stupid, except that Euxenus knows some geometry.

that it is like a ship's captain who is strong but deaf; and the one about the verses of poets, that they are like youths without beauty (for when
1407a the latter have lost their bloom of youth and the former their meter they do not seem the same).[52] And Pericles' simile for the Samians, that they are like children who accept the candy but keep crying, and his remark about the Boeotians, that they are like oaks (for oaks are felled by oaks,[53] and the Boeotians by fighting each other). And Demosthenes' [simile] about the citizen body, that it is like those sick on board ship.[54] And the way Democritus likened orators to nannies who, after swallowing the pabulum, moisten the baby's lips with their spit. And the way Antisthenes compared skinny Cephisodotus to incense, because "He gives pleasure by wasting away." All these can be spoken both as similes and as metaphors, so whichever are liked when spoken as metaphors clearly will make similes too, and similes are metaphors needing[55] an explanatory word. 4. Metaphor from analogy should always have a correspondence between the two species of the same genus: thus, if the wine cup is the "shield" of Dionysus, the shield can fittingly be called the "cup" of Ares.[56] Speech, then, is composed from these things.[57]

Chapter 5: To Hellēnizein, *or Grammatical Correctness*

■ In chapters 5–12 attention turns to style as seen in combination of words into sentences. The first subject discussed is what Aristotle calls "speaking Greek," by which he means observance of the rules of grammar and the conventions of idiom of the language, but much of what he says really relates more to clarity than to correctness. Perhaps the chapter is a survival of some earlier thoughts on clarity, placed here because it deals with composition rather than with word choice. Although Protagoras and other sophists

---

52. The passages are *Republic* 5.469e, 6.488a, and 10.601b, respectively.

53. Perhaps from thrashing in a storm, more likely from being cut down by oak-handled axes or with oak wedges.

54. Probably not Demosthenes the famous orator, whom Aristotle seems to avoid quoting, presumably because of his hostility to Macedon; perhaps the fifth-century B.C.E. general of the same name.

55. When the metaphor would be obscure or too violent, it "needs" to be recast as a simile.

56. On metaphor from analogy, see *Poetics* 21.11–14 in Appendix I.G, where the same example is given.

57. That is, from the different kinds of words discussed earlier: *kyria*, glosses, compounds, coined words, and metaphors, including epithets and similes.

had made a start at the study of grammar, it was in Aristotle's time still a relatively undeveloped field of study. Systematic grammars of the Greek language did not appear until the second century B.C.E., when they reflect the research of Stoic philosophers. The oldest surviving Greek grammar book is the work of Dionysius Thrax; he came from Alexandria and became a celebrated teacher at Rhodes in the years before and after 100 B.C.E.

1. The first principle [*arkhē*] of *lexis* is to speak [good] Greek [*to hellēnizein*]. 2. This is done in five ways:[58] first is in the [correct] use of connective particles, when a speaker preserves the natural response between those that are prior and those that are posterior to each other, as some require. Thus, *ho men* ["He on the one hand . . ."] and *ho ego* ["I on the one hand . . ."] require [in a subsequent clause] *de* ["on the other hand . . ."] and *ho de* ["he on the other hand . . ."] respectively. The correlatives should occur while the first expression is still in the mind and not be widely separated, nor should another connective be substituted for the one needed; for it is rarely appropriate: "But I, when he spoke to me (for there came Cleon both begging and demanding), went, taking them along." In these words many connectives are thrown in, in place of what is expected; and if the interval is long, the result is unclear.[59]

3. On the one hand, then, one merit is found in the use of connectives, a second, on the other hand, in calling things by their specific names and not by circumlocutions.[60] 4. Third is not to use amphibolies[61]—unless the opposite effect [obscurity] is being sought. People do this when they have nothing to say but are pretending to

---

58. Others could easily be added, and the chapter is one of the least satisfactory in the *Rhetoric*.

59. The example (perhaps a quotation) seems poorly chosen and does not involve the use of correlatives, though it does use a number of words that Aristotle would have regarded as connectives ("but, when, for, both, and"). Its faults come from the cumbersome syntax, not from separating connectives or failing to use the expected responses. As notes to earlier chapters indicate, Aristotle himself was capable of writing awkward sentences as bad or worse than this, including long parentheses where the reader can easily forget the beginning of the sentence—but of course the *Rhetoric* is neither a speech nor a work of artistic literature. In his published dialogues his language was regarded as elegant and correct; see, e.g., Quintilian 10.1.83.

60. Aristotle illustrates the correct use of correlatives, but fails to supply an example of this point.

61. An amphiboly (lit. "what shoots both ways") is an equivocation based on a word or phrase with an ambiguous meaning, often creating a fallacious argument; see 3.18.5.

say something. Such are those [philosophers] who speak in poetry, Empedocles, for example. When there is much going around in a circle, it cheats the listeners and they feel the way many do about oracles: whenever the latter speak amphibolies most people nod assent: "Croesus, by crossing the Halys [river], will destroy a great kingdom."[62] Since there is generally less chance of a mistake, oracles speak of any matter in generalities. In the game of knucklebones one can win more often by calling "odd" or "even" than by specifying a particular number of counters, and the same is true about *what* will happen in contrast to *when* it will happen, which is why soothsayers do not specify the time. All these things are alike, so they should be avoided except for the reason mentioned.

1407b

5. The fourth [rule is to observe] Protagoras' classification of the gender of nouns: masculine, feminine, and neuter. There should be correct grammatical agreement: "Having come and having spoken, she departed."[63] 6. Fifth is the correct naming of plural and singular: "Having come, they beat me." What is written should generally be easy to read and easy to speak—which is the same thing. Use of many connectives[64] does not have this quality, nor do phrases not easily punctuated,[65] for example, the writings of Heraclitus. To punctuate the writings of Heraclitus is a difficult task because it is unclear what goes with what, whether with what follows or with what precedes. For example, in the very beginning of his treatise he says, "Of this Logos that exists always ignorant are men." It is unclear whether "always" goes with what precedes [or what follows]. 7. Further, the lack of correspondence creates a solecism[66] if you do not join words with what fits both; for example, if you are speaking of sound and color, seeing is not common to them, but perceiving is. And it is unclear if you do not first set forth what you are talking about when you are going to throw in much in the middle; for example, "I

---

62. A famous ambiguous response by the Delphic oracle to Croesus, king of Lydia. He interpreted it as encouragement, but the kingdom destroyed was his own.

63. In Greek the participles modifying "she" have distinct feminine forms; in the next example the participle is in the masculine plural to agree with "they."

64. *Polloi syndesmoi*, or *polysyndeton*, regarded by later rhetoricians as a figure of speech involving a surfeit of conjunctions: i.e., A and B and C, etc., rather than A, B, C....

65. Classical Greek was generally written without punctuation and even without spacing between the words; it thus had to be "punctuated" by the reader.

66. A mistake in usage or syntax; in later grammatical and rhetorical theory contrasted to a "barbarism" or mistake in the form of a word.

intended, after talking with that man about this and that and in this way, to go," instead of "I intended, after talking with that man, to go" and then "This and that transpired and in this way."

Chapter 6: Onkos, *or Expansiveness, and* Syntomia, *or Conciseness*

■ *Onkos* literally means "bulk, mass, swelling"; here it implies "elevation, dignity," though in later writers it is often a pejorative term for swollen style. As Aristotle implies in section 7, *onkos* can be regarded as a stylistic form of *auxēsis*, amplification, of which some inventional aspects were discussed in 2.18.4, 2.19.26, and 2.26. Note the prescriptive tone of this chapter with its practical advice on how to amplify. As in the case of arguments in Books 1–2, Aristotle is setting out "available" techniques. Although it appears several times in Demetrius' treatise *On Style* (a work showing strong Aristotelian influence), *onkos* did not gain acceptance among later rhetoricians as a technical term.

1. The following things contribute to expansiveness [*onkos*] in expression: to use a definition instead of a word; for example, not *circle* but "a plane figure equidistant from the center." For conciseness [*syntomia*], [one should make use of] the opposite: the word for the definition. 2. And if something is shameful or inappropriate, if the shame is in the definition, use the word, and if in the word, use the definition. 3. And make something clear by metaphor and epithets, while guarding against the poetic. 4. And make the singular plural, as poets do: though there is a single harbor, they say "to Achaean harbors," and "the tablet's many-leaved folds."[67] 5. And do not join [words with a single definite article] but use one article with each: *tēs gynaikos tēs hēmeteras*; but for conciseness the opposite: *tēs hēmeteras gynaikos.*[68] And speak [expansively] with a conjunction, but if concisely, without a conjunction, yet not without grammatical connection; for example, "having gone and having conversed" com-   1408a pared with "having gone, I conversed."[69] 7. Antimachus'[69] technique of describing something on the basis of properties it does not have is also useful; he applies it to Teumessos [in the passage beginning],

---

67. Of a writing tablet made up of only two pieces of thin wood, joined together loosely.

68. Cope ([1877] 1970, 3:67) captured the difference in English by *that wife of ours* as contrasted with *our wife.*

69. Greek poet of about 400 B.C.E., author of an epic on the Theban cycle.

"There is a windy *little* hill. . . ." Amplification of this sort can go on indefinitely.[70] What it is not can be said of things good and bad, whichever is useful. This is the source of words the poets introduce such as *stringless* or *lyreless* music; for they apply privatives. This is popular when expressed in metaphors by analogy; for example, to say the trumpet is "lyreless music."

Chapter 7: To Prepon, *or Appropriateness, Propriety*

■ The beginning of chapter 2 identified appropriateness of style to subject as a necessary quality of good speaking or writing. In this chapter Aristotle explains the concept more fully.

1. The *lexis* will be appropriate if it expresses emotion and character and is proportional to the subject matter. 2. Proportion exists if there is neither discussion of weighty matters [*euonkōn*] in a casual way nor shoddy things solemnly and if ornament is not attached to a shoddy word. Otherwise, the result seems comedy, like the [tragic] poetry Cleophon composes. Some of what he used to say is like calling a fig "Madame." 3. Emotion is expressed if the style, in the case of insolence [*hybris*], is that of an angry man; in the case of impious and shameful things if it is that of one who is indignant and reluctant even to say the words; in the case of admirable things, [if they are spoken] in a submissive manner; and similarly in other cases. 4. The proper *lexis* also makes the matter credible: the mind [of listeners] draws a false inference of the truth of what a speaker says because they feel the same about such things, so they think the facts to be so, even if they are not as the speaker represents them; 5. and the hearer suffers along with the pathetic speaker, even if what he says amounts to nothing. As a result, many overwhelm their hearers by making noise.

6. Proof from signs is expressive of character, because there is an appropriate style for each genus and moral state. By *genus* I mean things like age (boy, man, old man; or woman and man or Spartan and Thessalian) and by *moral state* [*hexis*] the principles by which someone is the kind of person he is in life; 7. for lives do not have the same character in accordance with [each and] every moral state.[71] If, then,

---

70. Cf. Christian amplification of the glory of God or of Christ: "without beginning or end, ineffable, unbegotten, etc."

71. Cf. *Nicomachean Ethics* 2.1.

a person speaks words appropriate to his moral state, he will create a sense of character. A rustic and an educated person would not say the same thing nor [say it] in the same way. Listeners react also to expressions speechwriters[72] use to excess: "Who does not know?" "Everybody knows. . . ." The listener agrees out of embarrassment in order to share in the feelings of all others.

8. Opportune or inopportune usage is a factor common to all species [of rhetoric]. 9. There is a commonly used defense for every hyperbole: the speaker should preempt criticism;[73] for something seems true when the speaker does not conceal what he is doing. 10. Further, do not use all analogous effects [of sound and sense] together; for thus the hearer is tricked. I mean, for example, if the words are harsh, do not deliver them with a harsh voice and countenance. Otherwise, what you are doing is evident. But if sometimes one feature is present, sometimes not, you accomplish the same thing without being noticed. But if, as a result, gentle things are said harshly and harsh things gently, the result is unpersuasive.

11. Double words and frequent epithets and especially unfamiliar words suit one speaking passionately; for it is excusable that an angry person calls a wrong "heaven-high" or "monstrous." And [this can be done] when a speaker already holds the audience in his control and causes them to be stirred either by praise or blame or hate or love, as Isocrates does at the end of the *Panegyricus*: "[How great the] fame and name . . ." and [earlier] "who endured . . . [to see the city made desolate?"].[74] Those who are empassioned mouth such utterances and audiences clearly accept them because they are in a similar mood. That is why [this emotional style] is suited also to poetry; for poetry is inspired. It should either be used as described or in mockery [*eirōneia*], as Gorgias did and as in the *Phaedrus*.[75]

1408b

---

72. Logographers, i.e., professional writers, like Lysias, of speeches for clients to deliver in the law courts, some of whom were rather simple people.

73. The better manuscripts give *should add a censure*; but ancient rhetoricians (e.g., Quintilian 8.3.37) advised anticipation ("You may not want to believe what I am going to say, but . . ."). Some scribe may have wrongly inserted the single letter (sigma) that makes the difference in meaning.

74. Reference to Isocrates' *Panegyricus* 186 and 96, respectively, slightly misquoted, probably from memory. Isocrates' text of the first quotation has "fame and memory."

75. Cf. Gorgias' mockery of the swallow, cited in 3.3.4; Plato, *Phaedrus* 231d, 241e.

Chapter 8: Rhythm in Prose

■ A sense of rhythm begins to be evident in some Greek prose of the late fifth century B.C.E., but real feeling for it is first seen in the writings of Plato, Isocrates, and Demosthenes in the fourth. Demosthenes in particular (though ignored by Aristotle) avoids a succession of short syllables. The reader needs to keep in mind that Greek (and Latin in the classical period) rhythm was quantitative, based not on stress but on long and short syllables. With a few exceptions, a syllable was regarded as "long" if it contained a long vowel (e.g., eta or omega), a diphthong, or a short vowel followed by two or more consonants.

1. The form of the language[76] should be neither metrical nor unrhythmical. The former is unpersuasive (for it seems to have been consciously shaped) and at the same time also diverts attention; for it causes [the listener] to pay attention to when the same foot will come again—as when children anticipate the call of heralds (in the law courts): "Whom does the freedman choose as his sponsor?" [The children call out] "Cleon!"[77] 2. But what is unrhythmical is unlimited, and there should be a limit, but not by use of meter; for the unlimited is unpleasant and unknowable.[78] And all things are limited by number. In the case of the form of language, number is rhythm, of which the meters are segments. 3. Thus, speech should have rhythm but not meter; for the latter will be a poem. The rhythm should not be exact. This will be achieved if it is [regular] only up to a point.[79]

4. Of rhythms, the heroic [dactylic hexameter] is dignified and not conversational and needs musical intonation;[80] the iambic by itself is the language of the many; thus all people most often speak in iambics.

---

76. *To skhēma tēs lexeōs*, the term adopted by later rhetoricians for "figure of speech," but here meaning the language's rhythmical configuration.

77. The example does not well illustrate Aristotle's point and is rather odd in other ways. A herald is calling for some citizen to take the case of a non-citizen not legally entitled to speak. Cleon, the late-fifth century B.C.E. demagogue, apparently took such cases. Court rooms were unroofed and open to the public, and apparently children hung around there in search of amusement. It seems that children in Aristotle's time still chanted this call for Cleon, who was long dead.

78. A basic Aristotelian principle in metaphysics, physics, and other sciences; cf. *Metaphysics* 3.4.999a27.

79. Prose rhythm, like other aspects of style, should be a mean between the conversational and the poetic.

80. That is, it needs to be chanted. In Aristotle's time rhapsodists no longer accompanied themselves on the lyre as had been the case in earlier centuries.

But [oratory] should be dignified and moving. The trochaic meter is rather too much of a comic dance, as is clear from trochaic tetrameters; for they are a tripping rhythm. What remains is the paean; it 1409a came into use beginning with Thrasymachus, though at the time people did not recognize what it was. The paean is a third kind of rhythm, related to those under discussion; for it has the ratio of three to two [three short syllables and one long, the latter equal in time to two beats], whereas the others are one to one [the heroic, with one long and two shorts] or two to one [iambic and trochaic, a long and a short or a short and a long, respectively]. And one-and-a-half [the proportion of three to two] is the mean ratio and this is what a paean is. 5. The other rhythms should be avoided for the reasons given and because they are [poetic] meters; and the paean should be adopted; for it alone of the rhythms mentioned is not a meter, and thus its presence most escapes notice. As it is, only one paean is in use, both for beginning and ending, but it is necessary to distinguish the opening from the closing. 6. There are two species of paean opposite to each other, of which one [called a first paean] is suitable for an opening, as it is now used. This is the one that begins with a long syllable and ends with three shorts: *Dālogenes/eite Lukian* and *khryseokoma Hekate/pai Dios*; the other [called a fourth paean] is the opposite, where three shorts begin and a long ends: *meta de gān/hudata t' ōkeanon ēphanise nūx*. This makes an ending, for a short syllable [at the end] makes the expression seem cut short. It should instead be cut off with a long syllable and be a clear termination, not through the action of a scribe or the presence of a marginal mark[81] but through the rhythm. 7. That *lexis* should, therefore, be rhythmical and not unrhythmical and what rhythms make it well rhythmed and what they are like has been said.

■ Aristotle's account of prose rhythm is unsatisfactory in several ways. He seems to be the victim of an unrealistic theoretical approach. Despite what he says, the paean was sometimes used in lyric poetry; the examples of paeans he cites are all from poetry, probably from poems by Simonides of Ceos. Conversely, the paean is very rare in prose. Most serious is his failure to consider the cretic (long-short-long), which has the same proportions as the paean and is the commonest prose rhythm in Greek and Latin literary prose and oratory. Indeed, a paean can be regarded as a cretic with one of

---

81. *Paragraphē.* Though written punctuation was undeveloped in Aristotle's time, a mark was often made in the margin to indicate the change of speaker in a play or dialogue.

the long syllables resolved into two shorts. Finally, a short syllable at the end of a verse was regarded as lengthened by its position, and later rhetoricians extended this rule to prose rhythm; cf. Cicero, *Orator* 217 and Quintilian's comment in 9.4.93.

Chapter 9: Periodic Style

■ This chapter also has problems. One is the extent to which Aristotle thought of a period as essentially a rhythmical unit. He says it has magnitude, is limited, and has number; he equates it with a line of verse in section 4; and the need for rhythm might be assumed from the previous chapter, but he does not here specifically speak of rhythms or identify rhythms in the prose quotations that begin in section 7. (See Fowler 1982, who denied that rhythm is involved, and, on the other side of the question, Adamik 1984.)

The most conspicuous features of a period as Aristotle understands it, and of its subdivision called a *kōlon*, seem to be some syntactical completion (at least a complete phrase), unitary thought, and length that is a mean between "too short" and "too long," in order for the hearer to grasp the thought easily. Aristotle does not use the word *periodos* to mean one of the long, complex sentences of Isocrates (favored later by Cicero and many early modern English writers). He quotes *parts* of Isocrates' complex sentences as examples of periods, but does not analyze the sentences as a whole. Apparently he viewed a long Isocratean sentence as made up of several periods.

Periodos, from *peri* (around) and *hodos* (road), another of Aristotle's visual metaphors, suggests a circular motion, but as the examples cited show, the technique is more one of antithesis and balance than circularity. Aristotle may not have originated the use of *periodos* as a grammatical-stylistic term. The Byzantine encyclopedia *Suda* attributes it to Thrasymachus.

1. The *lexis* [of formal speech and artistic prose] is necessarily either *strung-on* [*eiromenē*][82] and given unity by connection, like the preludes in dithyrambs, or *turned-down* (*katestrammenē*) and like the antistrophes of the ancient poets. 2. The strung-on style is the ancient one;[83] for in the past all used it, but now not many do. I call that

---

82. Or "running," strung together with connectives. Though this is seen in what is called *paratactic* sentence structure such as "We met and we went for a walk and then we had a drink . . . ," Aristotle is probably thinking of smaller units, as in polysyndeton; for otherwise it is not the opposite of periodic style as he describes it.

83. The manuscripts insert here a misquotation of the opening of Herodotus' *Histories*: "Of Herodotus of Thurii this is the account of the investigation." Kassel (1976) double-bracketed this as a late addition by Aristotle. Though Herodotus' work regularly utilizes the strung-on style, this opening sentence does not illustrate it; see Dillery 1992.

strung-on which has no end in itself unless the thing being said has been completed. It is unpleasant because it is unlimited; for all wish to foresee the end. Thus, as they complete the course [runners] pant and are exhausted; for they do not tire before the goal is in sight.

3. This, then, is the strung-on style of composition, but the turned-down style is that in periods. I call a *period* an expression having a beginning and an end in itself and a magnitude easily taken in at a glance. Such a style is pleasant and easily understood, pleasant   **1409b** because opposed to the unlimited and because the hearer always thinks he has hold of something, in that it is always limited by itself, whereas to have nothing to foresee or attain is unpleasant. And it is easily understood because easily retained in the mind. This is because utterance in periods has number, which is the most easily retained thing. Thus, all people remember verse better than prose;[84] for it has number by which it is measured. 4. But a period should also be complete in thought and not cut off, as it is in iambic lines:

> Calydon is this land, of Pelops soil . . .[85]

Because of the line division it is possible to misunderstand the meaning, as though in this quotation Calydon was in the Peloponnesus.

5. A period is either divided into cola or simple.[86] *Lexis* in cola is both complete and divided and easily uttered by the breath, not in its division but in the whole. A colon is one of the two parts of a period. I call a period *simple* when it has only one colon. 6. The cola and the periods should be neither stubby nor long. A short one often causes the hearer a bump; for when [his mind] is rushing toward what is to come and its measure, of which he has his own definition, he is pulled up short by the speaker's pausing and trips, as it were, at the abrupt close. Long ones cause him to be left behind, as do those racers who go wide at the turning point;[87] for they, too, lose contact with their fellows. Similarly, long periods turn into a *logos* and are like a

---

84. *Khydēn*, "heaped up, indiscriminate."

85. Attributed by the manuscripts to Sophocles, but actually the first line of Euripides' *Meleager*. Aristotle here equates a period with a line of verse; the line is metrically complete but incomplete in thought. The next line, however, continued without grammatical break, making the geography clear: "Alas, across the straits facing pleasant plains, woe, woe!" Cf. Demetrius, *On Style* 58.

86. A colon (the visual image is that of the limbs of the body) is either a clause or phrase that has some grammatical independence. A period may be made up of either one or two cola; as section 7 will explain, if there are two they may be parallel or contrasted.

87. The interpretation of Harris 1974.

prelude. This is the source of the parody [of Hesiod, *Works and Days* 265–266] by Democritus of Chios, attacking Melanippides on the ground that he was composing preludes rather than antistrophes:

> A man does wrong to himself when he does it to another,
> And a long prelude is the worst thing for a composer.

Much the same applies to those who speak long cola, while those that are too short do not constitute a period. Thus they drag the hearer headlong.

7. *Lexis* in cola is either divided or contrasted. It is divided in this example: "Often have I admired those organizing panegyric festivals/and those instituting athletic contests." It is contrasted when in each colon opposite lies with opposite or the same is yoked with its opposites, for example, "They Helped both,/both those who stayed/ and those who followed; to the latter they provided more than they had at home/and for the former they left enough behind." *Staying* and *following* are opposites, as are *enough* and *more*. [Another example is] "And so both to those needing money/and those wishing to enjoy it"; here *enjoy* is opposed to acquisition. And again, "It happens often in these circumstances that the wise fail/and the foolish succeed" [and] "Straightway they were thought worthy of meeds of valor/and not much later they took command of the sea" [and] "To sail through the land/and to march through the sea,/yoking the Hellespont/and digging through Athos" [and] "And though citizens by nature,/by law deprived of their city" [and] "Some of them miserably perished,/ and others were shamefully saved." And [another is] "Privately to use barbarian servants,/and collectively to overlook the many who were enslaved," [and] ". . . either while living to hold it/or when dead to lose it."[88] And what someone said to Peitholaus and Lycophron[89] in the law court: "When these men were at home, they sold you, but coming to you now they have bought you." All these examples do what has been said. 8. Such a style is pleasing because opposites are most knowable and more knowable when put beside each other and because they are like a syllogism, for refutation [*elenkos*] is a bringing together of contraries.[90]

---

88. These quotations are all from Isocrates' *Panegyricus* (sections 1, 35, 41, 48, 72, 89, 105, 149, 181, and 186, respectively), but apparently from memory, since they are not very accurate. The most famous is the reference to Xerxes' invasion of Greece in 480 B.C.E., when he built a bridge of rafts across the Hellespont and dug a canal for his ships through the isthmus of Athos.

89. Assassins of Alexander of Pherai in 358 B.C.E. The text is uncertain but the antithesis is clear.

90. Cf. what was said about the refutative enthymeme in 2.23.30.

■ Up to this point in the chapter Aristotle has not used the word *antithesis* (some translators insert it) even though some of the examples are clearly antithetical, but now he speaks of antithesis as the sort of thing he is discussing. For his students and readers it was hardly a technical term, since its meaning was clear from its two roots, as in *op-position*. Antithesis was one of the characteristics of the prose style of Gorgias, and without mentioning him Aristotle proceeds to discuss other examples of what have come to be known as the "Gorgianic figures."

9. Antithesis, then, is one thing, as is *parisōsis* if the cola are equal [in the number of syllables] and *paromoiōsis* if each colon has similar extremities. This must occur either at the beginning or at the end [of the colon]. At the beginning it always takes the form of [similar] complete words, but at the end it may consist of [the same] final syllables or [the same] grammatical form or the same word. At the beginning are found such things as "**Agron** *gar elaben* **argon** *par autou*" and "**Dōrētoi** *t'epelontos* **pararrētoi** *t'epeesin*,"[91] at an end "*ōiēthēs an auton ou paidion* **tetokenai**, *all' auton paidion* **gegonenai**,"[92] or "*en pleistais de* **phrontisi** *kai en elakhistais* **elpisin**,"[93] and inflexion of the same word: "*axios de stathēnai* **khalkous**, *ouk axios ōn* **khalkou?**"[94] and recurrence of the same word: "You spoke of him in life meanly and now you write of him meanly". [One also finds] use of the same [concluding] syllable: "What would you have suffered so striking if you had seen the man shirking?" It is possible for one example to have all these features—for the same [colon] to be an antithesis, parison, and homoeoteleuton.[95] 10. The beginnings of periods have mostly been enumerated in the *Theodectea*.[96] There are also false antitheses, for example, the one [the comic poet] Epicharmus wrote,

1410b

---

91. "*Land* they took, *unworked*, from him," probably from a lost comedy. "Ready for *gifts* they were and ready for *persuasion* by words," from *Iliad* 9.526.

92. "You would have thought him not to have *begotten* a child, but himself to have *become* one," source unknown.

93. "In greatest cases and in smallest hopes," source unknown.

94. "Worthy of being set up in *bronze* but not worth a coin *of bronze*," source unknown.

95. Parison is another name for parisosis; homoeoteleuton is paromoiosis at the end of cola.

96. Patillon 1997 sought to identify the *Theodectea* with chapters 1–28 of *Rhetoric for Alexander*; in that case, the reference could be to the list of twofold statements in chapter 24 of that work; but see further Appendix II.A *ad fin*.

Sometimes I was in their house, sometimes I was with them.

Chapter 10: Asteia, *or Urbanities, and* Pro Ommatōn Poiein,
*or Bringing-Before-the Eyes, Visualization; with Further
Remarks on Metaphor*

■ *Astu* means "town," usually in the physical rather than the political sense, the latter being *polis*. In contrast to the country, towns often cultivate some degree of sophistication; thus, *asteia*, "things of the town," came to mean good taste, wit, and elegant speech (see Schenkeveld 1994). Latin *urbanitas* (from *urbs*, "city"), and thus English "urbanity," have similar meanings; cf. also "polite" from Greek *polis* (city state) and "civil" from Latin *civis* (citizen).

1. Since these things have been defined, there is need to say what are the sources of urbanities [*asteia*] and well-liked expressions [*eudokimounta*]. Now it is possible to create them by natural talent or by practice, but to show what they are belongs to this study. Let us say, then, what they are and let us enumerate them thoroughly, and let the following be our first principle [*arkhē*].

2. To learn easily is naturally pleasant to all people,[97] and words signify something, so whatever words create knowledge in us are pleasurable. Now glosses are unintelligible, but we know words in their prevailing meaning [*kyria*]. Metaphor most brings about learning; for when he[98] calls old age "stubble," he creates understanding and knowledge through the genus, since old age and stubble are [species of the genus of] things that have lost their bloom. 3. Now the similes of the poets also do the same thing; and thus, if they do it well, they seem urbane. (A simile is, as was said earlier, a metaphor differing by what is put first.[99] Thus, it is less pleasing because longer and because it does not say that this *is* that,[100] nor does [the listener's] mind seek to understand this.)

----

97. Cf. the first sentence of the *Metaphysics*: "All human beings by nature desire to know." But note that here Aristotle emphasizes the pleasure coming from learning *easily*; see section 4. As in the case of enthymemes (2.22.3), demands on a popular audience should not be great.

98. Homer in *Odyssey* 4.213.

99. *Prothesis*; on the meaning of the word here, see Tamba-Mecz and Veyne 1979.

100. Aristotle, unlike later classical rhetoricians, thus implies that metaphor is a form of predication, a major contention of Paul Ricoeur in *The Rule of Metaphor* (1977).

4. Those things are necessarily urbane, both in composition and in enthymemes, which create quick learning in our minds. This is why superficial enthymemes are not popular (by *superficial* I mean those that are altogether clear and which there is no need to ponder), nor those which, when stated, are unintelligible, but those [are well-liked] of which there is either immediate understanding when they are spoken, even if that was not previously existing, or the thought follows soon after; for [then] some kind of learning takes place, but in neither of the other cases. 5. In terms of the thought of what is said, such kinds of enthymemes are well-liked; in terms of the composition [an expression is urbane] on the one hand because of the figure, if it is spoken with some contrast (for example, "regarding the *peace* shared by others as a *war* against their own interests,"[101] where peace is opposed to war) 6. or on the other hand because of the words, if they have metaphor—and metaphor that is not strange[102] (for that would be difficult to perceive) nor superficial (for that causes nothing to be experienced). Furthermore, [urbanity is achieved] by means of bringing-before-the-eyes [*pro ommatōn poiein*, "visualization"]; for things should be seen as being done rather than as going to be done.[103] [To achieve urbanity in style] one should thus aim at three things: metaphor, antithesis, actualization [*energeia*].

7. Of the four kinds of metaphor,[104] those by analogy are most admired, as when Pericles said that the young manhood killed in the war vanished from the city as though someone took the spring from the year.[105] And Leptines, speaking about the Lacedaimonians, [said] that he would not allow [the Athenians] to stand by while Greece was deprived of one of its "two eyes." And when Chares was pressing to

1411a

---

101. Isocrates, *Philippus* 73, slightly misquoted. *Philippus* was completed in 346 B.C.E., and quotations from it here and elsewhere are the latest historical references in Book 3.

102. *Allotrios*; but according to *Poetics* 21.7 (see Appendix I.G), every metaphor is *allotrios* (alien).

103. Use of the present tense to describe future action; but the use of the "historic" present to describe past action is commoner. Through the rest of the chapter Aristotle uses *bringing-before-the-eyes* as a technical term. He will define it at the beginning of chapter 11.

104. Genus to species, species to genus, species to species, or from analogy; cf. *Poetics* 21.7 in Appendix I.G; Kirby 1997. In the traditional numbering, derived from the Bipontine Edition, 3.10.7, consisting of a series of examples of visualization, is the longest in the *Rhetoric*.

105. A simile, but Aristotle identifies simile as a form of metaphor. Quoted in slightly different form in 1.7.34; see the note thereon.

submit his financial account in the Olynthian war for approval,[106] Cephisodotus objected, saying he was trying to have his account approved while "strangling the state at the throat." And once, urging on the Athenians when they had secured supplies for a compaign to Euboea, he said they should march out "by the decree of Miltiades."[107] And Iphicrates, when the Athenians had made a truce with Epidaurus and the neighboring coast, complained that they had deprived themselves of "traveling expenses" for the war. And Peitholaus called the Paralus "the bludgeon of the people" and Sestus "the baker's board of the Peiraeus."[108] And Pericles demanded the removal of Aegina, "the eyesore of the Piraeus." And Moerocles said he was no more wicked than—(naming someone of the upper class); for that person was wicked "at thirty-three and a third percent interest" he himself "at ten." And Anaxandrides' iambic line about the daughters who were slow in marrying:

> The maidens, I note, are in arrears in their marriages.

And [another example] is the remark of Polyeuctes against the paralytic Speusippus, that he couldn't keep quiet though "bound by fate in a pillory of disease." And Cephisodotus used to call warships "colored millstones," and [Diogenes] the Cynic called fast-food shops "the Attic common mess." Aesion, moreover, said they had "poured" the city into Sicily;[109] for this is a metaphor, and bringing-before-the-eyes. And [his phrase] "so that Greece cried aloud" is in a certain way metaphor, and a bringing-before-the-eyes. And [so is] the way Cephisodotus demanded that they not hold many *syndromas*.[110] And Isocrates [provides another example] in regard to "those running together" in festivals.[111] And [consider] what is found in the Funeral

---

106. Probably about 347 B.C.E., when Aristotle left Athens, a relatively late reference in this book.

107. I.e., without further planning and preparation, as Miltiades is supposed to have decreed at the time of the Persian invasion in 490 B.C.E. Demosthenes (*On the Embassy* 303) uses the phrase to mean a historical call to action against enemy threats.

108. The Paralus was the ceremonial ship of the Athenian state. The city of Sestus had a strategic position on the trade route supplying grain from the Black Sea to the port of Athens. Except for Pericles (fifth century B.C.E.), the politicians mentioned in this section were older contemporaries of Aristotle whom he may have heard speak when he was in Athens.

109. In 414–413 B.C.E.

110. "The running together of a mob," a play on *synklētous*, said of a meeting "duly called."

111. *Philippus* 12.

Oration, that "it was proper at the tomb" of those dying at Salamis for Greece "to cut the hair in mourning, since freedom was being buried with their valor."[112] If he had said it was proper to shed tears since their valor was being buried, it would be a metaphor and before-the-eyes, but the words "freedom with valor" provide an antithesis. And when Iphicrates said, "My path of words is through the midst of Chares' actions," it was a metaphor by analogy, and "through the midst" is before-the-eyes. And to say, "Call dangers to the aid of dangers" is before-the-eyes and metaphor. And [consider] Lycoleon speaking on behalf of Chabrias: "not ashamed of his suppliant atti-tude in that bronze statue"; it was a metaphor at the time it was spoken, but not at all times, but it was before-the-eyes,[113] for when he was in danger, the statue [seemed to] supplicate, the lifeless for the living, the memorial of his deeds for the city. And [another example is] "in every way *practicing* lowly thinking";[114] for "to practice" is to increase something. And [another is] that "God kindled the mind as a light in the soul"; for both make something clear. [Another is] "For we do not settle ways, but postpone them"; both postponement and a peace of this sort are [a species of] delaying. And to say that treaties are a much better "trophy" than those won in wars;[115] for a trophy honors a moment and one success, while treatises apply to the whole war; both are signs of a victory. And [another is] that cities give "great financial account" in the censure of mankind; for a financial account is a legal form of damages. Thus, that urbanities come from metaphor by analogy and by bringing-before-the eyes has been explained.

1411b

Chapter 11: *Continued Discussion of Bringing-Before-the Eyes;* Energeia, *or Actualization; the Psychology of Metaphor and Its Similarity to Philosophy; Proverbs; Hyperbole*

■ This chapter completes Aristotle's discussion of devices of style that defamiliarize language and explains how they do so. The explanation is consistent with his cognitive psychology as found in other works, including

---

112. Lysias 2.60; but the reference there is to the Battle of Aegospotami (405 B.C.E.), not to Salamis.

113. Lycoleon indicated the bronze statue of the kneeling Chabrias; although not visible from the court, it would be familiar to the jurors. The statue commemorated his ordering his troops to await the enemy on their knees.

114. Isocrates, *Panegyricus* 151.

115. Isocrates, *Panegyricus* 180.

Poetics and *Nicomachean Ethics*: the hearer "sees" something in a different way and takes pleasure in learning. Though Aristotle has no concept of "figures" of thought or speech, some of what he discusses here corresponds to, but did not directly influence, the discussion of figures in later rhetorical treatises. Note the emphasis on the visual, which is characteristic of Aristotle. Rather oddly, Paul Ricoeur has called the beginning of this chapter "the most enigmatic passage of the *Rhetoric*" (see Ricoeur 1977:42 and 307–309).

1. But it is necessary to say what we mean by bringing-before-the-eyes and what makes this occur. 2. I call those things "before-the-eyes" that signify things engaged in activity. For example, to say that a good man is "foursquare"[116] is a metaphor, for both are "complete"; but it does not signify activity [*energeia*].[117] On the other hand, the phrase "having his prime of life in full bloom"[118] is *energeia*, as is "you, like a free-ranging animal"[119] and "now then the Greeks darting forward on their feet."[120] *Darting* is actualization and metaphor; for he means "quickly." And [*energeia*], as Homer often uses it, is making the lifeless living through the metaphor. 3. In all his work he gains his fame by creating activity, for example, in the following:

> Then to the plain rolled the ruthless stone,[121]

and "the arrow flew" and [also of an arrow] "eager to fly" and [of spears] "They stood in the ground longing to take their fill of flesh," and "The point sped eagerly through his breast."[122] In all of these something seems living through being actualized; for being "ruthless" and "longing" and the other examples constitute *energeia*. He applied these by using metaphor by analogy; for as the stone is to

1412a

---

116. Aristotle was probably thinking of the occurrence of this word (*tetragōnos*) in a poem by Simonides of Ceos (frag. 5): " 'Tis difficult for a man to be truly good, foursquare in hands and feet and mind without incurring blame. . . ."

117. The English cognate is *energy*. As a rhetorical term *energeia* may be translated "actualization" or "vivification." It is sometimes, but not always, "personification" and should be distinguished from *enargeia*, which means "clearness" or "distinctiveness"; see Eden 1986:71–75.

118. Isocrates, *Philippus* 10.

119. Isocrates, *Philippus* 127.

120. Euripides, *Iphigenia at Aulis* 80.

121. *Odyssey* 9.598.

122. The examples are from *Iliad* 13.587, 4.126, 9.574, and 15.541, respectively. But some of what seems personification in early Greek may have been literally understood by an archaic audience, still sharing something of an animistic worldview.

Sisyphus, so is the "shameless" one to the one "shamefully treated".
4. He does the same to lifeless things in his much admired similes:

> Arched, foam-crested, some in front, but others upon others.[123]

He makes everything move and live, and *energeia* is motion.

5. As was said earlier, metaphors should be transferred from things
that are related but not obviously so, as in philosophy, too, it is characteristic of a well-directed mind to observe the likeness even in
things very different.[124] Thus, Archytas [the Pythagorean philoso-
pher] said that an arbiter and an altar were the same; for one who has
been wronged flies to both. Or if someone said that an anchor and a
rope hung from a hook are the same; for both are the same [shape],
but they differ in that one is hung from above and one from below.
And to say that [the allotments of land in] cities "have been equal-
ized"[125] is the same thing in widely differing cases: the equality is in
the surface of land and the powers [assigned to each citizen].

6. Urbanities in most cases come through metaphor and from an
added surprise; for it becomes clearer [to the listener] that he learned
something different from what he believed, and his mind seems to
say, "How true, and I was wrong." The urbanity of epigrams derives
from their not meaning what is [literally] said; for example, that of
Stesichorus that "the cicadas will sing to themselves from the
ground."[126] Good riddles are pleasing for the same reason; for there is
learning, and they are spoken in metaphor, as is what Theodorus calls
ta kaina legein.[127] But this occurs when there is a paradox and not, as
he says, in opposition to previous opinion; rather, it is like the bogus
word coinages in jests. Jibes involving change of a letter [i.e., puns]
also have this effect; for they are deceptive. It occurs too in verses,
when they do not end as the listener expected:[128] "He came on,
having under his feet—blisters." The listener expected *sandals*. [To
be effective,] the point should be clear as soon as the word is said.
Changes of letter [as in a pun] make the speaker mean not what he

---

123. *Iliad* 13.799, where it is part of a simile comparing battle to waves of the sea.
124. Cf. 2.20.7.
125. Perhaps a reference to Isocrates, *Philippus* 40.
126. Meaning that the land will be devastated; cf. 2.21.8 and Demetrius, *On Style*
99, who attributes the epigram to Dionysius of Syracuse.
127. "Saying new things." The rhetorical handbook of Theodorus of Byzantium
was mentioned in 2.23.28 and by Plato in *Phaedrus* 266e6; cf. Appendix II.A.
128. This is technically known as *paraprosodokia*, "contrary to expectation."

says but what the word plays on, like the remark of Theodorus[129] to Nikon the harpist, *Thrattei se*. He pretends to say, "It disturbs you" and deceives, for he means something different. Thus it is pleasing to the learner, but if the latter does not understand that Nikon was a Thracian it will not seem urbane. And [consider] the remark *Boulei auton persai*.[130] 7. It is necessary for both examples to be said in the right way. Similarly also with urbanities, as in saying that the *arkhē* [command] of the sea was not the *arkhē* [beginning] of misfortunes for the Athenians; for they benefited; or as Isocrates says,[131] that the *arkhē* [empire] was the *arkhē* [beginning] of misfortunes; for in both cases someone says what would not be expected and its truth is recognized. To say that an *arkhē* is an *arkhē* is not very clever, but he means the words in different senses; and [in the first example the speaker] does not negate the *arkhē* he has spoken of but uses the word in a different sense.

8. In all these cases, if a word is introduced appropriately, either as a homonym or a metaphor, it is well done. For example, "Mr. Baring is unbearable."[132] The homonym is negated, but appropriately if he is unpleasant. And "You should be no stranger than a stranger," or no more than you should be. Or again, "It is not necessary for the stranger always to be strange," for one word [*xenos*] is used in different senses. Similar is the admired line of Anaxandrides: "Good it is to die before doing anything worthy of death." That is the same as saying someone is worthy of dying when not worthy of dying or worthy of dying when not being worthy of death or not doing anything worthy of death. 9. The species of the *lexis* in these examples is the same, but insofar as they are spoken concisely and with a contrast they are better liked. The cause is that knowledge results more from contrast but is quicker in brief form. 10. There should always be application to the person addressed or [an awareness of] what is rightly said, provided what is said is true and not superficial. It is possible to have one quality [e.g., truth] without the other [without teaching something in brief, striking form]; for example, "One should die while still faultless." But that is not urbane. "A worthy man should marry a

---

129. Probably the actor mentioned in 3.2.4.

130. Literally, "you wish to destroy," probably a pun on *Persai*, "Persian women."

131. *Philippus* 61 and *On the Peace* 101 (the former from 346, the latter from 355 B.C.E.).

132. *Lit.* "Anáskhetus is unbearable [*anaskhetós*]."

worthy woman." But that is not urbane [either]. But it *is* [urbane] if both [qualities] are present: "He is worthy to die when not worthy of dying." The more there is in the thought, the more it seems an instance of urbanity; for example, if the words are a metaphor and a metaphor of a certain sort and [if there is] antithesis and *parisōsis*[133] and it has *energeia*.

11. As has been said above [3.4], similes, which are well liked in some way, are also metaphors. They always involve two terms, as does metaphor from analogy. For example, we say the shield is the wine cup of Ares and his bow is a stringless lyre. Thus, their mean-   1413a ing is not that of the single word, as would be the case if we said the bow is a lyre or the shield a cup. 12. People also make similes this way; for example, a flute-player [can be] compared to an ape[134] or a near-sighted man to a lamp sprinkled with water; for both [eyelids and flame] flicker. 13. This is well done when there is metaphor; for it is possible to liken the shield to the cup of Ares and a ruin to the "rag" of a house and to say that Niceratus is a "Philoctetes bound by Pratys," a simile made by Thrasymachus after seeing Niceratus defeated by Pratys in a rhapsode contest, still disheveled and dirty [like Philoctetes in Sophocles' play]. If poets do not do this well, they most fail with the public; and if they do it well, they are popular. I mean when they make terms correspond: "He has legs like stringy parsley" [or] "like Philammon boxing the punching ball." All such things are similes, and that similes are metaphors has been repeatedly said.

14. Proverbs [*paroimiai*] are metaphors from species to species. For example, if someone brings home something, believing it is a good thing, and then suffers harm, it is "what the Carpathian says of the hare," for both have experienced what is described.[135] So the sources and cause of *asteia* have been more or less stated.

15. Well-liked hyperboles[136] are also metaphors; for example, of a man with a black eye, "You would have thought him a basket of mulberries"; for his face is somewhat purple, but there is much exaggeration. And in *like* this or that there is hyperbole differing in the form of expression: "like Philammon boxing the punching ball"

---

133. Defined in 3.9.9 as equality in the length of cola.

134. While playing, the flute-player takes a stance like a crouching ape.

135. Meaning uncertain, but cf. the Australian experience with the introduction of rabbits, which were originally thought to be useful but devastated crops.

136. Lit. "overshooting" the mark.

(you would think him to be Philammon fighting a sack), "He has legs like stringy parsley" (you would think him to have parsley for legs, so stringy they are). Hyperboles are adolescent; for they exhibit vehemence.[137] (Therefore those in anger mostly speak them:

> Not even if he gave me as much as the sand and the dust . . .
> But I will not marry the daughter of Agamemnon, son of Atreus,
> Not even if she rivals golden Aphrodite in beauty,
> And Athene in workmanship.)[138]

1413b   (The Attic orators especially use this.)[139] Thus, it is inappropriate for an older man to speak [in hyperbole].

Chapter 12: Oral and Written Style: Deliberative, Judicial, and Epideictic Styles

■ Aristotle does not make the distinction of the different "characters" or levels of style—grand, middle, and plain—that are a feature of later Greek and Latin rhetorical theory, but in this chapter he partly foreshadows that development by looking at style in an overall sense of what is appropriate for each of the three species of rhetoric as described in Book 1, and he also considers the stylistic differences between written and oral compositions. Before the end of the fifth century B.C.E. most oratory had been extempore and not published in written form. Gorgias and other sophists began the writing and publishing of epideictic speeches, and this was continued by Isocrates. In judicial oratory, speech writers (*logographers*), of whom Antiphon was probably the earliest and Lysias the most famous, had made a profession for themselves by ghostwriting speeches for clients to memorize and deliver in court, and some of these speeches were published. By Aristotle's time, political orators, including Demosthenes, were publishing written, polished versions of judicial and deliberative speeches they had earlier delivered, seeking a longer lasting influence on the public.

Though writing had been introduced into Greece in the ninth century B.C.E., "publication" in all genres long remained a matter of oral presentation. The period from the middle of the fifth to the middle of the fourth

---

137. The young overdo everything; cf. 2.12.4.

138. *Iliad* 9.385 and 388–389. Kassel (1976) double-bracketed the parenthesis as a later addition by Aristotle.

139. Deleted by some editors. Hyperbole is certainly a regular feature of fourth-century B.C.E. Greek oratory. If Aristotle added this sentence, he may not have been in Athens at the time; thus, between 347 and 335 B.C.E. See note on 3.17.10.

centuries has been called the time of a "literate revolution," comparable to the changes brought in the fifteenth century by the introduction of printing and in the twentieth century by the computer, for reliance on writing greatly increased in this period and affected the composition and reception of texts (see Havelock 1982; Ong 1982; and Kennedy 1998:191–195). Important Greek texts dealing with the effect of writing include the end of Plato's *Phaedrus*, his *Seventh Epistle* (341c–342a), and the essay by Alcidamas, *On Those Writing Written Speeches* (translations in Gagarin and Woodruff 1995; and Muir 2001). Written texts could be studied in detail in a way impossible with purely oral publication, and Aristotle's discussion of style would not have been possible without them (see Graff 2001).

1. One should not forget that a different *lexis* is appropriate for each genus [of rhetoric]. For the written and agonistic[140] styles are not the same; nor are the demegoric [deliberative] and the dicanic [judicial], and it is necessary to know both. [Debate] consists in knowing how to speak good Greek; [writing] avoids the necessity of silence if one wishes to communicate to others [who are not present], which is the condition of those who do not know how to write. 2. Written style is most exact; the agonistic style is very much a matter of delivery. Of the latter there are two species; for one form is ethical, the other emotional. Thus, actors are on the lookout for plays of these sorts, and the poets for these kinds of actors. But [poets] who write for the reading public are [also] much liked, for example, Chaeremon (for he is as precise as a professional prose writer [*logographos*]), and Licymnius among the dithyrambic poets. On comparison, some written works seem thin in debates, while some speeches of [successful] orators seem amateurish when examined in written form. The cause is that [their style] suits debate. Thus, things that are intended for delivery, when delivery is absent, seem simple minded, since they are not fulfilling their purpose; for example, *asyndeta*[141] and constant repetition are rightly criticized in writing but not in speaking, and the orators use them; for they lend themselves to oral delivery, 3. and it is necessary to speak the same thought in different words; this, as it were, leads the way for the delivery: "He is the one cheating you; he is the one deceiving you; he is the one trying to betray you." This is the sort of thing Philemon the actor used to do in *Old Man's Madness* by Anaxandrides when reciting [the passage about] Rhadamanthus

---

140. A speech in an actual debate (*agōn*).
141. Absence of connective words.

and Palamedes and in the "ego" passage of *The Pious Ones*. For if one does not act out these lines, it is a case of "the man carrying a beam."[142] Similarly with asyndeta: "I came, I met, I was begging"; 4. for it is necessary to act this out and not to speak it as one talking in the same character and tone. Furthermore, asyndeta have a special characteristic; many things seem to be said in an equal space of time; for the connectives make many things seem one, so if they are taken away, clearly the opposite results: one thing will be many.[143] Asyndeton thus creates amplification [*auxēsis*]: "I came; I spoke; I besought" (these things seem many), "he overlooked everything I said." This is Homer's intention also in the passage "Nereus, again, from Syme . . . Nereus, son of Aglaïa . . . Nereus who, as the handsomest man . . .";[144] for a man about whom many things are said must necessarily often be named. [Conversely,] people think that if someone is often named there must also be many things to say; thus [Homer] amplified [the importance of Nereus] (though mentioning him only in this passage) and by this fallacy made him memorable, though no account of him is given anywhere later in the poem.

5. Now the demegoric style seems altogether like shadow-painting;[145] for the greater the crowd is, the further the distance of view; thus, exactness is wasted work and the worse in both cases. Speaking in the law courts requires more exactness of detail,[146] and that before a single judge even more; for it is least of all a matter of rhetorical techniques; for what pertains to the subject and what is irrelevant is more easily observed [by a single judge], and controversy is gone, so the judgment is clear. As a result, the same orators are not successful in all these kinds of speeches.[147] Where there is most need of performance, the least exactness is present. This occurs where the voice is important and especially a loud voice. The epideictic

---

142. Probably a proverb descriptive of awkwardness: the man walks stiffly to keep the beam balanced.

143. As with metaphor, the listener learns something; see Blettner 1983.

144. *Iliad* 2.671–673.

145. Outline painting, without detail, intended to be seen at a distance and used for background scenery in the theater; cf. Plato, *Theaetetus* 208e and *Parmenides* 165c.

146. As Cope pointed out ([1877] 1970) in his commentary on this passage, Aristotle seems to confuse exactness of style—i.e., careful choice of words—with detailed treatment of argument. It is the latter that is important in a court room, and especially before a single judge, as in a tyranny.

147. Perhaps generally so, but conspicuous exceptions include Demosthenes, Cicero, and some moderns.

style is most like writing; for its objective is to be read. And the judicial style second[-most].

6. To make a further distinction of style that it should be pleasant and elevated is superfluous.[148] For why that, rather than chaste or liberal or any other virtue of character? Clearly, the things discussed will make the style pleasant if the virtue of *lexis* has been rightly defined. For otherwise, what is the point of being clear and not flat but appropriate? For if it is luxuriant, it is not clear, nor if it is [too] concise. But clearly the mean is suitable. And the things mentioned will make style pleasant if they are well mingled: the conventional and the strange, and rhythm, and persuasiveness from propriety. This concludes the discussion of *lexis*, both in general about all of it and in particular about each genus. It remains to speak about arrangement.

Chapters 13–19: *Taxis*, or Arrangement

■ Except in the case of some extempore oratory, inspired by an unexpected opportunity, an effective speech should be well organized; that is, it should consist of parts, each performing some function, but joined together into an artistic unity; Plato had called for this in *Phaedrus* 246. How these parts are arranged differs somewhat with the conventions of public address in different societies, the occasion, the speaker's perception of the audience's knowledge of the subject and attitude, and the speaker's individual character and style. Speeches in the Homeric poems already illustrated some of the structural patterns taught by later rhetoricians (see Martin 1989; Kennedy 1999:5–12). The first teachers of rhetoric in the Greek world seem to have recommended following a set order of parts in a judicial speech, beginning with an introduction to get the attention and good will of the audience, followed by a narration of the facts in the case, a statement of the speaker's position with reasons why the jury should believe it, and a conclusion summarizing the argument; some handbook writers exercised originality in identifying additional parts. For details, see Appendix II.A.

Aristotle's treatment of arrangement resembles his approach to invention at the beginning of Book 1[149] in that he initially takes an austere, rather Platonic, view of what, in an ideal society, should be adequate—facts and

---

148. This requirement is attributed to Theodectes by Quintilian (4.2.63).

149. See also his treatment of delivery in 3.1 as something regrettable, needed because of the corruption of the audiences.

arguments—and he then turns to consider the actual situation of his time and offers practical advice to his students. This probably reflects what he perceived as the necessities in teaching a course on rhetoric to a general audience in the Academy in the 350s B.C.E.; however, chapter 17, on the proof has probably been rewritten at a later time. It contains a discussion of enthymemes and a reference to Isocrates' *Philippus* of 346 B.C.E.

The word *taxis* is common in military contexts and carries the connotation of the arrangement of troops for battle. Similarly, the speaker needs to marshal the available means of persuasion for debate.

Chapter 13: The Necessary Parts of a Speech

1. There are two parts to a speech; for it is necessary [first] to state the subject with which it is concerned and [then] to demonstrate the argument. It is ineffective after stating something not to demonstrate it and to demonstrate without a first statement; for one demonstrating, demonstrates *something*, and one making a preliminary statement says it first for the sake of demonstrating it. 2. Of these parts, the first is the statement [*prothesis*], the other the proof [*pistis*], just as if one made the distinction that one part is the problem, the other the demonstration.[150]

3. Currently [writers on rhetoric] make ridiculous divisions; for a *diēgēsis* [or narration of the facts] surely belongs only to a judicial speech. How can there be the kind of narration they are talking about in epideictic or deliberative? Or how can there be replies to the opponent? Or an epilogue, in demonstrative speeches? *Prooemion* [introduction] and *antiparabolē* [reply by comparison] and *epanodos* [recapitulation] sometimes occur in public speeches when there is debate on two sides of a question [for there is often both accusation and response], but not insofar as there is deliberation.[151] Moreover, an epilogue is not a requirement of every judicial speech—for example, if the speech is short or if the subject is easily remembered; for an epilogue results from shortening [i.e., condensing] the length [of an argument]. 4. The necessary parts, then, are *prothesis* [proposition] and *pistis* [proof]. These are, therefore, the parts that really belong [in every speech]; and at the most, prooemion, proposition, proof, and

1414b

---

150. As in geometry.

151. Deliberation (*symboulē*), the coming to an agreement. In actual Greek speeches all these divisions can be found.

epilogue. For replies to the opposition belong to the proofs, and reply by comparison is amplification of the same, so it is a part of the proofs. One who does this demonstrates something, but the prooemion does not, nor the epilogue; the latter reminds [the audience of what has been demonstrated]. 5. If one continues making such divisions as the followers of Theodorus[152] make, there will be another *diēgēsis*, both the *epidiēgēsis* [supplementary narration] and *prodiēgēsis* [preliminary narration] and *elenkos* [refutation] and *epexelenkos* [supplementary refutation], but one should attach a name only when speaking of a distinct species and difference; otherwise, the category becomes empty and laughable, like those Licymnius created in his *Art*, [speaking of] "wafting" and "wandering" and "ramifications."[153]

Chapter 14: The Prooimion, or Introduction

■ *Oimos* literally means "stripe" or "layer" but metaphorically is used of the "course" or "strain" of a song. A *pro-oimion* is thus a "prelude." The word first occurs in Pindar's *Nemean Odes* 2.3. Transliterated into the Latin alphabet the word becomes *prooemion* or *proemium*, sometimes shortened in English to *proem*. The Latin term is usually *exordium*, in which the image is that of a warp set up on a loom for weaving. Other analogous words are *prologue*, used primarily of plays, and *preface*, from Latin *praefatio*, "what is said first," used in the case of prose works other than oratory. Among the works of Demosthenes is a collection of prooemia adaptable to a variety of speeches.

1. The prooemion is the beginning of a speech, what a prologue is in poetry and a *proaulion* in flute-playing; for all these are beginnings and, as it were, pathmakers for one who is continuing on. Now the *proaulion* is like the prooemion of epideictic speeches; for the flute-players, first playing whatever they play well, lead into the opening note of the theme, and this is the way to write epideictic speeches: after saying whatever one wants, to introduce the theme and join the parts together, as all [epideictic writers] do. An example is the prooemion of Isocrates' *Helen*, where there is nothing in common

---

152. The rhetorician mentioned in 2.23.28 and 3.11.6; on his handbook, see Appendix II.A.

153. Licymnius was a poet and may have applied these terms to dithyrambs or other poetry rather than to oratory; cf. 3.2.13.

between the eristics and Helen.[154] At the same time, even if [an epideictic writer] wanders from the subject, it is appropriate for the whole speech not to be uniform.

2. The prooemia of epideictic speeches are drawn from praise or blame. For example, in his *Olympic Discourse* Gorgias praises those who founded national festivals: "You are worthy of the admiration of many, O men of Greece."[155] Isocrates, on the other hand, blames them because they honored excellence of the body with gifts, but offered no prize to the wise (*Panegyricus* 1). 3. Another [source of epideictic prooemia is] from offering advice: for example, that one should praise the good, and thus the speaker praises Aristeides,[156] or such as are neither famous nor bad but are good while obscure, like Alexander the son of Priam.[157] [In these instances] the speaker offers **1415a** advice. 4. Another source is borrowed from judicial prooemia, that is, from appeals to the audience, if the speech is about something paradoxical or difficult or already much discussed, in order to obtain pardon [for discussing it], as the verse of Choerilus:[158] "Now, when [all the subjects of poetry] have been treated. . . ." These, then, are the sources of the prooemia of epideictic speeches: from praise, from blame, from exhortation, from dissuasion, from appeal to the audience. The opening note must be either unrelated or related to [the subject of the speech].

---

154. In the prooemion of the speech Isocrates attacks philosophers who argue for the sake of argument (eristic) or sophists who speak on trivial subjects. In contrast, he says, Gorgias chose a fine subject in his *Encomium of Helen* but then composed an apology rather than an encomium. This leads into the body of the speech where Isocrates shows how Helen should be celebrated.

155. Gorgias appeared at the Olympic games some time in the late fifth century B.C.E. and gave a speech, perhaps as part of an oratorical contest. The theme, much cultivated later by Isocrates, was need for concord among the Greeks. For what little is known about the speech, see Sprague 1972:49–50.

156. See 2.23.7.

157. Not the best possible example, since he became notorious. The point is that Paris was living alone in the country until chosen as a judge in the beauty contest of the goddesses. Aristotle has mentioned a declamation about Alexander in 2.23.8, 2.24.7, and 2.24.9.

158. Fifth-century B.C.E. epic poet, complaining of the limited subjects left for treatment by poets in his time.

JUDICIAL PROOEMIA

5. As for the prooemia of judicial speeches, one should grasp that they have the same effect as the prologues of plays and the prooemia of epic poems. (Those in dithyrambs are like those in epideictic. For example: "Through you and your gifts and then spoils. . . .")[159] 6. In [judicial] speeches and in epic there is a sample of the argument in order that [the audience] may know what the speech is about and [their] thought not be left hanging. The unlimited leads astray; he who gives, as it were, the beginning into the hand [of the hearer] allows him, by holding on, to follow the speech. This is the reason for "Sing, Goddess, the wrath . . ." [and] "Speak to me, Muse, of the man . . ." [and]

> Bring to me another theme, how from the land of Asia
> There came to Europe a great war.[160]

And the tragedians make the subject of the play clear—if not right away as Euripides does, at least somewhere in the prologue, as Sophocles does too: "My father was Polybus. . . ."[161] And the comedians similarly.

The most necessary and specific function of the prooemion is this: to make clear what is the purpose for which the speech [is being given]. As a result, if the subject is clear or short, there is no need of a prooemion. 7. The other kinds that are used are *remedies* [*iatreumata*] and are common [to all species of rhetoric]. These are derived from the speaker and the hearer and the subject and the opponent:[162] from the speaker and the opponent whatever refutes or creates a prejudicious attack [*diabolē*].[163] But these are not done in

---

159. Attributed to the fifth-century B.C.E. dithyrambic poet Timotheus (frag. 18).

160. The quotations are, respectively, the first lines of the *Iliad*, the *Odyssey*, and Choerilus of Samos' epic on the Persian wars.

161. *Oedipus the King* 774; not indeed from the prologue of the play but from the prologue of a long speech by Oedipus. Kassel (1976) double-bracketed the quotation as a late addition by Aristotle.

162. These are the topics of prooemia as identified in many Greek and Roman rhetorical treatises, e.g., *Rhetoric for Herennius* 1.8.

163. *Diabolē*, which recurs frequently in this chapter and the next, regularly means "slander, prejudice" and is so rendered through this passage by most translators. The cognate verb *diaballō*, however, which also occurs in the passage, means "attack," and Aristotle's discussion does not draw a sharp distinction between attacks that may be justified and those that are slanderous.

the same way. In the defendant's speech replies to attack come first, in the prosecution's [they come] in the epilogue.[164] The reason is not unclear; for the defendant, when he is going to introduce himself, has to remove whatever hinders his case and thus must first counteract the attack. But the attacker ought to put his attack in the epilogue in order that [the audience] may better remember it.

Remarks aimed at the audience derive from an effort to make them well disposed or make them angry and sometimes to make them attentive, or the opposite; for it is not always useful to make them attentive, which is why many speakers try to induce laughter. All sorts of things will lead the audience to receptivity if the speaker wants, including his seeming to be a reasonable person. They pay more attention to these people.

■ Aristotle regards the remedial functions of the prooemion as two: to make the audience well disposed [*eunous*] and attentive [*prosektikos*]. He then speaks of receptivity [*eumatheia*], apparently regarding it as much the same as attentiveness. Later Greek and Latin rhetorical works (e.g., *Rhetoric for Herennius* 1.7) usually speak of three functions: to make the audience receptive or teachable (Latin *docilis*), well disposed (*benivolus*), and attentive (*attentus*).

1415b   And they are attentive to great things, things that concern themselves, marvels, and pleasures. As a result, one should imply that the speech is concerned with such things. If they are not attentive, it is because the subject is unimportant, means nothing to them personally, [or] is distressing. 8. But one should not forget that all such things are outside the real argument: they are addressed to a hearer who is morally weak and giving ear to what is extrinsic to the subject, since if he were not such a person, there would be no need of a prooemion except for setting out the headings of the argument in order that the body [of the speech] may have a "head." 9. Furthermore, making the audience attentive is a feature common to all parts of a speech, if there is need of it [at all]; for these remedies are sought everywhere, not just when beginning. Thus, it is ridiculous to amass them at the beginning, when all listeners are most paying attention. As a result, whenever there is an opportunity, one should say [things

---

164. As in modern trials, the prosecution spoke first. The prosecutor, however, sometimes begins with an explanation of why he has been moved to bring the case to trial; cf. e.g., Lysias 12.1–3, Isocrates 17.1–2, Aeschines 1.1–2, etc.

like] "And give me your attention; for none of this pertains more to me than to you," and "I shall tell you something strange, the like of which you have never heard," or "[something] so marvelous." To do this is, as Prodicus[165] said, "to throw in some of the fifty-drachma lecture when the hearers nod." 10. But it is clear that this is not addressed to the hearer in his proper capacity as hearer; for all [who do it] are attacking others or absolving themselves in their prooemia. "Lord, I shall not speak as one in haste. . . ." "Why this proem . . . ?"[166] And [those do this] who have or seem to have a bad case [where] it is better to spend words on anything other than the subject. That is why slaves do not answer questions but go round in a circle and "prooem-ize."

11. The sources of creating good will have been mentioned and each of the other similar [states of mind].[167] But since it is well said,

Grant me to find among the Phaeacians friendship or compassion,[168]

these are the two things one should aim at. In epideictic, however, one should make the hearer think he shares the praise, either himself or his family or his way of life or at least something of the sort; for what Socrates says in the funeral oration[169] is true, that it is not difficult to praise Athenians in Athens, but among the Spartans [it is another matter].

DELIBERATIVE PROOEMIA

The prooemia of deliberative rhetoric are copied from those of judicial, but in the nature of the case there is very little need for them. Moreover, they are concerned with what the audience knows, and the subject needs no prooemion except because of the speaker or the opponents[170] or if the advice given is not of the significance they suppose, but either more or less. Then it is necessary to attack or absolve

---

165. Fifth-century B.C.E. sophist, best known from his role in Plato's *Protagoras* and his narration of the myth of "The Choice of Heracles" preserved in Xenophon's *Memorabilia* 2.1.21–34.

166. Sophocles, *Antigone* 223; Euripides, *Iphigenia Among the Taurians* 1162; double-bracketed by Kassel (1976) as late additions by Aristotle.

167. See 2.1.7, 2.4, and 2.8. This is probably a later addition to the text.

168. *Odyssey* 7.327.

169. Plato, *Menexenus* 235d.

170. When the speaker needs to explain why he rises to speak or what his opponents' hidden motives are; cf., e.g., Demosthenes 4.1.

and to amplify or minimize. It is for this that a prooemion is needed —or for ornament, since the speech seems carelessly done if it does not have one. An example of the latter is Gorgias' encomium to the Eleans: without preliminary sparring or warm-up[171] he begins abruptly, "Elis, happy city."

1416a

Chapter 15: *Ways of Meeting a Prejudicial Attack; the Question at Issue*

■ This subject is a logical continuation of the discussion of meeting attacks in the prooemion, but the strategies described may by applied anywhere in a speech. Much of what Aristotle discusses was later absorbed into *stasis* theory, the technique of determining the central question at issue in a trial —whether it was one of fact (called conjectural stasis), law, quality (e.g., illegal but just), or jurisdiction of the court, with many subdivisions and variations. Stasis theory was also applied to deliberative and epideictic oratory, though its primary function was in judicial speeches. The subject was first organized systematically by Hermagoras of Temnos in the second century B.C.E. and supplied the basis for inventional theory in the *Rhetoric for Herennius* and the rhetorical works of Cicero. In the second century C.E. new approaches were advanced, of which that found in *On Stasis* (or *On Issues*) attributed to Hermogenes of Tarsus was the most influential (see Heath 1995). Aristotle touched on the subject in 1.13.9–10 and will return to it in 3.17.1, but perhaps because of his lack of personal experience in litigation, he does not seem to have realized the rhetorical importance of determining the question at issue at the outset of planning a prosecution or defense (see Liu 1991). His lack of a systematic account of stasis is probably one reason why the *Rhetoric* was rather little studied in rhetorical schools of later antiquity.

1. One source of counteracting a prejudicial attack (*diabolē*)[172] is to use arguments to refute an unpleasant suspicion. It makes no difference whether someone has [actually] expressed the suspicion or not, so this is of general applicability. 2. Another topic is to make denial in regard to what is at issue: either that it is not true or not harmful or not to this person or not so much as claimed or not unjust, or not very,

---

171. The metaphors are from boxing. Epideictic was often thought of as analogous to athletic contests; cf. Isocrates, *Panegyricus* 1.

172. See note on this term in 3.14.7.

or not disgraceful or that it is not important. The question at issue [*amphisbētēsis*] concerns things like this, as in the reply of Iphicrates to Nausicrates; for he admitted that he had done what the other claimed and that it caused harm but not that he had committed a crime.[173] Or one may balance one thing against another when a wrong has been done, [saying that] although it was harmful, it was honorable [or that] though it caused pain, it was advantageous, or something of this sort.

3. Another topic: that [the act in question] is a mistake or bad luck or a necessity, as Sophocles said he was not trembling for the reason his accuser said—in order to seem old—but out of necessity; for it was not of his own volition that he was eighty years old.[174] And it is possible to offer a different reason: that one did not intend harm but some other objective and not what the accuser alleged, but the accidental result was harmful: "It would be just for you to hate me if I acted in order to bring this about."

4. Another [topic is recrimination], if the accuser has been involved [in the action or something similar], either now or in the past, either himself or one of those near him. 5. Another [is] if there are others with similar characteristics whom [the opponents] agree are not liable to the charge; for example, if a person who is fastidious about his appearance is [to be judged] an adulterer, then so-and-so must be. 6. Another [is] if the opponent or someone else has attacked others [in the past] or if, without arraignment, others have been under suspicion as the speaker now is and have been shown not guilty. 7. Another comes from counterattacking the accuser; for it will be strange if his words are believable when he himself is unbelievable. 8. Another if there has been a previous decision, as in Euripides' reply to Hygiainon in an *antidosis* trial when accused of impiety because he had written a line recommending perjury: "My tongue swore, but my mind was unsworn" (*Hippolytus* 612). He said [Hygiainon] was wrong to bring trials into the law courts that belonged in the Dionysiac contest; for he had given or would give an account of the

---

173. Iphicrates is the Athenian general often mentioned earlier; Nausicrates (called Naucrates by Roman writers) was a student of Isocrates; see Quintilian 3.6.3.

174. The reference is perhaps to Sophocles the dramatist, when accused by his son of mental incompetence as described in an anonymous biography prefixed to some manuscripts; otherwise the fifth-century B.C.E. general Sophocles whose trial Aristotle mentions in 1.14.3 and 3.18.6.

words there if anyone wanted to bring a complaint.[175] 9. Another is to use [the nature of] slander [*diabolē*] as a basis of attack, considering what a bad thing it is, and this because it alters legal judgments and
1416b does not rely on the facts. To speak of *symbola*[176] is a topic common to both sides; for example, in the *Teucer* [of Sophocles] Odysseus claims Teucer is a relative of Priam, for his mother Hesione was [Priam's] sister, but Teucer says that his father Telamon was Priam's enemy and that he had not betrayed the spies. 10. Another, for the accuser, is to find fault with some big thing briefly after praising some little thing at length or, after setting forth many good things [about the opponent] to find fault with the one thing that bears on the case.[177] Such [speakers] are most artful and most unjust; for they seek to harm by saying good things, mingling them with the bad. [A topic] common to accuser and defendant [occurs] when the same thing can have been done for many reasons; the accuser should attribute an evil motive, pointing to the worse interpretation, the defendant the better [motive]. For example, when Diomedes picked Odysseus [as a companion on an expedition in *Iliad* 10.242–46] one [speaker] might say that he regarded him as the best man, another, no, [he regarded him] as worthless, chosen because he alone would not be a rival.[178] Let this be enough about prejudicial attack.

Chapter 16: The Diēgēsis, *or Narration, and the Use of Narrative*

■ *Diēgēsis* literally means "a leading through" the facts. It has become usual to distinguish *narration* as a part of a speech from *narrative*, meaning any account of a course of events, but Greek *diēgēsis* (and Latin *narratio*) were sometimes used of both. Conversely, Greek *diēgēma*, "narrative," was

---

175. The trilogy of which the *Hippolytus* was a part had been given first prize by the judges in the dramatic contest of 428 B.C.E., and Euripides was claiming a charge of impiety should be brought before those judges. This is an example of what comes to be known as stasis of transference or jurisdiction, the claim that the charge is brought before the wrong court.

176. Often physical evidence, but here a probable sign: the assumption of family loyalty as contrasted with evidence from actions. Teucer was accused of treachery to the Greeks.

177. As Antony does in regard to Brutus in his funeral oration for Caesar in Shakespeare's *Julius Caesar*. That Brutus was an "honorable man" is repeatedly stated, but he is "ambitious."

178. As in the *Ajax* of Theodectes; see 2.23.20.

sometimes used of the narration of a speech, and in the second century C.E. *katastasis* became the common Greek word for a narration.

EPIDEICTIC NARRATIVE

1. *Diēgēsis* in epideictic speeches is not continuous but part-by-part,[179] for one should go through the actions that constitute the argument [*logos*]. The argument is composed partly from what is non-artistic, since the speaker is in no way the cause of the actions, and partly from art, which is a matter of showing either that the action took place, if it seems unbelievable, or that it was of a certain kind or importance or all these things. 2. For this reason, sometimes everything should not be narrated continuously, because this kind of demonstration is hard to remember. From some actions a man is shown to be brave, from others wise or just. A speech so arranged is simpler; the other approach[180] is confusing [*poikilos*] and not plain [*litos*]. 3. Well-known actions should [only] be recalled, [not described in detail]. Thus, many [epideictic speeches] have no need of narrative, for example, if you wish to praise Achilles; for all know of his actions. But it *is* necessary to make use of these. On the other hand, if you are praising Critias, you should [narrate his good actions] for not many know of them. . . .[181]

JUDICIAL NARRATIVE

4. But nowadays they[182] ridiculously say that the narration should be rapid [*taxeia*]. Yet, as the man said to the baker when asked whether he should knead the dough hard or soft, "What? Can't it be done *right?*" Similarly here, one should not narrate at length, just as one should not [unduly] lengthen prooemia, nor proofs either; for speaking well is not a matter of rapidity or conciseness but of moderation,

---

179. In judicial oratory narrative is largely confined to a continuous statement of the facts of the case and necessary background information. In epideictic, as Aristotle understands it, the speaker may identify the virtues of the person being praised one-by-one and add narrative passages in support of them.

180. I.e., a single narrative to which references are made later in the speech.

181. Critias was one of the Thirty Tyrants in Athens in 404 B.C.E. Something seems to have been lost in the text here; in what follows Aristotle is discussing narrative in judicial speeches. The manuscripts fill the gap by inserting a passage from 1.9.33–37; see note thereon.

182. Writers of handbooks and, perhaps, Isocrates and his followers.

and that means saying just as much as will make the thing clear or as much as will make [the audience] suppose that something has happened or that harm has been done or injustice, or that the facts are as important as you claim. 5. [As] the opposing speaker, [you] should do the opposite: seize an opportunity in the narration to mention whatever bears on your own virtue (for example, "By stressing justice, I kept admonishing him not to abandon his children") or bears on the opponent's wickedness ("But he answered me that wherever he might be there will be other children," which is what according to Herodotus[183] the Egyptian rebels replied [when begged by Psammetichus not to desert their wives and children]) or what is pleasing to the judges.

6. The defendant's narration can be shorter; for what is in doubt is whether something happened or whether it was harmful or unjust or not important, so one should not waste time on what is agreed unless something contributes to the defense; for example, if something has been done but not that it was unjust. 7. Further, actions should be spoken of in past tenses except for what brings in either pity or indignation when it is dramatized. The account of [what was told to] Alcinous is an example, in that it has been compressed into sixty verses for Penelope,[184] and [other examples] are the way Phaÿllus told the epic cycle and the prologue of the *Oeneus*.[185]

8. The narration ought to be indicative of character [*ēthikē*]. This will be so if we know what makes for character [*ēthos*]. One way, certainly, is to make deliberate choice [*proairesis*] clear: what the character is on the basis of what sort of choice [has been made]. And choice is what it is because of the end aimed at. Mathematical works do not have moral character because they do not show deliberate choice (for they do not have purpose), but the Socratic dialogues do (for they speak of such things). 9. Other ethical indications are attributes of each character; for example, that someone walks away while talking; for this makes his arrogance and rudeness of character clear. And do not speak from calculation, as they do nowadays, but

---

183. *Histories* 2.30.

184. The story told to Alcinous includes Odysseus' dramatic narration of his adventures, with much direct discourse, and stretches through *Odyssey* 9–12. In *Odyssey* 23.264–284 and 310–343 (not quite sixty verses) Odysseus gives Penelope a summary of his adventures.

185. Nothing is known of Phaÿllus; the *Oeneus* was a tragedy by Euripides, now lost.

from moral principle: "I desired it and I chose this for that reason, but if I did not benefit, it was better so." The former is characteristic of a prudent man, the latter of a good one; for the quality of a prudent man consists in pursuing his own advantage, that of a good man in pursuing the honorable. If [what you say] seems incredible, then add the cause, as Sophocles does. An example is the passage from the *Antigone*, arguing that there is more obligation to a brother than to husband or children; for the latter can be replaced if they die,

> But when mother and father have gone to Hades
> There is no brother who can be born again.[186]

If you do not have a reason to give, say that you are not unaware that what you say may seem incredible but [that] you are naturally this sort of [virtuous] person and [that] people never do believe [that] anyone willingly does anything except for some advantage. 10. Further, speak from the emotions, narrating both the results [of emotion] and things the audience knows and what are special characteristics of the speaker or the opponents: "And he went off, scowling at me." And as Aeschines says of Cratylus,[187] that he was hissing and violently shaking his hands; for these things are persuasive since they are indications [*symbola*] that the audience knows of those things they do not know. Many such things are to be found in Homer: **1417b**

> Thus she spoke, and the old nurse covered her face with her hands.[188]

For those who begin to cry place their hands over their eyes. And at the beginning you should introduce yourself—and the opponent—as a person of a certain character so that they will see you as such, but do it inconspicuously. That this is easy can be seen from messengers [in tragedy]; for we know nothing of what they are going to say, but we get some inkling of it [from their attitude]. Narrative should occur in many places and sometimes not at the beginning.

---

186. Sophocles, *Antigone* 911–912, with minor textual difference. The argument has been difficult for some modern critics to accept as something Sophocles would have written, but Aristotle's citation is evidence that it is genuine, and there is other evidence as well.

187. Aeschines here is not the orator but Aeschines called "Socraticus," contemporary of Plato, devoted follower of Socrates, and author of dialogues. Cratylus was a follower of Heraclitus and engages in debate with Socrates in Plato's dialogue *Cratylus*.

188. *Odyssey* 19.361.

DELIBERATIVE NARRATIVE

11. Narrative is least common in deliberative oratory, because no one narrates future events, but if there is narrative, it will be of events in the past, in order that by being reminded of those things the audience will take better counsel about what is to come (either criticizing or praising).[189] But then the speaker does not perform the function of an adviser. If something is unbelievable, promise to tell the cause of it immediately and to refer it to whomever they wish, as Iocasta in the *Oedipus* of Carcinus is always promising when someone is trying to find out about her son. And [similarly] Haemon in Sophocles.[190]

Chapter 17: The Pistis, or Proof, as Part of an Oration

■ This somewhat rambling chapter begins with discussion of proofs in judicial oratory, turns to epideictic and deliberative speeches and the differences among the species, returns to epideictic, comments on refutation, and ends with further remarks on the presentation of character. Aristotle seems in sections 5–9 and 12–17 to have revised and expanded the original text of his "afternoon" lectures by discussion of paradigms, enthymemes, and maxims which he had discussed in Book 2, chapters 20–22, at a late stage in the development of the text.

1. Proofs should be demonstrative [i.e., logically valid]. Since four points may be open to dispute [*amphisbētēsis*],[191] there is need to provide a demonstration bearing on what is disputed: for example, if the issue disputed in a trial involves a denial that something was done, there is most need to provide a demonstration that it was, and if [the act is admitted but one party alleges] that it did no harm, [the other needs to show] that it did; and if [it is denied] that it was important or [claimed] that it was done justly, similarly. And if the dispute is about whether something has been done [by one of the parties], 2. do not forget that it is necessary on this issue alone for one or the other to be a liar; for ignorance is not an excuse, as it might be if the dispute were

---

189. Double-bracketed by Kassel (1976) as one of Aristotle's late additions.

190. *Antigone* 683–723. Apparently Aristotle thought Haemon's loyalty to his father was unlikely.

191. Aristotle here again anticipates some categories of later stasis theory. His four questions are fact, harm, importance, and justice, of which the last three become subdivisions of stasis of quality.

about justice.[192] So in this case one should use [the topic of the opponent's wickedness], but not in others.

3. In epideictic speeches there will be much amplification about what is good and advantageous; for the facts need to be taken on trust, and speakers rarely introduce evidence of them, only if any are incredible or if someone else is held responsible.

4. In deliberative speeches one may debate whether the events predicted [by a previous speaker] will occur or admit that they will occur as he demands, but [claim they] will not be just or advantageous or important. One should also look to see if any incidental details are falsified; for these are sure signs [*tekmēria*] that he also falsifies other things more to the point.[193] 5. Paradigms [i.e., proof from examples] are most appropriate to deliberative oratory, enthymemes more suited to judicial; for the former is concerned with the future, so it is necessary to draw examples from the past; the latter is concerned with what are or are not the facts, which are more open to demonstration and a necessary conclusion; for the past has a necessity about it. 6. But the enthymemes should be mixed in and not spoken continuously; otherwise they get in each other's way. (There is a limit to how much an audience can take, [as in the line]

Oh friend, since you have spoken as much as a wise man would[194]

as much as, not *such things as*.) 7. And do not seek enthymemes about everything; otherwise you do what some philosophers do; the conclusions of their syllogisms are better known and more plausible than their premises. 8. And when you would create pathos, do not speak enthymemes; for the enthymeme either "knocks out" the pathos or is spoken in vain. (Simultaneous movements knock out each other and either fade away or make each other weak.) Nor should you seek an enthymeme when the speech is being "ethical"; for logical demonstration has neither *ēthos* nor moral purpose.[195]

1418a

---

192. In *Nicomachean Ethics* 5.10.1135b30 Aristotle somewhat qualifies this: if a speaker denies an action that he has performed because he has genuinely forgotten it, he is not necessarily wicked. But generally, when one person claims something was done and another denies it, one is lying.

193. This hardly meets the standards of *tekmēria* as discussed in 1.2.16, which may have been a later development in Aristotle's terminology.

194. *Odyssey* 4.204.

195. The rejection of enthymemes as too coolly rational in arousing emotion or portraying character (modified in section 12) is evidence against the view of Grimaldi and others that Aristotle's discussion of emotions and characters in Book 2 is intended to supply topics for enthymemes; see Wisse 1989:24–25.

9. Maxims should be used both in a narration and in a proof; for they are ethical: "I *have* given [the money], though knowing 'one should not trust.'"[196] Or [they should be used] if the context is emotional: "Though wronged, I have no regret; the profit belongs to him, the justice to me."[197]

10. Speaking in a deliberative assembly is more difficult than in a law court, as one would expect, since it is concerned with the future, the other with the past, which is known already, "even to prophets," as Epimenides the Cretan said (he used not to prophesy about the future but about things in the past that were unclear); and the law is a hypothesis in judicial cases: having a starting point, it is easier for one to find proof. And [deliberative oratory] does not have many opportunities for diatribes, for example, against the opponent or about oneself or to create pathos.[198] Least of all [species of rhetoric can deliberative do this], unless one digresses. Therefore, one should do this [only] when at a loss for something to say, as do the orators at Athens and Isocrates;[199] for even when giving advice, he uses invective, for example, against the Lacedaimonians in the *Panegyricus* and against Chares in the *Symmachicus*.[200]

11. In epideictic one should interweave the speech with praise, as Isocrates does; for he is always bringing in somebody [to praise]. What Gorgias used to say—that he was never at a loss for words—is similar: if he is talking about Achilles, he praises [his father] Peleus, then [his grandfather] Aeacus, then the god [Aeacus' father, Zeus]; similarly, with courage, that it does this and that or has certain qualities [that can be amplified]. 12. If one has logical arguments, one should speak both ethically and logically; if you do not have

---

196. The situation is that of a man who has deposited money with another.

197. Despite what Aristotle has just said, this seems to qualify as an enthymeme since a reason is given.

198. *Diatribē* literally means "spending time" on some subject, but came to mean a personal attack. To illustrate Aristotle's point, compare the general absence of personal invective against his Athenian opponents in Demosthenes' deliberative speeches with his extended invective in judicial speeches, including *On the Crown*. In Hellenistic philosophical schools a diatribe was an informal personal speech, sometimes like a sermon, addressed by a teacher to his students, often in response to questions.

199. On orators at Athens, see note on 3.11.15. Isocrates, though an Athenian, did not speak in public, which may be why he is mentioned separately.

200. Aristotle regarded the *Panegyricus* as a deliberative speech since it gave advice on the need of the Greeks to join together under Athenian leadership against Persia; because of its extensive praise of Athens it is often classified as epideictic. The *Symmachicus* is better known as *On the Peace*.

enthymemes, speak ethically. And to seem virtuous suits a good person more than an exact argument does. 13. Refutative enthymemes are better liked [by audiences] than demonstrative ones because what makes a refutation is more clearly syllogistic; for inconsistencies are clearer when placed side-by-side. 14. Refutations of the opponent are not a separate species but belong to proofs.[201] Some disprove by objection [to a premise or conclusion], some by [a counter-]syllogism.[202] In both deliberation and in court the opening speaker should state his own premises first, then should meet those of his opponent by disproving and tearing them to pieces before he can make them.[203] But if the opposition has many good points to make, put the refutations first, as Callistratus did in the Messenian assembly; for first removing the objections they were going to voice, he then spoke his own case.[204] 15. But if you speak second you should reply first to the opposing speech, refuting and offering opposed syllogisms, especially if what was said seems to have met with approval. Just as the mind is not receptive toward a person who has been previously criticized, in the same way it is not [receptive] toward a speech if the opponent seems to have spoken well. One should thus make room in the hearer's mind for the speech one is going to give, and this will happen if you take away [the impression that has been left]. Thus, after fighting against everything or the most important things or the popular things or the easily refutable things, one should then make one's persuasive points:

1418b

> First shall I be a defender of the goddesses,
> And shall show she does not speak justly.
> For I do not think that Hera. . . .[205]

---

201. Cf. 2.26.3. Aristotle does not regard the refutation as a distinct part of an oration, as did Theodorus (cf. 3.13.5), but later writers often so list it; cf., e.g., *Rhetoric for Herennius* 1.4. In *Rhetoric for Alexander*, chapters 7 and 13, refutation is one of several subheadings of proof.

202. Cf. 2.25.1.

203. In an Athenian court the speakers would have known most of the arguments of their opponents from the preliminary hearing.

204. On an embassy to the Messenians in 362 B.C.E. Callistratus began with reasons why they should not ally with Thebes before introducing arguments why they should join with Athens (see Nepos, *Epaminondas* 6). When an orator confronts a hostile audience it is often most effective to face immediately the arguments or prejudices in their minds. Cicero's speech *For Cluentius* is a large-scale example.

205. Euripides, *Trojan Women* 969–1032, where Hecuba begins her reply to Helen by defending the action of the goddess (Aphrodite) in the judgment of Paris. *She* is Helen.

In these lines [Hecuba] seizes first on [Helen's] most foolish argument. So much for arguments [*pisteis*].

16. In regard to ethos, since there are sometimes things to be said about oneself that are invidious or prolix or contradictory, and about another that are abusive or boorish, it is best to attribute them to another person, as Isocrates does in the *Philippus* and in the *Antidosis*[206] and as Archilochus does in censure; for he introduces the father speaking of his daughter in an iambic poem: "Nothing is unexpected nor declared impossible on oath"[207] and [introduces] Charon the carpenter in [another] iambic work, which begins "Nothing to me the [wealth of] Gyges." And as Sophocles does, making Haemon speak to his father about Antigone on the basis of what others say.[208] 17. Sometimes it is advisable to change enthymemes into maxims; for example: "Sensible men should seek reconciliations when successful; for thus they get the greater advantage." As an enthymeme this would be "If it is necessary to seek reconciliations whenever such changes are most profitable and most advantageous, then it is necessary to seek changes when one is successful."[209]

Chapter 18: Erōtēsis, *or Interrogation*

■ In Athenian judicial procedure indictment resulted from a preliminary hearing before one of the archons, or magistrates, at which some prima facie evidence of a wrong was presented and witnesses offered testimony. It is likely that the defendant could interrogate the witnesses and try to show that there was no merit in the charge. The evidence of the witnesses was taken down in writing and then read out by a court secretary if a trial took place. (On judicial procedures in Athens, see Bonner and Smith 1930–1938.) Interrogation was also used in auditing officials on the completion of a term in office. Though the prosecution and defense in trials often discuss the evidence of witnesses, there was no cross-examination of them there in the modern sense. The principals in the trial could, however, ask questions

206. *Philippus* 4–7 and *Antidosis* 132–139 and 141–149 attribute flattering remarks to Isocrates' friends.

207. Archilochus, sixth-century B.C.E. poet, when disappointed in love for Neobule, attributed opprobrious remarks about her to her father in a passage beginning with this line.

208. *Antigone* 689–700.

209. In syllogistic form, if A = B when B = C, then A, since B = C. The maxim cited here, however, fulfills the requirements of an enthymeme as given in 2.21.2, since it already has a supporting reason.

directly of each other and demand an answer, which is principally what Aristotle here discusses; examples of the procedure can be found in Plato's *Apology* (24c–27d), Lysias' speech *Against Eratosthenes* (12.25), and elsewhere, but rhetorical questions, not expecting an answer, are far more common. Chapter 5 of *Rhetoric for Alexander* discusses investigational oratory (*exetasis*) and has some similarities to Aristotle's chapter but does not mention the possibility of replies. *Erōtēsis* did not become a distinct part of rhetoric nor is investigation a species of oratory in the standard teaching of Greek and Roman rhetoricians (for further discussion, see Carawan 1983).

1. As for interrogation (*erōtēsis*), it is most opportune to use it when an opponent has said one thing and, if the right question is asked an absurdity results. For example, Pericles questioned Lampon about **1419a** the holy rites of the Savior Goddess. When he replied that it was not permitted for an uninitiated person to hear about them, Pericles asked if he knew them himself. Since he admitted he did, [the next question was,] "And how, since you are uninitiated?" 2. A second situation is when something is self-evident and it is clear to the questioner that the opponent will grant another point. Receiving the expected answer to this, one should not ask about what is self-evident but should state the conclusion to which it points, as Socrates did when Meletus denied that Socrates believed in the gods. He asked if *daimones* ["spirits," in which Meletus admitted Socrates believed] were not either children of gods or something divine, and when Meletus said "They are," Socrates asked, "Does anybody think there are children of gods but not gods?"[210] 3. Another situation is when [the speaker] intends to show that [the opponent] is contradicting himself or saying something paradoxical. 4. And a fourth when it is not possible to answer the question except sophistically; for if he answers that it is and isn't or "Some yes, some no" or "In a way, but in another way not," [the audience] calls out that he is at a loss. Otherwise, do not attempt interrogation; for if the opponent resists, you seem to be defeated; for it is not possible to ask a series of questions because of the weakness of the audience. (For the same reason one should condense enthymemes as much as possible.)[211]

---

210. The exchange is incorporated in Plato's *Apology* 27d, which Aristotle apparently regarded as a faithful record of what Socrates said, at least in this case. The conclusion is a rhetorical question, addressed to the jury.

211. Cf 1.2.13, where it is said that a general audience cannot follow an extended argument.

5. Amphibolies[212] need to be answered by examining them logically and in some detail, supplying a resolution of seeming contradictions directly in the answer before [the opponent] asks a follow-up question or draws a conclusion; for it is not difficult to see to what the train of argument may lead. Let how to do this and how to make replies be evident from the *Topics* [book 8]. 6. If a conclusion takes the form of a question, explain the reason for the conclusion; for example, when Sophocles[213] was asked by Pisander if he had approved establishing the government of the Four Hundred, as the others on the committee to draft legislation did, he admitted it. "But why? Did these measures not seem to you to be wicked?" He agreed. "Did you not then do these wicked deeds?" "Yes," he said, "but there were no better alternatives!"[214] And as the Spartan replied, when rendering an account of his term as ephor: being asked if it did not seem to him that the others on the board had justly been put to death, he agreed. The examiner asked, "Did not you take the same measures as they?" He admitted it. "Therefore would it not be just to put you also to death?" "Not at all," he replied, "for they took bribes to do these things; I did not, but acted in accordance with my own judgment." Thus, one should not ask any further question after drawing a conclusion nor couch the conclusion as a question unless the balance of truth is in one's favor.

1419b

7. As for humor, since it seems to have some use in debate and Gorgias rightly said that one should spoil the opponents' seriousness with laughter and their laughter with seriousness, the number of forms of humor have been stated in the *Poetics*,[215] of which some are appropriate for a gentleman to use and some not. Each speaker will take up what suits him. Mockery [*eirōneia*] is more gentlemanly than buffoonery [*bōmolokhia*]; for the mocker makes a joke for his own amusement, the buffoon for the amusement of others.

Chapter 19: The Epilogos, *or Conclusion of a Speech*

■ *Epilogos* simply means a *logos* that is added on (*epi*). The Latin is *peroratio*. Note the references in this chapter to a "natural order" in the arrangement

---

212. See note on 3.5.4. Here an amphiboly is an ambiguous statement, or question that cannot be answered in the terms asked. A notorious modern instance is "Have you stopped beating your wife yet?"

213. The orator involved in the oligarchic revolution of 411 B.C.E., not the dramatist.

214. Cf. Lysias, *Against the Grain Dealers*, sec. 5, in Appendix I.C.

215. In the lost second book. This section is probably a late addition to the chapter.

of the material. In contrast to the previous chapters, the discussion does not consider epilogues in each of the three species of rhetoric. What Aristotle says here is chiefly applicable to judicial rhetoric, but could be applied in an extended deliberative speech where the audience needs a recapitulation of the arguments.

1. The epilogue is made up of four things: disposing the hearer favorably toward the speaker and unfavorably toward the opponent; amplifying and minimizing; moving the hearer into emotional reactions [*pathē*]; and [giving] a reminder [of the chief points in the argument]. After he has shown himself to be truthful and his opponent false, the natural thing is [for a speaker] to praise and blame and drive home the point. One should aim at showing one or the other of two things: either that the speaker is a good man in terms of the issues or that he is good generally; or either that the opponent is a bad man in terms of the issues or that he is bad generally. The topics from which such characterizations are derived have been discussed [in Book 1, chapter 9]. 2. After this, in natural order, is the amplification or diminution [of the importance] of what has already been shown [in the proof]; for what has been done should be agreed upon before talking about its importance. Similarly, the growth of bodies comes from the pre-existent.[216] The topics which should be used for amplification and diminution have previously been laid out.[217] 3. After this, when the nature and importance [of the facts] are clear, lead the hearer into emotional reactions. These are pity and indignation and anger and hatred and envy and emulation and strife. Their topics have also been mentioned earlier.[218] What remains, then, is to remind the audience of what has been said earlier. 4. This may be fittingly done in the way that [writers of rhetorical handbooks] wrongly speak in discussing prooemia. They require that points be made several times in order to be easily learned. In the prooemion it is right to identify the subject, in order that the question to be judged not escape notice, but in the epilogue one should speak in recapitulation of what has been shown.

---

216. Aristotle regarded politics, poetry, rhetoric, etc. as developing analogously with biological organisms; their matter and form have potential to be actualized.

217. Presumably the reference is to 2.19, though to call them "topics" here confuses the distinction otherwise maintained between that term and *koina*.

218. In Book 2, chs. 2–11, but neither *topic* nor any other rhetorical term is used of the propositions set out there. This cross-reference is probably a later addition by Aristotle.

The starting point [of the epilogue] is to claim that one has performed what was promised, 5. so there should be mention of what these things are and why. The discussion is [sometimes] derived from comparison with the case of the opponent. Compare what both have said on the same subject: "But he says this about that, while I say this and for these reasons." Or use mockery: "He says this, I that. And what would he have done if he had shown this but not that?" Or

1420a   use interrogation:[219] "What has not been shown?" or "What did he show?" Either do this by comparison or in the natural order as the statements were made, first one's own and again, if you want it,

1420b   the opponent's claim separately. 6. Asyndeton is appropriate for the end of the discourse, since this is an *epi-logos*, not a *logos*: "I have spoken; you have listened, you have [the case], you judge."[220]

---

219. Here meaning rhetorical question, not expecting a reply.

220. Cf. the end of Lysias, *Against Eratosthenes* (12.100): "You have listened, you have seen, you have suffered, you have [the case]. You be the judge."

APPENDIX I
SUPPLEMENTARY TEXTS

A. GORGIAS' *ENCOMIUM OF HELEN*

■ The traditional cause of the Trojan War in the early days of Greek history was the abduction of Helen, wife of Menelaus of Sparta, by the handsome young Trojan prince known as Paris or Alexander, resulting in the Greek expedition against Troy and a war that lasted ten years. The persons involved in these heroic events became central figures in Greek tragedy and also in the epideictic oratory of the sophists. Paris had been promised the most beautiful woman in the world as a bribe for choosing Aphrodite, goddess of love, when he judged a beauty contest between her, Hera, and Athena. Helen's role in the abduction is not specified in the Homeric poems and was variously interpreted by later writers. In this celebrated speech Gorgias attempted to free her from all blame. It serves to illustrate sophistic epideictic as well as Gorgias' poetic style, on which Aristotle remarks in 3.1.8–9, 3.3.1, 3.3.4, 3.7.11, and 3.17.16. The translation seeks to recapture some features of Gorgias' prose style, including antithesis, alliteration, pairing of clauses, homoeoteleuton, and other forms of paronomasia which came to be known as "Gorgianic figures." Gorgias had come to Athens from Sicily in 427 B.C.E. The date of composition of the speech is unknown; he may have given it repeatedly as a demonstration of his art and may have provided written copies to his followers or allowed them to make transcriptions. In addition to his stylistic mannerisms, the speech illustrates techniques of amplification and the logical method of dividing a question and seeking proof by refuting the alternative possibilities. Gorgias' remarks on the power and nature of speech and opinion have been of special interest to modern students of rhetoric. This translation is based on the text as edited by Francesco Donadi (Rome, 1983).

Prooemion

1. Fairest ornament to a city is a goodly army and to a body beauty and to a soul wisdom and to an action virtue and to speech truth, but their opposites are unbefitting. Man and woman and speech and deed and city and object should be honored with praise if praiseworthy, but on the unworthy blame should be laid; for it is equal error and ignorance to blame the praiseworthy and to praise the blameworthy. 2. It is the function of a single speaker both to prove the needful rightly and to disprove the wrongly spoken. Thus, I shall refute those who rebuke Helen, a woman about whom there is univocal and unanimous testimony among those who have believed the poets and whose ill-omened name has become a memorial of disasters.[1] I wish, by giving some logic to language, to free the accused of blame and to show that her critics are lying and to demonstrate the truth and to put an end to ignorance.

Narration

3. Now that by nature and birth the woman who is the subject of this speech was preeminent among preeminent men and women, this is not unclear, not even to a few; for it is clear that Leda was her mother, while as a father she had in fact a god, though allegedly a mortal, the latter Tyndareus, the former Zeus; and of these the one seemed her father because he was, and the other was disproved because he was only said to be; and one was the greatest of men, the other lord of all. 4. Born from such parents, she possessed godlike beauty, which getting and not forgetting she preserved. On many did she work the greatest passions of love, and by her one body she brought together many bodies of men greatly minded for great deeds.[2] Some had the greatness of wealth, some the glory of ancient noblesse, some the vigor of personal prowess, some the power of acquired knowledge. And all came because of a passion that loved conquest and a love of honor that was unconquered. 5. Who he was and why and how he sailed away taking Helen as his love, I shall not say;[3] for to tell the

---

1. Cf., e.g., in Aeschylus' *Agamemnon* (line 689), a play on Helen's name: "Hell to ships, hell to men, hell to the city."
2. Helen had many suitors before marrying Menelaus.
3. That is, Paris or Alexander, who is named in section 19.

knowing what they know is believable but not enjoyable. Having now exceeded the time allotted for my introduction, I shall proceed to my intended speech and propose the causes for which Helen's voyage to Troy is likely to have taken place.[4]

Proposition

6. For either by fate's will and gods' wishes and necessity's decrees she did what she did or by force reduced or by words seduced or by love induced.

Proof

Now if for the first reason, the responsible one should rightly be held responsible:[5] it is impossible to prevent a god's predetermination by human premeditation, since by nature the stronger force is not prevented by the weaker, but the weaker is ruled and driven by the stronger; the stronger leads, the weaker follows. But god is stronger than man in force and in wisdom and in other ways. If, therefore, by fate and god the cause had been decreed, Helen must of all disgrace be freed.

7. But if she was seized by force and illegally assaulted and unjustly insulted, it is clear that the assailant as insulter did the wrong and the assailed as insulted suffered wrongly. It is right for the barbarian who laid barbarous hands on her by word and law and deed to meet with blame in word, disenfranchisement in law, and punishment in deed, while she who was seized and deprived of her country and bereft of her friends, how should she not be pitied rather than pilloried? He did dread deeds; she suffered them. Her it is just to pity, him to hate.

8. But if speech (*logos*) persuaded her and deceived her soul, not even to this is it difficult to make answer and to banish blame, as follows. Speech is a powerful lord that with the smallest and most invisible body accomplishes most godlike works. It can banish fear and remove grief and instill pleasure and enhance pity. I shall show how this is so. 9. It is necessary for it to seem so as well in the opinion of my hearers.

---

4. The speech will thus be characterized by argument from probability (*eikos*).
5. Aphrodite, goddess of love, who had promised Helen to Paris.

All poetry I regard and name as speech having meter. On those who hear it come fearful shuddering and tearful pity and grievous longing, as the soul, through words, experiences some experience of its own at others' good fortune and ill fortune. But listen as I turn from one argument to another.

10. Divine sweetness transmitted through words is inductive of pleasure, reductive of pain. Thus, by entering into the opinion of the soul the force of incantation is wont to beguile and persuade and alter it by witchcraft, and the two arts of witchcraft and magic are errors of the soul and deceivers of opinion. 11. How many speakers on how many subjects have persuaded others and continue to persuade by molding false speech? If everyone, on every subject, had memory of the past and knowledge of the present and foresight of the future, speech would not do what it does; but as things are, it is easy neither to remember the past nor to consider the present nor to predict the future; so that on most subjects most people take opinion as counselor to the soul. But opinion, being slippery and insecure, casts those relying on it into slippery and insecure fortune. 12. What is there to prevent the conclusion that Helen, too, when still young, was carried off by speech just as if constrained by force? Her mind was swept away by persuasion, and persuasion has the same power as necessity, although it may bring shame; for speech, by persuading the soul that it persuaded, constrained her both to obey what was said and to approve what was done. The persuader, as user of force, did wrong; the persuaded, forced by speech, is unreasonably blamed.

13. To understand that persuasion, joining with speech, is wont to stamp the soul as it wishes, one must study, first, the words of astronomers who, substituting opinion for opinion, removing one and instilling another, make incredible and unclear things appear true to the eyes of opinion; second, forceful speeches in public debate, where one side of the argument pleases a large crowd and persuades by being written with art even though not spoken with truth; third, the verbal wrangling of philosophers in which, too, a swiftness of thought is exhibited, making confidence in opinion easily changed. 14. The power of speech has the same effect on the condition of the soul as the application of drugs to the state of bodies; for just as different drugs dispel different fluids from the body, and some bring an end to disease but others end life, so also some speeches cause pain, some pleasure, some fear; some instill courage, some drug and bewitch the soul with a kind of evil persuasion.

15. Thus, it has been explained that if she was persuaded by speech she did no wrong but was unfortunate. I shall now go on to the fourth cause in a fourth argument. If it was love that did these things it will not be difficult to escape the charge of error that is alleged: for we see not what we wish but what each of us has experienced: through sight the soul is stamped in diverse ways. 16. Whenever men at war, enemy against enemy, buckle up in the armaments of bronze and iron, whether in defense or offense, when their sight beholds the scene, it is alarmed and causes alarm in the soul, so that often they flee in terror from future danger as though it were present. Obedience to law is strongly brought home by fear derived from sight which, coming upon people, has made them desire both what is judged seemly by law and thought good by the mind, 17. but as soon as they have seen terrible sights they have abandoned the thought of the moment. Thus, discipline is extinguished and fear drives out the concept. And many fall victim to imaginary diseases and dreadful pains and hard-to-cure mental aberrations; thus does sight engrave on the mind images of things seen. And many terrors are left unmentioned, but those that are omitted are very like the things that have been said. 18. Moreover, whenever pictures of many colors and figures create a perfect image of a single figure and form, they delight the sight. How much do the production of statues and the workmanship of artifacts furnish pleasurable sight to the eyes! Thus is it natural for the sight sometimes to grieve, sometimes to delight. Much love and desire for many objects is created in many minds. 19. If, then, the eye of Helen, pleased by the body of Alexander, gave to her soul an eagerness and response in love, what wonder? If love, a god, prevails over the divine power of the gods, how could a lesser one be able to reject and refuse it? But if love is a human disease and an ignorance of the soul, it should not be blamed as a mistake but regarded as a misfortune. For she went caught by the nets around her soul, not by the wishes of her mind, and by the necessity of love, not by the devices of art.

Epilogue

20. How, then, can blame be thought just? Whether she did what she did by falling in love or persuaded by speech or seized by violence or forced by divine necessity, she is completely acquitted. By speech I have removed disgrace from a woman. I have abided by the principle I posed at the start of my speech: I have tried to refute the injustice of

defamation and the ignorance of allegation. I wished to write a speech that would be Helen's encomion and my own *paignion*.[6]

B. SOCRATES' CRITIQUE OF SOPHISTIC RHETORIC

■ In Plato's *Gorgias* (written about 380 B.C.E.) Socrates is portrayed in dialogue with Gorgias, his student Polus, and Callicles on the subject of rhetoric. Socrates, as often, represents himself as in search of understanding and open to conviction, but he clearly has deep moral reservations about "what is called rhetoric" and whether it is a legitimate art. He compares it to medicine, mathematics, and other subjects, and wants to know what is its province. In the course of his argument he advances one of his favorite paradoxes, that if a person knows what is good he will do it. The question of the subject of rhetoric and the morality of the orator are important issues for Aristotle as well, and in *On Rhetoric* he seeks to provide a response.

458e SOC. Hear then, Gorgias, what I wonder at in what you have been saying; for probably you are speaking correctly but I am not correctly understanding you. Do you say that you are able to make a person into a rhetorician if he wants to learn from you? GOR. Yes. SOC. So as to be persuasive on all subjects in front of a crowd, not **459a** teaching them but persuading them? GOR. Certainly. SOC. You were saying just now that a rhetorician will even be more persuasive than a doctor about health. GOR. That's what I said, at least in front of a crowd. SOC. By this phrase "in front of a crowd" you mean among non-experts, don't you? He will surely not be more persuasive than a doctor among medical experts. GOR. You're right. SOC. Now if he will be more persuasive than a doctor, is he not more persuasive than an expert? GOR. Certainly. SOC. Even though he is not a doctor, isn't that so? GOR. Yes. SOC. Clearly one who is not a doctor is ignorant about things that a doctor knows. GOR. Clearly. SOC. One who lacks knowledge, then, will be more persuasive than one with knowledge among those without knowledge whenever the rhetor is more persuasive than the doctor. Is this the conclusion or isn't it? GOR. It is the conclusion, at least

---

6. I.e., plaything, amusement.

in this case. SOC. Isn't the rhetorician and rhetoric also in the same situation in regard to all other arts? There is no need for rhetoric to know the nature of the actual facts, only to have found some device of persuasion so as to seem to the ignorant to know more than the experts.

GOR. Isn't that a wonderfully easy way of doing things, Socrates? Not to be outdone by the experts when you haven't learned the other arts, only this one!

SOC. Whether the rhetor is outdone or not outdone by the others because of this we'll consider in a moment, if it is relevant. But let us consider this first, whether it happens that the rhetorician is in the same situation in regard to justice and injustice and the shameful and the honorable and good and bad as in the case of health and other things of which there are other arts: although not knowing what is good or what is bad or what is honorable or what is shameful or just or unjust, but devising persuasion about them so as to seem to know when he lacks knowledge in front of those without knowledge, rather than being one of those who knows. Or is there a necessity to have knowledge and should he have already learned these things before coming to you to learn rhetoric? Otherwise, you, the teacher of rhetoric, will teach none of these things to one who comes to you—for it is not your function—but you will make him seem to know such things in front of many people when he does not and to seem to be good when he is not. Or is it completely impossible for you to teach him rhetoric unless he already knows the truth about these subjects? What is the situation here, Gorgias? By Zeus, just as you promised a little while ago, pull the veil from rhetoric and say what is its power (*dynamis*).[7]

460a

GOR. But I think, Socrates, if he happens not to know these things he will also learn them from me.

SOC. Stop there; for what you are saying is good. If you make someone a rhetorician, it is necessary for him to know what things are just and unjust, either before he comes or later, learning them from you. GOR. Certainly. SOC. What then? Is a person who has learned building a builder, or not? GOR. Yes. SOC. And one who has learned music is a musician? GOR. Yes. SOC. And one who has learned medicine is a doctor. And in the same way, does a person who has learned each subject acquire the character that the

---

7. Cf. Aristotle's definition of rhetoric as a *dynamis*, 1.2.1.

knowledge creates in each? GOR. Certainly. SOC. In the same way also, someone who has learned justice is just? GOR. Certainly, of course. SOC. The just man does just things, I presume. GOR. Yes. SOC. Thus it is necessary, isn't it, for the rhetorician to be just and for the just man to wish to act justly? GOR. So it seems, anyway. SOC. Never will the just man, at least, wish to do wrong. GOR. Necessarily. SOC. From this argument it is necessary for the rhetorician to be just. GOR. Yes. SOC. The rhetorician, then, will never wish to do wrong. GOR. At least it does not seem so.

SOC. Do you remember what you said a little while ago, that trainers shouldn't be blamed or expelled from the city if a boxer uses his knowledge of boxing and uses it unfairly and commits an unjust act, and in the same way if a rhetor uses rhetoric unjustly his teacher should not be blamed and expelled from the city, but blame should be laid on the person doing the wrong and not using rhetoric rightly? Isn't that what was said? GOR. That was said. SOC. But now this same person, the rhetorician, it seems would not ever do wrong. Is that not so? GOR. So it seems. SOC. And in the first part of our discussion, Gorgias, it was said that rhetoric was a matter of words, not words about odd and even numbers, but words about justice and injustice. Is that right? GOR. Yes. SOC. Even then I supposed that you were saying that rhetoric would never be an unjust thing, since what it always talks about is justice. And when a little later you said that the rhetor might even use rhetoric unjustly, I was very astonished, and thinking that what was being said was inconsistent, I made the statement that if you thought it profitable to be refuted, as I did, it would be worthwhile to discuss the matter, and if not, to say goodbye. But now that we are examining it again, you see as do I, that it has again been agreed that the rhetorician is incapable of using rhetoric immorally and of wanting to do wrong. To figure out, Gorgias, by the Dog of Egypt, what is the truth will require no small amount of discussion to examine the matter adequately.

461a

■ At this point Gorgias' student, Polus, interrupts impatiently, complaining that Socrates is taking an unfair advantage of Gorgias. Polus demands that Socrates say what he thinks rhetoric is. Socrates replies by labeling it a form of flattery. This then leads to the famous comparison of the true and the false arts, with Socrates' assertion that rhetoric is analogous to cookery, something that dresses up bad ideas to make them persuasive, just as a cook tries to make bad food palatable.

C. LYSIAS' SPEECH *AGAINST THE GRAIN DEALERS* (386 B.C.E.)

■ This selection is provided as an example of a judicial speech given in an Athenian law court and of the work of a logographer, a professional writer of speeches for others (cf. *Rhetoric* 3.7.7). It was written by Lysias for memorization and delivery in court by an unnamed member of the Athenian Council in prosecution of retail grain dealers who had allegedly been buying up larger supplies from importers than the law allowed, at first bidding against each other, but then entering into a conspiracy to keep the price down and charging inflated prices to consumers in a time of scarcity.[8] Athens could not feed its own large population and regularly imported grain from the island of Cyprus or from Greek cities on the Black Sea. Athens' enemies, including the Spartans, tried to disrupt this trade, with some success. In composing this speech Lysias was concerned to awaken the jury's confidence in the speaker, to break down the defendants' plea that they had acted with official permission, and to play upon the jury's emotions against grain dealers as extortioners and public indignation at anything that raised the price of staple goods. There are thus factors of ethos, logos, and pathos at work in the speech, and a form of non-artistic persuasion is seen in the introduction of Anytus as a witness. Whether or not Aristotle had read this speech we do not know; the clarity and simplicity of the style should have earned his approval. What he says about the parts of a judicial speech in Book 3, chapters 13–19 can be compared with Lysias' treatment throughout. Note especially the interrogation in section 5 of the speech in terms of what Aristotle says in chapter 18 of Book 3.

Prooemion

1. Many people have come to me, Gentlemen of the Jury, in surprise that I made an accusation against the grain dealers in the Council, and saying that even if you think they are doing great injustice, nonetheless you regard those who speak against them also as opportunistic slanderers. Thus I want to say first why I feel forced to prosecute them.

---

8. The importers were required to sell at least two-thirds of the cargo brought by each ship.

Narration

2. When the executive committee in charge at the time brought a report about them to the Council there was such great anger against them that some of the speakers said they ought to be handed over to the proper authorities to be put to death without a trial. I thought, however, that it was a dreadful thing for the Council to accustom itself to do things of this sort, and I stood up and said that it seemed to me the grain dealers should be tried in accordance with the law. It was my belief that if they deserved to be put to death, you serving on a jury would be no less able than the Council to come to a just decision, and if they were not guilty they ought not to die without a trial. 3. After the Council agreed to this, attempts were made to slander me by saying that I made these remarks in hopes of saving the grain dealers. Now when the case came before the Council for a preliminary hearing I answered the charge by my action. While the others kept quiet, I stood up and accused these men and made it clear to everyone that I was not speaking on their behalf but in support of the established laws. 4. Well, I became involved in the case for these reasons, but I think it would be shameful to abandon it before you have given whatever verdict you wish.

Interrogation

5. So first, I summon [one of the grain dealers] to come up here. Tell me, sir, are you a resident alien? "Yes." Do you live here intending to obey the laws of the city or to do whatever you want? "To obey the laws." Do you judge you deserve to die if you have acted in violation of the laws for which death is the penalty? "I do." Then answer me: Do you acknowledge that you with others bought more grain than the fifty baskets that the law allows? "I bought it on the orders of the grain commissioners."

Proof

6. Well then, Gentlemen of the Jury, if he shows that there is a law that orders the grain dealers to buy up grain if the commissioners command, acquit them. But if not, it is just for you to convict them; for we have produced the law that forbids anyone in the city from buying up more grain than fifty measures at a time. *The law is read.*

7. This accusation of mine ought to have been enough, Gentlemen of the Jury, since he agrees that he bought up grain when the law makes it clear it was forbidden, and you have sworn to vote in accordance with the laws. Nevertheless, in order that you may be persuaded that they are lying in their statements against the commissioners, I must speak at greater length about them. 8. For since these men shifted the blame upon them, we called the commissioners before us and questioned them. Two denied any knowledge of the matter, but Anytus[9] said that in the previous winter, when grain was dear and these men were outbidding each other and fighting among themselves, he advised them to stop their competition, thinking that it was to the advantage of you who bought from them that they should buy grain [from the importers] at the most reasonable price possible; for they were required to sell at no more than an obol higher. 9. That he did not order them to buy up and hold grain but only advised them not to bid against each other, I will produce Anytus himself as witness to you. *Anytus' testimony is read by the clerk and acknowledged.*

The witness spoke these words at last year's Council, but these men seem to be buying up grain this year. *Testimony of additional witnesses is read.*

10. Well then, you have heard that it was not at the order of the commissioners that they bought up the grain. But I think that even if they are telling the whole truth about these matters, they will accuse the commissioners rather than clear themselves. For in circumstances where laws have been expressly written to govern the case, shouldn't both those not obeying the laws and those ordering them to do the opposite be punished?

11. But in fact, Gentlemen of the Jury, I think they will not have recourse to this argument, but probably will say, as before in the Council, that it was as a favor to the city that they bought up the grain in order to sell it to you at as reasonable a price as possible. But I shall tell you a great and very clear proof that they are lying. 12. If they were doing this for your benefit, they ought to have been seen selling for many days at the same price until what they had bought was exhausted, but as it is, on one and the same day they were selling at a profit of more than a drachma as though buying at one basket at a time. I furnish you yourselves as witness of this. 13. And it seems to me strange if, when they have to contribute to a war tax which everyone is going to know about, they refuse and give their poverty as an

---

9. This may well have been the same Anytus who was one of the prosecutors of Socrates.

excuse,[10] but in the case of acts for which death is the penalty and where it was in their interest to escape notice, these they alleged they illegally did out of good will to you. And yet you all know that they are people from whom such statements are least appropriate. 14. Their interests and those of others are opposed to each other. They make the most profit when they sell grain dearly after some bad news reaches the city. They are so delighted when they see your disasters that they get news before anyone else, and some rumors they make up themselves, saying that the ships have been lost in the Black Sea or captured by the Lacedaimonians on the outward voyage, or the ports are closed or the truce is about to be broken, and they plot against you on the same occasions as do your enemies. 15. For whenever you happen to be in most need of grain, these men snap it up and do not wish to sell in order that we may not argue about the price but be glad if we come away having bought from them for any price however high. The result is that sometimes during peace we are besieged by these men. 16. The city recognized their wickedness and disaffection so long ago that although you have appointed market supervisors for all other purchases, for this one trade alone you have chosen grain controllers by lot. And often to date you have inflicted the extreme penalty on them even though they were citizens because they were not able to defeat the villainy of these men. What now should the actual offenders suffer at your hands when you put to death even those unable to control them?

17. You must keep it in mind that it is impossible for you to vote to acquit them. For if you absolve them when they are agreeing that they are combining against the importers, you will be shown to be plotting against those traders. If they were making any other defense, nobody could object to their being acquitted, for it rests with you which side you wish to believe, but as it now stands how would you not seem to be doing something dreadful if you dismiss unpunished those confessing they broke the law? 18. Remember, Gentlemen of the Jury, that although many in the past met with this charge, denied it, and produced witnesses, you condemned them to death, thinking the speeches of their accusers more persuasive. Surely it would be astonishing if in passing judgment on the same offenses you are more interested in getting justice from those who deny the charge [than from these who admit it]. 19. And moreover, Gentlemen, I think it is

---

10. Of this no evidence is provided, the speaker assuming it is well known.

clear to all that suits of this kind are of the widest concern to people in the city, and thus they will inquire what judgment you have about them, thinking that if you condemn these men to death, the others will be brought to better order, but if you let them go unpunished, you will have voted them full license to do whatever they want. 20. It is essential, Gentlemen of the Jury, to punish them, not only because of what has come to pass but as an example of what is going to be; for even so they will be barely tolerable. Keep in mind that a very large number of those in this trade have been put on trial for their lives, and even so they make so much profit from it that they prefer every day to risk their lives rather than cease milking you unjustly. 21. Moreover, not even if they implore and beseech you would you be justified in pitying them; rather, pity those citizens who have died because of their wickedness and the importers against whom they have combined. You will gratify them and make them more zealous by punishing these men. Otherwise, what do you think their state of mind will be when they learn that you acquitted the retailers who confessed to forming a conspiracy against the importers?

Epilogue

22. I do not know what more there is to say. In the case of other evil-doers, when put on trial, you have to get information from the accusers, while the villainy of these men you all know. If then you convict them, you will both do justice and buy your grain at a fairer price, but if not it will be dearer.

D. INTRODUCTION TO DIALECTIC FROM ARISTOTLE, *TOPICS* 1.1–3

■ In *On Rhetoric* 1.1.1. Aristotle describes rhetoric as a "counterpart" to dialectic, a subject with which students in his school were assumed to be familiar. His principal discussion of dialectic is found in the *Topics*. It does not provide a formal definition of dialectic, but in the following passage distinguishes it from other kinds of reasoning and discusses its uses (see Evans 1977).

1. The purpose of this treatise is to find a method from which we **100a18** shall be able to syllogize about every posed problem on the basis

of generally accepted opinions [*endoxa*] and while upholding an argument ourselves say nothing self-contradictory. First, then, there should be a statement of what a syllogism is and what are its different kinds, in order that the dialectical syllogism may be grasped; for that is what we are seeking in the treatise at hand.

Now syllogism is a statement [*logos*] in which, certain things having been posited, something other than the posited necessarily results through what is posited. *Apodeixis* [logical demonstration] occurs whenever the syllogism is drawn from things that are true and primary or from things that are of the sort as to have taken the first principle of knowledge of them from what is primary and true;[11] but a syllogism is dialectical when drawn from generally accepted

100b18   opinions. Things are true and primary when they are persuasive through themselves, not through other things; for in the case of scientific principles there is no need to seek the answer to *why* but each of the first principles is persuasive in and by itself. Generally accepted opinions [*endoxa*], on the other hand, are those that seem right to all people or most people or the wise—and in the latter case all the wise or most of them or those best known and generally accepted [as authorities]. Syllogism is *eristical* [or contentious] when derived from what appears to be generally accepted opinions but are not and when it appears derived from generally accepted or apparently generally accepted opinions; for every opinion that appears to be generally accepted is not generally accepted; for none of the apparently accepted opinions has an altogether obvious manifestation, as results in the case of the first principles of eristic argument, where immediately and for the most part the nature of the falsehood is obvious to

101a   those with even a small capacity of comprehension. Therefore, let the former kind of syllogism that has been termed eristical also be called *syllogism*, and the other not syllogism but *eristical syllogism*, since it appears to syllogize but does not syllogize.

Furthermore, in addition to all the syllogisms that have been mentioned there are *paralogisms* drawn from premises concerned with specific sciences, as in fact occurs in geometry and subjects related to it; for this form seems to differ from the syllogisms that have been mentioned. One who draws a faulty [geometrical] diagram does not syllogize from what is true and primary nor from generally

---

11. *Apodeixis* begins with what are called a priori propositions, such as the axioms of geometry, or from propositions proved in some other science, as physics uses propositions from mathematics.

accepted opinions. He does not fall within the definition; for he does not take [as premises of his argument] what seems so to all nor to the majority nor to the wise (and among the latter all or most or the most authoritative) but makes the syllogism from assumptions peculiar to the science but not true; for he makes a *paralogism* by drawing semicircles or by extending lines in a way they should not be extended.

Let the species of syllogisms, then, to take them in outline, be as has been said. Speaking in general about all the matters discussed and those to be discussed later, let us make definitions [only] to this degree [or precision], because we do not propose to offer an exact account of any of them but want to give an account to the extent of an outline, thinking it quite sufficient in accordance with the method we have set to be able to recognize each of them in some way.

2. What would follow the matters discussed is to say for how many and what [purposes] the study [of dialectic] should be useful.[12] It is useful for three purposes: for mental training, for [serious] conversation, and for the sciences along philosophical lines. That it is useful for mental training is obvious in itself; for by having a method we shall be able more easily to undertake discussion of any proposed question.[13] [It is useful] for conversation because after enumerating the opinions of the many we shall engage in discussion with others on the basis of their own beliefs rather than that of others, restating whatever they seem to be saying to us when it is not well said. [The study is useful] for the sciences along philosophical lines because if we are able to raise difficulties on both sides of the issue, we shall more easily see in each case what is true and what false. Further, [it is useful] in regard to what things are primary in each science; for it is impossible to say anything about them on the basis of the specific first principles of each proposed science, since the principles are primary in all cases,[14]   **101b**

---

12. Cf. Aristotle's account of why rhetoric is useful in *Rhetoric* 1.1.12–13.

13. Aristotle is here thinking of the dialectical exercises or disputations that were a common feature of ancient philosophical schools (and continued to be practiced in some form until the early modern period). Two students were set against each other to debate a question. One stated a proposition in a universal positive form (e.g., I say that pleasure is the only good). The other, by asking a series of questions that can be answered *yes* or *no*, sought to refute the proposition.

14. No science (mathematics, physics, metaphysics, etc.) can prove its own first principles; they have to be taken from somewhere else, either from what is proved in another science or from assumptions accepted generally or by the wise. Thus, in the beginning of his *Physics* Aristotle raises the question whether there is one or several first principles of physics and considers the opinions of earlier Greek thinkers on this subject in search of some agreed-upon starting point.

and it is necessary to discuss them on the basis of generally accepted opinions in each case. This is specific and most proper to dialectic; for since it is investigative, it leads the way to the first principles of all methods. 3. We shall possess the method completely when we are in the same situation as in rhetoric and medicine and such faculties: that is, [able] to accomplish what we choose from the available means;[15] for neither will the one with rhetorical skill persuade by every means nor will the doctor heal, but if none of the available means is neglected we shall say that he has knowledge adequately.

■ The *Topics* then continues with discussion of propositions and problems, an account of the four "predicables" (definition, property, genus, and accident), and definitions of the ten "categories" (essence, quantity, quality, relation, place, time, position, state, activity, and passivity). The categories are mentioned in *Rhetoric* 1.7.21 and 2.7.6

E. TWO SELECTIONS FROM ISOCRATES

1.   From *Against the Sophists*

■ *Against the Sophists* was written about 390 B.C.E. when Isocrates first opened his school in Athens. In it he attacks contemporary sophists and outlines his own project for teaching rhetoric. The long sentences are characteristic of all of Isocrates' writing; they are, however, in Greek, remarkably clear as a result of the purity of his word choice and the smoothness of his composition. Only the first twenty-two sections of the speech survive; see the translation by David Mirhady in *The Oratory of Classical Greece*, edited by Michael Gagarin, vol. 4 (*Isocrates I*) University of Texas Press, 2000), pp. 61–66.

14. If I should not only rebuke others but also make clear my own mind, I think that all intelligent people will agree with me that while many of those who have studied philosophy have remained in private life, others who have never associated with any of the sophists have become skilled at speaking and engaging in public life. Abilities both of speech and of all other activities occur in those well endowed

---

15. Cf. *Rhetoric* 1.2.1.

by nature and those schooled by experience. 15. Formal education (*paideusis*) makes such people more skilled and more resourceful in seeking things out; for it teaches them to take from readier sources what they now hit upon at random,[16] but it would not fashion those without natural aptitude into good debaters or writers, although it would lead them on to improvement and to a greater degree of understanding on many subjects.

16. Since I have gone this far I want to speak more clearly about these things. I assert that to gain knowledge of the particulars (*ideai*) from which we speak and compose all speeches is not one of the very difficult things, if one entrusts himself not to those making rash promises but to those knowing something about these matters. To chose from these [particulars] those which are needed for each of the subjects and to join them to each other and to arrange them properly, and further not to miss opportunities but also to adorn the whole speech appropriately with enthymemes[17] and to speak in words rhythmically and melodiously, 17. these things require much study and are the function of a manly and imaginative mind.[18] The student, in addition to having some natural aptitude, must learn the different species (*eidē*) of speeches and practice himself in their uses, and the teacher must be able to expound the subject so accurately as to leave nothing out, and for the rest, he must furnish himself as such an example [of oratory], 18. so that the students who have taken form and become able to imitate him will straight away in speaking show themselves more flowery and graceful than others. When all these things come together completely, the devotees of philosophy will have success, but in proportion as any one of the things mentioned is left out, necessarily will the students be worse positioned in this respect.

2. From *Antidosis*

■ About 354 B.C.E. Isocrates became aware of criticism of himself and his school and undertook a defense in a long disquisition entitled *Antidosis*, in which he imagines he is on trial in court. Aristotle had recently begun his "afternoon" lectures in the Academy, which are thought to have been

---

16. Cf. *Rhetoric* 1.1.2.
17. In this context apparently meaning "striking thoughts."
18. Parodied in Socrates' remarks to Gorgias in Plato's *Gorgias* 463a.

provoked by disapproval of Isocrates' teaching, and it is possible to read portions of *Antidosis* as Isocrates' rejoinder.[19]

84. Surely it would be evident that I am more truthful and useful than those affecting to turn people toward self-control (*sōphrosynē*) and justice (*dikaiosynē*).[20] They exhort people to a kind of virtue (*aretē*) and wisdom (*phronēsis*) unknown by others and disputed among themselves,[21] whereas I urge people to what is agreed by all [to be wisdom]. 85. For them it is enough if they can attract some to their company by the reputation of their names, while I will be shown as never urging any private individuals to join me; instead, I try to persuade the city as a whole to undertake the sort of actions from which the citizens will become prosperous and which will deliver the other Greeks from their present evils. . . .

261. I think that teachers skilled in eristics[22] and those engaged in studies of the stars and geometry[23] and other such learning benefit and do not injure their associates—benefit them less than they promise but more than others think. 262. Most men suppose such studies empty talk and hair-splitting; for none of them are useful in either private or public affairs, nor do any of them long remain in the memory of students because they do not accord with life nor make any contribution to our activities, but are wholly removed from our needs. 263. This is neither my opinion nor am I far removed from it. Those thinking this kind of education is of no use in practical life seem to me to hold the right view, and those praising it also speak the truth. The reason I have made this contradictory statement is that these studies are different in nature from the others by which we are taught, 264. Other studies naturally help us after we have acquired knowledge of them, whereas these would not benefit those who master them, except if they chose to make their living from teaching them, but they do benefit us while we learn them. In spending time on the detail and precision of study

---

19. For the complete speech, see the translation by Yun Lee Too in the *Oratory of Classical Greece*, edited by Michael Gagarin, vol. 4: *Isocrates I* (University of Texas Press 2000), pp. 201–264.

20. Given the interest of Plato and Aristotle in these virtues the reference applies to them.

21. As in Socratic dialogues and exercises in dialectic in the Academy.

22. E.g., Aristotle. As elsewhere, Isocrates makes no distinction between eristics and dialectic; cf. Aristotle's account of the differences and the usefulness of dialectic in *Topics* 1.1.

23. E.g., Eudoxus and others in the Academy.

of the stars and geometry, 265. and being forced to apply the mind to difficult things, and being habituated to speak and struggle with what is being said and shown and not let our minds wander, we gain the ability, after being exercised and sharpened on these studies, of grasping and learning more easily and more quickly those subjects of more importance and greater value. 266. I do not, however, think it right to give the name "philosophy" to training that is no help in the present, neither in speech nor in action; rather I call this exercise "mental gymnastic" and preparation for philosophy, something more mature than what boys pursue in schools, but for the most part rather like it. . . .

270. I have said enough advice about these studies. As for wisdom (*sophia*) and philosophy (*philosophia*), it would not be fitting for someone pleading another case to speak about these terms (for they are distinct from all litigation), but since I am being tried on such grounds and claim that what is called philosophy by some is not that, it is fitting for me to define and explain to you what it is when rightly understood. 271. My view, as it happens, is very simple. For since it is not within the nature of mankind to acquire certain knowledge (*epistēmē*) by which we might know what one should do or say [in every case], from what remains possible I think those are wise (*sophoi*) who can come upon opinions that are best for the most part, and those are philosophers who occupy themselves with studies from which they will most quickly gain practical understanding (*phronēsis*) of that sort. . . .

274. I think that the kind of art (*tekhnē*) that can impart virtue (*aretē*) and justice (*diakaiosynē*) in those naturally depraved neither has existed in the past nor does now, and that those making promises about it in the past will cease speaking and stop their nonsense before any such education is found, 275. but I do think that people can become better and worthier if they conceive an ambition to speak well, and if they have a passion to be able to persuade their hearers, and in addition if they set their hearts on seizing the advantage (*pleonexia*), not advantage as understood by foolish people, but advantage in the true meaning . . .

F. SELECTIONS FROM *RHETORIC FOR ALEXANDER*

■ The *Rhetoric for Alexander* is a composite work, consisting of a forged introductory letter, purporting to be by Aristotle writing to Alexander the

Great, and two separate rhetorical handbooks by different authors, covering some of the same contents but differently organized. Both authors make up their own examples to illustrate their rules, rather than quote known sources, as Aristotle frequently does. The second treatise has a few similarities to teachings attributed to Isocrates, suggesting that the author may have studied with him. The first treatise (chs. 1–18) takes up each of seven species of rhetoric in turn. The topics discussed have some resemblance to portions of Book 1 of Aristotle's *Rhetoric*, but the author does not distinguish the three means of persuasion central to Aristotle's theory and the work lacks any counterpart to Aristotle's discussion of the emotions and characters found in Book 2. The second treatise (chs. 19–38) is organized around the arrangement of the different species of rhetoric and thus has a superficial similarity to *Rhetoric* 3.13–19. Whether the authors knew Aristotle's *Rhetoric*, or conversely Aristotle knew one or both of the treatises, remains uncertain but is unlikely. An historical reference in the first treatise (ch. 8.1429a18) can be dated to 341 B.C.E., so this part of the work was written after that date at the earliest and perhaps much later. Portions of the first treatise were found on a papyrus from Hibeh in Egypt in 1906, and it is thought to have been written about fifty years after Aristotle's death. The two parts were probably combined by an editor who composed the introduction at some time during the later Roman Empire. On the basis of a reference in Quintilian (3.4.9) it has long been customary to attribute both parts of *Rhetoric for Alexander* to Anaximenes of Lampsacus, a contemporary of Aristotle, Michel Patillon (1997) has argued that the first treatise should be identified with the *Theodectea*, a work on rhetoric mentioned by Aristotle in *Rhetoric* 3.9.10, and that the second part is an expanded version of the handbook tradition stemming from Tisias (Corax) and Theodorus. See further Appendix II.A. A translation of the complete work by H. Rackham can be found in the second half of the Loeb Classical Library edition of Aristotle's *Problems* xxii–xxxviii (Harvard University Press, *1957*).

1421b7   *Chapter 1*: [There are three kinds (*genē*) of political speech: deliberative and epideictic and judicial. Of these,][24] there are seven species: protreptic, apotreptic; encomiastic, invective; accusatory, apologetic; and investigative (the latter either by itself or in relation to another species). The species of speeches are of this number and we shall use them in general public debates and in litigation about contracts and in

---

24. Perhaps an addition to the text by the editor, adjusting it to the standard post-Aristotelian tradition.

private meetings. We may be able to speak about them most readily if we take the species one by one and enumerate their functions and uses and arrangements. And first [let us treat] protreptic and apotreptic, since there is use for these most in private meetings and in general public debates.

To speak in general terms, a *protreptic* is an exhortation to decisions or speeches or actions, and an *apotreptic* a dissuasion from decisions or speeches or actions. Since these are their definitions, one making an exhortation must show that the things which he urges are just and lawful and advantageous and honorable and pleasant and easy to be done; but if not, whenever he urges disagreeable actions they should be shown to be possible and that it is necessary to do them. The one dissuading should apply hindrance by the opposite arguments, [saying) that something is not just and not lawful and not advantageous and not honorable and unpleasant and not practicable, and if he cannot argue this, that it is laborious and not necessary. These qualities belong to all actions, so no one having one or the other of these hypotheses should be at a loss. These are the things that those exhorting or dissuading ought to aim at; and I shall try to define what each of them is and to show from what source we can secure a good supply for each of our speeches.

Now what is *just* [*dikaion*] is the unwritten custom of all people or of most, distinguishing honorable things from base. It is honorable to honor parents and do good to friends and repay a favor to benefactors; for written rules do not enjoin these and things like them to humans, but they are observed by unwritten custom and law everywhere.   1422a

Law [*nomos*] is the common agreement of a city setting out in writing how each thing must be done.

What is *advantageous* [*sympheron*] is the preservation of existing good things or acquisition of those we do not possess or rejection of existing evils or prevention of harmful things expected to occur. It is divided in the case of individuals into what is advantageous to body and mind and externals. Now for a body, the advantageous is strength, beauty, health; for a mind courage, wisdom, justice, and externals are friends, money, possessions; and their opposites are disadvantages. For a city, advantageous things are such as concord, power against an enemy, financial resources, abundance of revenues, good and numerous allies. And briefly, we think all things like these are advantageous, and their opposites are disadvantageous.

Honorable things [*kala*] are those from which some good repute and some distinguished honor will come to doers, and *pleasant*

things [*hēdea*] are those causing delight, and *easy* [*rhaidia*] those accomplished with very little time and toil and expense, and *practicable* [*dynata*] all those that can be done, and *necessary* [*anankaia*] those that do not lie with us to do, but are as they are by some divine or human necessity.

Such then are the just and legal and advantageous and the honorable and pleasant and easy and practicable and necessary. We shall find plenty to say about them both from what has already been said about them and analogies [*homoia*] to them and their opposites and previous judgments by gods or men of repute or judges or by our opponents.

Now we have previously shown what sort of thing is the just. An analogy to the just is something of the following sort: "Just as we think it just to obey our parents, in the same way it is right for sons to imitate the actions of their fathers." And "just as it is just to do good in return to those who do us good, so it is just not to harm those who do us no evil." This then is the way we should use analogy to the just, and we must make the example clear from its opposites: "Just as it is just for those doing something bad to be punished, so also is it fitting for benefactors to be benefited in turn." The judgment of some men of repute about the just you will take thus: "But we are not alone in hating and doing harm to enemies, but both Athenians and Lacedaimonians judge it just for enemies to be punished." This is then how you will use the just, pursuing it in many ways.

■ There follow topics (though that word is not used), with examples made up by the author, for treating the issue of legality and advantage, concluding with the statement that honor, ease, pleasure, practicability, and necessity can be treated in a similar way. In chapter 2 the author describes the subjects of debate in councils and assemblies; those listed differ from the list in Aristotle (1.4.7) by including religious ritual, separating legislation from constitutional provisions, and adding alliances and treaties. These are discussed in much greater detail than in Aristotle's *Rhetoric*, after which the author turns to epideictic and then to judicial rhetoric. Beginning in chapter 6, the author discusses elements common to all species of rhetoric. Included are remarks about paradigms and enthymemes that make an interesting contrast to Aristotle's teaching.

1428a *From chapter 7*: There are two modes [*tropoi*] of proofs [*pisteis*]: some are derived from actual words and actions and persons, others are supplementary [*epithetoi*] to what is said and done. Probabilities, examples, inferences, enthymemes, maxims, and refutations are proofs drawn from actual words and persons and actions; the opinion of the speaker, evidence of witnesses, evidence under torture, and oaths are supplementary. We ought, then, to understand what sort of thing each of these is and the sources from which we will have an abundance of arguments and [understand] how they differ from each other.

A *probability* [*eikos*] is something said of which the hearers have examples in their minds. I mean, for example, if someone should say that he wanted his country to be great and the inhabitants to prosper and their enemies to be unfortunate and things like this in general, the statements would seem probable; for each of the hearers would be conscious of having some such desires as these himself about these and things like them. Thus it is necessary for us always to pay attention in our speeches to whether we shall find out hearers sharing knowledge of what we are saying.

■ The author then distinguished three species [*ideas*] of probability in arguing about motivation for action: one based on common human emotions, one on what various groups of people are accustomed to do, and one based on desire for profit.

From chapter 8: Examples [*paradeigmata*] are actions that 1429a21 have occurred in the past and are similar or opposed to what we are now discussing. One should use them when what you are saying is incredible and you want to make it clear [by examples] if it cannot be proved by argument from probability, so the audience may more trust what you are saying now when they realize that some other action has occurred like to what you are claiming.

■ Two types [*tropoi*] of paradigms are distinguished, those supporting a reasonable expectation and those illustrating something that is contrary to expectation. Numerous examples are supplied.

Chapter 9: Inferences [*tekmēria*] are things that have happened 1430a14 contrary to what is asserted in the [opponent's] speech and things in which his speech contradicts itself. Most hearers infer [*tekmairontai*] from inconsistencies in argument or action that nothing that is being said or done is sound. You will obtain a supply of inferences by considering whether your opponent's speech contradicts itself or whether his action is inconsistent with his words. Such is the nature of *tekmēria* and how you will make the most supply of them.

■ The author appears to regard *tekmēria* as necessary signs, the meaning given them by Aristotle in *Rhetoric* 1.2.16–18, but differs in limiting them to negative proofs. This applies also to the author's description of enthymemes, which follows immediately in the next chapter. Cf. Quintilian 5.14.2.

Enthymemes [enthymēmata] are not only things counter to words or actions, but also to all other things. You will obtain many by following the method described for investigatory oratory and by considering if the speech contradicts itself in any way, or whether what has been done is contrary to justice or law or self-interest or honor or feasibility or facility or probability or the character of the speaker or the usual course of events.

1445b24   *Chapter 38. Conclusion of the second treatise*: Both those speaking and those writing ought, as much as possible, to try to make their speeches accord with what has been said earlier, and to accustom themselves to use all these precepts readily. For purposes of speaking artistically in private and in public contests and in intercourse with others we shall have from them the largest number of technical resources. It is necessary also to give careful attention not only to speeches but also to one's own life, regulating it by the particulars that have been mentioned; for our way of life contributes both to persuasion and to attaining a good reputation.

First, then, you must divide up the material in accord with the overall arrangement learned from your studies, attending to what should be first or second or third or fourth; then you must make a presentation of yourself, as we described the relationship to the audience in discussing prooemia. Now you will make their feelings well disposed toward you if you stand by your agreements and keep the same friends throughout life and show yourself as not changeable in other ways but always using the same principles. And they will pay atten-

1446a   tion to you if you deal with great and honorable actions and those to the advantage of many people. Having gained their good will, when you come to practical proposals for avoidance of evils and securing benefits, they will accept these as advantageous to themselves and they will disapprove those that produce the opposites.

For the sake of the narration being spoken rapidly and clearly and distinctly and not unconvincingly, it is necessary for your actions to be as follows. You will complete the narration rapidly [if you do not try to treat every point at once];[25] and clearly if you do not try to treat

----

25. A few words are lost in the text.

everything all together, but describe the first thing first and then what followed; and distinctly if you do not quickly drop one subject and turn to another before finishing the first; and not unconvincingly if you do not act at variance with your character, and in addition do not pretend that the same persons are your enemies and friends.

From among the proofs, we shall adopt the plan of completing our proposals in accord with explanation of our knowledge, but in matters of which we happen to be ignorant in terms of what occurs for the most part; for it is safest to act on these things with an eye on what is usual.

As regards the contest with opponents, we shall obtain confirmation for our case when it is a question of the words by which something has been said, and in the case of contracts we shall do this if we deal with them in terms of written and unwritten laws, with the best evidence within fixed limits of time.

In the epilogue we shall remind the hearers of what has been said, giving a summary of what has been done in recapitulation, and we shall remind them of what has been done in the past on the basis of what we are doing on the same lines, whenever we are taking in hand the same or similar actions to those of the past.

The audience will be favorably disposed to us if we follow lines of action from which they think they have benefited or are likely to benefit. We shall accomplish great things if we take in hand the causes and actions of many honorable people.

This is the way one must regulate his personal conduct, while practicing himself on the basis of the system of speech previously stated.

G. ON WORD CHOICE AND METAPHOR, FROM ARISTOTLE'S *POETICS*

■ Chapters 20–22 of the *Poetics* discuss *lexis*, with special attention to poetic diction. In chapter 20 Aristotle surveys what he calls the "parts" of *lexis*, which are element (or intelligible sound), syllable, connective, noun, verb, conjunction (or article?), inflection, and proposition (*logos*). He then continues with the following account of the species of words, of which metaphor is one. The passage is of special interest in connection with *Rhetoric* Book 3, chapters 2, 4, 10, and 11.

1457a20 *Chapter 21*: 1. The species [*eidē*] of word[26] are, on the one hand simple (and by *simple* I mean not composed of signifying elements, for example, *earth*), and on the other double, 2. and of the latter one form is made up of a signifier and non-signifier (though not [separately] signifying and non-signifying in the [composite] word) and the other of [two] signifiers.[27] 3. There would also be triple and quadruple and

1457b multiple compounds (like) *Hermo-kaïko-xanthos*.

4. Every word is either a *kyrion*[28] or *glōtta*[29] or metaphor or ornament, or coined or lengthened or abbreviated or altered. 5. I call *kyrion* what everybody uses and *glōtta* what other people use;[30] 6. so it is apparent that both a *glōtta* and a *kyrion* can be the same, but not to the same people. *Sigynon* [spear] is *kyrion* among the Cyprians but a *glōtta* to us.

7. Metaphor is the movement [*epiphora*] of an alien [*allotrios*] word from either genus to species or from species to genus or from species to species or by analogy.[31] 8. I call from *genus to species*, for example, "My ship stands here"; for to be at anchor is [a species] of standing. 9. [I call] *from species to genus*, "Yea, Odysseus did ten thousand noble deed"; for ten thousand is a species of much, used here for "many." 10. [I call] *from species to species*, for example, "drawing off his life with bronze" and "cutting with tireless bronze"; for here "to draw off" means "to cut" and "to cut" means "to draw off."[32] 11. I call it *analogy* when the second thing is related to the first as the fourth is to the third; for [a poet] will say the fourth for the second or the second for the fourth. 12. And sometimes they add something to which it relates in place of what it [usually] refers to. I mean, for example, the cup is related to Dionysius as the shield to Ares.[33] 13. Or since old age is to life as evening is to day, then he will call evening the old age of day or, like Empedocles, call old age the

---

26. *Onoma*, "name, noun"—but including what we call adjectives and pronouns.

27. E.g., *unearthly* (non-signifying plus signifying) and *earthborn* (two signifying elements; but each has only a single signification).

28. The prevailing or "proper" meaning; cf. *Rhetoric* 3.2.2.

29. "Strange, foreign"; see *Rhetoric* 3.3.2 and note thereon.

30. I.e., speakers of another dialect or language or from a different time.

31. For detailed examination of this statement, see Ricoeur 1977 (esp. 9–43), Tamba-Mecz and Veyne 1979, and Levin 1982.

32. In the first case *bronze* is apparently a spear, in the second a cupping vessel; cf. *Rhetoric* 3.2.12.

33. These are the "iconographic" symbols of the god of wine and the war god in literature and art.

evening of life or "life's gloaming." 14. In some cases there is no corresponding term within the analogy, but nonetheless a likeness will be expressed; for example, scattering seed is "sowing," but in the case of the sun the [dispersion of] light has no name [in Greek].[34] Nevertheless, this has the same relation to the sun as scattering has to seed, so it is expressed as "sowing divine fire."

15. It is possible to use this turn [*tropos*] of metaphor in another way, too, by applying the alien term while denying one of its attributes; for example, if someone were to say not that the shield is Ares' cup but [that it is] a "wineless" cup.

■ The chapter continues with brief discussion of the other categories of words and an attempt to identify the grammatical gender of nouns on the basis of their final letters. Chapter 22 then begins with a statement similar to that in *Rhetoric* 3.2.1: "The virtue of *lexis* is to be clear and not flat."

H. DEMOSTHENES' *THIRD PHILIPPIC* (341 B.C.E.)

■ Demosthenes (384–322 B.C.E., an exact contemporary of Aristotle) has been universally regarded as the greatest classical Greek orator, the premier defender of Athenian liberty and patriotism, who became an important model for Cicero and many later speakers. For example, his works were studied by early Americans, both in Greek and in English translations, as models of the grand style and eloquent summons to the defense of liberty. In 1781, John Adams wrote to his son, John Quincy Adams, then a student in Europe, insisting that he begin study of Demosthenes as soon as possible: "If there is no other way, I will take you home, and teach you Demosthenes and Homer myself."[35] In 1822, Thomas Jefferson recommended the study of Demosthenes to college students: "In a country and government like ours," he wrote, "eloquence is a powerful instrument, well worthy of the special pursuit of our youth. . . . For senatorial eloquence, Demosthenes is the finest model, for the bar Cicero. The former had more logic, the latter more imagination."[36]

---

34. In English it is *beaming*.

35. *Adams Family Correspondence*, vol. 4., ed. L. H. Butterfield (Cambridge: Harvard University Press, 1973), p. 144.

36. *The Writings of Thomas Jefferson*, vol. 15, ed. A. E. Bergh (Washington, D.C.: Thomas Jefferson Memorial Association, 1905), p. 353.

Demosthenes' numerous published orations include deliberative speeches delivered in the Athenian Council or Assembly, judicial speeches in important political trials, some delivered by himself, others written for clients, and speeches in private civil and criminal trials. In 352 B.C.E. he became alarmed at the growth of the power of Philip, king of Macedon in northern Greece, who was absorbing cities allied with Athens; at Philip's threats to control the straits between Europe and Asia, through which Athenian ships had to pass bringing grain from the Black Sea; and eventually at the possibility that Philip might invade southern Greece and threaten Athens, all of which eventually came to pass. Much of Demosthenes' political activity in the ten years between 351 and 341 was an attempt to persuade the Athenians of the reality of this danger and to get them to take the necessary steps to fund and organize military resources and alliances. The speeches known as the "Philippics" were a part of this effort. The specific occasion of the *Third Philippic* (341 B.C.E.) was a request received from mercenary forces sent by Athens to hold the Chersonesus for supplies to resist the advance of Philip's army. The Chersonesus, mentioned repeatedly in the speech, is the long peninsula on the European side of the Dardanelles, in modern Turkey. Several of the cities there were originally Athenian colonies and maintained close ties with Athens, but Philip had now captured Cardia, the largest city on the peninsula.

The Athenian Assembly, in which any adult male citizen could participate and vote, met out-of-doors, either on the side of the Pnyx hill, in the theater, or elsewhere where there were good acoustics. Unlike modern orators, Demosthenes often used very long sentences. We should imagine the long sentence that begins this speech as spoken slowly, with short pauses after each phrase or clause. Note the way this sentence builds to its ironic conclusion. Later parts of the speech were probably delivered more rapidly, especially rhetorical questions and passages containing anaphora. Demosthenes was very conscious of the importance of delivery. As a young man he practiced exercises in elocution and there is a story that when asked what was the most important factor in effective rhetoric he replied, "Delivery." What is second? "Delivery." And third? "Delivery."

When he had the opportunity, Demosthenes probably wrote out in advance a draft of a speech that he intended to deliver and memorized part or all of it. He would have wanted to give the appearance of speaking spontaneously and thus would not have read a speech from a written text, though he might have consulted some notes or an outline. The versions of his speeches that we read today were, however, written up after the fact, often with revisions to improve arguments or style. Copies on papyrus scrolls were then prepared by scribes and given or sold to the public to enhance the orator's political agenda and his reputation as an orator. At an early time the speeches were studied by students of rhetoric. It is worth noting, however, that in his treatise *On Rhetoric* Aristotle never cites Demosthenes as a model of rhetoric and only once refers to him as a politician,[37] despite his many references and quotations of Isocrates and other fourth-century B.C.E. orators. But Philip had appointed Aristotle to supervise the education of Alexander, he had many ties with Macedon, and probably little sympathy for the greatest Athenian opponent of Macedonian power. He could not have heard Demosthenes delivering the *Third Philippic*, but he may well have read it when copies reached Macedon.

Cicero repeatedly says that Demosthenes had been a student of Plato.[38] This view, however, was based on a letter falsely attributed to Demosthenes; Plutarch and other biographers do not mention it, and it is probably wrong. Demosthenes was, however, familiar with Plato's writings; his description of the orators of his time as flattering the public rather than speaking the truth echoes Socrates' description of rhetoricians in Plato's *Gorgias*. In the late first century B.C.E. a Peripatetic philosopher, name unknown, argued that Demosthenes acquired his rhetorical skills from studying Aristotle's *Rhetoric*. This provoked a reply from the historian-rhetorician Dionysius of Halicarnassus, whose *First Epistle to Ammaeus* argues on the basis of Aristotle's historical references that the *Rhetoric* was composed after most of Demosthenes' speeches. It might be added that *On Rhetoric* was not published until many years later and would have been available only in Aristotle's personal library, to which Demosthenes is not apt to have had access.

A student of rhetoric will find it instructive to undertake an analysis of this speech using Aristotelian concepts of logos, ethos, and pathos, identifying paradigms, enthymemes, and topics, as well as metaphors and other stylistic and compositional features discussed by Aristotle.

This translation is based on the Oxford Classical Text, 2nd ed., vol. 1 by M. R. Dilts (Oxford: Clarendon Press, 2002).

There have been many speeches, Men of Athens, at almost every meeting of the Assembly concerning the aggressions of Philip ever since he made the Peace,[39] aimed not only against you but against

---

37. *Rhetoric* 2.24.8; other mentions of Demosthenes are probably to another person with the same name.

38. Cicero, *On the Orator* 1.189, *Brutus* 121, and *On Duties* 1.4.

39. In 347 B.C.E. a mutual non-aggression treaty had been negotiated between Philip and Athens. Demosthenes subsequently brought allegations of treason against some of the ambassadors.

others; and although I know that all would say, even if they do not act on their words, that there is need of speech and action so that he will cease from his insolence and pay the penalty, I see the whole matter undermined and neglected to the extent that I fear it is offensive but true to say that if all those coming forward wanted to speak and you wanted to vote what was going to make the situation the worst possible, I do not think the result could be worse than it is now. 2. There are probably many reasons for this and the situation did not come about from one or two causes, but most of all, if you examine the matter rightly, you will find that it is because of men choosing to speak to please rather than to say what is best, some of whom, Men of Athens, are guarding their own reputations and influence and take no thought for the future, nor do they think you should do so; others, accusing and slandering those active in public life, are doing nothing other than getting the city to punish itself, be concerned with this, and let Philip say and do whatever he wants. 3. Policies like this are familiar to you and the cause of the evils. I ask, Men of Athens, if I say some truths frankly that I incur no anger from you. Look at it this way. You think there should be freedom of speech to all in the city on other matters, so that you even give a share of it to foreigners and slaves, and one might see many servants among us saying whatever they want with greater liberty than citizens have in some of the other cities, but you have utterly banished this liberty from political debate. 4. The result of this has been that in meetings of the Assembly you give yourselves airs and enjoy the flattery, listening to everything with pleasure, while in the real world of events you are now in the greatest degree of danger. If that is your state of mind now, there is nothing I can say. But if you want to hear without flattery what is in your best interests, I am ready to speak. Even if the situation is very bad and much has been lost, nevertheless, if you are willing to do what needs to be done, everything can still be set right. 5. What I am going to say is perhaps a paradox, but yet true: the worst thing in the past is what is really the best for the future. What then is this? That your affairs have gone badly while you have been doing nothing you ought to do, great or small, since, of course, if you were doing everything you should and were still in this situation, there would be no hope that things will get better. But now Philip has prevailed over your indolence and indifference,—but he has not prevailed over the city! You have not been defeated; you haven't even stirred!

6. Now if we all agreed that Philip is making war on the city and violating the Peace, there would only be need for someone to come

forward to speak and advise how we can most safely and easily resist him, but since some people are so strangely disposed, that while he is capturing cities and holding many of your possessions and wronging all mankind, they tolerate certain speakers in meetings of the Assembly saying often that some of *us* are the ones making war. Since that is so, it is necessary to be on guard and to set the record straight. 7. There is a danger that anyone proposing and advising that we resist may incur the accusation of having brought about the war. First of all I say this and I define whether it is in our power to deliberate as meaning whether we ought to keep the Peace or go to war. 8. If, therefore, it is possible for the city to maintain the Peace and if this is up to us, to begin with that, I myself say we ought to do so, and I think it is right for anyone saying this to introduce motions and take action and not to mislead us. But if another person, holding weapons in his hands and having a large force behind him, holds out to you the *name* of peace but employs the *deeds* of war, what else is there to do but to resist? Though if you want to claim to be maintaining the Peace in the way he does, I don't disagree. 9. But if anybody supposes this is peace, when that man will advance against us after capturing everything else, first of all such a person is out of his mind, and secondly he is talking about peace for him from you, not for you from him. What Philip buys with all the money he spends is for him to be at war *with* you but not to be warred on *by* you. 10. And surely if we wait to the point that he admits he is making war on us we'll be the most simple-minded of all; not even if he comes into Attica itself and to the Peiraeus[40] will he admit this, if we are to judge by what he has done to others. 11. Remember what he said to the Olynthians when he was only forty stades[41] from their city: that one of two things must happen, either they must cease living in Olynthus or he in Macedon, while during all the previous time if someone accused him of anything of the sort, he was indignant and sent messengers to answer the charge. And again he marched toward the Phocians as though they were his allies, and ambassadors of the Phocians were following with him as he marched, and many among you argued that his journey would do no good to the Thebans.[42] 12. Not only that, but recently he seized Pherae, coming into Thessaly as though a friend and ally, and he holds it now. And lastly he told those wretched folk

---

40. The port of Athens.
41. About five miles.
42. Athens and Thebes were traditionally hostile to each other.

in Oreus[43] that he had sent his soldiers out of kindness, claiming he had heard they were suffering from disease and faction and it was the duty of allies and true friends to be present in such circumstances. 13. Then do you think that he chose to deceive these people, who would have done him no harm but perhaps might have prevented themselves from suffering, rather than using force after he warned them, but that he will attack you only after a formal declaration, so long as you are willing to be deceived? 14. That's impossible! He would be the stupidest man alive if, when you make no complaints against him of being harmed, but are blaming some of your own people, he dissolved your quarrels with each other and invited you in advance to turn against him and abolished the claims of those he has bribed, by which they put you off, saying that he at least is not at war with the city.

15. In the name of Zeus, is there a man in his senses that would judge someone keeping peace or making war on him from his words rather than his deeds? Clearly no one. From the beginning, when the Peace had just been made and Diopeithes was not yet holding his command and the soldiers now in the Chersonesus had not yet been sent, Philip was taking Serrion and Doriscus[44] and was expelling our forces from the citadel of Serrion and the Sacred Mount[45] where your general had installed them. 16. Well then, what was he doing when he did this? He had sworn a Peace. And let no one say, "What do these things amount to?" Or "What do they matter to the city?" Whether these are trifles or no concern of yours would be another question. Honor and justice have the same value whether someone violates them in small ways or great. Come now. When he sends mercenary troops into Chersonesus, which the Persian king and all the Hellenes[46] have acknowledged to be yours, and claims to be going to their aid and states this in a letter, what is he doing? 17. He denies he is making war, but I am so far from agreeing that in doing this he is keeping the Peace with you, that by his attack on Megara and by establishing a tyrant in Euboea and now advancing on Thrace and plotting in the Peloponnesus, and by doing all the things he does with his forces, I say he is violating the Peace and making war on you, unless you claim that someone bringing up siege engines is keeping the Peace until they actually plant them on the walls. But you will not claim that; for

---

43. On the island of Euboea; Philip was here only about a hundred miles from Athens.
44. Athenian garrisons in Thrace.
45. A fortification on the northern side of the Chersonesus peninsula.
46. The collective term for the Greeks.

he who is doing and contriving things by which I would be captured is at war with me, even if he has not yet thrown a spear or shot an arrow.

18. Now what are the things that would endanger you if they came to pass? The alienation of the Hellespont,[47] your enemy becoming master of Megara and Euboea, causing the Peloponnesian cities to sympathize with him. Then shall I claim that the one erecting such a war machine against the city is keeping the Peace with you? 19. Far from it, but I define the beginning of his being at war from the day when he annihilated the Phocians.[48] If you defend yourselves now, I say you will be wise, but if you desist, you will not be able to do so when you want to. And I so differ from other advisers, Men of Athens, that it does not seem to me now a question about the Chersonesus or Byzantium, 20. but while we ought to go to their aid and see to it no harm befalls them, it is a question of consulting about all the Hellenes as standing in great danger. I want to tell you why I am so fearful about the situation, in order that, if I am reckoning rightly, you may share in my reasoning and exercise some forethought for yourselves, at least, if you don't in fact want to do so for others, and if I seem to be talking nonsense and am besotted, you need not pay any attention to me as a sane man, neither now or in the future.

21. That Philip became great from a small and humble beginning, and that the Hellenes are mistrustful and quarrelsome among themselves, and that it was much more beyond belief that he became what he is from what he was, than that now, when he has secured so much, he should subject the rest to his power, and all the other things I could say, all this I shall pass over. 22. But I see that all mankind, beginning with you, has conceded to him what has been the issue at all other times in all Hellenic wars. What is this? To do what he pleases, and to fleece and pillage the Hellenes one by one in the way he is doing, attacking and enslaving their cities. 23. For seventy-three years you were the leaders of Hellas and for thirty years less one the Lacedaimonians were, and the Thebans too have had some power in recent years after the battle of Leuctra.[49] But nevertheless, never, Men of

---

47. The Chersonesus and surrounding area on the Dardanelles.

48. Phocis was the mountainous territory separating Thessaly and Macedon to the north from southern Greece through the Pass of Thermopylae. To control it offered an invader a base for invasion of Boetia (Thebes) and Attica (the territory of Athens).

49. Athens from victory in the Persian War 477 B.C.E. to defeat in the Peloponnesian War in 405; Sparta from 405 to defeat at the battle of Naxos in 376; Thebes after its victory over Sparta at the battle of Leuctra in 371.

Athens, not to you nor to the Thebans nor to the Lacedaimonians, was it conceded by the Greeks to do anything you wanted, far from it. 24. But all thought it necessary to go to war with you, or rather with the Athenians of the time, when they seemed to some to be conducting themselves immoderately, and all, even those having nothing to complain of on their own, thought it necessary to join the injured states in war against you. And again when the Spartans were supreme and came into the same powerful position you once had, when they tried to go too far and were disturbing the established order of things beyond measure, all went to war against them, even those having nothing to complain of. 25. What need is there to speak of others? We ourselves and the Lacedaimonians, although having at the beginning no wrong to complain of from each other, nevertheless thought it necessary to go to war because of the wrongs we saw done to others. And yet the faults of the Lacedaimonians in their thirty years in power and of our ancestors in seventy, are less, Men of Athens, than the wrongs Philip has inflicted on the Hellenes in under thirteen years, or rather not a small part of them. 26. That is easy to show in a few words. I pass over Olynthus and Methone and Apollonia and thirty-two cities in Thrace, all of which he has annihilated so brutally that someone going there could not easily tell if they had ever been inhabited. I am silent about the extirpation of the large race of Phocians. But what is the condition of Thessaly? Has he not destroyed their constitutions and even their cities and established tetrarchies in order that they may be enslaved not only city by city, but tribe by tribe?[50] 27. Are not the cities on Euboea even now ruled by tyrants, and that on an island near Thebes and Athens? Does he not expressly write in letters "I am at peace with those who are willing to obey me"? He does not write these words and fail to act upon them, but he goes to the Hellespont, before that he went to Ambracia; he holds the great city of Elis in the Peloponnesus; recently he plotted against Megara; neither Hellas nor barbary[51] can contain the man's ambition. 28. All Hellenes see and hear these things but we do not send ambassadors about them to each other and indignantly complain; we are in so bad a state of mind and have dug such divisions between cities, that up until today we have

---

50. In 342 Philip divided Thessaly into four regions, each ruled by a tyrant of his own appointing. The regions corresponded to membership in four traditional tribes.

51. The classical Greeks regarded all people who did not speak Greek as "barbarians," people whose speech sounded like "bar-bar-ba." Barbarians thus include ancient civilized people throughout the Near East.

not been able to do anything our interest and duty require, nor to unite nor to create any commonality of aid and friendship, 29. but we look on while the man becomes greater, each one thinking to profit during this time when another is destroyed, as it seems to me, not caring or acting how the affairs of the Hellenes can be saved, for that like a course of fever or attack of some other disease he is coming even to him who now thinks himself far removed, no one can be ignorant. 30. And consider this: whatever the Hellenes suffered from the Lacedaimonians or from you, they were wronged at least by genuine sons of Hellas, and one might have thought of this in the same way he would if a legitimate son born to much wealth administered it badly and wrongly, in this way deserving blame and censure, but it could not be said that he was doing this when not akin and heir to this property, 31. but if a slave or suppositious son ruined and spoiled what did not belong to him, by Heracles, how much more dreadful and deserving anger all would declare it to be. Yet they have no such feelings in the case of Philip and what he is doing now, a man not only not a Hellene, and not related in any way to Hellenes,[52] but not even a barbarian from a place decent to mention, a curséd Macedonian from a place where in the past it was not even possible to buy a slave worth anything.

32. Moreover, what degree of insolence does he omit? In addition to annihilating cities does he not dare to sponsor the Pythian games,[53] the national contest of the Hellenes, and send slaves to preside in his absence? Is he not master of Thermopylae and of the passes into Hellas and does he not hold these places with garrisons and mercenaries? Does he not have the right to be the first to consult the god,[54] shoving us aside and the Thessalians and Dorians and the other members of the Amphictyonic League, a privilege not even shared by all Hellenes? 33. Does he not write to the Thessalians what kind of government they must have? Does he not send some mercenaries to Porthmos to expel the democratic party of Eretria and others to Oreus

---

52. Despite Demosthenes' claims, the Macedonians were related to the other Greeks and spoke a Greek dialect.

53. The Pythian games were held at Delphi in Phocis in the third year of each Olympiad.

54. Representatives of cities or private persons went to Delphi to consult the god Apollo about the future or what they should do; answers (often ambiguous) were delivered by an inspired priestess, coached by the priests. There was an established order of precedence. After defeating the Phocians Philip assumed their right of first consultation.

to set Philistides up as tyrant? But yet the Hellenes see this and put up with it in the way they seem to me to view a hailstorm, each praying that it not come upon themselves and no one trying to prevent it. 34. Not only does no one take any measures against the outrages Hellas is receiving at his hands, but no one does so for the wrongs that each state is suffering. This is the most outrageous aspect of the situation. Has he not attacked Ambracia and Leucas that belong to the Corinthians? Has he not sworn to hand over Naupactus, belonging to the Achaeans, to the Aetolians? Has he not taken Echinus away from the Thebans, and is he not now marching on Byzantium, though allies? 35. And of your own possessions, to pass over the rest, does he not hold Cardia, the greatest city of the Chersonesus? This is how we are being treated and we are all hesitating and soft and we look to our neighbor, distrusting each other but not the man wronging us all. And yet he who is using us so outrageously, when he has become master of us all one by one, what do you think he will do?

36. What then is the cause of these things? For it was not without reason and just cause that the Hellenes were once so ready to defend freedom and now to be slaves. There was something then, there was, O Men of Athens, something in the minds of the people that is not there now, something that defeated the wealth of Persia and kept Hellas free and did not give way in the face of battle by sea or land, and now that it has perished everything is spoiled and all things turned upside down. 12. What was this thing? It was the fact that everyone hated those who took money from men wanting to rule or destroy Hellas, and to be convicted of bribery was a most grievous thing, and they punished this with the heaviest penalty. 38. Thus the critical moment in actions, which chance often provides even to the careless, could not be bought from speakers and generals, nor was their concord with each other for sale nor their distrust of tyrants and barbarians nor any thing of this sort. 39. But now all these have been sold like goods in the market and there have been substituted for them things by which Hellas has been ruined and made sick. What are these things? Envy if someone has taken something. Laughter if he admits it. Forgiveness to those proved guilty. Hatred of anyone who blames them. And all the other things involved with bribery. 40. Ships and manpower and abundance of funds and other resources, and other things by which one judges cities to be strong, are now more numerous and greater in all the cities than they used to be, by much. But these things are made useless, ineffective, unprofitable by those who buy and sell them.

41. That this is the present situation you all doubtless see and do not need my testimony, and that in past times the opposite held I shall make clear, not by any words of my own but from an inscription that your ancestors set up on a pillar of bronze on the acropolis, not to be useful to them (for they knew what was right without these writings), but in order that *you* might have reminders and examples of the zeal appropriate in such cases. 42. What does the inscription say? It says, "Arthmius, son of Pythonax, of Zeleia is an outlaw and enemy of the city of the Athenians and their allies, both he and his family." Then the reason why is inscribed: "because he brought the gold from the Medes into the Peloponnesus."[55] That is what it says. 43. Consider, by the gods, what was the intention of the Athenians of the time when they did this or what their estimate of what was right? A certain man of Zeleia named Arthmius, a slave of the king (for Zeleia is in Asia), because, in his master's service, he brought gold into the Peloponnesus, not to Athens, was declared to be their own enemy and that of their allies, both himself and his family, and outlawed. 44. This is not what one would ordinarily call being outlawed. What would it matter to a man from Zeleia to have no rights in Athens? That is not what it means. There is a provision in the laws of murder dealing with those not subject to prosecution for murder where killing someone is a holy act, "and let him die an outlaw" it says. This means that anyone who kills such a person is not religiously polluted. 45. Thus they thought that the safety of all Greeks should be a concern to them. Unless this was their belief it would not have mattered to them if someone bribes some people in the Peloponnesus and corrupts them, and they were accustomed to punish in this way and take vengeance on those they saw doing it to the extent of setting up this inscription. As a consequence, in all probability the Hellenes were a source of fear to the barbarian, not the barbarian to the Hellenes. But it is not so now. That is not your attitude toward such things nor toward other matters, but what is your attitude? 46. You know yourselves. What need is there for me to accuse you on all counts? And all the rest of the Hellenes, are no better than you. For that reason I am saying that the present situation requires much earnestness and good planning. What should we do? Do you demand I tell you? And will you promise not to be angry?

47. Well then, there is a simple-minded argument on the part of those wishing to reassure the city. They say that "Philip is not yet

---

55. He was sent by King Artaxerxes I of Persia to stir up trouble in Greece in the mid-fifth century B.C.E. Mede is often used to include the Persians in this period.

what the Lacedaimonians once were when they ruled the sea and all the land and had the Persian king as an ally and nothing stood in their way, but nevertheless the city resisted them and was not swept away." All things, so to speak, have made much progress, and nothing now is like what it once was, and I think that nothing has changed and developed more than the art of war.[56] 48. First of all, I hear that the Lacedaimonians then and all the others would invade some territory for four or five months, during the real summer, and after ravaging the countryside with heavy armed troops and citizen soldiers they would return home again. So old-fashioned were they, or rather so city-oriented in their ways, that they did not buy anything from anyone with money, but their warfare was something legitimate and open. 49. Now you doubtless see that the traitors cause the most losses and nothing happens in open conflict or battle. You hear of Philip going where he wants not by leading a column of infantry but by recruiting skirmishers, cavalry, archers, mercenaries—that kind of army. 50. At the head of such troops, whenever he falls on cities internally diseased where no one comes out to meet him in defense of the territory because of distrust of one another, he brings up his battering rams and besieges them. I say nothing of the fact that summer and winter make no difference to him and that there is no season exempt while he leaves off. 51. If you all know these things and take account of them, you must not let war come into our territory nor be thrown headlong into ruin while looking back to the simplicity of the former war with the Lacedaimonians, but you must be on your guard with plans and preparations to keep him as far away as possible and prevent him from stirring from home, and by no means engage with him in a decisive battle. 52. We have many natural advantages for war, Men of Athens, if we wish to do our duty: the nature of the land, much of which we can harry and pillage and damage, and thousands of other things, but for a pitched battle he is better prepared than we are.

53. Not only must you recognize these things and not only resist him by operations of war, but by reasoning and judgment you must come to hate those speaking among you on his behalf, keeping in mind that it is not possible to prevail over the enemies of the city until you punish those in the city itself that are serving them. 54. By Zeus and the other gods, you will be unable to do this, for you have come to this state of folly or madness or—I don't know what to call it, for

---

56. An important change was the increased reliance on mercenary troops in the fourth century B.C.E. and the reduction in the number of citizen soldiers, but there were also developments in tactics and siege warfare.

often fear has come upon me that some demonic power may be driving our affairs—with the result that you call on men who have been bribed to speak in order to enjoy their abuse, malice, scurrility, or for whatever other reason, and some of these men would not even deny this description, and you laugh if they abuse others. 55. Although this is bad it is still not the worst. You have given greater safety in politics to these men than to those who speak in your own interests. Well, look at what disasters willingness to listen to such men lays up in store for you. I shall mention facts that you all know.

56. There were in Olynthus some in public life on the side of Philip and serving him in everything, and some, on the other hand, of the better side, acting to prevent the citizens from being enslaved. Which group destroyed their country? Which betrayed the cavalry, after which Olynthus perished? Those sympathetic with Philip; those who, while the city still existed, brought dishonest and slanderous charges against the patriots, with the result that in the case of Apollonides the people of Olynthus were even persuaded to banish him.

57. It was not only among them and nowhere else that this habit of thinking wrought all manner of evils. In Eretria, after the tyrant Plutarch and his mercenaries had been gotten rid of and the democratic party held that city and Porthmos, some wanted to turn things over to you, others to Philip. Listening for the most part to the latter, the wretched and ill-fortuned Eretrians were finally persuaded to banish the advocates of their own best interests. 58. As you know, Philip, their "ally"!, sent Hipponicus and a thousand mercenaries, dismantled the walls of Porthmos, and established three tyrants, Hipparchus, Automedon, and Cleitarchus; and since then he has already twice expelled from the country those wanting to save themselves, first sending mercenaries with Eurylochus, then those with Parmenio.

59. What need is there to list all the many instances? Enough to say that in Oreus Philistides was working for Philip as were Menippus and Socrates and Thoas and Agapaeus, who now control the city, as everyone knew at the time, and a certain man called Euphraeus, who once lived among us, was tying to keep them free and slaves of no one. 60. To describe all the ways he was insulted and slandered by the people would be a long story, but the year before the capture of the city he brought a charge of treason against Philistides and his fellows, perceiving what they were doing. Many men joined together, having Philip as their financer and producer,[57] and led Euphraeus off to

---

57. Demosthenes uses a metaphor from the financing and producing of dramatic plays in Athens.

prison on the charge of disturbing the peace. 61. On seeing this the democratic party of Oreus, instead of going to his aid and beating the traitors to death, displayed no anger against them and said Euphraeus deserved it and declared their pleasure. After this the conspirators acted with all the freedom they wanted for the capture of the city and prepared for the outcome. If any of the democratic party noticed, he kept silent and was frightened, remembering what Euphraeus suffered. So dreadful was their situation that no one dared to raise a voice at the evil coming on them until the enemy was ready and advanced to the walls. Then some tried to resist while others betrayed the city. 62. When the city had been captured in this shameful and base way, one party ruled and tyrannized; they exiled some and killed others of those who had previously tried to save themselves and been ready to do anything to Euphraeus, and the good Euphraeus cut his throat, by his act bearing witness that he had justly and with pure motives opposed Philip on behalf of the citizens.

63. What then was the cause, perhaps you are wondering, that the Olynthians and Eretrians, and Oreitans were better disposed to speakers favoring Philip than to those speaking in their own best interests? The same reason that exists among you, because it is not possible for those speaking what is for the best, not even if they want to, to say anything for your pleasure, since it is necessary for them to examine how the situation will be saved, while the others are cooperating with Philip in the act of seeking popularity. 64. One group demanded that taxes be raised, the other claimed there was no need; one to go to war and not trust Philip, the other to remain at peace, until they had been caught in the snare; everything else in the same way, I think, not to go into particulars. One group was saying things by which they were going to win favor, the other things by which they were going to be saved. In many cases the people finally gave way, not so much to please or out of ignorance, but quietly submitting when they thought all was lost. 65. By Zeus and Apollo, I fear that this will be your experience when on reflection you see that you can do nothing. And yet, may things never come to that, Men of Athens. Better to die a thousand deaths than do anything to flatter Philip. A beautiful return have the people of Oreus now received for entrusting themselves to Philip's friends and thrusting Euphraeus aside. A beautiful return the democracy of Eretria received for driving away your envoys and giving in to Cleitarchus. They are slaves, whipped and butchered. Beautifully did he spare the Olynthians, who elected Lasthenes to command the cavalry and banished Apollonides. 67. It is foolishness

and cowardice to cherish such hopes, giving way to bad advice and wanting to do nothing one should but listening to those who speak on behalf of the enemy, thinking to dwell in a city so great that whatever happens one will suffer no harm. 68. Surely it is shameful to say sometime later, "Who would have thought these things would happen? By Zeus, we ought to have done or not done such and such." Many things could the Olynthians tell of now that would have kept them from destruction if they had foreseen them; many things the Oreitans, many the Phocians, many each of the cities destroyed. 69. What good does it do them now? So long as the ship is safe, whether large or small, so long must sailor and helmsman and every man in turn be alert and watch out that no one willingly or unwillingly capsize it. But when the sea overwhelms it, efforts are in vain.

70. What then about us, Men of Athens? So long as we are safe, with the greatest city, the most resources, the finest reputation, what are we to do? Probably someone has long been sitting wanting to ask this question. I shall tell you, by Zeus, and I will introduce a motion so that you may vote if you wish. I say we ourselves, first, should resist and make preparations with ships and money and soldiers; for even if all the others give way to slavery, we at least must fight for freedom. 71. When we ourselves are prepared and make this clear, let us call next upon the others and send ambassadors to teach these things everywhere,—I mean into the Peloponnesus, to Rhodes, to Chios, to the king (for it is not to his interest either to let Philip subjugate the world), so that, if you persuade them, you may have partners to share the dangers and expenses, should there be need, and if not, you may at least delay events. 72. For since the war is with one man and not against the force of a united state, even delay is not unuseful, nor were those embassies and accusations last year when I and Polyeuctus, that best of men, and Hegesippus and others went around the Peloponnesus and forced Philip to hold back and not attack Ambracia and not set out for the Peloponnesus. 73. I am not, however, saying that we should call upon the others to help unless we are willing to do what is necessary for ourselves; for it is foolish to sacrifice what is one's own and claim to care about what belongs to others and while neglecting the present to alarm others about the future. I don't say to do that, but I do say you must send money to the forces in the Chersonesus and do all they ask, and we must make preparations ourselves and summon, convene, instruct, warn the other Hellenes. That is something worthy of a city as great as yours. 74. If you think the people of Chalcis are going to save Hellas,

or the Megarians, while you run away from events, you are not thinking rightly; for it is enough for them if each can save themselves. *You*
must do this. To *you* your ancestors bequeathed this honor, acquired
through many great dangers. 75. But if each person sits down seeking
what he wishes and looking to see how he can do nothing himself, in
the first place he will never find anyone to do it, and in the second I
fear that the necessity may come upon us of doing everything we
don't want all at the same time.

76. This is my proposal and I move we do this. And I think even
now affairs would be set right if these things were done. If anyone has
a better plan, let him speak and advise us. Whatever seems best to
you, I pray to all the gods it may prove good.

■ As a result of Demosthenes' speech the Athenian Assembly rejected
negotiations with Philip, chose Demosthenes as their leader, and made
preparations for war. Aid was sent to the forces in the Chersonesus, and
alliances were made with several Greek cities. Philip, however, continued his
expansionist aggression. In November 339 B.C.E. he invaded central Greece,
and despite Demosthenes' efforts, the allied Greek armies were defeated at
the Battle of Chaeronea in August 338. This date is regarded by historians
as the end of the classical period of Greek history. What followed is called
the "Hellenistic Age" in which Greek culture was spread across the Near
East and western Asia as a result of the conquests of Alexander the Great.
After Chaeronea, Philip controlled all of Greece. Demosthenes organized
the city to withstand a siege, but Philip did not attack Athens, which was
allowed to administer its domestic affairs. Demosthenes was chosen to
deliver the funeral oration in memory of the many Athenian dead in the
battle and continued active in Athenian public life, despite difficulties,
though somewhat weakened politically.

APPENDIX II
SUPPLEMENTARY ESSAYS

A. THE EARLIEST RHETORICAL HANDBOOKS

At least since the time of Cicero, the traditional view has been that the formulation of rhetorical rules in Greek began in Sicily in the second quarter of the fifth century B.C.E. with two shadowy figures named Corax and Tisias, who sought to fill a practical need to speak effectively on the part of litigants in cases regarding ownership of land in the newly established democracy of Syracuse.[1] Rhetorical teaching then developed at Athens during the later part of the century in the schools of sophists[2] and in the form of handbooks of rhetoric, a small part of the literate revolution of the times. The name for a rhetorical handbook was *tekhnē logōn*, an "art of words." These small books on papyrus could be bought or borrowed and studied by someone anticipating the need to speak in public, especially in a court of law where litigants were ordinarily required to speak on their own behalf. The standard collection of sources relating to the early development of Greek technical rhetoric has for over fifty years been *Artium Scriptores* (*Reste der voraristotelischen Rhetorik*) by Ludwig Radermacher (1951), to which I shall repeatedly refer here.

The publication of handbooks of judicial rhetoric was largely distinct from the teaching of the sophists, an account of which was given

---

1. This essay is a much revised and updated replacement for an article I published many years ago, "The Earliest Rhetorical Handbooks," *American Journal of Philology* 82 (1959):169–178, which is best forgotten.

2. English translations of the fragments and testimonia of the sophists, based on Diels-Kranz, *Die Fragmente der Vorsokratiker*, can be found in Sprague 1972; additional translations appear in Gagarin and Woodruff 1995:173–312.

in section B of the Introduction to this book. A crucial passage for understanding how rhetorical technique was taught by a leading sophist is what Aristotle says at the end of *Sophistical Refutations* (183b16–184b7). Aristotle was trying to create a theoretical and systematic art of dialectic to replace an unscientific eristic; the beginning is difficult, he says (183b23), but once started, progress will be made, as has been the case in rhetoric (*tous rhētorikous logous*) with a succession of writers leading from Tisias,[3] to Thrasymachus, Theodorus, and others. With this he contrasts (183b36) the educational technique of Gorgias in which, he says, students were assigned ready-made speeches to memorize, "as though a shoemaker were to try to teach his art by presenting his apprentice with an assortment of shoes." In Plato's dialogue *Gorgias* (449b), Gorgias claims to be able to make people into rhetors like himself, but as he appears in both Plato and Aristotle he lacks the ability to conceptualize his views of rhetoric. His students were expected to learn by imitation; perhaps he offered some criticism of their efforts. Gorgias did publish prose works other than speeches, but the few references to his statements about rhetoric do not seem to include a handbook like those described here.

Tisias, Thrasymachus, and Theodorus are among the writers of books (*biblia*) "on the art of speech" (*peri logōn tekhnēs*) mentioned by Plato in *Phaedrus* 266d5–267d9. There is no mention of Corax in this passage. Socrates says that according to these books a speech should begin with a *prooemion*, but he does not explain the function and form that should take. Second there should come a *diēgēsis*, which becomes the standard Greek term for a narration or statement of the facts. The books under review apparently continued with the requirement that the facts narrated should be supported by witnesses. Third come *tekmēria*, proof from signs, and fourth are *eikota*, probabilities. Theodorus of Byzantium is mentioned at this point as "an admirable adorner of speeches" whose book provides for a *pistōsis* and an *epipistōsis*, proof and supplementary proof, which have a counterpart in *elenkhos* and *epexelenkhos*, refutation and supplementary refutation. The proposed content of these supplements is not known. According to Socrates, Tisias and Gorgias "saw that probabilities are more honored than truth, and they make small things seem great and great things small by the strength of words, and new things

---

3. "Tisias after the first." Whom Aristotle regarded as "the first" is uncertain. One possibility is Empedocles (Diogenes Laertius 7.57–58; Quintilian 3.1.8). As will emerge later, "the first" probably did not refer to Corax.

old and the opposite new, and they discovered both brevity of speech and unlimited length on all subjects" (267a6–b2). If they showed how to do this in books on the art of speech, the most practical way would have been with examples of each technique.[4] We can see conventional topics being employed in the prooemia of extant judicial speeches by the earliest speech writers, Antiphon and Lysias. The narration of the speech, of course, dealt with a specific case, but Plato's mention of brevity and amplification suggests that examples could have been given of how to elaborate or compress statements of fact. Aristotle notes (*Rhetoric* 3.16.4) that contemporary handbooks required the narrative of a speech to be "rapid" (*takheia*), which probably can be taken to mean concise and brief, and which he thought was laughable. *Rhetoric for Alexander* (ch. 30, 1438a22–23) gives what became the standard doctrine: that it should be clear, brief, and persuasive. The sections of a handbook on proof from signs and probabilities and refutations doubtless also consisted largely of examples, perhaps introduced by a brief statement of the function of each part. Aristotle (*Rhetoric* 1.1.9) criticizes writers of handbooks for their obsession with prooemia and narrations and the other parts of a speech,[5] complaining that they concern themselves with how to put an audience in a certain frame of mind and neglect enthymemes.[6]

In the case of argument from probability (*eikos*), a famous example is cited both by Plato (*Phaedrus* 273a–b), where it is attributed to Tisias, and by Aristotle (*Rhetoric* 2.24.11), who says it constitutes "the art of Corax," probably meaning the most distinctive feature of his teaching. This is the case of a man charged with assault. If he is a weakling he should argue that it is improbable he would have attacked a stronger man, but if he appears to be the stronger one, he can argue that it is probable he would have refrained, knowing that he would be easily suspected. This may seem a bit of sophistry, but some male students in a class I was teaching claimed they were personally familiar with such an argument when there was a question of who had started a fight, and the message being given is to see if argument for one side of a case can be turned around to support the other side. Aristotle also (*Rhetoric* 2.23.28) instances a form of argument from

---

4. See Cole 1991a:88–94.

5. See also *Rhetoric* 3.13, where he criticizes the "ridiculous" divisions of a speech specified by some technical writers.

6. For enthymemes as described in a handbook contemporary with Aristotle, see *Rhetoric for Alexander* in Appendix I.F.9.

probability based on what it would have been a mistake for someone to do, saying "this topic and species of enthymeme is the whole art before Theodorus."[7] In contrast to his complaint in 1.1.9 he is here acknowledging the existence of at least one form of enthymeme exampled in the early handbooks.

Before exploring these matters further, we need to return briefly to Socrates' account of the books on the art of speech. After the references to Tisias and Gorgias quoted earlier, and to the views of the sophists Prodicus and Hippias on amplification as practiced by Tisias and Gorgias, Socrates turns to what seem to be early examples of artistic diction: Polus' "museums" of words—diplasiology, gnomonology, and eikonology—and Protagoras' *Orthoepeia*, on correct language, noting also Thrasymachus' ability to use words to evoke emotions. These are clearly separate works containing examples of usage, part of the development of language study of the time, not something found in judicial handbooks of the type Theodorus wrote, but the account of the latter is then completed by mention of the end (*telos*) of a speech, called *epanodos* (recapitulation) or by "other names" (i.e., *epilogos*). Its function is agreed to be reminding the audience of what has been said and summarizing each heading.

Most later Greek and Latin, and many early modern rhetorical handbooks as well, retained the organization of precepts, either entirely or partially, on the basis of the parts of a speech: prooemion, narration, proof, and epilogue and sometimes other parts (proposition, partition, digression, etc.). It seems clear that this structure was used by Theodorus of Byzantium, but whether he initiated it is uncertain. Plato seems to imply that it was already a feature of Tisias' handbook. In fact, this structure can be found in Odysseus' speech to Achilles in *Iliad* 9.225–306 and in other speeches in poetry and history, and late writers also attribute something like it to Corax.[8] A word of caution: most references to a rhetorician named Theodorus in writings of the Roman period mean Theodorus of Gadara, the teacher of the emperor Tiberius and author of a well-known rhetorical treatise organized around the parts of a speech.

The esoteric works of Aristotle were largely unavailable in the Hellenistic period, but some of his teaching had been transmitted

---

7. In Aristotle's example Medea can argue that she did not kill her children because if she had been intent on doing so it would have been a mistake not to kill Jason as well.

8. See Radermacher 1951:B II 8 and 23.

through his followers. When the young Cicero wrote *On Invention* around 90 B.C.E., despite his claim to wide reading in the sources (2.4) he probably had no firsthand knowledge of Aristotle's rhetorical works but had heard from his teachers about some of his rhetorical teaching:

> Aristotle sought out and brought together in one place the ancient writers of the art, starting with the first inventor, Tisias, and wrote a clear account, naming the authors, of the precepts of each, which he examined with great care and set out carefully in an annotated form; and he so surpassed the inventors of the subject in attractiveness and brevity of speaking that no one learns their precepts from their own books, but all who want to know what they taught turn to him as to a much more useful explicator. Thus, he himself has made available for us both his own teaching and that of those before him, so that we learn about others and about him through him. (*On Invention* 2.6–7)

The work of Aristotle described here is the *Synagōgē tekhnōn*,[9] or, in Latin, *Artium Scriptores*. Its genesis, probably at the time of his first teaching of rhetoric when a member of Plato's Academy in the 350s B.C.E.,[10] can perhaps be compared to that of the collection of constitutions made by or for Aristotle in connection with his studies of politics and his frequent practice in other treatises of reviewing earlier theories of the subject at hand. By the time he wrote *Brutus*, some forty-five years after *On Invention*, Cicero had studied in Athens and Rhodes with major rhetoricians and perhaps had heard again something about the *Synagōgē* or even seen it, but his account, doubtless from memory, seems very confused. The passage (*Brutus* 46–48) is too long to quote here, but can be summarized. According to Aristotle, Cicero says,[11] Corax and Tisias in Sicily were the first to compile a rhetorical *ars* and *praecepta* at the time when tyranny was abolished (in Syracuse) and people were trying to recover their property by suits in the courts of law. Protagoras, Gorgias, and

---

9. In Diogenes Laertius' list of Aristotle's works (5.24.10–11) it appears as *Tekhnōn synagōgē a' b'* (i.e., in two papyrus scrolls). It is quite possible that much of the research was done by Aristotle's assistants.

10. The principal sources for this course in rhetoric are Philodemus, *Rhetoric* 6, col. 48 (vol. 1, p. 50 Sudhaus); Cicero, *On the Orator* 3.141; Quintilian 3.1.14; Aulus Gellius 20.5.

11. Cf. also *On the Orator* 1.91.

Antiphon wrote collections of *loci communes*. "Lysias at first was accustomed to teach the art of speaking; then, because Theodorus was subtler in art but drier in speech, he began to compose orations for others and abandoned teaching. Similarly, Isocrates at first denied that there was an art of speaking, but was accustomed to write speeches for others which they used in the lawcourts; but when he himself was often brought into court because he was alleged to have broken a law that forbade anyone from being unjustly convicted, he stopped writing speeches for others and transferred his activities to compiling *arts* (*ad artes componendas*)." In *Education of the Orator* 2.17.7 Quintilian refers to Tisias and Corax as the first "teachers" of rhetoric, and in 3.1.8–12 he gives a survey of early rhetoricians, apparently based on what Cicero said in *Brutus* with some additions from Plato's account in *Phaedrus*.

From all this, we can reasonably conclude that the *Synagōgē* surveyed the history of rhetoric, based on written material, from the earliest systematic teaching in Syracuse in the 460s B.C.E. down to the time of Isocrates, and that individuals mentioned included Tisias, Gorgias, Thrasymachus, Theodorus, Lysias, Isocrates, and probably others.

There is a second tradition about the beginnings of Greek rhetoric that seems to owe nothing to Plato or Aristotle and is known to us only from Greek writings of the imperial and Byzantine periods. Its earliest extant appearance is in Sextus Empiricus' attack on the claims of rhetoric to be an art (*Adversus Mathematicos* 2.95–96), probably written in the late second century C.E., but Sextus says the story was reported by "many" earlier writers. A possible candidate for its original source seems to be Timaeus of Tauromenium, the third-century B.C.E. historian who was of a highly rhetorical bent and narrated events in Sicily in detail.[12] Timaeus is a major source for Diodorus Siculus (fl. 60–30 B.C.E.), who describes (12.53.1–4) Gorgias' embassy to Athens and his innovative prose style, but says nothing about Corax, who is one of the two actors in Sextus' passage. The other is called simply "a young man." Sextus is trying to show that those who employ an *amphisbētēsis*, here meaning a double argument, intensify the dispute and confuse the minds of the judges. Evidence for this is a story told about Corax. A young man passionately wanted to learn rhetoric and promised he would pay Corax his fee if he won his first case. When the youth began to show skill in rhetoric, Corax demanded his fee, but was refused. Corax then

---

12. Cf. Radermacher 1897.

took him to court. Then, "they say," he was the first to use an *amphisbētēsis* of this sort, claiming that whether he won the case or lost it, he ought to receive his fee. If he won he should get it because he had won, if he lost he was owed it by the terms of the agreement, for his opponent had agreed to pay if he won his first case. The judges applauded, but the young man reversed the argument. He need not pay, he said, if he wins, because he has won, and if he loses he has lost his first case and is excused from paying. The judges were perplexed at the equal strength of the arguments and drove Corax and the young man from the court, crying, "A bad egg from a bad crow (*korax*)." Sextus leaves the pun unremarked as being self-evident. A similar story is told about Protagoras and his student Euathlus (Diogenes Laertius 9.56), but of course without the pun. Probably quarrels between teachers and students over fees were not uncommon among Greeks, encouraged by the nature of the subject.

The story of the bad egg from the bad crow reappears in late antiquity in the "prolegomena" composed as introductions to the study of rhetoric and prefixed to collections of the rhetorical treatises of Hermogenes and others. The earliest (number 5 in Hugo Rabe's 1931 *Prolegomenon Sylloge*) may be that attributed to Troilus, a teacher in Constantinople around 400 C.E. He begins by defining *epistēmē*, *tekhnē*, and *empeiria* and then organizes his discussion around four questions: Does rhetoric exist? What is rhetoric? What kind of thing is it? Why does it exist? The influence here and in what follows of Neo-Platonic dialectic, ultimately derived from Aristotle, is clear.

Troilus, not surprisingly, concludes that rhetoric does exist. It has come to be by nature and art, which involves consideration of the place, time, manner, cause, and person of its origin.[13] These are provided for by the story of Corax, which contains details not earlier found. Troilus claims that Corax had been an administrative assistant to the tyrants Hieron and Gelon. When tyranny was replaced by democracy (about 467 B.C.E.) Corax realized that he could not persuade a whole populace in the way he had a tyrant:

> For that reason he contrived *prooemia*, in order that by their use he might draw the hearer to good will, followed by a *prokataskeuē* in order to remove any complaint against him; then the *prokatastasis*, being an entrance and beginning for the *katastasis*, and the *katastasis*, a bald exposition of what had been done; then the *agones*, demonstration and proof of what had been merely narrated; then

---

13. Rabe 1931:51–52.

the *parekbasis* ("digression"), being a demonstration of the life of the person being tried; for he had observed that when an accusation is made on the basis of a single complaint, the defendant will be acquitted, and for this reason he thought up the idea of the digression; and finally epilogues, recapitulations of what had been said because of the probability that the judges, after hearing many things, were becoming forgetful.

He then went around Syracuse inviting anyone who wanted to learn his technique at a fixed charge of a thousand drachmas. There follows the story of Corax and the student who refused to pay, who here is identified as Tisias, concluding with the proverbial "From a bad crow comes a bad egg." The account then continues with mention of Gorgias and his embassy to Athens, followed by discussion of definitions of rhetoric, without any reference to their sources except in the case of Aristotle. It is possible that the initial account of the activities of the person here called Corax comes from Timaeus or another historical source, but otherwise the passage seems to be an invention based on probable speculation about the situation on the part of some unidentified rhetorician of the Roman period who was not familiar with Aristotle's *Synagōgē*. There is no reference to Thrasymachus, Theodorus, Lysias, or Isocrates. A tell-tale sign of the late date is the use of the terms *prokataskeuē*, *prokatastasis*, *katastasis*, and *parekbasis*, which are not standard names for the parts of an oration in the classical or Hellenistic periods but became common in the second century C.E. and later.[14]

In the *Rhetoric* Aristotle says nothing about the rhetorical theories of Corax except that they involved argument from probability. The passage in which he mentions him by name, as noted earlier, is basically similar to the example of argument from probability attributed by Plato to Tisias. Plato, in contrast, never mentions Corax. Cicero, in *On Invention* 2.6, was of the opinion that Aristotle's *Synagōgē tekhnôn* began with Tisias, though later in *Brutus* he says Corax and Tisias "wrote" an art of precepts of rhetoric. Modern teachers of rhetoric have long been accustomed to refer to Corax and Tisias as the earliest professors of their discipline, but Thomas Cole is almost certainly right in conjecturing that the two are in fact one and the same person.[15] Corax, the Crow, is an unlikely proper name for a

---

14. On the terminology, see Martin 1974:54–55.
15. See Cole 1991b.

Greek, but a perfectly appropriate pejorative nickname. Some support for this is provided by an otherwise inexplicable reference to Tisias in *Phaedrus* 273c8: "It was a wondrously hidden art (i.e., reversible argument from probability) that Tisias or another seems to have discovered, *whoever he really was and whatever he likes to be called!*" and then there is a passage in Lucian's *Pseudologistes* (sec. 30) where there is mention of "Tisias' handbook, that work of an ill-omened crow [*dyskorakos*]."

Radermacher's collection of testimonia and fragments contains a few additional items about Tisias, Thrasymachus, and Theodorus that need to be noted. Pausanias (6.17.7–9), speaking of the statue of Gorgias at Olympia, says that Gorgias and Tisias came to Athens together on the embassy from Sicily, that Tisias improved the art of rhetoric, and "wrote" the most persuasive speech of his time in support of the claim to some property by a woman of Syracuse (Radermacher 1951:B II 2). Most references to Thrasymachus (Radermacher 1951:B IX) are to speeches, his prose style and use of rhythm, and his ability to arouse emotions. His work entitled *Eleoi*, or "Plaints" (Aristotle, *Rhetoric* 3.1.7), seems to have been a collection of passages illustrating these techniques. Plato (*Phaedrus* 267c–d) notes passages on old age and poverty. The Byzantine encyclopedia *Souda* (Radermacher 1951:B IX 1) attributes to Thrasymachus some deliberative speeches, a *Tekhnē rhētorikē, Paignia* (jokes, amusing stories, trivia of various sorts), and *Aphormai rhētorikai*. A scholiast on Aristophanes' *Birds*, line 880, refers to his *Megalē tekhnē*, or "Large Art," for a bit of historical information. According to the commentary on the *Phaedrus* by the Neo-Platonist Hermias, Thrasymachus taught that one must arouse the judges to sorrow and solicit their pity, bewailing one's age, poverty, children, and the like. This suggests that Thrasymachus' handbook resembled others at least in treating judicial oratory.[16] The meaning of *aphormai* is uncertain: possibly prooemia, more likely "resources" or "starting points" in the sense of a collection of commonplaces or arguments (cf. *Rhetoric for Alexander* 38).

Aristotle attributes to Theodorus several subdivisions of the parts of a speech outlined earlier (3.13.5). According to the *Souda* (Radermacher 1951:B XII 1) he "wrote" speeches against Thrasybulus and against Andocides and "some other things." This helps to confirm a late fifth-century B.C.E. floruit.

---

16. For translations of the fragments of Thrasymachus, see Sprague (1972:86–93).

In his account of the *Synagōgē* (*Brutus* 48) Cicero says that Isocrates wrote *artes*, by which he is unlikely to have meant Isocrates' famous orations. In *On Rhetoric* Aristotle often quotes or refers to Isocrates, and it seems likely that the *Synagōgē* did include summary of a *tekhnē* attributed to him. Radermacher followed this lead and in B XXIV printed forty-one passages from later writers that relate to a *tekhnē*, including some that deny that it existed or claim that it is a forgery, as well as twenty-three pages (163–187) of selections from Isocrates' extant speeches that bear on his views on rhetoric. His most explicit statement about his teaching is found in *Against the Sophists* (secs. 15–16), which also includes (secs. 19–20) sharp criticism of the writers of rhetorical handbooks. Terry Papillon (1995) has recently reexamined the subject in detail, concluding that Isocrates probably did not write a *tekhnē* of the sort attributed to Tisias and Theodorus, but that he may have assembled a body of material consisting of his own rhetorical texts and analysis for use by his students. It is also possible that the "Isocratean Art" was an abstract by one or more of his students of his lectures on rhetoric along the lines suggested in *Against the Sophists* (cf. Appendix I.E.1).

What now seems to me to be a possible account of the development of rhetorical handbooks in Greece can be summarized as follows.

Teaching of rhetoric began in Sicily around 466 B.C.E. when a democracy was established. In the democratic courts, as at Athens, litigants were ordinarily expected to speak in their own behalf. Litigation arose about the ownership of property that had been confiscated by the tyrants. Tisias, nicknamed "the Crow," developed and taught a simple way to compose a judicial speech, with examples. An account of this was written in a small book, copies of which reached Athens later in the century. In Tisias' system a judicial speech began with a prooemion to secure the interest and good will of the judges, followed by a narrative of the facts, confirmed by probabilities. Whether witnesses and signs were mentioned is uncertain. A speech ended with an epilogue recapitulating the argument. Short examples of these techniques were provided; argument from probability was illustrated by the case of the weak and strong men involved in a brawl as later recounted by Plato and Aristotle. Gorgias probably knew Tisias personally and was familiar with his system, but Gorgias' teaching in Athens, beginning after 427 B.C.E., was based largely on imitation of his own epideixis. Lysias may also have known Tisias, perhaps at Thurii in the late 440s B.C.E. (Pseudo-Plutarch, *Lives of the Ten Orators*, in *Moralia* 835C–D). To judge from Plato's *Phaedrus*,

Lysias may at one time have taught rhetoric by means of epideixis; after the Peloponnesian War his rhetorical activity chiefly took the form of logography, writing speeches for clients to memorize and deliver in court. Antiphon had initiated this earlier and Theodorus may have written for clients but soon abandoned the practice. Judicial speeches by Antiphon and Lysias often employ the divisions and techniques of the handbook attributed to Tisias.

Theodorus of Byzantium came to Athens around the same time that Gorgias did. He wrote a handbook of judicial rhetoric similar to that attributed to Tisias, but perhaps in greater detail, dividing the proof into confirmation (logical argument), supplementary confirmation, refutation, and supplementary refutation. Thrasymachus also wrote a work known as the "Great Art," which may have included similar material, but he was best known for his "Plaints" and collections of examples of other emotional appeals. Protagoras earlier and later Polus and Licymnius wrote short works on language and style, perhaps little more than lists. Isocrates founded the first permanent rhetorical school in Athens about 390 B.C.E. His own teachers are said (*Lives of the Ten Orators* = Plutarch's *Moralia* 836F) to have included Prodicus, Gorgias, Tisias, and Theramenes, but this may only be speculation. Although be had practiced as a logographer (six of his judicial speeches for clients survive), he abandoned it early in the fourth century B.C.E. His form of instruction combined epideixis and practice speeches by his students with analysis of rhetorical techniques and some theoretical precepts. The *Art of Rhetoric* attributed to him in later times may have been a compendium of theory and extended examples, perhaps composed by some of his students.

In connection with his "afternoon" lectures on rhetoric while still a member of Plato's Academy in the 350s B.C.E., Aristotle compiled, or had an assistant compile, the *Synagōgē tekhnōn* on the basis of rhetorical teachings from Tisias to Isocrates. According to Cicero, this work had the effect of replacing all the early judicial handbooks, which were rapidly forgotten. In his later study of rhetoric Aristotle dismissed these handbooks as of little significance.

Handbooks continued to be written in the fourth century B.C.E. Aristotle (2.28.14 and 20) cites topics from the handbook of Calippus, a student of Isocrates (cf. *Antidosis* 93), and Radermacher[17] includes testimonia relating to several other writers. The most important figures seem to be Anaximenes of Lampsacus and the Athenian

---

17. 1951:192–200.

Theodectes. According to Dionysius of Halicarnassus (*On Isaeus* 1:122) Anaximenes wrote histories and technical works and tried his hand at deliberative and judicial oratory but was not very good at any of it.[18] Theodectes was a tragedian and orator of some distinction. He was a close friend of Aristotle, who cites several of his plays, and according to the Byzantine encyclopedia, *Souda*, he wrote an *Art of Rhetoric* in verse (*en metrōi*). Both Anaximenes and Theodectes have been connected by modern scholars with the only other Greek treatise on rhetoric surviving from the classical period, the *Rhetoric for Alexander*, preserved as a work of Aristotle. This is an important document in the history of Greek rhetoric, for it shows a development in detail, especially in treatment of invention, far beyond what was contained in the earlier handbooks and parallels Aristotle's approach.

It begins with a curious letter claiming to be by Aristotle addressing Alexander the Great and sending him the treatise that follows, which each is to keep secret from others for their lifetime, perhaps an attempt to explain why the work was not well known before being edited in late antiquity. The main body of the text falls into two parts. The first part (chs. 1–28) provides advice, topics, and illustrations for composing seven species of rhetoric: exhortation, dissuasion, encomion, vituperation, accusation, defense, and investigation.[19] (For a translation of chapter 1, see Appendix I.F.) There are some parallels to what Aristotle says in Book 1 of *On Rhetoric*. The second part (chs. 29–38) is a handbook approaching the subject in terms of the parts of an oration, but considering all seven species rather than limiting the contents to judicial rhetoric as had earlier handbooks. This part thus roughly corresponds to Aristotle on the parts of an oration in Book 3, chapters 16–19. Despite obvious parallels to Aristotle's *Rhetoric*, and the probability that the two works are roughly contemporary, it does not seem possible to say that Aristotle knew and used *Rhetoric for Alexander* nor that the author or authors of the latter made direct use of Aristotle's *Rhetoric*, which was an unpublished, esoteric work existing only in Aristotle's own library. They could have known something about Aristotle's teaching from former students. The author of both parts has commonly been thought to be Anaximenes on the basis of a statement in Quintilian 3.4.9 that Anaximenes

18. Testimonia in Radermacher 1951:200–202.
19. For discussion of problems relating to this, see David C. Mirhady, "Aristotle, the *Rhetorica ad Alexandrum* and the tria genera causarum," in Fortenbaugh and Mirhady 1994:54–65.

specified seven species of rhetoric, an unusual approach. There are, however, some inconsistencies in teaching and terminology between the two parts, so only one part is likely to be the work of Anaximenes.

At the end of the introductory epistle the person who assembled the two parts into their present form many centuries later, pretending to be Aristotle, says that he has adopted the contents from other writers and specifies two sources, "material in the Arts written by me (i.e. Aristotle) for Theodectes," and "the other that of Corax." This latter reference can be understood to mean the tradition of rhetorical teaching stemming from Tisias (Corax) and Theodorus. The reference to a work on rhetoric by Aristotle for Theodectes, if it means anything, must be to the first part. Now the list of Aristotle's works as given by Diogenes Laertius (5.24) includes a second *Synagōgē*, "of the Art of Theodectes in one book." Aristotle refers to this work in *Rhetoric* 3.9.10: "The beginnings of periods have mostly been enumerated in the *Theodectea*." Michel Patillon (1997) has speculated that the first part of the *Rhetoric for Alexander* is to be identified with the *Theodectea* and that when Aristotle mentions the latter in *Rhetoric* 3.9.10 he is referring to chapter 24 of *Rhetoric for Alexander*, which lists forms of "twofold statements."[20] Aristotle's reference to the *Theodectea* sounds as though it was something he had written himself,[21] and the listing in Diogenes Laertius (probably ultimately derived from the catalogue of the Alexandrian Library) seems to confirm this. Why would Aristotle take the trouble to write such a work in addition to the other *Synagōgē*? Was the *Theodectea* an earlier work by Aristotle *dedicated* to Theodectes? Or was it an abstract of Theodectes' rhetorical theory or practice, whether made by Aristotle or someone else? Could Theodectes have asked him for a text on which to base his projected versified "Art of Rhetoric"?[22]

---

20. "The beginnings of periods have mostly been enumerated in the *Theodectea*" (Patillon 1997:n.47).

21. He does not refer to works by others in this form. Valerius Maximus (8.14. ext. 3) has a curious story that Aristotle allowed Theodectes to claim authorship of one of his own works, then became jealous of the fame and inserted a reference in his writings to show he had written it. Quintilian (4.2.11) was uncertain whether the *Theodectea* was a work by Aristotle or by Theodectes.

22. A versified "Art of Rhetoric" is not completely absurd, and the excuse for it would have been that rhetorical precepts could be learned and remembered more easily if in verse. The tradition of writing on technical subjects in verse goes back to Hesiod's *Works and Days* and is seen in Aratus' *Phaenomena*. Michael Psellus' eleventh-century versified summary of Hermogenic rhetoric survives and can be found in volume 3 of Walz's *Rhetores Graeci*.

Patillon acknowledged that the text may not seem well enough written to be a genuine work by Aristotle, but says (1997:124, n.43) that the author of a *synagōgē* in principal did not intervene in what was said in the original text. There is in fact no need to assume that Aristotle personally wrote out the text. If he had anything to do with it at all he probably dictated it, and it is possible that it was largely written by an assistant and thus lacks what Patillon calls "la vigeur de la pensée aristotélienne." But there are other objections that seem to rule out the identification. Cicero (*Orator* 173 and 194) and Quintilian (4.2.11 and 9.4.88) refer to teachings of Theodectes that do not appear in *Rhetoric for Alexander*. The text is certainly not an abstract of Aristotle's "afternoon lectures" of the mid-350s B.C.E., and a reference to a Corinthian expedition to Syracuse (ch. 8, 1429a18) shows that the work must be dated after 341 B.C.E. Nor is it based on knowledge of the text of the *Rhetoric* or lectures by Aristotle in the Lyceum after 335, for it departs from Aristotle's basic teachings in many respects, including such crucial matters as the three modes of persuasion and the definition of paradigm and enthymeme (cf. Appendix I.F.7–8). It remains possible that the original author of one or both parts of *Rhetoric for Alexander* was Anaximenes of Lampsacus and also that Aristotle did at some time, probably early in his teaching of rhetoric, provide a sketch of the subject now lost, for Theodectes to use as a basis for a versified treatment.

B. THE HISTORY OF THE TEXT AFTER ARISTOTLE

The geographer Strabo (13.1.54), an often well-informed writer of the late first century B.C.E., and the historian-philosopher Plutarch (*Sulla* 26.1–2), writing a hundred years later, are the major sources for the early history of the text of the esoteric works of Aristotle. They are in general agreement and probably drew on the same source. The tale they tell has not always been believed, but in the case of *On Rhetoric* it is consistent with the very limited knowledge of the treatise shown by Greek and Latin writers from the late fourth to the middle of the first centuries B.C.E. The story goes as follows.

Aristotle apparently left behind most of the papyrus rolls of his esoteric works—the texts for his lectures—in the Lyceum when he left Athens in 323 B.C.E. His most famous student, Theophrastus, became head of the school and inherited the library on Aristotle's death the following year. Theophrastus wrote on several aspects of rhetoric, and though these works have not survived, from brief references to them in Cicero and other writers they often seem to have been an extension of Aristotle's thinking.[23] "Topics," "enthymemes," delivery,[24] and style were all treated by Theophrastus, his work *On Lexis* being especially influential. Here he seems to have reformulated Aristotle's discussion of the virtue of style in terms of diction and composition under four headings: correctness, clarity, ornamentation, and propriety (see esp. Cicero, *Orator* 79). At Theophrastus' death (about 285 B.C.E.) copies of some of Aristotle's still unpublished manuscripts perhaps remained in the Peripatetic school in Athens, and copies of some in whole or part were perhaps made for research libraries, of which the most important was the great Library at Alexandria in Egypt. There is, however, no proof that *On Rhetoric* was among these books. Aristotle's library was inherited from Theophrastus by the philosopher Neleus and much or all of it was taken to Scepsis in Asia Minor, where it fell into the hands of people who were not scholars. To prevent the books from being seized by agents for the great Stoic library at Pergamum, these owners hid them and then forgot about them. Thus, according to Strabo, the Peripatetics after Theophrastus did not have the original esoteric works of Aristotle, or at least not most of them. They did not continue philosophical research along the lines begun by Aristotle and Theophrastus except for dialectic and seem to have been primarily interested in debating theses for practice (Quintilian 12.2.25). They did have, of course, Aristotle's published works, including the *Gryllus*, and we can probably imagine debate about whether rhetoric was an art, as discussed there and in Plato's *Gorgias*. The head of the Peripatetic school in the middle of the second century B.C.E. was Critolaus. According to Quintilian (2.15.23) he denied that rhetoric was a faculty (Aristotle's *dynamis*), a science (*epistēmē*), or an art (*tekhnē*), and called it a *tribē*, a "knack," as had Socrates in Plato's *Gorgias*. Hostility to the formal study of rhetoric was shared by the other philosophical schools in Athens in the second century (Cicero, *On the Orator* 1.46–47), perhaps because the appearance of rhetorical schools attracting Roman students constituted a threat to their own survival. Subsequently, perhaps about 100 B.C.E., Aristotle's library,

---

23. For fragments and testimony on Theophrastus' rhetorical works, see Fortenbaugh 1992:2.508–559.

24. See Fortenbaugh 1985.

now in a damaged condition, was sold by the heirs of those who had hidden it to Apellicon of Teos, living in Athens. After Apellicon's death it was seized by the Roman general Sulla and sent to Rome around 83 B.C.E. There the grammarian Tyrannio "arranged" the works and furnished copies to Andronicus of Rhodes, who "published" them and drew up lists of the works.

It has often been assumed that some editing was done by Tyrannio and Andronicus, and one possibility is the combining of Books 1–2 of *On Rhetoric* with Book 3, including adding one of the transitional passages (probably 3.1.1–2). The reference to Aristotle's *Lexis* in Demetrius (*On Style* 116) may imply that he regarded it as a separate work, and Diogenes Laertius (5.24), writing much later, lists an *Art of Rhetoric* in two books, not three, as well as a work *On Lexis* in two books (one on style, one on arrangement?). Possibly two traditions existed, one containing all three books, one containing only Books 1 and 2. The version known to Quintilian (2.17.14) in the late first century C.E. had three books.

When Cicero wrote *On Invention* as a very young man, before the arrival of the library of Apellicon in Rome, he knew that Aristotle had written a work on rhetoric, describes it as providing aids and ornaments to the art (1.7), and attributes to Aristotle the view that the duty (*officium*) of the orator was exercised in three *genera*: demonstrative, deliberative, and judicial. That, of course, is not quite what Aristotle says in 1.4, but it does indicate that the division of rhetoric into three species was traditionally associated with Aristotle. This may well represent an oral tradition that goes back to Aristotle's own students in the fourth century B.C.E. rather than knowledge of the full text in the intervening centuries.

Even if *On Rhetoric* was available to some scholars in Athens and Alexandria between 300 and 50 B.C.E., new developments in rhetorical theory rendered it obsolete as a school text. Hermagoras of Temnos, in the middle of the second century B.C.E., had worked out stasis theory, a systematic way to determine the central question at issue in a speech. Aristotle shows some awareness of such matters in 1.13.9–10 and 3.15.17 but failed to present a full account. By Cicero's time stasis theory was the foundation of the study of rhetorical invention, and continued so for centuries. In the study of style, the Stoics had developed the theory of tropes and figures of speech, concepts unknown to Aristotle, and these also were major concerns of later rhetoricians. Aristotle's topical theory did remain a subject of interest, though modified by subsequent Latin writers including Cicero, Quintilian, and Boethius.

When Cicero wrote *On the Orator* in 55 B.C.E. he clearly had some knowledge of *On Rhetoric* from the edition of Tyrannio and Andronicus, and the discussion of invention in *On the Orator* 2.114–306 is considerably more Aristotelian than what is found in *On Invention* or in the other early Latin treatise, *Rhetoric for Herennius*. Cicero refers to *On Rhetoric* repeatedly in *On the Orator* and even makes his character Antonius claim to have read it in Athens in the late second century B.C.E. (2.160). This could possibly have occurred if he had access to the library of Apellicon. Aristotelian influences in *On the Orator* include the role of logical proof, presentation of character, and emotional appeal (2.115), described later in *Orator* 69 as the three *officia* of the orator—to prove, to delight, and to move—and then associated with the three kinds of style: plain, middle, and grand, concepts that may have been developed by Theophrastus. This represents an important and long influential restatement and extension of Aristotle's basic concepts in *On Rhetoric* 1.2.

Aristotle's philosophical works were reedited and extensively studied in later antiquity, beginning with Alexander of Aphrodesias around 200 C.E.,[25] but the works on rhetoric that became authoritative in this and later periods in Greek were the treatises on stasis and style attributed to Hermogenes of Tarsus. Some Aristotelian influence is visible, however, in a compendium of rhetoric known as *Anonymous Seguerianus* and in the *Arts of Rhetoric* by Apsines of Gadara and Cassius Longinus, rhetoricians of the third century C.E.[26] In the Neo-Platonist reorganization of the Aristotelian corpus *On Rhetoric* was assigned to the *Organon*, following the *Topics* and preceding the *Poetics*. Rhetoric was thus regarded as a logical tool, not as a practical or productive art. There are only occasional references to the treatise in Greek writers of the Roman Empire or early Middle Ages, but it did survive because of its Aristotelian authorship. Our earliest— and often best—Greek manuscript of the text is *Parisinus* 1741, written in the thirteenth century. It is a compilation of rhetorical treatises by Menander (two works on epideictic), Dionysius of Halicarnassus (works on style), and others, plus *On Rhetoric* and *Poetics*. There are two rather short Greek commentaries written in the twelfth century, one attributed to a certain Stephanus, one anonymous.[27] *On Rhetoric* was also known to Arabic scholars of Greek philosophy. The most important of these was al-Farabi (died 950 C.E.). In his treatise on *The*

---

25. See Lord 1986.
26. See Dilts and Kennedy 1997:ix–x.
27. Texts in Rabe 1896; on Byzantine study of the *Rhetoric*, see Conley 1990b.

Philosophy of Aristotle he was concerned with the logical status of rhetoric and provided a commentary to the first three chapters of *On Rhetoric*.[28] He did not know Greek and probably relied on a Syriac translation.[29] Since there was no tradition of civic oratory in Arabic, al-Farabi understood rhetoric to be one of the skills of a philosopher-king, a concept derived from Plato and probably known to him by way of teachings of Themistius.[30] In the thirteenth century Hermannus Alemannus in Spain introduced Aristotle's *Rhetoric* to the western world by a Latin translation of al-Farabi's commentary. Greek manuscripts of the *Rhetoric* existed in libraries in Greek-speaking southern Italy and became the source of two Latin translations in the thirteenth century. The first of these, known as the "Old Translation," was perhaps the work of Bartholomew of Massina; the second was made by William of Moerbeke at the urging of Thomas Aquinas. Giles of Rome then wrote a Latin commentary, but (as this commentary indicates) what interested readers of the time was not the rhetorical theory, for which they kept to the Ciceronian tradition, but its chapters on politics and ethics.[31]

In the fifteenth century George of Trebizond brought Aristotle's theories to the attention of Italian humanists and prepared a new Latin translation, which was the first printed version of the *Rhetoric* (about 1477) and the first to divide the work into chapters.[32] The complete Greek text was not printed with early editions of Aristotle's philosophical works and first appeared in 1508 in the Venice edition of the collected *Rhetores Graeci*, published by Aldus Manutius. Thereafter, new editions of the Greek text began to appear and new translations were made.[33] The work occasionally became the subject of university lectures; for example, John Rainolds lectured on the *Rhetoric* at Oxford in the 1570s.[34] In 1637 the political philosopher Thomas Hobbes published (anonymously) the first English version of the text, more an outline and summary than a full translation.[35] In the eighteenth and early nineteenth centuries numerous new rhetorics bearing little

---

28. Cf. Murphy 1974:90–92; Aouad 1989; Watt 1995.
29. See John W. Watt, "Syriac Rhetorical Theory and the Syriac Tradition of Aristotle's *Rhetoric*," in Fortenbaugh and Mirhady 1994:243–260.
30. Cf. Watt 1995.
31. See Murphy 1974:89–101.
32. See Monfasani 1976:241–299.
33. See Brandes 1989.
34. Cf. Green 1986. Only the first nine lectures survive.
35. Modern edition by Harwood 1986.

debt to Aristotle were published and came into use in schools and universities; the most famous are those of George Campbell, Hugh Blair, and Richard Whately. Although it has often been thought that Aristotle's *Rhetoric* fell into neglect at this time, Carol Poster has shown that study of the text from a humanistic viewpoint was prevalent at Oxford in the early part of the nineteenth century and later from a more philological approach at Cambridge.[36] A major development was the publication by the Cambridge University Press in 1877 of the fine commentary in three volumes by E. M. Cope, edited and completed by J. E. Sandys and still of great value. In the twentieth century, with the reemergence of rhetorical studies in connection with the teaching of composition, critical studies, linguistics, and speech communication, *On Rhetoric* secured a place in the curricula of colleges and universities and is now read by more people than at any time in history.

---

36. Poster 2001.

GLOSSARY

All syllables and letters of the Greek terms should be pronounced. The original pitch accent on Greek nouns occurred on one of the last three syllables of a word but can only be determined for a particular noun or adjective by consulting a dictionary. It is, however, acceptable to pronounce the Greek in accordance with Latin rules of stress accent. In the following list, *ē* represents eta, pronounced as long *a* as in English *make*, *ō* is omega, long o as in English *hope*; *nk* represents an original gamma kappa (*gk*), which was nasalized; *y* represents Greek upsilon, roughly equivalent to *u* as in French *lune*. Latin writers used the letter *c* to represent Greek kappa (*k* in the words here), and Latin spelling continues to be used by some today: thus *arkhē* or *archē*, *kōlon* or *colon*, and so on. The definite articles in Greek are, in the singular, *ho* (masculine), *hē* (feminine), *to* (neuter); in the plural *hoi, hai, ta*, respectively. In the following list gender is indicated by m., f., or n. References to the text are a sample of usages, not a complete list of passages in which the words appear. For a full index of Greek words see Kassel's edition (1976:199–254) or Wartelle's *Lexique* (1981).

adikia (f.): injustice (1.9.7, etc.).
amphibolos, amphibolon, pl. *amphiboloi, amphibola* (m., n.):
   equivocation, ambiguity (1.15.10, 3.5.4, 3.18.5).
amphisbētēsis, pl. *amphisbētēseis* (f.): the question at issue, what
   is being debated (1.13.10, 3.15.2, 3.16.6, 3.17.1).
antistrophos, pl. *antistrophoi* (m.): counterpart, correlative
   (1.1.1, 3.9.1, 3.9.6).
antithesis, pl. *antitheseis* (f.): antithesis, contrast or opposition of
   words, phrases, or ideas (3.9.9, 3.10.6, 3.11.10).
apodeixis, pl. *apodeixeis* (f.): logical demonstration (1.1.11, 1.9.40,
   2.21.4, etc.).

313

apologia, pl. *apologiai* (f.): a speech in self-defense (1.3.3, 1.10.1, 1.12.7, 3.13.3).

aretē, pl. *aretai* (f.): excellence, moral virtue (1.6.6–10, 1.9.4, etc.); the virtue of style (3.2.1).

arkhē, pl. *arkhai* (f.): beginning, starting point, first principle (1.2.21, 1.7.12, etc.). The word has a variety of meanings; see 3.11.7.

asyndeton, pl. *asyndeta* (n.): asyndeton, absence of connectives (3.6.6, 3.12.2, 3.19.6).

atekhnos pistis, pl. *atekhnoi pisteis* (f.): non-artistic proof, evidence used but not invented by the speaker (1.2.2); by later writers often called "extrinsic." The forms discussed in 1.15 are laws, witnesses, contracts, tortures, and oaths. In 3.16.1 the facts in an epideictic speech are called *atekhnon*.

auxēsis (f.) or *to auxein* or *to auxētikon* (n.): amplification or intensification of a statement to heighten its effect; characteristic of epideictic oratory (1.9.38–39, 3.6.7, 3.12.4), but used in all species (2.18.4); not to be regarded as a topic of enthymemes (2.26.1–2). Its opposite is *meioun* (depreciation).

blaisōsis (f.): a "twist," given to refute the enthymeme of an opponent by showing that two opposite conclusions can follow from the premises (2.18.15).

diabolē, pl. *diabolai* (f.): prejudicial attack or slander in a speech (3.15).

diairesis, pl. *diaireseis* (f.): division of an argument into logical headings (1.7.31, 1.10.10, 2.23.10, 2.24.3); division of a period into *kōla* (3.9.5).

dialektikē (f.): dialectic, the art of logical argument on general issues of a political or ethical nature; practiced as an exercise by students of philosophy in the form of question-and-answer dialogue (1.1; Appendix I.D).

dianoia (f.): thought, used in 1.26.3 to mean rhetorical invention.

diatribē, pl. *diatribai* (f.): dwelling on a subject; usually personal invective, often in digressions (2.6.20, 3.17.10).

diēgēsis, pl. *diēgēseis* (f.): the narration or narrative passages in a speech (1.1.9, 3.16).

(to) dikaion, pl. *(ta) dikaia* (n.): what is just, the subject of judicial oratory (1.3.5; 1.13, etc.); its opposite is *adikia*: injustice (1.9.7).

dikanikos (logos), pl. *dikanikoi* (m.); *dikanikon (genos* or *eidos)*, pl. *dikanika* (n.): judicial speech, as in a court of law (1.3.1–6, 1.10–15).

dikastēs, pl. *dikastai* (m.): judges, jurors (1.1.5, 1.1.7, 1.3.2, 1.15.24, etc.).

dikē, pl. *dikai* (f.): justice (1.12.8, 2.1.2); also a trial relating to alleged violation of someone's rights (1.3.3, 1.12.25).

dynamis, pl. *dynameis* (f.): potentiality, ability, or faculty of doing or becoming something (1.2.1); in Aristotelian philosophy contrasted with *energeia*, actualization (2.2.3).

eidos, pl. *eidē* (n.): appearance, form, class, species, in contrast to *genos* (1.4.12, 2.19.11, etc.); in 1.2.22 *specific* topics in contrast to *common* topics.

eikōn, pl. *eikones* (f.): simile (3.4).

eikos, pl. *eikota* (n.): probability (1.2.15, 2.24.10–11, 2.25.8–11).

eiromenē: see *lexis eiromenē*.

eirōneia (f.): dissimulation, mockery (2.2.24).

ekklēsiastēs, pl. *ekklēsiastai* (m.): a voting member of a citizen assembly (1.3.2).

elenkhos, pl. *elenkhoi* (m.): refutation (3.17.13–15).

energeia (f.): actualization (2.2.3), representing inanimate things as animate (3.11.2).

enkōmion, pl. *enkōmia* (n.): praise of the deeds of a person (1.9.33).

enstasis, pl. *enstaseis* (f.): objection to a premise in an opponent's argument (2.25.1–7, 2.26.3).

entekhnos pistis, pl. *entekhnoi pisteis* (f.): artistic means of persuasion, derived from the character of the speaker as trustworthy, moving the emotions of the audience, or the use of logical argument (1.2.3, 2.1).

enthymēma, pl. *enthymēmata* (n.): enthymeme; a rhetorical syllogism (1.2.8–22, 2.22, etc.).

epagōgē, pl. *epagōgai* (f.): inductive argument (1.2.8).

epainos, pl. *epainoi* (m.): praise, the positive form of epideictic (1.3.3, 1.9.33).

epideiktikos-ē-on, pl. *epideiktikoi-ai-a* (adj., often used as a noun): epideictic, demonstrative rhetoric (1.3.1–6, 1.9, 3.12, etc.).

epieikeia (f.): fair-mindedness (1.2.4); *epieikes* (n.): fairness.

epilogos, pl. *epilogoi* (m.): epilogue, peroration, conclusion of a speech (3.19).

epistēmē, pl. *epistēmai* (f.): knowledge; in Aristotle's other works often scientific knowledge, in contrast to *tekhnē*, or art; in *Rhetoric* used of a discipline, such as politics or ethics, that has a systematic body of thought (1.1.1, etc.).

epitheton, pl. *epitheta* (n.): epithet (3.2.14, 3.3.3).

erōtēsis, pl. *erōtēseis* (f.): interrogation, questioning of an opponent in court (3.18).

ēthos, pl. *ēthē* (n.): character, the moral character of the speaker or someone else (1.2.3–4, 1.8.6, 1.9.1, 2.1.1–7, 2.12–17, etc.).

(ta) eudokimounta (n. pl.): expressions that are well-liked by audiences (3.10.1, 3.10.2).

glōtta, pl. *glōttai* (f.): a gloss; a strange, obsolete, or foreign word (3.3.2, 3.10.2).

gnōmē, pl. *gnōmai* (f.): a maxim, gnomic saying relating to life (2.21, 3.17.9).

(to) hellēnizein (n.): speaking good grammatical Greek (3.5).

homoioteleuton, pl. *homoioteleuta* (n.): *paromoiōsis*, or rhyme at the end of two or more cola (3.9.9).

hyperbolē, pl. *hyperbolai* (f.): hyperbole, exaggerated metaphor (3.11.15).

hypokrisis (f.): acting, delivery in oratory (3.1.3–7).

idiai (protaseis, pisteis) (f. pl.); *idion*, pl. *idia* (n.): specific (propositions or proofs); the special topics of politics and ethics in contrast to common topics (1.2.21–22, etc.).

(to) kalon, pl. *(ta) kala* (n.): what is fine, good to look upon, honorable, or noble, as praised in epideictic (1.3.5, 1.9, etc.).

katēgoria, pl. *katēgoriai* (f.): accusation, prosecution (1.3.3, 1.10.1).

koinai pisteis (f.): logical means of persuasion, common to all three species of rhetoric: paradigm, maxim, and enthymeme (2.20–22).

koinoi topoi: see *topos*.

(to) koinon, pl. *(ta) koina* (n.): subjects for argument common to all species of rhetoric: the possible and impossible, past and future fact, degree of magnitude (1.3.7–9, 1.7, 1.14, 2.19).

kōlon, pl. *kōla* (n.): colon, one of the two parts of a period (3.9.5).

krisis, pl. *kriseis* (f.): judgment, as made by an assembly or jury (1.1.4, 2.1.2, etc.).

kritēs, pl. *kritai* (m.): judge, a member of a jury, a member of a deliberative assembly (1.3.2, etc.).

kyrios-a-on, pl. *kyrioi-ai-a* (adj.): in grammar, the prevailing or proper meaning of a word (3.2.2.); in other contexts the word has a variety of meanings (e.g., "authoritative" in 1.8.2).

lexis, pl. *lexeis* (f.): how something is said, style, often word choice, sometimes composition of sentences or speeches (3.1–12).

lexis agōnistikē (f.): the style of a speech spoken in actual debate (3.12.1).

lexis eiromenē (f.): the "strung-on" or running style of composition (3.9.1).

lexis katestrammenē (f.): the "turned-down" or periodic style of composition (3.9.1).

logographos, pl. *logographoi* (m.): a prose writer (2.11.7, 3.12.2); a speech writer for litigants in court (3.7.7).

logos, pl. *logoi* (m.): word, sentence, argument, reason, speech, tale, esteem (*passim*).

lysis, pl. *lyseis* (f.): refutation of an argument by "undoing" its logic (2.25).

metaphora, pl. *metaphorai* (f.): metaphor (3.2, 3.10, 3.11); the movement or transfer of an alien word from genus to species, species to genus, species to species, or by analogy (*Poetics* 21.7–15 in *Appendix* I.G).

nomos, pl. *nomoi* (m.): law (1.4.12, 1.15.3–12). Law is either *gegrammenos* (written) or *koinos* (common to the tradition of all) (1.10.3, 1.13.2).

onkos (m.): expansiveness in style (3.6).

paian, pl. *paianes* (m.): paean, a metrical foot consisting of one long and three short or three short and one long syllables (3.8.5–6).

parabolē, pl. *parabolai* (f.): comparison, a form of example (2.20.2–4).

paradeigma, pl. *paradeigmata* (n.): paradigm, inductive argument from example (1.2.8–10, 2.20).

parison, pl. *parisa* (n.): or *parisōsis*, pl. *parisōseis* (f.): an equal number of syllables in each of two cola (3.9.9).

paromoiōsis, pl. *paromoiōseis* (f.): similarity in sound at the beginning or ending of cola (3.9.9).

pathos, pl. *pathē* (n.): emotion, a temporary state of feeling awakened by circumstances; in the *Rhetoric* esp. the emotions of members of an audience as moved by a speaker (1.2.5, 2.1–11).

periodos, pl. *periodoi* (f.): an expression having a beginning and end in itself and consisting of one or two cola (3.9).

pistis, pl. *pisteis* (f.): proof, means of persuasion, non-artistic or artistic, by character, emotion, or logical demonstration. See esp. 1.2; but in 3.17.15 and probably in 1.1.3 *pistis* refers only to logical argument.

(to) prepon (n.): the appropriate, propriety as a quality of style (3.2.1, 3.7).

proairesis (f.): deliberate choice or moral purpose, a decision made on the basis of character (1.1.14, 1.8.6, 3.16.8).

prooimion, pl. *prooimia* (n.): the proem, or exordium, or introduction of a speech (3.14).

pro ommatōn poiein (n.): bringing-before-the-eyes, visualization in artistic style (3.10–11).

protasis, pl. *protaseis* (f.): a proposition or premise of an argument (1.3.7).

prothesis, pl. *protheseis* (f.): the statement of a case at the beginning of a speech (3.13.2).

psogos, pl. *psogoi* (m.): blame, invective, the negative form of epideictic (1.3.3).

(ta) psykhra (n. pl.): frigidities, or faults, of style (3.3).

rhētor, pl. *rhētores* (m.): a speaker (1.1.14, etc.).

rhētorikē (tekhnē) (f.): rhetoric, the ability in each particular case to see the available means of persuasion (1.2.1, etc.).

rhythmos, pl. *rhythmoi* (m.): recurring proportion in the quantity (long or short) of syllables, giving a sense of limit to language, esp. at the beginnings and endings of sentences and clauses (3.8).

(to) saphes (n.): clarity, the virtue of style (3.2.1).

sēmeion, pl. *sēmeia* (n.): sign, a probable or necessary indication that something is so (1.2.14–18).

semnos-ē-on (adj.): stately or solemn in style (3.3.3–4).

soloikizein (inf.): to make a mistake in word usage (3.5.7); cf. English "solecism."

sophistēs, pl. *sophistai* (m.): sophist, a person who engages in specious argument (1.1.14, etc.).

stoikheion, pl. *stoikheia* (n.): element, identified with topics in 2.22.13 and 2.16.1.

syllogismos, pl. *syllogismoi* (m.): syllogism, a deductive argument in dialectic consisting of major premise, minor premise, and conclusion (1.2.8, etc.; Appendix I.D).

symbouleutikos (logos) (m.), *symbouleutikon (eidos)* (n.): deliberative speech, as before a civic assembly (1.3.5, 1.6.1).

(to) sympheron, pl. *(ta) sympheronta* (n.): what is advantageous or beneficial to a speaker or audience, the subject of deliberative oratory (1.3.5, 1.6.1, etc.).

taxis (f.): arrangement, esp. of the parts of a speech in a conventional order (3.13–19).

tekmērion, pl. *tekmēria* (n.): a necessarily valid sign (1.2.16–18).

tekhnē, pl. *tekhnai* (f.): art (1.1.2, etc.), a reasoned habit of mind in making something (*Nicomachean Ethics* 6.4.3).

theōros, pl. *theōroi* (m.): a spectator or observer, one who listens to a speech but is not asked to take action, as in epideictic (1.3.2).

topos, pl. *topoi* (m.): topic; a mental "place" where an argument can be found or the argument itself; in 1.2.21, a form or strategy of argument, to be distinguished from an *idion*, which is a proposition specific to some body of knowledge. In 2.23 twenty-eight *topoi* are described, but in 1.15.19 *idia* are referred to as topics. See also note on 3.15.2.

BIBLIOGRAPHY

MODERN EDITIONS OF THE GREEK TEXT OF THE *RHETORIC*

Dufour, Médéric, and André Wartelle. 1960–1973. *Aristote, "Rhétorique,"* with French translation. 3 vols. Paris: Les Belles Lettres.

Kassel, Rudolf. 1976. *Aristotelis "Ars Rhetorica."* Berlin: De Gruyter.

Ross, W. David. 1959. *Aristotelis "Ars Rhetorica."* Oxford: Clarendon Press.

ENGLISH TRANSLATIONS OF THE *RHETORIC*

Cooper, Lane. [1932] 1960. *The Rhetoric of Aristotle.* New York: Appleton-Century-Crofts.

Freese, John H. 1926. *Aristotle, "The 'Art' of Rhetoric,"* with Greek text. Loeb Classical Library. Cambridge: Harvard University Press.

Lawson-Tancred, H. C. 1991. *Aristotle, "The Art of Rhetoric."* London: Penguin Books.

Roberts, W. Rhys. 1924. *Rhetorica* in *The Works of Aristotle*, vol. 11. Oxford: Clarendon Press. Rpt. 1954 in *Aristotle, "Rhetoric" and "Poetics,"* trans. W. Rhys Roberts and Ingram Bywater. New York: Modern Library. Also rpt. with corrections, 1984, in *The Works of Aristotle*, ed. Jonathan Barnes, vol. 2.2152–2269. Princeton: Princeton University Press.

BOOKS AND ARTICLES REFERRED TO IN THE NOTES, WITH ADDITIONAL WORKS USEFUL FOR STUDY OF THE *RHETORIC*

Adamik, Tomás. 1984. "Aristotle's Theory of the Period," *Philologus* 128:184–201.

Allard-Nelson, Susan K. 2001. "Virtue in Aristotle's *Rhetoric*: A Metaphysical and Ethical Capacity," *Philosophy & Rhetoric* 34:245–259.

Aouad, M. 1989. "Aristote de Stagire: *La Rhétorique*. Tradition syriaque et arabe," *Dictionnaire des philosophes antiques*. Paris, CNRS, 1:455–472.

Arnhart, Larry. 1981. *Aristotle on Political Reasoning*. DeKalb: Northern Illinois University Press.

Atwill, Janet M. 1997. *Rhetoric Reclaimed; Aristotle and the Liberal Arts Tradition*. Ithaca: Cornell University Press.

Barnes, Jonathan, Malcolm Schofield, and Richard Sorabji, eds. 1979. *Articles on Aristotle: Psychology and Aesthetics*. London: Duckworth.

Benoit, W. L. 1980. "Aristotle's Example: The Rhetorical Induction," *Quarterly Journal of Speech* 66:182–192.

Blettner, Elizabeth. 1983. "One Made Many and Many Made One: The Role of Asyndeton in Aristotle's *Rhetoric*," *Philosophy & Rhetoric* 16:49–54.

Boegehold, Alan J. 1999. *When a Gesture was Expected: A Selection of Examples from Archaic and Classical Greek Literature*. Princeton: Princeton University Press.

Bonner, Robert, and Gertrude Smith. 1930–1938. *The Administration of Justice from Homer to Aristotle*. 2 vols. Chicago: University of Chicago Press.

Brandes, Paul D. 1989. *A History of Aristotle's* "Rhetoric." Metuchen, N.J.: Scarecrow Press.

Brill's New Pauly: Encyclopaedia of the Ancient World. 2000–. Ed. Hubert Cancik and Helmut Schneider. Leiden: Brill.

Brunschwig, Jacques. 1996. "Rhetoric as a Counterpart to Dialectic," in Rorty (1996), pp. 34–55.

Burkert, Walter. 1975. "Aristoteles im Theater: Zur Datierung des 3. Buch der *Rhetorik* und der *Poetik*," *Museum Helveticum* 32:67–72.

Carawan, E. M. 1983. "*Erotesis*: Interrogation in the Courts of Fourth-Century Athens," *Greek, Roman, and Byzantine Studies* 32:209–226.

Carey, Christopher. 1994. "'Artless' Proofs in Aristotle and the Orators," *Bulletin of the Institute of Classical Studies* (London) 39:95–106.

Chroust, Anton-Hermann. 1964. "Aristotle's Earliest Course of Lectures on Rhetoric," *L'Antiquité Classique* 33:58–72. Rpt. in Erickson (1974), pp. 22–36.

———. 1965. "Aristotle's First Literary Effort: The *Gryllus*, a Lost Dialogue on the Nature of Rhetoric," *Revue des Etudes Grecques* 78:576–591.

Clayton, Edward W. 2004. "The Audience for Aristotle's *Rhetoric*," *Rhetorica* 22:183–203.

Cole, Thomas. 1991a. *The Origins of Rhetoric in Ancient Greece*. Baltimore: Johns Hopkins University Press.

———. 1991b. "Who Was Corax?" *Illinois Classical Studies* 16:65–84.

Conley, Thomas. 1982. "*Pathe* and *Pisteis*: Aristotle, *Rhet.* II 2–11," *Hermes* 110:300–315.

———. 1984. "The Enthymeme in Perspective," *Quarterly Journal of Speech* 70:168–187.

———. 1990a. *Rhetoric in the European Tradition*. New York: Longman.

———. 1990b. "Aristotle's *Rhetoric* in Byzantium," *Rhetorica* 8:29–44.

Consigny, Scott. 1989. "Dialectical, Rhetorical, and Aristotelian Rhetoric," *Philosophy & Rhetoric* 22:281–287.

Cope, Edward M. [1867] 1970. *An Introduction to Aristotle's "Rhetoric."* Rpt. Hildesheim: Olms.

———. [1877] 1970. *The "Rhetoric" of Aristotle, with a Commentary.* 3 vols. Ed. J. E. Sandys. Rpt. Hildesheim: Olms.

Corbett, Edward P. J. 1990. *Classical Rhetoric for the Modern Student.* 3rd ed. New York: Oxford University Press.

Dillery, John. 1992. "Herodotus' Proem and Aristotle, *Rhetorica* 1409a," *Classical Quarterly* 42:525–528.

Dilts, Mervin, R., and George A. Kennedy, eds., 1997. *Two Greek Rhetorical Treatise from the Roman Europe.* Leiden: Brill.

Donadi, Francesco. 1983. *Gorgiae Leontini in Helenam Laudatio.* Rome: Bretschneider.

Douglas, Alan E. 1955. "The Aristotelian *Synagoge Technon* after Cicero *Brutus*, 46–48," *Latomus* 14:536–539.

Dover, Kenneth J. 1974. *Greek Popular Morality in the Time of Plato and Aristotle.* Berkeley: University of California Press.

———. 1978. *Greek Homosexuality.* Cambridge: Harvard University Press.

Düring, Ingmar. 1957. *Aristotle in the Ancient Biographical Tradition.* Göteborg: Göteborg University.

———. 1966. *Aristoteles: Darstellung und Interpretation seinen Denken.* Heidelberg: Carl Winter Verlag.

Edel, Abraham. 1982. *Aristotle and His Philosophy.* Chapel Hill: University of North Carolina Press.

Eden, Kathy. 1986. *Poetic and Legal Fiction in the Aristotelian Tradition.* Princeton: Princeton University Press.

Enos, Richard Leo, ed. 1982. "The Most Significant Passage in Aristotle's *Rhetoric*: Five Nominations," *Rhetoric Society Quarterly* 12:2–20.

Erickson, Keith, ed. 1974. *Aristotle: The Classical Heritage of Rhetoric.* Metuchen, N.J.: Scarecrow Press.

———. 1975. *Aristotle's "Rhetoric": Five Centuries of Philological Research.* Metuchen, N.J.: Scarecrow Press.

Erlich, Victor. 1981. *Russian Formalism: History-Doctrine.* New Haven: Yale University Press.

Evans, J. D. G. 1977. *Aristotle's Concept of Dialectic.* Cambridge: Cambridge University Press.

Fleming, David. 2003. "Becoming Rhetorical: An Education in the Topics," in Petraglia and Bahri (2003), pp. 93–116.

Fortenbaugh, William W. 1970. "Aristotle's *Rhetoric* on Emotion," *Archiv für Geschichte der Philosophie* 52:40–70. Rpt. in Erickson (1974), pp. 205–234, and in Barnes et al. (1979), pp. 133–153.

————. 1975. *Aristotle on Emotion: A Contribution to Philosophical Psychology, Rhetoric, Poetics, Politics, and Ethics*. New York: Barnes & Noble; 2000. 2nd ed., with Epilogue. London: Duckworth.

————. 1985. "Theophrastus on Delivery," *Rutgers University Studies* 2:269–288.

————. 1986. "Aristotle's Platonic Attitude Toward Delivery," *Philosophy & Rhetoric* 19:242–254.

————. 1992. "Aristotle on Persuasion Through Character," *Rhetorica* 10:207–244.

Fortenbaugh, William W., et al., eds. 1992. *Theophrastus of Eresus; Sources for His Life, Writings, Thought and Influence*. 2 vols. Leiden: Brill.

Fortenbaugh, William W., and David Mirhady, eds. 1994. *Peripatetic Rhetoric After Aristotle*. New Brunswick, N.J.: Transaction Publishers.

Fowler, R. L. 1982. "Aristotle on the Period," *Classical Quarterly* 32:89–99.

Frede, Dorothea. 1994. "Mixed Feelings in Aristotle's *Rhetoric*," in Rorty (1996), pp. 258–285.

Fuhrmann, Manfred. 1960. *Das Systematische Lehrbuch*. Göttingen: Vandenhoeck & Ruprecht.

Furley, David J., and Alexander Nehamas. 1994. *Aristotle's Rhetoric: Philosophical Essays. Proceedings of the Twelfth Symposium Aristotelicum*. Princeton: Princeton University Press.

Gagarin, Michael. 1996. "The Torture of Slaves in Athenian Law," *Classical Philology* 91:1–18.

Gagarin, Michael, and Paul Woodruff. 1995. *Early Greek Political Thought from Homer to the Sophists*. Cambridge: Cambridge University Press.

Gaines, Robert N. 1986. "Aristotle's Rhetorical Rhetoric," *Philosophy & Rhetoric* 19:194–200.

————. 2000. "The Contemporary Arts of Practical Discourse," in Gross and Walzer (2000), pp. 3–23.

Garver, Eugene. 1986. "Aristotle's *Rhetoric* as a Work of Philosophy," *Philosophy & Rhetoric* 19:1–22.

————. 1988. "Aristotle's *Rhetoric* on Unintentionally Hitting the Principles of the Sciences," *Rhetorica* 6:381–393.

————. 1994. "Deception in Aristotle's *Rhetoric*: How to Tell the Rhetorician from the Sophist and Which One to Bet On," *Rhetoric Society Quarterly* 24:75–94.

Genette, Gérard. 1982. *Figures of Literary Discourse*. Trans. Alan Sheridan. New York: Columbia University Press.

Goebel, George H. 1989. "Probability in the Earliest Rhetorical Theory," *Mnemosyne* 42:41–53.

Graff, Richard. 2001. "Reading and the 'Written Style' in Aristotle's *Rhetoric*," *Rhetoric Society Quarterly* 31:19–44.

———. 2005. "Prose versus Poetry in Early Greek Theories of Style," *Rhetorica* 23:303–335.

Green, Lawrence D., ed. and trans. 1986. *John Rainold's Oxford Lectures on Aristotle's* Rhetoric. Newark: University of Delaware Press.

———. 1990. "Aristotlian Rhetoric, Dialectic, and the Traditions of *Antistrophos*," *Rhetorica* 8:5–27.

Grimaldi, William M. A. 1972. *Studies in the Philosophy of Aristotle's "Rhetoric."* Wiesbaden: Steiner Verlag.

———. 1980–1988. *Aristotle, "Rhetoric": A Commentary.* 2 vols. New York: Fordham University Press.

Gross, Alan G., and Arthur E. Walzer, eds. 2000. *Rereading Aristotle's "Rhetoric."* Carbondale: Southern Illinois University Press.

Guthrie, W. K. C. 1978. *A History of Greek Philosophy:* Volume Five, *The Later Plato and the Academy.* Cambridge: Cambridge University Press.

Harris, H. A. 1974. "A Simile in Aristotle's *Rhetoric* (III.9.6)," *Classical Review* 24:178–179.

Harwood, John T., ed. 1986. *The Rhetorics of Thomas Hobbes and Bernard Lamy.* Carbondale: Southern Illinois University Press.

Hauser, Gerald A. 1968. "The Example in Aristotle's *Rhetoric:* Bifurcation or Contradiction?" *Philosophy & Rhetoric* 1:78–90.

———. 1985. "Aristotle's Example Revisited," *Philosophy & Rhetoric* 18:171–179.

———. 1999. "Aristotle on Epideictic," *Rhetoric Society Quarterly* 29:5–23.

Havelock, Eric A. 1982. *The Literate Revolution in Greece and Its Cultural Consequences.* Princeton: Princeton University Press.

Heath, Malcolm. 1995. *Hermogenes on Issues: Strategies of Argument in Later Greek Rhetoric.* Oxford: Clarendon Press.

Heidegger, Martin. 1962. *Being and Time.* Trans. John Macquarries and Edward Robinson. New York: Harper & Row.

Hellwig, Antje. 1973. *Untersuchungen zur Theorie der Beredsamkeit bei Platon und Aristoteles.* Göttingen: Vanderhoeck & Ruprecht.

Hill, Forbes. 1981. "The Amorality of Aristotle's *Rhetoric*," *Greek, Roman, and Byzantine Studies* 22:133–147.

Jaeger, Werner. 1934. *Aristotle: Fundamentals of the History of His Development*, trans. from the 1923 German ed. by Richard Robinson. London: Oxford University Press.

Johnstone, C. L. 1980. "An Aristotelian Trilogy: Ethics, Rhetoric, and the Search for Moral Truth," *Philosophy & Rhetoric* 13:1–24.

Kassel, Rudolf. 1971. *Der Text der Aristotelischen "Rhetorik."* Berlin: De Gruyter.

Kennedy, George A. 1983. *Greek Rhetoric Under Christian Emperors.*
Princeton: Princeton University Press.
———. 1994. *A New History of Classical Rhetoric.* Princeton: Princeton
University Press.
———. 1998. *Comparative Rhetoric: An Historical and Cross-Cultural
Introduction.* New York: Oxford University Press.
———. 1999. *Classical Rhetoric and Its Christian and Secular Tradition
from Ancient to Modern Times.* 2nd ed. Chapel Hill: University of
North Carolina Press.
Killeen, J. F. 1971. "Aristotle, *Rhet.* 1413a," *Classical Philology*
76:186–187.
Kirby, John T. 1997. "Aristotle on Metaphor," *American Journal of
Philology* 118:517–554.
Lear, Gabriel R. 2004. *Happy Lives and the Highest Good: An Essay on
Aristotle's* Nicomachean Ethics. Princeton: Princeton University Press.
Leighton, Stephen R. 1982. "Aristotle and the Emotions," *Phronesis*
27:144–174.
Levin, Samuel R. 1982. "Aristotle's Theory of Metaphor," *Philosophy &
Rhetoric* 15:24–46.
Lienhard, Joseph T. 1960. "A Note on the Meaning of *Pistis* in
Aristotle's *Rhetoric*," *American Journal of Philology* 87:446–454.
Liu, Yameng. 1991. "Aristotle and the Stasis Theory: A Reexamination,"
Rhetoric Society Quarterly 21:53–59.
Lord, Carnes. 1981. "The Intention of Aristotle's *Rhetoric*," *Hermes*
109:326–339.
———. 1986. "On the Early History of the Aristotelian Corpus,"
American Journal of Philology 107:137–141.
Lossau, Manfred. 1974. "Der Aristotelische *Gryllos* antilogisch,"
Philologus 11:12–21.
Lynch, J. P. 1972. *Aristotle's School: A Study of a Greek Educational
Institution.* Berkeley: University of California Press.
Martin, Joseph. 1974. *Antike Rhetorik: Technik und Methode.* Munich:
Carl Beck'sche Verlag.
Martin, Richard P. 1989. *Language of Heroes: Speech and Performance
in the* Iliad. Ithaca: Cornell University Press.
Matson, Patricia P., Philip Rollinson, and Marion Sousa, eds. 1990.
Readings from Classical Rhetoric. Edwardsville: Southern Illinois
University Press.
McAdon, Brad. 2001. "Rhetoric Is a Counterpart of Dialectic,"
Philosophy & Rhetoric 34:113–149.
———. 2004. "Two Irreconcilable Conceptions of Rhetorical Proofs in
Aristotle's *Rhetoric*," *Rhetorica* 22:307–325.
McCall, Marsh. 1969. *Ancient Rhetorical Theories of Simile and
Comparison.* Cambridge: Harvard University Press.

MacKay, L. A. 1953. "Aristotle, *Rhetoric*, III, 16, 11 (1417b12–20)," *American Journal of Philology* 74:281–286.

Merlan, Philip. 1954. "Isocrates, Aristotle, and Alexander the Great," *Historia* 3:68–81.

Miller, Carolyn R. 1987. "Aristotle's 'Special Topics' in Rhetorical Practice and Methodology," *Rhetoric Society Quarterly* 17:61–70.

Mills, Michael J. 1985. "*Phthonos* and its Related *Pathe* in Plato and Aristotle," *Phronesis* 30:1–12.

Mirhady, David C. 1991. "Non-Technical *Pisteis* in Aristotle and Anaximenes," *American Journal of Philology* 112:5–28.

———. 1994. "Aristotle, the *Rhetorica ad Alexandrum*, and the Tria Genera Causarum," in Fortenbaugh and Mirhady (1994), pp. 54–65.

———. 1995. "A Note on Aristotle, *Rhetoric* 1.3 1358b5–6," *Philosophy & Rhetoric* 28:405–409.

Monfasani, John, 1976. *George of Trebizond. A Biography and a Study of His Rhetoric and Logic*. Leiden: Brill.

Muir, J. V. 2001. *The Works and Fragments of Alcidamas*, with introduction, translation, and commentary. London: Bristol Classical Press.

Murphy, James J. 1974. *Rhetoric in the Middle Ages: A History of Rhetorical Theory from Saint Augustine to the Renaissance*. Berkeley: University of California Press.

Natali, Carlo. 1989. "*Paradeigma*: The Problems of Human Acting and the Use of Examples in Some Greek Authors of the Fourth Century B.C.," *Rhetoric Society Quarterly* 19:141–152.

Nikolaides, A. G. 1982. "Aristotle's Treatment of the Concept of *Praotes*," *Hermes* 110:414–422.

Nussbaum, Martha C. 1986. *The Fragility of Goodness*. Cambridge: Cambridge University Press.

Ober, Josiah. 1989. *Mass and Elite in Democratic Athens: Rhetoric, Ideology, and the Power of the People*. Princeton: Princeton University Press.

Ong, Walter J. 1982. *Orality and Literacy: The Technologizing of the Word*. New York: Methuen.

Oravec, C. 1976. "Observation in Aristotle's Theory of Epideictic," *Philosophy & Rhetoric* 9:162–173.

Palmer, Georgiana P. 1914. *The Topoi of Aristotle's "Rhetoric" as Exemplified in the Orators*. Chicago: University of Chicago Press.

Papillon, Terry. 1995. "Isocrates' *Techne* and Rhetorical Pedagogy," *Rhetoric Society Quarterly* 25:129–143.

Patillon, Michel. 1997. "Aristotle, Corax, Anaximène, et les Autres dans la *Rhétorique à Alexandre*," *Revue des Etudes Grecques* 110:104–125.

Pearson, Lionel. 1962. *Popular Ethics in Ancient Greece*. Stanford: Stanford University Press.

Pease, A. S. 1926. "Things Without Honor," *Classical Philology* 21:27–42.

Petraglia, Joseph, and Deepika Bahri, eds. 2003. *The Realms of Rhetoric: The Prospects for Rhetoric Education.* Albany: SUNY Press.

Poster, Carol. 1997. "Aristotle's *Rhetoric* Against Rhetoric: Unitarian Reading and Eroteric Hermeneutics," *American Journal of Philology* 118:219–249.

———. 2001. "Pedagogy and Bibliography: Aristotle's *Rhetoric* in Nineteenth-Century England," *Rhetoric Society Quarterly* 21:5–35.

Rabe, Hugo, ed. 1896. *Commentaria in Aristotelem Graeca.* Vol. 15 (Byzantine Commentaries on the *Rhetoric*). Berlin: Reimer.

———, ed. 1931. *Prolegomenon Sylloge.* Leipzig: Teubner.

Radermacher, Ludwig. 1897. "Timäus und die Ueberlieferung über die Ursprung der Rhetorik," *Rheinisches Museum für Philologie* 52:412ff.

———, ed. 1951. *Artium Scriptores (Reste der voraristotelischen Rhetorik). Sitzungsberichte* 227, 3. Vienna: Oesterreichische Akademie der Wissenschaften. Abhandlung.

Radt, Stefan. 1979. "Zu Aristoteles Rhetorik," *Mnemosyne* 32:284–306.

Reinhardt, Tobias, ed. 2003. *Marcus Tullius Cicero, Topica.* Text, translation, and commentary. Oxford: Oxford University Press.

Richards, I. A. 1936. *Philosophy of Rhetoric.* Oxford: Oxford University Press.

Ricoeur, Paul. 1977. *The Rule of Metaphor.* Trans. Robert Czerny, Kathleen McLauglin, and John Costello. Toronto: University of Toronto Press.

———. 1996. "Between Rhetoric and Poetics," in Rorty (1996), pp. 324–384.

Rist, John M. 1989. *The Mind of Aristotle: A Study in Philosophical Growth.* Toronto: University of Toronto Press.

Rorty, A. O. 1984. "Aristotle on the Metaphysical Status of *Pathe,*" *Review of Metaphysics* 37:521–546.

———, ed. 1996. *Essays on Aristotle's "Rhetoric."* Berkeley: University of California Press.

Rosenmeyer, Thomas G. 1955. "Gorgias, Aeschylus, and *Apate,*" *American Journal of Philology* 76:225–260.

Rountree, Clarke. 2001. "The (Almost) Blameless Genre of Classical Greek Epideictic," *Rhetorica* 19:293–305.

Ryan, Eugene E. 1984. *Aristotle's Theory of Rhetorical Argumentation.* Montreal: Bellarmin.

Schenkeveld, Dirk M. 1994. "*Ta Asteia* in Aristotle's *Rhetoric,*" in Fortenbaugh and Mirhady (1994), pp. 1–14.

Schiappa, Edward. 1990. "Did Plato Coin *Rhetorike?*" *American Journal of Philology* 111:457–470.

Schröder, Joachim. 1985. "Ar. *Rhet.* A2. 1356a35–b10, 1357a22–b1," *Hermes* 113:172–182.

Schütrumpf, Eckart. 1994a. "Some Observations on the Introduction to Aristotle's *Rhetoric*," in Furley and Nehamas (1994), pp. 99–116.

———. 1994b. "Non-Logical means of Persuasion in Aristotle's *Rhetoric* and Cicero's *De Oratore*," in Fortenbaugh and Mirhady (1994), pp. 95–110.

Solmsen, Friedrich. 1929. *Die Entwicklung der Aristotelischen Logik und Rhetorik*. Berlin: Weidmann.

———. 1938. "Aristotle and Cicero on the Orator's Playing upon the Feelings," *Classical Philology* 33:390–404.

———. 1941. "The Aristotelian Tradition in Ancient Rhetoric," *American Journal of Philology* 62:35–50 and 169–190. Rpt. in Erickson (1974), pp. 278–309.

Sprague, Rosamond Kent, ed. 1972. *The Older Sophists*. Columbia: University of South Carolina Press.

Sprute, Jürgen. 1982. *Die Enthymemtheorie der aristotelischen Rhetorik*. Göttingen: Vandenhoeck & Ruprecht.

———. 1994. "Aristotle and the Legitimacy of Rhetoric," in Furley and Nehamas (1994), pp. 117–128.

Stanford, William B. 1936. *Greek Metaphor*. Oxford: Blackwell.

Tamba-Mecz, Irène, and Paul Veyne. 1979. "Metaphora et comparaison selon Aristote," *Revue des Etudes Grecques* 92:77–98.

Thür, Gerhard. 1977. *Beweisführung vor den Schwurgerichthöfen Athens*. Vienna: Oesterreichische Akademie der Wissenschaften.

Toulmin, Stephen. 1958. *Uses of Argument*. Cambridge: Cambridge University Press.

Trevett, J. C. 1996. "Aristotle's Knowledge of Athenian Oratory," *Classical Quarterly* 46:371–379.

Walton, Douglas. 1997. *Appeal to Pity; Argumentum ad Misericordia*. Albany: SUNY Press.

Wartelle, André. 1981. *Lexique de la "Rhétorique" d'Aristote*. Paris: Les Belles Lettres.

Watt, John W. 1995. "From Themistius to al-Farabi: Platonic Political Philosophy and Aristotle's *Rhetoric* in the East," *Rhetorica* 13:17–41.

Weidemann, Hermann. 1989. "Aristotle's Inference from Signs, *Rhet.* 1.2.1357b1–25," *Phronesis* 34:343–351.

Wians, William, ed. 1996. *Aristotle's Philosophical Development*. London: Rowman & Littlefield.

Wieland, Wolfgang. 1968. "Aristoteles als Rhetoriker und die Exoterischen Schriften," *Hermes* 86:323–346.

Wilcox, Stanley. 1943. "Corax and the Prolegomena," *American Journal of Philology* 44:1–12.

Wisse, Jakob. 1989. *Ethos and Pathos from Aristotle to Cicero*. Amsterdam: Hakkert.

Woerther, Frédérique. 2005. "La *lexis ēthikē* (stylistique) dans le Livre III des la *Rhétorique* d'Aristotle. Les employs d'*ēthikos* dans le corpus aristotlécien," *Rhetorica* 23:1–33.

Wooten, Cecil W. 1973. "The Ambassador's Speech: A Particularly Hellenistic Genre of Oratory," *Quarterly Journal of Speech* 59:209–212.

INDEX

Aristotle: *Analytics*, 34, 40, 42, 43, 191;
attitude toward Plato, 2–3;
Categories, 2, 69n, 138, 178n;
classification of rhetoric, 10, 37;
Constitution of the Athenians, 55;
dialogues, 4, 5; esoteric works, 3,
18, 306–7; *Eudemian Ethics*, 56,
60, 80n, 88n; *Gryllus*, 5, 14, 18,
307; lectures, 4–5, 6, 79; life of,
1–7; *Metaphysics*, 3n, 16, 67, 68,
212n, 218n; *Methodics*, 40;
Nicomachean Ethics, 1, 3n, 16,
31n, 37, 56, 57, 61, 62, 69, 76n,
77n, 87, 121n, 219n, 222, 243n;
On Interpretation, 40n, 196n;
On Rhetoric, *see* Aristotle's *On
Rhetoric*; *Poetics*, xv, 18, 56, 91n,
92, 139, 197, 198, 199, 200, 203n,
205, 206n, 222, 248, 275–77;
Politics, 3, 52, 55n, 72, 74n,
107n, 108, 219n, 309; *Sophistic
Refutations*, 12, 18, 184, 294;
Synagoge Tekhnon, 5, 10, 18, 297,
300, 302–3; theory of knowledge,
16; *Topics*, 2, 35, 37, 40, 51, 65,
69n, 70n, 170, 176, 177, 178, 190,
192, 248, 263–66, 309
Aristotle's *On Rhetoric*: audience for,
17–20; composition of, 18, 56;
contents, 23–25; history of the
text, xv, 306–33; strengths and
limitations, 20–23; title, xv;
translations, 310, 321
Arrangement, 31–32, 229–50
Arts or handbooks of rhetoric, ix, x, 5,
9, 10, 12, 28, 31, 39, 179, 181, 188,
229, 230, 239n, 249, 269, 293–306
Asyndeton, 227–28, 250
Athens and Athenians, 2, 9, 39, 79–80,
102, 107n, 136, 169–70, 177, 235,
278–79
Athletics, 9, 59–60
Attic orators, 8, 226, 244
Autocles, 178

Bartholomew of Massina, 310
Beauty, 59–60
Bekker, Immanuel, xv
Bias, 151
Boethius, 308
Bryson, 201

Callias, 200
Callippus, 31n, 96, 179, 181
Callisthenes, 127
Callistratus, 67, 100, 245
Calmness, 121–24
Carcinus, 183, 242
Carthaginians, 95
Categories, 69, 138, 266. *See also*
Aristotle, *Categories*
Cephisodotus, 206, 220
Chabrias, 68, 221
Chaeremon, 184, 227
Chance, 86. *See also* Luck
Character, 15, 38–39, 74, 168, 210. *See
also* Ethos
Chares, 105, 219–20, 221, 244
Chiasmus, 31n
Chilon, 150, 177
Choerilus, 232
Cicero, x, 115, 228n, 236, 277, 279,
293, 306, 307–9; *Brutus, 302;
For Caelius*, 149; *For Cluentius*,
245n; *On Invention*, 297–98, 308;
On the Manilian Law, 46n, 60n;
On the Orator, 4n, 49n, 197,
309; *Orator*, 197, 214, 306, 309;
Topics, 172
Cimon, 154
Clarity, 197–200, 307
Cleon, 207, 212
Cleophon, 105, 210
Colon, 214–17
Common topics, 45–46, 50–51, 298. *See
also* Koinon
Comparison, 162, 163, 230, 231. *See
also* Simile
Compound words, 202, 211
Conciseness, 209–10
Confidence, 13–32
Conon, 178, 183
Constitutions, 3, 54–55, 72–75
Contracts, 106–7
Corax, 188–89, 293–303. *See also*
Tisias
Cratylus, 241
Critias, 12, 105, 239
Critolaus, 307
Cydias, 136

Darius, 162
Deduction. *See* Enthymeme; Syllogism

Printed in the USA/Agawam, MA
August 28, 2019

710360.001